Student Personnel Services
in Colleges and Universities

STUDENT PERSONNEL SERVICES——

SOME FOUNDATIONS,
TECHNIQUES, AND PROCESSES
OF PROGRAM ADMINISTRATION

1961   New York   Toronto   London

——IN COLLEGES
AND UNIVERSITIES

E. G. Williamson

Dean of Students
Professor of Psychology
University of Minnesota

McGRAW-HILL BOOK COMPANY

STUDENT PERSONNEL SERVICES
IN COLLEGES AND UNIVERSITIES

70562

789101112–BPBP–1098

To the Staff
of the Office of the Dean of Students
University of Minnesota

Whose loyal, energetic, and ingenious
daily (and nightly) efforts, over these many years,
have brought our program of services
to its present stage of effectiveness.

How simple then is our duty—loyalty to life, to the ship's company and to ourselves, that it may not be through our surrender that the great experiment of existence, whose issue remains in doubt, comes to an end in nothingness. "We must not obey," said Aristotle, "those who urge us, because we are human and mortal, to think human and mortal thoughts; in so far as we may we should practice immortality, and omit no effort to live in accordance with the best that is in us."

What a handful of dust is man to think such thoughts! Or is he, perchance, a prince in misfortune, whose speech at times betrays his birth? I like to think that, if men are machines, they are machines of a celestial pattern, which can rise above themselves, and, to the amazement of the watching gods, acquit themselves as men. I like to think that this singular race of indomitable, philosophising, poetical beings, resolute to carry the banner of Becoming to unimaginable heights, may be as interesting to the gods as they to us, and that they will stoop to admit these creatures of promise into their divine society.

W. M. DIXON, *The Human Situation*

Preface

This book is not a "how-to-do" handbook for deans of students and other administrators. It is nonetheless concerned with the processes of day-to-day operation and management of services to student clientele[1]—those services customarily referred to as student personnel services or Student Personnel Work. The diversity of these services is shown in the organizational-functional charts of Chapters 1, 3, and 4.

As an introduction to Parts One and Two, the traditional services found on most campuses are defined in Chapter 1, briefly, and the underlying educational philosophy and historical development are cited. In this first chapter, as in following ones, I quote and refer to findings in, and related materials from, adjacent fields of knowledge, especially industry, government services, social psychology, higher education, and educational philosophy. I believe these borrowings illuminate and enhance the concepts and techniques of our program of services.

The first four chapters set the stage for Parts Two and Three, in which I describe and evaluate some of the highly dynamic processes and techniques of administration. I have selected several services which, to me, are currently in need of critical reassessment and re-examination. In Chapter 5, for example, I examine some aspects of administration of discipline resulting from the shift, during the past several decades, from discipline as punishment to discipline as rehabilitative counseling. This chapter also deals with the changing

[1] This new terminology was first used in a recent speech to be published later in our Minnesota Series, by Professor W. H. Cowley, Stanford University, who earlier contributed so much to the literature of our field in the 1920–1940 period of development.

administrative processes in a second major evolution in discipline, the transition from administration enforcement of administration-made restrictive rules to the new administration, by joint action of administration and student-faculty judiciaries, of rules jointly made by administration, faculty, and students.

In Part Three, I formulate, provisionally, some philosophical foundations for certain emerging new forms of services. At the same time I present institutional case illustrations of administrative processes and techniques as they have been identified in the development of these new services.

These cases are, of course, only sample illustrations of the many forms of processes employed in administering a program of services. I call attention to the underlying hypothesis especially relevant to these particular forms of services, controversial and disruptive as they are, in sharp contrast with the noncontroversial professional service of counseling. The underlying hypothesis of Chapters 9, 10, and 11 is this: Some educational good (learning) can result from campus-wide controversies if the personnel staff is skillful enough to play the effective role of an educator rather than, or in conjunction with, the necessary role of administrator. This hypothesis is extended in modified form in Chapter 13, with clarifying reference back to Chapter 7, to the extracurriculum in general as a possible source of intellectual learning.

Chapter 12 explores the legalities of the relationship of students with the institution, especially with the central administration, in order to arrive at a clarification and understanding of them. I believe Chapter 9 also will clarify the confusion that characterizes much futile and disruptive discussion of what constitutes the "givens" of students' academic freedoms.

Obviously, no claim is even implied that I have isolated and described all the important administrative processes, or even those that are universally applicable. There is so much that is unique in any one community of scholars that we are not well experienced in transposing experience from one community to another. All I can do is to provide for the reader as accurate as possible a description and interpretation of the case incidents I have observed in my own institution. I hope that others will provide us with other case incidents, in sufficient detail, so that more light can be thrown through the making of thoughtful comparisons. The comparative method has yielded rich rewards in cultural anthropology, but thus far we have not learned to apply it with complete effectiveness to the administration of student personnel services.

Our own staff, like that of many other universities, has been encouraged and aided by the institution's climate of opinion and by the generous provision of facilities to experiment in program development. That is, the tradition of research in laboratories extends even to our program facilities. This institutional tradition of transferring to the problems of higher education the many research methods, and an experimental point of view in education, has produced a sizable contribution to the research literature of higher education. It also has contributed to the literature of program development of many parts of higher education. Through both types of contribution to the literature, a distinctive attitude of critical evaluation, rather than bland assumptions of effectiveness, has added continuing freshness to the climate of opinion in which personnel services are being developed and reconstructed.

It is my hope that we who have been privileged to experiment in student personnel program development have extended and continued this tradition with the generous and intelligent, enthusiastic support of the central administration, especially President J. L. Morrill and Vice-president M. M. Willey, the faculty, and certainly the students themselves. And I hope that this book will be evaluated according to that criterion.

By way of further orientation to my concept of administration, let me state that the main thesis underlying my treatment of administration is that our services are in the nature of *educative relationships* with students. In certain instances, these service relationships assume the function of preparation for other types of educative relationships which take place in the classroom, laboratory, and library. In some they are *restorative* of skills, motivations, and necessary orientation to the classroom type of education. But still other educative relationships occur outside of the formal classroom relationship. For example, the learning that occurs in the disciplinary counseling relationships is experienced in that relationship or, usually, not at all—at least, not as restructuring of values and perceptions in rehabilitation. Likewise much, but sometimes not all, of the learning about concepts of authority, freedom, rights, and responsibilities of students, especially in respect to the complex problem of their separate membership and dual role in the institution contrasted with their retained community citizenship—all these learnings are acquired, if at all, in those controversies which continuously rage in the extracurriculum over the issue of control and rights.

Although student personnel work consists of educative relationships, it cannot be isolated from the surrounding culture. In order to understand student personnel work as it is integrated with education, we must understand the societal context within which these institutional programs operate, and with which they are integrated. This point of view illuminates such recent studies of American education as *A History of Education in American Culture,* by R. Freeman Butts and Lawrence A. Cremin.[2]

One more aspect of my main thesis needs brief mention. Without assuming any degree of cultural isolation, I hold that the collegiate experience, especially Mather's "collegiate way of living in"[3] a dormitory or fraternity, is such an exciting and stimulating experience in itself—or it can so become—that we personnel workers need to reevaluate that experience critically as basic in higher education.

To return to the collegiate way of living, in a moment of nostalgia I relived many rich experiences in the reading of that imaginative compilation, *The College Years* edited by A. C. Spectorsky.[4] On the advertising jacket we read these words so relevant to the defining of our task and our opportunity for inventive leadership:

Of the many things we cherish among our memories, truly none is so dearly thought of, so never-to-be-forgotten, as the 'college years,' for this is the period of life which marks the major dividing line between adolescence and adulthood.

Near the close of a long period spent in revising this manuscript, I stumbled upon a new gold mine of relevant concepts. And there I found this wise observation:

No book can ever be finished. While working on it we learn just enough to find it unmature that moment we turn away from it.[5]

[2] Published by Henry Holt and Company, Inc., New York, 1953.
[3] Cotton Mather, *Magnalia Christe Americana: Or the Ecclesiastical History of New England.* Hartford: Silas Andrus and Son, 1953, vol. II, pp. 9–10.
[4] Published by Hawthorn Books, Inc., New York, 1958.
[5] Karl R. Popper, *The Open Society and Its Enemies.* Princeton, New Jersey: Princeton University Press, 1950, p. vii.

What an exciting and new challenge opens up before us—to re-explore the relevancy of our program efforts in student personnel work as among the means, perhaps minor in significance but nevertheless relevant to the age-old revolution—the transition from an absolutistic society of rigid traditionalism to an open society in which, in Popper's words, "Individuals are confronted with personal decisions." [6]

. . . an open society which rejects the absolute authority of the merely established and the merely traditional while trying to preserve, to develop, and to establish traditions, old or new, that measure up to its standards of freedom, of humaneness, and of rational criticism.[7]

Surely such a philosophy of human society provides some role of significance for our educative services in so far as they aid students to develop into full humanity—a development which President Pusey of Harvard University declared to be the goal of American education.[8]

[6] *Ibid.*, p. 169.
[7] *Ibid.*, p. viii.
[8] Nathan M. Pusey, "The Exploding World of Education," *Fortune*, September, 1955, p. 204.

Addendum

In writing this book, I sought to define functions of the dean of students in his role of educational leader, not merely as a manager of day-to-day services as, if, and when requested by student clientele for remediation of their problems and troubles, but as one with educative goals of his own to be achieved through that program of services. But alas, Popper's dictum is true—a book is never finished! After writing and rewriting this entire manuscript and this preface, I returned to my office to find Philip Selznick's *Leadership in Administration.* He has described elegantly, though for larger organizations, a model and concept adequate for the dean of students as administrator of services to student clientele in an educational institution. I recommend it as basic orientation. And now a dozen or so other relevant titles, but recently uncovered, await reading in search of Popper's measure of maturity of understanding of my topic and theses.

E. G. *Williamson*

Acknowledgments

For the information contained in the organizational and func
tional charts of Chapters 1, 3, and 4, I am obligated to my fellow
deans.

I desire to express special gratitude to my staff of efficient and
imaginative secretaries and bibliographic assistants, whose searches
for the correct quotation and the right reference have added accuracy to this manuscript and, as well, corrected my faulty memory.
These assistants have borne the major responsibility for this necessary
editorial accuracy: Virginia Willems, June Stein, Alice Blackman,
Virginia Levy, Alice Tracy, Shirley Vogel, Gwendolyn Fillman,
LaDonna Mossefin, Joan Engberg, and Barbara C. Osman.

I was aided in reconstructing the record in Chapter 11 by my
former associates who participated in the development of the policy
and program of conduct control, B. J. Borreson, Theron Johnson,
Gordie Smith, and Bud Williamson. W. H. Cowley and Walter Johnson identified many points in the original manuscript needing restatement. Over the years I have accumulated many obligations to
Professor Cowley—obligations for aid in writing English, the concept of "holism," the story of Lowell's reform of the Harvard tradition of a "Gentleman's C" grade, the story of the colonial colleges,
and for clarifying emphasis upon the dependency of our work upon
the historical context of American higher education. I am also
deeply indebted to students and faculty serving on the Senate Committee on Student Affairs, especially to its former chairman, Kenneth Clark, for cooperative aid in organizing supervision over student affairs (its basic responsibility) to emphasize the search for

learning from crises and issues some of the generalizations which serve as foundations for my theses and hypotheses about the educational and instructional potentialities of student personnel services, especially our staff's relationships with students' extracurriculum.

E. G. Williamson

Contents

PART ONE

Services and Administrative Processes

CHAPTER I

The Campus Program of Services

In current usage, the term "student personnel work" refers both to a program of organized services for students and to a point of view about these students. As an organized program, we may identify on every campus certain services designed to help students solve a problem in logic, develop a study skill, enjoy associations, learn to read rapidly, or organize a charitable drive. In expressing their point of view about students, we hear workers speak of these students in terms of their many-sided development: physical, moral, scholastic, and social. And we readily identify in the worker's attitude toward each student a respect for individuality and a concern for development of the many facets of that individuality.

It is, of course, true that some educators write of the college's supervisory authority over students as an extension of parental authority.[1] Such a perspective emphasizes, and sometimes is limited to, the custodial control of excessive behavior and defines the functions in these words: "Colleges are custodial as well as educational; college administrators spend much time dealing with or preventing breaches of mores." [2] Such restrictive definitions of our field are, we believe, currently incomplete and in part inaccurate. Still, it is necessary for the reader to see himself as some others, usually faculty associates, perceive him in his distinctive role on the campus. Such an understanding will serve to highlight many of the findings and experiences covered in later chapters on students' freedoms—academic freedoms, freedom of discussion, and

[1] American Civil Liberties Union, *Academic Freedom and Civil Liberties of Students*, 1956. Revised May, 1959.
[2] Robin M. Williams, Jr., *American Society: A Sociological Interpretation.* New York: Alfred A. Knopf, Inc., 1955, p. 300.

3

related controversial issues that impinge upon academic concerns of the faculty.

Because the tangible programs of the period following the First World War are still in evidence in many colleges and have proved adequate even in the current expansion of enrollment, some observers may have concluded that student personnel work originated during those decades. But earlier programs have been identified, and one may take some pride in the observation that we are not recent interlopers on the educational scene. Rather ours has long been an integral part of the American pattern of higher education. As an introduction to our description of services, we shall refer briefly to some of the highlighted events in the long-range development of our work.

As is true of so many parts of contemporary American education, some services originated in our early colonial colleges and persisted into the past century with little change in form. Leonard identified the early development of a number of these services during the first century and a half of our country's settlement.[3] These include a concern for housing, discipline, activities, and certain simple forms of counseling. Citizens and teachers alike were then as much concerned with students' riotous manners and depraved morals as with their intellectual development. Perhaps the convictions of the deeply religious *emigré* from Europe, threatened by the reckless and immoral life of the American frontier, forced intense preoccupation with many phases of the out-of-class life of students and thus led to development of early programs of extra-teaching relationships.

During the nineteenth century, a number of events signaled the further development of extraclassroom services for students. Oberlin College opened her doors to women in 1833; this move led to the appointment of lady principals or preceptoresses to give special attention to problems of women students. Out of this experience later emerged the position of dean of women.[4] In 1870 Harvard appointed a dean of the college whose duties included a number

[3] Eugenie Andruss Leonard, *The Origins of Personnel Services in American Education.* Minneapolis: University of Minnesota Press, 1956.
[4] Lulu Holmes, *A History of the Position of Dean of Women in a Selected Group of Co-educational Colleges and Universities in the United States.* New York: Columbia University Press, 1939.

of personnel functions. And in 1890 Harvard appointed Professor LeBaron Russell Briggs to serve as what Cowley called a "dean of student relations." [5] Morison describes his duties in the following words: "He performed the miracle of exercising a personal influence on a large and increasing student body. The humanity, perception, and kindly humor, which enliven his printed reports, were so evident to the undergraduates that it is said men used deliberately to 'get in trouble with the office' in order to talk with the Dean." [6]

These innovations in academic functions were made possible, in some respects, by the changes taking place during the mid-century period within the office of the college president. These changes have been well described by Schmidt.[7] In the colonial-type college of an earlier period, the president had served as chief student personnel worker, dealing with discipline, morals, morale, manners, and spiritual development. Williams described changes in the function and structure of higher institutions as "the superimposition of a centralized quasi-bureaucratic organization upon the old 'college' as a community of scholars and teachers." [8] The overworked teaching president of the college needed help in performing his varied duties and special assistants were appointed.

Originating as they did, largely within the college president's orbit of responsibilities—and sometimes as his personal duty— student personnel services became a presidential concern, and so they remain in many respects. Perhaps this is one reason why deans of students today continue to function in close administrative relationship with the president's staff. And such origination may well be one reason why we have often experienced some difficulties in enlisting sustained faculty participation in the expanding program of services. Central administration must, by necessity, be institution-wide in perspective and responsibility and concern itself with more than classroom teaching functions. Such a broad perspective

[5] W. H. Cowley, "The Disappearing Dean of Men," *Proceedings of the Nineteenth Annual Conference of the National Association of Deans and Advisers of Men.* Austin, Tex.: University of Texas, 1937. (Mimeographed.)

[6] Samuel Eliot Morison (ed.), *The Development of Harvard University.* Cambridge, Mass.: Harvard University Press, 1930, p. xxxv.

[7] George P. Schmidt, *The Old Time College President.* New York: Columbia University Press, 1930.

[8] Williams, *op. cit.,* p. 296.

invites close attention to out-of-class adjustments and problems. And this perspective also invites the public of parents and others to pressure the central administration directly regarding students' activities, misbehaviors, worries, and problems. Perhaps many presidents were following both precedent and sound principle of administration when they turned to a central staff officer for assistance with such pressures, as early happened with Clark at Illinois. Thomas Arkle Clark, appointed in 1901 as dean of men, said of his appointment, "I relieved the President of some very unpleasant duties." [9]

Perhaps we should think of the emerging student personnel services as related to and a part of basic changes in American education itself. During the middle decades of the nineteenth century, a number of changing conditions in our democratic society forced reorganization of structure, content, and instructional methods of collegiate education. These forces produced new institutions, land grant colleges, with missions radically different from those of the colonial colleges. Many changes in student personnel services resulted from these institutional changes. Prior to these drastic changes, student life was not the elaborate and complex way of living it became in the last quarter of the century.[10] Clubs and athletics and elaborate social affairs were a half century in the future. "The undergraduate life, too, in all these individual colleges, was essentially the same. It was plain, orderly, studious, thoughtful. It was free from distractions." [11] And it was not until later years that one finds the effects on the college program of such factors as the proliferation of the extracurriculum, application of discoveries in psychology, the accelerated expansion of enrollment in land grant colleges to include larger numbers of students from the economic middle classes, and the radical change in the curriculum to embrace vocational and other nonclassical subjects.[12] These

[9] Thomas Arkle Clark, *Secretarial Notes on the Fourth Annual Conference of Deans and Advisers of Men,* April 20–23, 1922, Lexington, Ky., University of Kentucky, p. 5.

[10] Charles F. Thwing, *A History of Higher Education in America.* New York: D. Appleton & Company, Inc., 1906.

[11] *Ibid.*

[12] Edward Danforth Eddy, Jr., *Colleges for Our Land and Time: The Land-grant Idea in American Education.* New York: Harper & Brothers, 1957, pp. 54–55, 79–80, 89.

changes brought to the old colonial-type college new concepts of education, new urban conditions of crowding and societal complexity, and new financial and personal problems to be faced by students. The program of student services had been evolving slowly for some years; then in the latter half of the nineteenth century, accelerated changes in the character of higher institutions and their students produced conditions which made the greater development of these services both possible and urgent. Following the First World War, they assumed the forms that we see today. And, of course, we recognize that the accelerated growth in related research and technology, occurring during this period, not only made other services possible but at the same time produced the societal and family conditions and changes which made such services requisite if the modern American universities were to fulfill their changed mission.

While the evolutionary extensions of colonial-day functions were interacting with the results of technological and educational revolutions, a contrary influence was imported at mid-century by Tappan of Michigan, following his personal experiences in German universities.[13] He turned the dormitory into classrooms and disclaimed institutional responsibility for all but instructional relationships with students. In a number of Midwestern state universities student personnel work was weakened, if not eliminated, as these universities adopted the continental conviction—that university students develop into men through handling their own problems and affairs outside of the classroom. The prevailing theory of those days was a reflection of European points of view, best exemplified in Paulsen's statement: "Rousseau's words are as true here as elsewhere: 'We must risk boys if we would gain men.'"[14]

Such a viewpoint is, of course, unlike those of student personnel workers as we define them in a subsequent section. At this point, we emphasize that the evolution of our part of higher education often has been interrupted and diverted by the force of other competing philosophies of education—in which the full development of the students, many types of students, was not the core concept of edu-

[13] Henry P. Tappan, *University Education.* New York: G. P. Putnam, 1851.
[14] Friedrich Paulsen, *The German Universities, Their Character and Historical Development.* New York: The Macmillan Company, 1895, p. 209.

cation. And even currently one finds on some campuses the vestiges of German "sink or swim" philosophy in education.

This point of view prevailed in many institutions until the overwhelming pressure of students and their problems forced colleges to consider a host of new problems,[15] especially those concerned with identifying and predicting scholastic aptitude in order to reduce the alarming rate of scholastic failures.[16]

It was fortunate that Army psychologists with their wartime manpower experiences were at hand on campuses in 1919, at this time of greatest need for improved means of classifying and counseling students. But one must not conclude that nothing occurred in this field prior to the war years. Lloyd-Jones has reminded us of general developments in the use of psychological tests by Cattell at Columbia in 1894 and by Kitson at Chicago University in 1917.[17]

In this connection we should also revise our historical orientation by rereading a speech by William Rainey Harper. He early outlined and argued for the use of diagnostic procedures to give understanding of students and their instructional and personal needs and capabilities before instruction was given to them.[18] This idea originated long before the technological developments made its application possible, and it served as a significant ideological underpinning for the evolving program of personnel services.

A number of events illuminate the development of organized programs of services during the second decade of the nineteenth century. A plan for individual guidance of students was developed by a special committee on individual training and guidance at Stanford University in 1911, perhaps influenced by the work of Parsons in Boston in 1908.[19] Other collegiate developments prior to

[15] W. H. Cowley, "The History and Philosophy of Student Personnel Work," *Journal of the National Association of Deans of Women,* vol. 3, pp. 153–162, June, 1940.

[16] Johnston, J. B.: "Predicting Success in College at the Time of Entrance," *School and Society,* vol. 23, pp. 82–88, Jan. 16, 1926.

————: *Education for Democracy.* Minneapolis: University of Minnesota Press, 1934.

[17] Esther Lloyd-Jones, *Student Personnel Work at Northwestern University.* New York: Harper & Brothers, 1929, p. 4.

[18] William Rainey Harper, *The Trend in Higher Education.* Chicago: University of Chicago Press, 1905, chap. 20, "The Scientific Study of the Student," pp. 317–326.

[19] Lewis Adams Maverick, *The Vocational Guidance of College Students.* Cambridge, Mass.: Harvard University Press, 1926, chap. II.

1926 are described by Maverick. The first Master of Arts and diploma of Dean of Women was granted at Teachers College, Columbia University, in 1914.[20] And in 1915 Dr. Lois Mathews Rosenberry, dean of women of the University of Wisconsin, published a book *The Dean of Women*[21] outlining student personnel functions for women students. Findlay reported that, while Dean Clark was appointed in 1901 as the first dean of men, the median date of appointment for deans of men in eighty-nine colleges and universities was 1924, after the greatly expanded student enrollment following the First World War.[22] An understanding of the scope and content of these early programs of services is given in Blake's survey of a number of women's colleges.[23] But perhaps the most nearly definitive description is to be found in Hopkins's intensive survey of fourteen institutions.[24] While many significant changes have come about since 1926, especially in organized counseling, the general structure and organization established in those years is found today in most institutions.

Our identification of some of the milestones in our long historical background will serve to buttress our point about the relevance of our work in education. Clearly, in different circumstances and in different types of colleges, some teachers observed at first hand the many personal problems of students and were consequently motivated to organize some kind of service to alleviate conditions that interfered with education. These pioneering teachers had little technological knowledge of human development but they did respect individuality and human needs. With this respect, they designed services to improve the lot of the student and to aid him in his search for development through educational experiences.

After this brief sketch of historical antecedents, we shall now examine the philosophy and point of view concerning students

[20] Esther Lloyd-Jones, "The Beginnings of Our Profession," in *Trends in Student Personnel Work*. Minneapolis: University of Minnesota Press, 1949, part 9.

[21] Published by Houghton Mifflin Company, Boston, 1915.

[22] J. N. Findlay, "The Origin and Development of the Work of the Dean of Men in Higher Education," *Association of American Colleges Bulletin*, vol. 25, p. 280, 1939.

[23] Mabelle Babcock Blake, *Guidance for College Women*. New York: D. Appleton & Company, Inc., 1926.

[24] L. B. Hopkins, "Personnel Procedure in Education," *The Educational Record Supplement*, no. 3, October, 1926.

which, in retrospect, can be identified through the evolution of these services. After this discussion we shall turn to a description of the services as they are organized and as they function currently.

PHILOSOPHY OF EDUCATION UNDERLYING
THE EMPIRICALLY DERIVED PROGRAM

Earlier in our opening remarks we defined student personnel work as a tangible expression in the programs of a basic philosophy of education. One philosophic view has been expressed by Taylor in these words:[25]

In place of a fixed aim or fixed principles for education, the instrumentalist position is that aims and principles are to be defined in terms of the growth of maturity and of personal qualities within the student and not in terms of an intellectual discipline for training the reason.

And again:[26]

In operation, an educational system of this kind places its emphasis upon the individual student and the quality of his experience and tries to arrange an educational environment in which it is possible for the individual to find his own way toward full development.

Sidney Hook stated his philosophy, relevant to personnel work, and identified it with the progressive education movement:[27]

The philosophy of progressive education had from the outset been committed to the belief that only in a democracy, and in a continuously expanding social democracy, can the end of individual growth be achieved. This follows from the concern with which the needs of every child were to be considered, the necessity of harmonizing these needs to permit their fruitful expansion, and the recognition that genuine equality of educational opportunity demands social democracy at one end and industrial democracy at the other.

A similar point of view has been given as a basic social philosophy

[25] Harold Taylor, "The Philosophical Foundations of General Education," *The Fifty-first Yearbook of the National Society for the Study of Education.* Chicago: University of Chicago Press, 1952, part I, p. 36.

[26] *Ibid.,* p. 37.

[27] Sidney Hook, *Education for Modern Man.* New York: The Dial Press, Inc., 1946, p. 53.

of education for democracy by the President's Commission on Higher Education in the following statement:[28]

The social role of education in a democratic society is at once to insure equal liberty and equal opportunity to differing individuals and groups, and to enable the citizen to understand, appraise, and redirect forces, men, and events as these tend to strengthen or to weaken their liberties.

And the Commission again stated this point of view:[29]

The first goal in education for democracy is the full, rounded, and continuing development of the person. The discovery, training, and utilization of individual talents is of fundamental importance in a free society. To liberate and perfect the intrinsic powers of every citizen is the central purpose of democracy, and its furtherance of individual self-realization is its greatest glory.

Thus, personnel workers have at hand an explicit philosophy of education; this philosophy has, in effect, been implicit in the personnel program itself for many decades. And it is clear that personnel work is related to, or extends from, that philosophy of education which concerns itself with the total development of the individual student. But we note that many of our services were empirically developed before such an explicit philosophy was formulated. This sequence of evolvement is of great significance because it means that our work has had a grass-roots development in the daily experiences and difficulties of students and teachers. We find that the current programs of personnel work have emerged out of attempts to do something positive to aid students who experience certain kinds of difficulty. For example, the vocational guidance movement, as developed by Parsons, was an attempt to help the adolescent avoid adult failure caused by the choice of an inappropriate occupation; and to increase the likelihood of his success and happiness through the wise and sound choice of an occupation. Stated another way, observation of the effects of the wrong choice, with its accompaniment of human maladjustment and industrial inefficiency, led to attempts to develop a pre-

---

[28] The President's Commission on Higher Education, *Higher Education for American Democracy*, vol. 1, *Establishing the Goals*. Washington: 1947, p. 5.
[29] *Ibid.*, p. 9.

ventive type of personnel service. In like manner, the observation by deans of women concerning the undesirable or harmful effects of poor housing on studying, morale, morals, and social experiences led to early attempts to aid students in maintaining higher standards in approved residences under supervision.

Another type of service will illustrate our point that personnel programs originate in the daily-life problems of students rather than as deductions from an explicit philosophy. Psychologists, after the First World War, observed the high failure rate among students who lacked requisite aptitudes or interest. Their observations led to efforts to perfect objective tests that could be taken by the students before they entered upon their course of study. Students were thus helped to avoid choosing curricula in which they found a high probability of failure. It is probably this peculiar origination of testing that has led us to relate closely testing and counseling as an integrated service to students.

PROBLEM-CENTERED CONTEXT

We may observe today certain vestiges of the origination of services—in the identification and remediation of students' daily-living problems, for example. The identification of reading difficulties, inadequate aptitude, wrong choice of curriculum and vocational objective, and the occurrence of riots and misbehavior—all such phenomena have resulted in the assignment of staff to correct undesirable conditions and behavior. Eventually procedures were adopted to prevent untoward occurrences before they resulted in scholastic failure or in disruptive behavior, as the case might be. In most instances, remediation and prevention proved to be effective contributions to the achievement of the college's mission—graduation of students.

But preoccupation with the failing or the misbehaving student precluded, in some respects, our giving attention to the scholastically successful and the behaviorally satisfactory student. We seemed to have little to contribute to the student who was not in trouble of some kind. And, to many of our academic colleagues, we seemed to be irrelevant to the mission of the college as they defined it—the instruction of the scholastically superior student. We may well seem to be preoccupied with the problem student whom the faculty thinks should be dismissed, and we have thus little to contribute to education of the adequate student. We shall discuss this aspect of our work at greater length in Chapter 13.

A POINT OF VIEW CONCERNING STUDENTS

We have made the point several times that our program of services has evolved empirically out of human efforts to correct situations that interfere with the full development of students. Such a human impulse to help someone in difficulty is found in many cultures and is explicit in the Judaeo-Christian view of human life, the prevailing *Weltanschauung* in Western civilization. Our student personnel philosophy has some aspects in common with broader systems of thought; of course, it is not, in itself, an articulate and explicitly organized philosophy about human development and human values. Nevertheless, we may identify at least five major aspects of our own point of view. These are expressed in the growing literature of the movement and implicit both in the nature of the services and in the way in which they operate through the distinctive quality of human relationships between worker and student client. We shall note that this type of human relationship is significantly related to the point of view.

A number of years ago, Cowley used the term "holism" [30] to describe one facet of this viewpoint, to denote *our central concern with all aspects of the development of human individuality.* We do not restrict our effort to intellectual development alone, even though this is essentially the major concern and belief of many educators. Indeed, we recognize that, throughout the history of Western education, there has been major confidence in the proposition that man can maintain control of himself and his environment if he develops his intellectual powers.

In contrast, our point of view constitutes a reaction against the development of the intellect as the dominant concern of higher education. Our movement was an early protest against the fragmentation of the individual into separable parts, a movement that ignored the early abandonment of faculty psychology as a foundation for education. Such a fragmentation of the individual rejects

[30] W. H. Cowley, "Nourishing Future Alumni," *The Educational Record,* vol. 19, no. 4, p. 494, October, 1938.

the social, interpersonal, moral, vocational, emotional, and other aspects of the individuality as peripheral in higher education—although they are not denied a place of importance in the individual's daily living. They are rather relegated to the home, the church, and the community as a major concern—to the end that the university can center on what is considered to be the pivotal, strategic potential of the individual, namely, the development of his intellectual powers.

A second aspect of our point of view concerns *the unique individuality of each student*. It is true that selective admission processes reduce the full possible range of individuality to be found in the college. Nevertheless there still remain a tremendous variety of different and individual human beings. Our own centering of attention upon the individual is in itself a reaction to and protest against mass education with the consequent neglect of the individual. It is also a protest against the ever-present dangerous pressures toward standardization in Western culture.

As a philosophic perspective, the concept of individuality relevant to education is described in the writings of George H. Mead.[31] In science, journalism, and literature, problems are treated and analyzed not in universals, as in earlier centuries, but as encountered in daily life by human individuals. A world perceived by an individual is not the same as one viewed by a side-line observer from another planet. Individuality or self as perceiver of experiences is the dominant perspective adopted in many parts of American education; certainly it is dominant in the way personnel workers view the problems of students. A personnel worker would find much illumination of his own way of looking at the world of students through studying Mead's critical appraisal of the past century. The problem of individuality as it concerns relationships with other individuals (the interpenetration of separate selfs) is considered by Mead, in Chapter 19 of the work cited and by others.[32]

Our point of view concerning the interpenetration of separate selfs is not so much a reaction and protest against conformist

[31] George H. Mead, "Individuality in the Nineteenth Century," chap. 19 in Merritt H. Moore (ed.), *Movements of Thought in the Nineteenth Century* Chicago: University of Chicago Press, 1936.

[32] See, e.g., Christian Bay, *The Structure of Freedom*. Stanford, Calif.: Stanford University Press, 1958.

tendencies within the individual; it is more a reaction against the pressures of college programs which oftentimes seem to treat all students as though they were alike in aptitudes and aspirations. To us it is axiomatic that students must not remain "faceless." As Gideonse says—[33]

The student personnel program is an unavoidable corrective for some of the weaknesses that are inherent in the size of a college. It is a *compensatory* influence, offsetting some of the by-products of bigness and impersonality, a neutralizer for the acid of indifference which size engenders, the catalyst which so often spurs the educational experience into activity, or the counterweight which provides equilibrium to the bewildering stress and strains of young people.

A third aspect of our point of view concerns *the assertion that teaching in the classroom is not enough, or sufficient, in the education of some students.* Our experiences indicate the need of some services for some students—supplemental to the classroom, laboratory, and library. The rehabilitation of failing students of high potential ability and the prevention of misuse of abilities are important areas of service.[34] We seek to avoid, if possible, wastage of human resources by organizing both preventive and remedial services in education.

Our advocacy of such a plan has drawn the charge that we desire or seek to coddle students, particularly those possessing modest or limited scholastic aptitude. In many instances, such a charge may be appropriate. However, when we operate at our best, we seek to help each individual achieve that level of effectiveness of which he is capable. We must admit that, to some of our critics, it may seem that we frequently help low-ability students find easy courses in which to enroll. Then, too, it may very well be that our efforts to help superior students achieve the optimum of their potential are not sufficiently visible to our faculty colleagues. Indeed, we readily observe that a tremendous amount of our effort is devoted to the failing and the near-failing student, who desperately comes for counseling or some other kind of

---

[33] Harry D. Gideonse, "Brooklyn College and Self-evaluation: A Challenge in Complacency," *Biennial Report of the President of Brooklyn College 1955–1957,* July, 1957, p. 15.
[34] See Donald G. Paterson, "The Conservation of Human Talent," *The American Psychologist,* vol. 12, no. 3, pp. 134–144, March, 1957.

service to avoid severance from alma mater. In spite of such partial observations, the record indicates that our complementary services have helped salvage and conserve human resources at all levels of capability.

A fourth aspect of our point of view concerns *the use of methods and relationships of an educative rather than an authoritarian or chain-of-command type.* This is related to the general democratization of higher education for students which has been so clearly evident during the past three decades—ever since the First World War brought to the campus more mature students with increasing demands to participate in institutional decision making. In response to their demands, we strive to use relationships of every sort to help the students develop through their greatly changed roles and status as student leaders in their relation to the administration of the college. Moreover, this new point of view has led us to substitute efforts at rehabilitation through counseling for the earlier repressive punishment which followed misbehavior. In other types of services there have been corresponding changes or shifts from less to more active roles for students in their relationship with the college. In the decades ahead, this switch from authoritarian to educative methods and relationships may well lead to fruitful experimentation with the development of new roles for students to replace the passive role of recipient of our services. Possibly, most personnel services can be reorganized so the students do not *receive* services, but instead actively *participate* in managing services for their own development. Such a revolutionary experiment probably will meet with some resistance among those accustomed to *giving* this service rather than *playing a part* in helping students acquire the educative products of the service.

A fifth aspect of our point of view concerns *the incorporation into services of new knowledge of human nature and its development.* Such new information comes from many fields—the psychology of learning, the psychology of affect, aptitude, and mental health. Many expanding fields provide appropriate new and rich understanding about human development. In effect, our recent philosophy represents a basic modification—through new understanding of human growth—of the method of *personal persuasion and admonition* (personal evangelism or character development) formerly used by some deans of men and women. The contrast between the earlier and later viewpoints is well illustrated in these remarks of a former dean at Purdue University:[35]

I have felt more and more of mechanism and more and more of methods, and less and less of heart and soul are coming to the deans of men's offices. My friends, he is not an idealized policeman, administering justice; nor should he be a prosecuting attorney to whom the faculty gives all information of misconduct. Why are we here anyway? Are we big enough for the job? I must say what is in my heart. The first time I met with the Deans of Men was at Illinois; we discussed the same problems as now. The next time the same old problems were discussed, as well as the next time. We had little of mechanical devices for solving those problems. Today we have so surrounded ourselves with mechanical records that we may have ceased being personalities and have become machines.

In effect, our present point of view has led us to professionalize our movement through advanced graduate training and the incorporation of technical know-how into techniques. Two points may be made about our attempt to professionalize our work. In the first place, a substitution of technical knowledge for the earlier common-sense approach to adolescents' development may very well improve our effectiveness—as has been the case in other professions. That is, improvement in accuracy and profundity of knowledge about human development should provide a more effective underpinning for our services. Secondly, such an incorporation of technical know-how does not need to produce, as Dean Coulter anticipated, a cold, impersonal, scientific type of relationship between worker and student. This was a documented fear of some of the early advocates of the common-sense approach—that we would become so coldly scientific that we would look upon our students as case numbers. It was just such a fear that recently prompted Dean Goodnight to admonish his fellow workers to ask themselves these questions:[36]

1. Is Coulter's contention—which he personally demonstrated so

[35] Stanley Coulter, in an address given in Boulder, Colo., in 1929, as quoted by Scott H. Goodnight, in *Proceedings of the National Association of Student Personnel Administrators,* April, 1957, p. 217.

Another description of the pattern of activities of a dean of students is found under a whimsical title. See W. Storrs Lee, *God Bless Our Queer Old Dean.* New York: G. P. Putnam's Sons, 1959.

[36] Goodnight, *op. cit.,* pp. 219-220.

often and so well—correct, namely, that a sincere and earnest appeal to a student's better nature is more effective than any other?

2. If so, have I given sufficient thought and earnest effort to disciplining my own mind and heart and strengthening my own character to prepare me well for the effective guidance of youth?

3. Am I relying too much upon records, tests, and other mechanical or material data to the neglect of the study of the student himself and finding the way to his heart and conscience to influence him directly?

4. Am I more concerned with the mental and physical welfare of students and with their material advancement than with their character development?

5. Do I properly fall under Dean Ten Hoor's indictment, that I am far more apt at discovering motes in other eyes than beams in my own? Or, putting it another way, have I the basic integrity to work diligently and effectively in this great field of student guidance and with no feeling of sham or hypocrisy?

No doubt there have been many instances in which this apprehension has been well grounded. Moreover, we face a constant danger that our desire for more technical know-how will make us forget that we have a peculiar kind of human relationship with students; we seek to help them to *approximate self-management* of their own development through educational experiences. With proper safeguards against these real dangers, we are committed today to the expansion of the technology undergirding our services.

Another point needs emphasis—not all types of personnel service have advanced at the same pace toward professionalization. Counseling has made the greatest advances, possibly because here there is more technical knowledge and current research in the adjacent fields of psychotherapy, aptitude testing, human development, psychiatry, and the like. But much less progress toward professionalization is evident in services for housing, extracurricular activities, and financial counseling and assistance. If these services are to contribute effectively to the accomplishment of the objectives intrinsic to our point of view, we shall need to expand and extend our research efforts and methods of assistance.

There are other aspects of the student personnel point of view that come to mind. However, the five mentioned will indicate that we view our service in education as complementary to that of classroom teachers—in so far as the individual student's intellectual development is concerned. With respect to other areas of his development, we are the principal educators. That is, when we counsel students regarding emotional disturbances or choice of occupation, we are helping them to learn more about themselves. This learning can be profound and may involve much of the technical knowledge available in the lectures of a professor. But we differ from teachers in our educational role; we deal with students as individuals and groups of individuals who are concerned with many aspects of *their own development*. In a sense, this is the curriculum of student personnel work—the student's *own* full development.[37]

CONTENT OF THE PROGRAM

Our principal thesis is not the historical development of personnel work, but rather *its present form of administration*.[38] We begin discussion of this topic by noting that administrative processes do not operate in a vacuum; they have no existence apart from the content of the program being administered. That is, administration is an organized pattern of means and processes geared to achieve formulated but ever-changing objectives. Thus administration does not exist in and of itself—apart from the processes and program content which are related to objectives. Moreover, administration is not a mechanical, depersonalized, button-pushing machine; rather, it consists of patterns of personal skills involved in the conduct of a program of services. The pattern of administration is not fixed in a mechanical rigidity. Indeed, both the structure and functions of administration are continually changed in terms of the personalities of the staff and administrators, the clientele served, and the changing content of the program of services.

Therefore, the word "administration" does not carry full meaning apart from the program content and the end objectives of the program. Thus it is that we review the content of the program in terms of what staff members actually do to achieve specified objectives. Also we shall stress the content of the program as an integral part of an institution's educational aim, not as something apart from the context of education. As a matter of fact, student personnel work

[37] E. G. Williamson, "The Dean of Students as Educator," *The Educational Record*, July, 1957, pp. 230–240.

[38] An extensive and critical evaluation of the program was made by Ruth Barry and Beverly Wolf, *Modern Issues in the Guidance and Personnel Work*. New York: Bureau of Publications, Columbia University, 1957.

does not and could not exist apart from an institution of learning as we know it today. One may note similarities between such programs and services and those found in industries and governmental agencies. However, we shall stress the unique and peculiar characteristics of programs that help college adolescents to achieve self-development. A typical matched listing of student needs and services might be as follows:[39]

Students and Their University Problems	Student Personnel Services
Orientation to the college environment through interpreting the college's objectives, selecting students and informing students of processes, procedures, and resources of the college.	Information and counseling prior to, and at the time of, admission to college; orientation during freshman week, freshman camps, and other programs.
Problems involved in intellectual mastery of studies and effective effort to learn new subject matter. Experience of deep motivation to learn more of the results of man's conquest of ignorance about himself and his universe.	Vocational and educational counseling; maintenance of records and diagnostic data useful in helping the college and the student understand his capabilities and his progress; special remediation services concerning reading, study habits, speech, and emotional development.
Choosing an occupational goal consistent with his aptitudes and interests and making progress in the requisite training for that goal.	Counseling about educational, vocational, and personal goals through interpretation of relevant case data, including tests of aptitude and interest.

[39] Adapted from "The Student Personnel Point of View," A Report of a Conference on the Philosophy and Development of Student Personnel Work in College and University, American Council on Education Studies, ser. 1, vol. 1, no. 3, Washington, June, 1937.

More comprehensive descriptions of the content of services are presented in these books:

Arbuckle, Dugald S.: Student Personnel Services in Higher Education. New York: McGraw-Hill Book Company, Inc., 1953.
——, and Joseph F. Kauffman.: "Student Personnel Services in Liberal Arts Colleges," The Personnel and Guidance Journal, vol. 37, pp. 296–299, December, 1959.
Knapp, Robert H.: Practical Guidance Methods. New York: McGraw-Hill Book Company, Inc., 1953.
Lloyd-Jones, Esther, and Margaret Ruth Smith: Student Personnel Work as Deeper Teaching. New York: Harper & Brothers, 1954.
Wrenn, C. Gilbert: Student Personnel Work in Colleges and Universities. New York: The Ronald Press Company, 1951.

Students and Their University Problems	Student Personnel Services
Progressive maturity in understanding and valuation of himself as a unique individual in relation to his associations with other unique individuals participating in the same democratic community.	Friendly and personal relationships maintained by teachers and staff with individual students as an accepted institutional practice; growing understanding and self-reference concerning value orientation and commitments and religious philosophy.
Development and maintenance of a sense of belonging to the collegiate institution; group morale achieved through active membership in small groups of congenial and like-minded students; student participation in management of institutional and student affairs; balanced social-recreational-intellectual participation.	Assistance to students in the development and redevelopment of constructive and meaningful group activities—social, recreational, political, professional, etc.; development of effective and satisfying group leadership and membership roles.
Means of developing new and significant interests and deepening old ones which continue to have meaning for the student.	Extended reading in the literature of man's experiences; participation in special lectures and discussions and in organized activities.
Assistance and encouragement in learning the arts of living, playing, and working effectively and amicably with others.	Improvements in residential facilities and experiences; effective membership and participation in activities.
Finding suitable quarters and living effectively away from home and parents.	Assistance in locating healthful and congenial living quarters; inspecting and maintaining the satisfactory standards of such quarters.
Progress in emotional development and in deeper insight into students' own emotional nature.	Personal relationships with teachers and counselors concerning developmental experiences.
Physical and mental health.	Physical and mental health services which help maintain sound personal conditions in the community.
Continuous development of ethical and moral understanding apace with other phases of growth.	A program of coordinated interfaith religious activities and encouragement of strong denominational programs by churches; religious and moral counseling.
Continuous reexamination and establishment of institutional and student rules of conduct.	Student judicial responsibility and organization within all organized groups and in the college as a whole; disciplinary counseling as

Students and Their University Problems	Student Personnel Services
	opposed to restriction and imposed discipline.
Financial self-support in a manner which adds to intellectual, social, and emotional growth.	A program of financial counseling through which students learn how to live on their resources and to use the cultural, social, and intellectual activities of the college; assistance in finding and profiting from remunerative work which may add to the student's personal and professional growth.
Preparation for satisfying and socially acceptable sexual adjustment.	Sound and special counseling regarding both physical and psychological adjustments in marriage.
Preparation for satisfactory postcollege adjustment in home, at work, and in the community.	Assistance in finding initial postgraduation employment in which the student's training and aspirations will be advantageous.

ORGANIZATIONAL STRUCTURE OF SERVICES

In the preceding section we outlined the traditional and customary student personnel services found on many campuses. But these were generalized or even idealized statements of functions without regard for the modifications and variations to be found on every campus. Diversity rather than uniformity is characteristic of student personnel services, as of every other phase of an institution of higher education in America. This diversity grew out of two sources: the personalities and idiosyncrasies of the originators; and the unique developmental history of each institution. An understanding of the uniqueness of each institution's program is necessary for a full comprehension of its services. We include in this and later chapters material illustrative of diversity, charts showing organization or structures of services. The first chart, on page 26, is that of Brigham Young University, by courtesy of Dean Wesley Lloyd, whose program is said to be the most comprehensive of all. Other charts will illustrate the uniqueness of each campus program. The reader will note that not every one of the generalized descriptions will be found on every campus and that many additional services will be embraced. Additional institutional organizational charts are given in Chapter 3 for Washington State University, University of Denver, Ohio State University, and Florida State University. At this point we include a generalized statement describing still another form of organization for a small liberal arts college, Occidental College, by courtesy of Dean Mary Laing Swift. Dean Swift describes Occidental's program in a private letter:

The broader aspects of counseling and the general problems of all college students are handled by a Counseling Committee composed of the Dean of the Faculty, the Dean of Women, the Dean of Men, the Registrar, the Director of Vocational Guidance, the Chaplain, and representatives from the departments of Psychology and Religion. The counseling relationship at Occidental College aims to provide each student opportunities for personal growth and development. It is a belief of the Counseling Committee that the primary purpose of counseling is neither advice nor reprimand nor suggestion; that advice at the best is disregarded and at the worst is a way of evading responsibility on the part of the student.

The primary responsibility for counseling is concentrated in the offices of the Dean of Men and the Dean of Women. This fact is communicated to all students who seek counseling help in these two offices. Many resources are available to the Deans in assisting students in their adjustment to college life. These resources include the services of the members of the Department of Psychology, the Health Staff with two College Physicians, the College Chaplain, the Committee for International Students, and the office of Vocational Guidance and Placement.

Academic guidance is primarily in the hands of departmental chairmen and the Registrar although both the Dean of Men and the Dean of Women serve in this area with students who have not made the choice of a definite major.

In contrasting the formal and elaborate structure of Brigham Young with that of Occidental College, one should note that on a small campus with fewer students, the organizational structure is much more casual and informal. Such informality is associated with, or even caused by, the small volume of business due to the small number of students, and also by the traditional informality associated with face-to-face relationships possible only in small institutions. Thus far, no one has been able to invent an organizational structure involving large numbers of persons—both staff and students—which maintains and permits the continued informality of the small institution such as Occidental College. Larger organizations inevitably become more formal and sometimes, unfortunately, impersonal. But large institutions still can seek for new ways to maintain informality of relationships in spite of the large numbers of students served. This is a major responsibility of administrators of student personnel services. We shall have more to say about this type of administrative leadership in subsequent chapters.

DESIRABLE NEW DEVELOPMENTS PROPOSED

In June of 1950, several university administrators and student personnel workers representing different special fields met in Washington to formulate a statement of desirable next steps in the development of the over-all program. Their deliberations were made in the light of past experience in different kinds of institutions. The results are found in the following statement of twelve needed aims in higher education:[40]

1. To achieve a better degree of integration between the student personnel programs in secondary schools and institutions for higher education.
2. To achieve a higher degree of integration between the student personnel services and instructional programs.
3. To assist college administrators in translating the student-centered concept of education into specific institutional objectives against which the effectiveness of the institution can be measured.
4. To establish high standards of selection and of professional competence for the specialized personnel worker.
5. To aid college president, academic deans, and departmental chairmen in recognizing that one of the criteria for advancement in rank and salary should be the competence of individual faculty members in advising students and in their overall personnel relationships with students.
6. To bring about wider recognition of the fact that if adequate personnel services are desired they must have a substantial and secure place in the institutional budget.
7. To develop overall administrative plans and procedures which will enable the specialized personnel staff to integrate their work with the other phases of the institutional administration.

[40] *Future Needs in Student Personnel Work.* Washington: American Council on Education, 1950. A statement prepared at a conference of college and university educators.

8. To recognize and take advantage of the occupational motivation of the student.

9. To improve systems of personnel records and their utilization within the institution.

10. To improve both quality and quantity of research on the instruments, processes, and programs of student personnel work.

11. To provide for the active participation of students in shaping policies and procedures of the student personnel program.

12. To have personnel workers deliberately apportion time for work with the superior and gifted students.

Changes in Earlier Formulations

Certain emphases, points of view, and content have been retained during the past several decades in student personnel programs. For example, emphasis is still placed upon the individual student and his development. The student is not, however, seen as an isolated individual; equally heavy emphasis is laid upon the campus school in which he achieves his development. But there are certain changes in the formulation. For example, in Hopkins's early statement of the content of personnel programs,[41] much emphasis was laid upon the value of personnel work as it could individualize classroom instruction and education in general. For example, Hopkins stated—[42]

The concept I have had before me has been that it means work having to do specifically with the individual in education. One might question how this differs from the concept of education itself. I do not assume that it does differ. . . . One of the functions, therefore, of personnel administration in education is to bring to bear upon any educational problem the point of view which concerns itself primarily with the individual.

In line with this conception, D. G. Paterson, an early associate of Hopkins, was often heard to say that counseling, one of several personnel functions, was an attempt to "individualize mass education."

In recent years this view of personnel work as a means of individualizing education has been somewhat replaced. There has been more preoccupation with direct services to students by specialists and less emphasis upon individualization efforts involving other

[41] L. B. Hopkins, "Personnel Procedure in Education," *The Educational Record Supplement*, no. 3, October, 1926.

[42] *Ibid.*, p. 5.

BRIGHAM YOUNG UNIVERSITY, Administrative Organization
Chart for Student Personnel Services

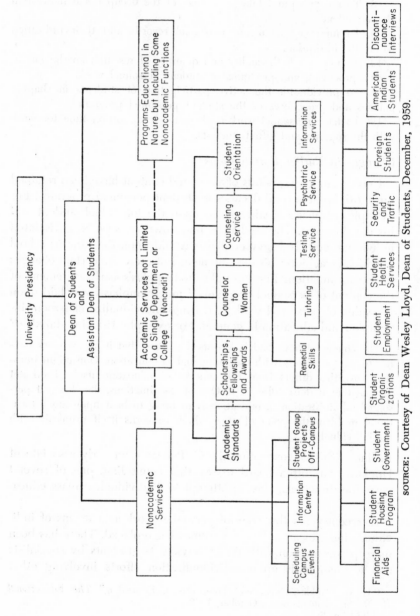

SOURCE: Courtesy of Dean Wesley Lloyd, Dean of Students, December, 1959.

staff members, notably classroom teachers. For example, counselors today are less concerned with helping teachers develop improved examinations and with similar matters which loomed large in the literature of a few decades ago.[43] As a matter of fact, a new specialty in examination construction has recently developed apart from the student personnel program. In the earlier literature of student personnel work there was much discussion of the use of placement tests for selecting, classifying, and assigning students to different levels of instruction within the classroom; of improved examinations to secure more valid criteria against which to check scholastic aptitude tests; and of similar matters directly related to the institution's instructional program. Such topics are seldom discussed in the contemporary literature of student personnel work.

Other earlier emphases have persisted, but are given much less attention. We refer to the use of members of the teaching faculty for advising and counseling students. Such a discussion received marked attention in Hopkins's 1925 survey:[44]

As far back as we have knowledge of the American college there is indication that, among the faculty members, there were certain individuals who thoroughly enjoyed personal contact with their students. These were the men also to whom the students went for counsel and advice. At a later date, in many institutions, there developed the recognition of a need for more of this type of service, and it became more or less the accepted thing to formalize this service by the appointment of faculty advisers.

In contrast, much of the current literature on counseling stresses the development of more technical and specialized psychological services performed by psychologically trained counselors. It is evident that the development of a technology underlying counseling has created the need for technically trained counselors. We are not here arguing the case of psychologists versus faculty advisers, since we believe that to be a false issue. Rather are we pointing to some of the significant recent changes in personnel work. Elsewhere we will indicate our interpretation and evaluation of some of these changes.

Another recent change in emphasis should be noted. The earlier

[43] See mention of this personnel function in *Ibid.*
[44] *Ibid.*, p. 25.

literature centered attention on the optimum development of the individual student within the limits of his capacity. This emphasis has not been lost in the changes of the past few decades. But a perusal of the 1949 formulation of the student personnel point of view reveals additional stress upon the societal context of the growth of the individual pupil.[45] That is, the philosophy of growth for growth's sake has been modified to include growing in relationships with other individuals. This socialization phase of instruction and personnel work appears earlier in some of the discussions of dormitory life, student activities, and the like. The 1949 formulation, however, is an explicit statement of this essential area of individual development.

A third major addition may be found by contrasting Hopkins's statement of objectives and content with the 1949 formulation of the American Council on Education. In the earlier literature, the emphasis was placed upon the value of service in assisting the individual to grow; his growth was taken as an end in itself, containing its own end value. Perhaps this concept was a remnant of the influence of the nineteenth-century political philosophy of individualism. At any rate, today more emphasis is placed on the importance —for society itself—of the optimum development of the individual. The individual is not deprived thereby of any of the enjoyment of his own development; rather, his development is seen as having far-reaching social significance. Therefore, failure to develop is seen not only as a source of dissatisfaction and unhappiness to the individual, but also as a loss to society. Every individual who does not reach his full growth cannot be expected by society to play his full maximum role in that society—economically, socially, politically, or in any other way. For this reason, we find increased emphasis upon the societal importance of the maximum growth of the individual in the conservation of human talent.[46]

A fourth current emphasis emerged in the formulation of personnel programs in the conference sponsored jointly by the U.S. Office of Education and the American Council on Education. In a sense, this new emphasis is a return to Hopkins's stress upon personnel work as a means of individualizing education. The 1950

[45] *The Student Personnel Point of View,* American Council on Education Studies, rev. ser. 6, vol. 13, no. 13, Washington, September, 1949.
[46] Paterson, *op. cit.*

conference stressed the need for a closer and more effective integration of personnel programs with the instructional programs of an institution. In the same year, the movement was criticized for its neglect of this very integration by a friendly critic in the following words:[47]

It [student personnel work] has been less alert and apt in relating its professed concern with students to the work of teachers and to the philosophy and program of the educational enterprise as a whole. It is still true, as it always has been, that the crucial roles in higher education are those of the teacher and the student, and any program or development which is not fundamentally concerned with their main work is bound to continue as a marginal service, however important it may be.

We shall have more to say about this point in later sections.

Modern Student Personnel Services

We may describe the content of student personnel services in still another way, categorizing services into the following rubrics:

Advising by Members of the Instructional Staff and Faculty. For the most part, this program has to do with assisting students in meeting the faculty's requirements for graduation. More and more advisers and counselors are becoming proficient in using data to diagnose the student's capabilities and in making such diagnoses before the individual gives evidence of inability to master the curriculum. This is, of course, the plan advanced so eloquently by William Rainey Harper as early as 1899.[48] And it is a major change from earlier days when students were permitted to choose a curriculum and then a faculty adviser told them what was required in order to meet their desired degree or diploma. Also, faculty advisers increasingly are accepting implications of the philosophy of student personnel work, with its major emphasis upon the individual student as a growing entity and on that growth as the central purpose of our education. The common adoption of this point of view makes for effective relationships between teacher and student; heightened morale for both; optimum learning of the formal

[47] *25-year Report*, 1925–1950. New Haven, Conn.: The Edward W. Hazen Foundation, p. 34.

[48] William Rainey Harper, *The Trend in Higher Education.* Chicago: University of Chicago Press, 1905, chap. 20, "The Scientific Study of the Student."

content of the curriculum; and other improvements in the general effectiveness of the institution.

Psychological Testing for Counseling at the Time of Admission. Evaluation of course credits for admission to college or for transfer from one institution to another is not student personnel work. But the use of psychological tests to evaluate the capabilities and interests of the individual before admission is a personnel function—or it may be viewed as a contribution of personnel workers to the reorganization and restructuring of the admission function. That is, even though personnel workers do not administer or participate in the admissions process in many colleges, they do contribute data, technical services, and consultation to those who do make decisions concerning the institution's formal admissions requirements.[49]

In some institutions, the admissions and registrar's office is part of the office of the dean of students. And in complex institutions, admissions are part of the responsibilities of the personnel program within the university. Such variations in programs make difficult generalizations concerning organizations, functions, and program content. Arbuckle also contributed to our understanding of the personnel program by analyzing and describing classroom teaching from a counselor's perspective of what teachers can and should do concerning students' personal problems and needs.

Orientation and Induction to College Life. Two phases of orientation are of concern to the personnel worker. First, the personnel worker usually coordinates the manifold subprograms involving most departments of the institution. Therefore, this is a phase of student personnel work, even though it involves correlating the work of some departments not formally included in the personnel program. For example, the payment of tuition and fees must be correlated with the other orientation and induction processes. However, this matter is handled by the institution's business department and is not within the personnel program. Many other phases of the total orientation program are direct responsibilities of the personnel departments. For example, the administration of the social program, orientation lectures, lectures on how to study, introductory convo-

---

[49] An excellent description of admissions practices and programs is included in D. S. Arbuckle, *Student Personnel Services in Higher Education.* New York: McGraw-Hill Book Company, Inc., 1953, chap. 3.

cations, and other comparable events are usually integral parts of the personnel program.

Special Skills or Remediation Clinics. Increasingly, modern research in human development has provided a foundation for professional services to aid individuals whose scholastic development is not proceeding satisfactorily in some respects. Remediation clinics on reading, study habits, psychological therapy, and speech are administratively part of the student personnel program, although not in all institutions.

Counseling. Many forms are included. They range from intensive and extensive time-consuming counseling by professionally oriented psychological counselors to a more simplified counseling by members of the faculty. Currently, counseling programs of modified and special character are being organized for special groups such as foreign students, who present special problems not always within the competence and training of psychotherapists or vocational guidance experts. In like manner, we shall see that within each type of college residence, new forms of simplified counseling are being developed apart from the centralized clinical types but correlated with them.

Housing Services. These services include securing housing; maintaining standards of hygiene, safety, and behavior in dormitories, fraternities, sororities, and private rooming houses; residential counseling; and stimulating students to participate in governing and administering the dormitories and other residences.

Health Services. Diagnostic identification of health problems and the maintenance of students' physical and mental health through medical services are included.

Religious Programs. Staff officers coordinate and stimulate interfaith programs and various denominational religious programs which are not legally a part of the institution but are of great importance in the total development of individual students.

The Extracurriculum. Responsibilities include supervision and development of the extracurriculum—to the end that it shall not be a negative intellectual and social influence in the college community, but rather shall contribute positively to the normal development of individual students. Activities may be utilized for many types of learning; students gain competence in handling controversy and conflict and in participating effectively in the management of the institution.[50]

Discipline. The handling of misbehavior is a necessary function; it needs to be carried out so that positive contributions are made to the rehabilitation of the individual student.

Financial Counseling. Students are counseled with regard to the use of their money. Loans and scholarships are granted to assist scholastically able students who most need such support.

Premarriage Counseling. This specialized form of counseling concerns itself with relationships in dating and in preparation for marriage.

Job Placement. Service and information are given students to secure jobs following graduation or severance from the university.

STRUCTURING PERSONNEL FUNCTIONS

The content of a program of services for students is divided; responsibilities are assigned to different members of the staff. As we shall see in Chapter 3, workers are assigned to bureaus, centers, offices, or staffs, each responsible for a relatively homogeneous group of services or functions. Sometimes a comparison of these departmental groups with the listing of services or functions given above reveals differences. That is, some bureaus may carry responsibility for several of the functions listed and, in addition, may carry some administrative responsibilities not specified among program services. Later, we shall discuss the problem of administrative structuring and organizing of service functions. At this point, we shall complete our discussion of the content of the student personnel program, naming some parts which are not readily classified above or in subsequent chapters. For example, in all bureaus and in the central personnel office, a variety of records must be available for continuous use in administrative decision making, in budget making and expenditure, in evaluation of services, and in various other

[50] Williamson, E. G.: "The Extracurriculum and General Education," *The Fifty-first Yearbook of the National Society for the Study of Education.* Chicago: University of Chicago Press, 1952, part I, pp. 230–249.

————: "The Dean of Students as Educator," *The Educational Record,* vol. 38, no. 3, pp. 230–240, July, 1957.

————, and B. J. Borreson: "Learning to Resolve Social Conflicts," *The Educational Record,* vol. 31, no. 1, pp. 26–38, January, 1950.

ways. Record keeping is clearly not the same type of function as is orientation. The former may be called a "supportive function," necessary to a direct service to students; the latter is itself a direct service. We shall see that there are many such supportive functions. Indeed, *administration, our central topic, is almost entirely a supportive personnel function.*

Other supportive services include the following:

1. Coordination of religious programs and staff workers employed by church foundations. Usually these are outside the legal responsibility of the college, but still operate within the greater university program of services to students.

2. Coordination of the manifold counseling and supervisory services operating within dormitories and residences, fraternities, sororities, and rooming houses.

3. Special direct and coordinating services involved in the needs and adjustments of foreign resident students.

4. Coordination of content, facilities, place, and date of the many recreational programs, events, and activities carried on by student organizations, student unions, university departments of athletics and physical education, music, theater arts, and others.

5. Maintenance of traffic order within the campus; handling violation of parking and traffic regulations and the possession and use of cars.

6. A host of other special assignments peculiar to each institution and growing out of local traditions and the dynamic interplay of personalities, needs, functions, and resources.

This book will discuss and evaluate the central and special problems, techniques, and processes involved in the management of programs of services and functions. Other descriptions of the program content of services are available. We shall describe ways in which the program of services is organized, conducted, and administered. To be sure, from time to time, we shall comment on particular services or illustrate an administrative technique by special reference to a particular personnel service. But in the main we shall restrict ourselves to describing and evaluating administrative processes involved in the day-to-day management of services to students and to those involved in the over-all integration of these services into an organized institution-wide program.

We have thus far itemized traditional student services found in the literature of our work. These services have evolved over the past few decades in organized form; they are presently staffed by increasingly professionalized specialists who supplement the efforts of the teaching faculty. In calling these services traditional, we mean to characterize them as well established in the programs and budgets of most colleges. To be sure, there are variations and unique forms. This is appropriate to the established principle of diversity in American higher education. But there is a growing edge in student personnel work parallel to that identified by Riesman in the classroom curriculum.[51] Some services have expanded and changed more rapidly than others. For example, we have noted that counseling has exceeded all other services in its technical-research development and in its degree of professionalization.

Some new services—beyond those listed in 1925 by Hopkins and in 1949 by the Committee of the American Council on Education—have developed and emerged to the point where their form and objective are visible. Deans of students and other personnel workers have been forced by changing campus and student life to forge new content and new techniques. For instance, the advanced maturity and background experiences of war veterans may have accelerated and changed in form the restructuring of students' relationship with the university's central administration. In Chapter 12 we shall discuss some of the new services which are arising because of these forces. Campus and student life has been profoundly changed by local and national upheavals. Consider the effects of the frantic search for security from fifth-column penetration, and the tidal wave of reformist sentiment caused by racial and ethnic inequalities. As a result of the interplay of campus and community, today's students present to us new personal problems. Sometimes these come from individuals—but frequently there are group inquiries and pressures for reforms of the college itself. In the case of some new services, we have first outlined the problem situation and traced its historical and philosophical development.

[51] David Riesman, *Constraint and Variety in American Education*. Lincoln, Neb.: University of Nebraska Press, 1956. Riesman used the figure of the differing rates of speed and positions of the head, middle, and tail of a snake as it propelled itself forward. Different parts of an institution grow and expand at different rates and therefore are at different states of development at any one time.

This procedure is followed in Chapters 9 and 10 concerning the puzzling aspects of what is called "civil liberties" for students, as these liberties have been blended with the historic academic-freedom concept imported from German universities. In Chapter 10, we traced some of the administrative processes involved in one institution's efforts to resolve the associated conflict situation by reformulating an institutional policy, adapting it to fit the temper of the times. In Chapter 12, we traced some administrative processes used in restructuring the adolescent's traditional conflict with authority-administration over student conduct and behavior. The development of a new form of partnership in the exercise of student judiciary responsibilities was the situation problem which served to illuminate these administrative processes.

In describing the content and form of new services evolving around such new student problems, we departed from the style of other chapters which dealt with traditional services already adequately described in available literature. With these exceptions, we have stressed the subject of this book—administrative processes and techniques used in organizing and managing certain services for our student clientele.

SUMMARY

We thus see that student personnel work has arisen out of things gone wrong. It is, in many instances, first a corrective and later a preventive program, which increases the likelihood of the optimum development of each individual. But it is not restricted to one method or one technique or one program. Rather it is as broad in purposes and methods as is the range of human nature, as wide as the ever-expanding and deepening knowledge of human nature, and as deep as our slowly increasing fund of verified knowledge of ways and means to aid individuals in developing optimally through the organized learning experiences available in our colleges and universities. Our task is to uncover and to evaluate the administrative processes and techniques necessary in managing these many services in day-to-day relationships with students.

CHAPTER 2

The Art of Administration

Administration is the organizing and carrying out of a program of activities and functions to achieve desired and specified objectives.[1] Or we may define our subject operationally in these words: "Administration is accomplished through the behavior of administrators in interaction with others."[2]

Barnard stated that "the life of an organization depends upon its ability to secure and maintain the personal contributions of energy . . . necessary to effect its purposes."[3]

We may add to his statement one by Hemphill indicating a signifi-

[1] Student personnel staffs and organizations have not become sufficiently large and complex to arouse fear of producing an "organization man." Nevertheless the theory and fact of organizations would be incompletely understood without some orientation to Whyte's analysis of the process of replacement of the Protestant ethic of hard work and frugality by the social ethic of conformity to the requirements of the organized group. See William H. Whyte, Jr., *The Organization Man*. New York: Simon and Schuster, Inc., 1956.

The reader should also read a critical review of Whyte's work. See Robert Lekachman, "Organization Men: The Erosion of Individuality," *Commentary*, March, 1957, pp. 270–276.

[2] Andrew W. Halpin (ed.), *Administrative Theory in Education*. Chicago: Midwest Administration Center, 1958, p. 32.

[3] Barnard, Chester I.: *The Functions of the Executive*. Cambridge, Mass.: Harvard University Press, 1948, p. 92.

Halpin (ed.), *op. cit.*

Moore, Wilbert E., and Richard C. Snyder: "The Conference on Theory of Organization," *Items*, vol. 6, no. 4, Social Science Research Council, December, 1952.

Parsons, Talcott: "Suggestions for a Sociological Approach to the Theory of Organizations," *Administrative Science Quarterly*, vol. 1, pp. 225–239, September, 1956.

Barnard's principal concepts were used to outline in simple form and style the scope and dimensions of administration. See Melvin T. Copeland, "The Job of an Executive," *Harvard Business Review*, Winter, 1940, pp. 148–160.

cant necessary condition for organizing the teamwork effort of several individuals: "The component parts of the task are seen to be dependently related to one another and to the solution of the initial problem." [4] And Getzels adds to our perception of administration another facet: [5]

. . . we may conceive of administration *structurally* as the hierarchy of subordinate-superordinate relationships within a social system. *Functionally*, this hierarchy of relationships is the locus for allocating and integrating roles and facilities in order to achieve the goals of the social system. It is here, in these relationships, that the assignment of statuses, the provision of facilities, the organization of procedures, the regulation of activity, and the evaluation of performance takes place.

These generalized statements touch on many parts of a complicated enterprise. First, there must be common tasks and mutual problems and content which require administration in the enterprise. For instance, in the field of student personnel work, the content is the program of services to students, as outlined in the preceding chapter. The desired and specified objectives, tasks, or problems of such a program arise out of the institution's educational philosophy and the staff members' points of view. The workers must perceive their separate operations as parts of an integrated whole. The phrase used earlier, "the organizing and carrying out of a program," refers to the use of procedures, techniques, and other means to achieve the program objectives or to solve common problems. Lastly, our definition implies that there are special agents whose function or role it is to assist the workers who carry on the day-to-day services—to help them perform these services so that the objectives of the program will be achieved. Barnard defines the function of these special agents in the following way: [6]

In a unit organization there are executive functions to be performed, but not necessarily by a single individual continuously. They may be performed alternately by the several persons who contribute to the organization. In complex organizations, on the other hand, the necessities

[4] John K. Hemphill, "Administration as Problem-solving," in Halpin (ed.), *op. cit.*, chap. V.
[5] Jacob W. Getzels, "Administration as a Social Process," in Halpin (ed.), *op. cit.*, chap. VII, p. 151.
[6] Barnard, *op. cit.*, p. 111.
Parsons refers to the "managerial" system. See Halpin (ed.), *op. cit.*, p. 43; Parsons, *op. cit.*, p. 44.

of communication result almost invariably in the localization of the executive functions of the subordinate unit organizations normally in one person. This is necessary for reasons of formal communication, but it is also necessary to establish executive organizations, that is, those units specializing in the executive functions. The executives of several unit organizations as a group, usually with at least one other person as a superior, form an executive organization.

Halpin also called attention to the fact that ". . . the managerial organization [is] controlled by the 'institutional' structure and agencies of the community . . . no organization is ever wholly independent." [6a]

In a real sense, we shall see that every staff member of any program of student personnel services not only carries on certain technical services; he also performs administrative or executive functions while carrying on these technical services. Thus, while there are specialized administrators who deal with the over-all, overlapping, and interdepartmental dovetailing of specialized programs, every staff member must perform some administrative functions if he is to work effectively as part of a team of workers. Sears referred to the decentralization of administrative processes as unique in the democratic concept of administration:[7]

There are two widely different concepts of how an organization should be made and how it should operate. According to one, the power that holds the organization together and directs it resides in and is applied by one person; according to the other, that power may be unified, but, as for its origin and use, originates in and is distributed to all parts of the organization. The governing principle of the one type we call autocracy; of the other, democracy. Both provide for unity of action, for cooperation, but in one case power to direct or to command does not, in the other it does, have to answer to those who are commanded. Or, in the one case, policies and plans are formed by the executive and handed down; whereas, in the other, they are built up by all who help to execute them.

Throughout our discussion, we shall stress this dual localization of administrative duties in (1) specialized administrators whose

[6a] Halpin (ed.), *op. cit.*, p. 44.
[7] Jesse B Sears, *The Nature of the Administrative Process.* New York: McGraw-Hill Book Company, Inc., 1950, pp. 93–94.
See also Harold Benjamin (ed.), *Democracy in the Administration of Higher Education.* New York: Harper & Brothers, 1950.

principal task is to help others carry on their programs; and in (2) each member of the staff who performs some administrative functions as an integral part of his own technical services.

Need for Administration?

We may properly begin our discussion of the nature of administration by answering this question. Speaking of the relationships of experts and administrators, Parsons pointed out that "the 'reference group' to which the expert looks in connection with his competence and the definition of its standards is not his 'managerial' boss but his professional peers and colleagues."[8] This principle clearly operates in colleges and universities. Indeed, writers sometimes assert that the educational enterprise needs only trained teaching and research specialists who carry on their own specialties. And in some academic circles, such an attitude toward administrators has been borrowed from European institutions, but without transfer of the unique type of administrative structure. As described by Abraham Flexner—[9]

The German university is ultimately governed by a central authority, the education ministry of each of the eight federated states . . . the business affairs of the university are looked after by the local *kurator* both through subordinates on the ground and through his own immediate contact with the ministry; the confidential representative of the government, he likewise is the trusted representative of the university in its dealings with the administration.

To a considerable extent, the European attitude of faculty members toward administrators has been carried over to American institutions. As a result, many critical comments are made about the lack of any necessity for deans and other administrators. One evaluation of college administrators described the university president as "an agreeable but purely decorative feature, his chief function being, as one of my colleagues said, to obviate the difficulties created by his office. I have never shared this view."[10] Such a faculty attitude toward administration has been given most cutting expression in the trenchant words of Veblen: "All that is here intended to be said

[8] Halpin (ed.), *op. cit.*, p. 47.
[9] Abraham Flexner, *Universities: American, English, German.* New York: Oxford University Press, 1930, pp. 316–317.
[10] Carl L. Becker, *Cornell University Founders and the Founding.* Ithaca N.Y.: Cornell University Press, 1943, pp. 199–200.

is nothing more than the *obiter dictum* that, seen from the point of view of the higher learning, the academic executive and all his works are anathema, and should be discontinued by the simple expedient of wiping him off the slate. . . ." [11]

Perhaps Veblen's caustic obiter dictum is but one individual's expression of a prevalent and persistent American attitude, the "right to distrust and criticize our public officials." Perhaps it is even an offshoot or special case of "a deep distrust of government and particularly of central government."[12]

Such an attitude as Veblen's toward the need for administrators is often associated with a reaction against the claimed attitude of administrators toward the faculty. In the words of J. McKeen Cattell: "The president and trustees hold the reins of power and exercise supreme control, while the professors are legally in the position of employees of the corporation."[13]

There is an opposing viewpoint concerning the issue of control versus participation in academic government of an institution. This opposing point of view was voiced by the president of Wabash College, a liberal arts institution: "While we have lamentable examples of presidents and boards of trustees who regard the professor as a hired hand, expected to approach administration deferentially with hat in hand, we have even more examples of faculty attitudes toward administrative officers and trustees which are just as lamentable and no more easily justified."[14] Trippet develops his argument from the assertion that the role of the faculty "in university management did not originate in academic freedom. Academic freedom means that the professor must be protected in his teaching and his research from the president, the dean, the board of trustees, and the public. It does not mean that he and he alone has the right

[11] Thorstein Veblen, *The Higher Learning in America.* Stanford, Calif.: Academic Reprints, 1954, p. 286.

[12] Henry Steele Commager, "The University and the Commonwealth," *Proceedings of the Centennial Symposium of the Continuing Education Service of Michigan State College,* February 25–26, 1955, East Lansing, Mich., p. 19.

[13] J. McKeen Cattell, *University Control.* A Series of Volumes for the Promotion of Scientific Research and Educational Progress, The Science Press, New York, 1913, vol. III, p. 474.

[14] B. K. Trippet, "The Role of a Faculty in College Administration," *Bulletin of the American Association of University Professors,* September, 1957, p. 489.

to say what the character and mission of the university shall be."[15]

We shall discover that the concepts of academic administration and academic freedom have become confused by many. Actually, they are separate, but related, issues in the history of American higher education. For our present discussion, we avoid such confusion, observing that the cause of faculty participation in academic government rests upon valid and historical assumptions which are related to those underlying the cause of freedom of teaching. However, these assumptions are more significantly a part—the essential part—of the search for effective management of the institution, but they are not the whole of the scope of management. We shall elaborate this thesis in the discussion of many aspects of the personnel program.

One other counter-Veblen point of view may be borrowed from a broader evaluation of the role of government: "The notion that the sole concern of a free society is the limitation of governmental authority and that government is best which governs least is certainly archaic . . . that government is best which governs best."[16]

We will not explore this side of the American pattern of administration in higher education. Rather, we urge the reader to look into this background, which has considerable potential influence on the acceptance and operation of student personnel work. Somehow or other, in the context of such faculty attitudes toward the central administration, we must seek to win faculty support and sympathy. A sophisticated understanding of this recent history would help to avoid some of the difficulties that we note as we endeavor to find a relevant place for our services in an institution where faculty strive to become more than Trippet's "hired hands."[17]

---

[15] *Ibid.*, p. 488.

[16] Robert M. Hutchins, "Is Democracy Possible?" *The Saturday Review*, Feb. 21, 1959, p. 58.

[17] Hofstadter, Richard, and Walter P. Metzger: *The Development of Academic Freedom in the United States.* New York: Columbia University Press, 1955.

Cowley, W. H.: "The American System of Academic Government," in *Addresses, Higher Education and Its Publics: Supports and Controls.* San Francisco. Calif.: Western College Association, November 9–12, 1955, pp. 25–34.

What Is Administration?

Pigors defines administration in these words:[18]

How did the innovations of yesterday become the institutions of today? An idea does not institutionalize itself. It has to be organized. When the initiator has proposed a plan and inspired a group of followers with the desire to pursue it, he must devise a way in which their joint purpose can be realized. It is this process of organization and management which I call administration. No group movement endures without it.

The implication in Pigors's generalization is that, if more than one person is involved in the performance of any common or joint function, personal relationships must be maintained in an organized manner if the central purpose is to be achieved and if chaos and anarchy are to be avoided. Barnard says: "An essential element of organization is the willingness of persons to contribute their individual efforts to the cooperative system."[19]

One special feature of the academic scene requires some modification of Barnard's generalization. Perhaps in our illustrations of the attitude of some college faculties toward administrators, there is a reflection of the traditionally independent lone wolf, the college teacher. In part, this independence grows out of the adopted policy of autonomy within each classroom and within each specialty in seperate fields of knowledge. College professors traditionally specialize in single units, i.e., they divide a field so that at least one specialist operates in each restricted field. Therefore, the need for organization concerning interfield and college-wide problems of maintenance and development is less evident, and too often neglected. And perhaps we cannot find that much coordination of specialists is needed—unless we search outside the organization of the departmental curriculum for models to serve in our field of education.

Administration Functions

For the most part, the structure of student personnel work remained simple in staff, budget, and other aspects of organization for some decades. But if someday we are to include a larger pro-

---

[18] Paul Pigors, *Leadership or Domination?* Boston: Houghton Mifflin Company, 1935, p. 246.
[19] Barnard, *op. cit.*, p. 139.

portion of the student body within our service program, then we shall be faced with the necessity of organizing larger and more complex programs of services performed by more and more independently operating members of the staff.

No doubt some readers will argue the question: Why do we need to become more complex in organization? Will we not lose the personalized relationships which have been an essential component of our philosophy and mode of operation? In reply, we believe that most institutions have no choice but to become larger and more highly differentiated in specialized functioning. And it is true that, unless we search for ways of retaining individualization of functioning, we shall indeed lose the desirable personal relationships of the past. Paradoxically, our task becomes one of retaining individualization in our services as we extend our coverage to students by a larger staff. We need to examine the efforts of large corporations to solve this paradox. Perhaps we cannot retain all aspects of the small, intimate colonial college, but we must make great efforts, and no doubt much can be done. We need to remind ourselves that the large universities, in the period 1930 to 1940, made very great progress in individualization of mass education despite huge expansions. We need not conclude beforehand that we have exhausted the possibilities of individualization.

In anticipation of expansion of coverage and services, we begin our present discussion of administration. We can profit from the experiences of organizations that have attained a much more advanced stage of complexity and maturity. They also highlight our own growing pains and experiences. We turn to the writings of students of administration in industry and government for some generalizations and concepts which may be useful in developing more effective organizational and administrative programs. In later chapters, we shall frequently apply these generalizations to our field of work in education. A most useful compilation of these experiences, encyclopedic in scope, is Albert Lepawsky's *Administration: The Art and Science of Organization and Management*.[20] We shall make extensive use of this source, although not limiting ourselves to it.[21]

[20] Published by Alfred A. Knopf, Inc., New York, 1949.

[21] A different approach to a concept of administration with respect to training administrators may be found. See Dan Throop Smith, "Education for Administration," *Harvard Business Review*, Spring, 1945, pp. 360–371.

In the discussions of administration in industry and government, certain terms denoting concepts and generalizations appear with great frequency. Common usage and practice has attached a central meaning to each term; it is this meaning which we shall endeavor to paraphrase for our discussion. We shall discuss very briefly four terms: *policy making, program content, administration and management,* and *organizational structure.*

The "policy" which determines the nature of an enterprise is quite frequently so all-pervasive, and has existed for such a long time, that it is frequently taken for granted and sometimes not even understood in detail. In other cases, the policy may be even unwritten but it is an oral operational statement of central objectives and plans of the institution and its separate parts. The social enterprise within which student personnel service operates, namely, the university, college, or school, has a long and complex developmental history. Policy has emerged out of a series of interrelated, overlapping, often duplicating policies or objectives which have been acquired throughout the decades of operations. Moreover, the policy of any one educational institution is not a unitary thing; it consists of many parts, some of which are at times in conflict and some of which are mutually exclusive in operation. And scarcely a decade goes by but what society imposes new policies or objectives upon the schools and colleges—sometimes without fully abandoning the old, even though they may be contradictory to the new. Other modifications grow out of technological advances. That is, the application of research studies constantly modifies policies to bring them in line with current knowledge of human nature and its development. These and other factors operate to determine the central policies within which personnel work operates in a state of flux. Clearly, a certain amount of flexibility and adaptability in program operations is required.

A second term we shall deal with is "program content." By this term we refer to what is done in the institution to achieve the purposes and objectives stated in the basic policy. The nature of the program content is frequently omitted from discussions of administration, as though administrative practices could operate universally without regard to any and all types of program content. But too wide a divorcement between content and techniques of administration would surely lead to some undesirable lessening of the effectiveness of the enterprise itself. This point has been recognized by Meriam, who says—[22]

The most important thing that has been omitted from that fascinating word "posdcorb" is knowledge of a subject matter. You have to plan something; you have to direct something. When you have to select your staff, you have to determine what the different classes of employees will have to do and then what they will have to know in order to do it. Intimate knowledge of the subject matter with which an administrative agency is primarily concerned is indispensable to the effective, intelligent administration of that agency.

"Administration" involves those operations and techniques which determine policy, develop sources of finance, and coordinate the uses of finances with production and distribution of the services and goods produced by the enterprise. Administration controls the executive management of the enterprise and consists of many specific functions which will be outlined in a later section.

"Management" is the execution of policy and the use of the organization and its facilities and staff to achieve the objectives stated in the policy of the enterprise.

The "organization" is the structure of the enterprise, but the term does not refer solely to the structure and hierarchy of authority as these are usually oversimplified in traditional organizational charts. Rather, organization refers to the integration of the work of the staff with the facilities used in achieving the objectives and policies. Organization includes, therefore, both personnel and matériel.

The term "personnel" refers to the workers and to the managers and executives who use facilities to achieve the objectives of the enterprise. It is the members of the staff who perform the functions or services; in our opinion, they are the most important element in any organization and any enterprise. This point of view shall be the underlying emphasis in our discussion. Members of the staff achieve the objective; they use facilities such as machines and other equipment to achieve these objectives. But they themselves are the real agents; they are the enterprise in its actual functioning.

In order to emphasize further the interrelation of these phases of an enterprise, we quote from Schulze:[23]

[22] Lewis Meriam, *Public Service and Special Training.* Chicago: University of Chicago Press, 1936, pp. 2–3.

[23] J. William Schulze, "Some Definitions," *Bulletin of the Taylor Society*, vol. 4, no. 4, pp. 3–4, August, 1919.

Administration is the force which lays down the object for which an organization and its management are to strive and the broad policies under which they are to operate. . . . An organization is a combination of the necessary human beings, materials, tools, equipment, working space and appurtenances brought together in systematic and effective correlation, to accomplish some desired object. . . . Management is the force which leads, guides, and directs an organization in the accomplishment of a predetermined object.

Some Administrative Functions

We may further clarify the prevailing concept of the nature and content of administration by paraphrasing Gulick's list of functions of the Chief Executive. Gulick developed this list following a study of the functions performed by the President of the United States. But these functions are useful suggestions at all levels of operations and in all kinds of administration. For our purposes, we should not think of these functions as being performed by a single administrator; they are distributed throughout an organization and performed in different ways by different personnel. Gulick coined the nonsense word "posdcorb," each letter of which refers to a specific function performed by administrators. These functions are as follows:[24]

Planning: Working out in schematic form the things that need to be done and the methods for accomplishing the purposes of the enterprise, that is, over-all plan making.

Organizing: Establishing the formal structure of authority through which work is performed, assigned, and coordinated; that is, laying out the program of the enterprise and assigning responsibilities and functions to members of the staff.

Staffing: Hiring and training members of the staff and maintaining favorable working conditions.

Directing: Continued supervision of workers and their work, making decisions, and leading the enterprise. It is obvious that this function is performed at all levels of authority and in all divisions or departments of the enterprise.

[24] Luther Gulick, "Notes on the Theory of Organization," *Papers on the Science of Administration,* Institute of Public Administration. New York, 1937, p. 13.

Thompson has suggested that this nonsense word be rewritten as "pscobord" (silent p) to facilitate memorization through pronunciation. See Halpin (ed.), *op. cit.,* p. 26.

Coordinating: That is, interrelating the parts of the total enterprise into a harmonious whole and avoiding conflicts and duplications which interfere with the entire enterprise.

Reporting: Keeping all members of the staff informed of what goes on in order that they may be able to perform their part of the whole enterprise in a harmonious and coordinated way.

Budgeting: Fiscal planning, accounting control, and maintaining the financial stability of the enterprise.

As we indicated above, these seven administrative functions are not performed without regard to the content of the program. Rather, they are applied in flexible and modified ways, depending on the nature of the enterprise itself. Indeed, later in our discussions of colleges and universities, we shall see that some of these functions are performed by other than personnel workers. For instance, in very few instances do personnel workers or their top administrators perform many budgetary functions. Rather it is a common practice for budgetary allotment to be made to personnel programs; from there on the institution's bookkeeping and accounting controls are applied. In contrast, in certain parts of the educational enterprise, such as a cafeteria or a dormitory, the director of the dormitory or cafeteria must be concerned with earning money and not merely with expending it in performing services for students.

Some Special Features of Administration

Certain generalizations may be derived from the experiences of men in business and governmental administration concerning the requirements of effective organization of services and functions. We may profitably review the literature to learn answers to this question: What operating conditions are found in effective administration as contrasted with ineffective administration? We shall mention six such conditions, including *unity of command, delegation of responsibility, span of control, unifunctional alternative structure, democratic control versus technical competence,* and *coordination.*

"Unity of command" may be paraphrased in the adage "No man can serve two masters." This is self-evident if the two masters issue conflicting orders and requirements; it is not true if the two sources of direction are complementary rather than antagonistic.

That is, there is a special exception to the unity-of-command concept. And Lepawsky says[25]

Dual supervision or joint command is possible despite the organizational tradition that no man can serve two masters. Command in military as in other forms of administration consists in practice not only of (1) simple command, to which the essential power to hire and fire is attached, but also (2) "technical command," which involves giving specialized directions outside the sphere of the recognized commander's competence though within his command jurisdiction.

An increasing number of student personnel services are based upon technical knowledge derived from research; therefore, services increasingly require professional competence of a technical sort. We shall find that this exception to the unity of command has important implications for our treatment of administration. We shall also see that it is difficult to employ administrators—at any level of responsibility—who are equally competent in administration and in the technical content of their programs. And even if the administrator is competent in one specialty within a field, he is not competent in all specialties. For example, even within a counseling program, it is difficult to find an administrator who is both competent and interested in two areas of administration: (1) budget and staff training ranging from secretarial to technical counseling; and (2) specialized fields of aptitude testing, personality theory, achievement testing, psychotherapy, projective testing, and vocational guidance. Personnel work will become increasingly specialized through application of research results. As it does, we will be compelled to modify our current administrative practices to meet the difficulty of encompassing all the techniques and competencies required in the broad-gauged program of personnel services.

Our second feature of effective administration has to do with the "delegation of responsibility." Indistinct, confused, overlapping, and conflicting assignment of duties to members of the staff produces overlapping, duplication, conflict, and inefficiency of operation. Therefore, effective administration involves constant clarification and redefinition of responsibilities of all members of the staff. Such redefinition may occur periodically, as part of an annual review of programs and responsibilities. Or it may take place episodically in

[25] Lepawsky, *op. cit.*, p. 333.

the restructuring of a program that has experienced a cessation or interference of functioning. Restructuring and reassignment of duties occurs when there is a resignation, criticism by students, or the desire to improve service by incorporating a newly discovered technique.

Another aspect of this point is important. This is the necessity for delegation or assignment of authority commensurate with the responsibility. It is apparent that no worker can operate effectively if he does not have the authority to carry out his responsibilities. But this does not mean full, complete, and absolute authority over each and every related process and function. Such a generalization holds true at all levels of management and administration; it does not affect only the top executive. We shall stress the point throughout our discussion that delegation of responsibility and authority is not made sweepingly or even permanently. Rather it constantly undergoes change as the nature of the work changes, as the policies change, and as the workers themselves change in competence and attitude.

In the field of student personnel work, we have still another reason for constant review of authority and responsibility. Our work is an application of research findings in education and psychology; as such, the fundamental nature of our services is constantly changing with new knowledge concerning human nature and its possible and desirable modification through learning and development.

A third characteristic of effective administration is referred to as the "span of control." That is, at all levels of organization, those in charge should not supervise the work of more staff members or immediate subordinates than they can effectively direct and coordinate. There is, of course, no universal maximum number in such a span. The number varies with the competence of the supervisor, the nature of the operation performed, the effectiveness of the relationships between supervisor and worker, and many other factors.

A fourth important characteristic of effective administration is the often repeated dictum that no one best type of administration or organization can be found for any particular enterprise. The factors entering into the determination of effective administration and organization are so varied that we should be aware of Gulick's generalization with respect to the "unifunctional basis" [26] upon

²⁶ Gulick, *op. cit.*, pp. 31–32.

which one selects an organizational structure appropriate to the functions performed. That is, there are alternative factors on which to base an organization, and one must arbitrarily select one basis of organization and proceed. As Lepawsky says, "The main task is to choose a major factor that is intrinsic to the main objective of the organization, and then to see that the unifunctional choice is carried out as consistently as possible."[27] That is, one must decide on the major objectives one seeks to accomplish and then organize an enterprise with the most appropriate structure to accomplish them. For example, if the purpose of a counseling bureau is to add to the technical understanding of the nature of the counseling process, then the selection and training of the staff and supervision of the counselors are geared to this particular objective. The administrator will undoubtedly organize seminars and plan precision research, seeks grants for research, and assist the counselors to utilize time and effort so that they produce research products. If, on the other hand, the major objective is to provide service for clientele directly without research implications, interviewing students will be the most important function.

A fifth important factor involved in effective administration has to do with the way in which authority is exercised and the manner in which members of the staff are called upon to determine policies and to make decisions about program content and processes of administration. Lepawsky says, "One can, of course, extract from a careful study of American administration a long list of basic administrative qualities, but they would all tend to fall between the two dominant American predilections for (1) democratic participation or control and (2) technical competence and efficiency." [28]

Increasingly in industry and government the trend is to maximize the participation of all members of an enterprise in the formulation of policies, programs, and plans and to avoid the unrestricted and absolutistic directing by single top executives.[29] This trend in shared

[27] Lepawsky, *op. cit.*, p. 390.

[28] *Ibid.*, p. 107.

[29] Mary P. Follett, "The Illusion of Final Authority," *Bulletin of the Taylor Society*, vol. 11, no. 6, pp. 243–250, December, 1926.

A related exploration of the exercise of authority in the case of those in positions of leadership is found in The Ohio State University studies of that topic, published by the Bureau of Business Research, College of Commerce Administration, The Ohio State University, Columbus, Ohio.

participation is as intrinsic a part of administration as is the increasing emphasis upon technical competence of staff members and the more rigorous determination of the achieved outcomes of a program. Such a trend has very interesting implications in our field of education. Not only should the principle of democratization be applied increasingly to participation by the technical members of a personnel staff, the recipients of personnel services—the students themselves—should also participate increasingly in management and administration. We shall refer in later chapters to the role of students in administration.

Follett's concept of the source of authority is thoroughly democratic, and therefore congruent with the American tradition of participation by many members of an enterprise in the determination of policies and programs. She stated this point in the words ". . . workers are sometimes managing." The traditional function of the top executive, or the board of directors, as the sole or principal source of authority is criticized. Rather does Follett stress the principle that, to be effective, an enterprise must enlist the good will and loyalties of all workers. This authority of loyalties is the "highest source of authority." She also refers to an executive decision as "a moment in a process" which is a long series of acts by many members of the staff. The final decision taken by the top management is not isolated, but must be preceded by a long series of preparatory decisions. She characterizes this as "pluralistic authority" as opposed to the hierarchy of administrative authority in which the top management is "on top."[30]

While the board of directors may be theoretically the governing body, practically, as our large businesses are now organized, before their decisions are made there has already taken place much of that process of which these decisions are but the last step. . . . Instead then of supreme control, ultimate authority, we might perhaps think of cumulative control, cumulative authority.

Campbell, Donald T.: *Leadership and Its Effects upon the Group.* Research Monograph, no. 83, 1956.

Stogdill, Ralph M., et al.: *A Predictive Study of Administrative Work Pattern.* Research Monograph, no. 85, 1956.

Stogdill, Ralph M., and Carroll L. Shartle: *Methods in the Study of Leadership.* Research Monograph, no. 80, 1955.

———: *Patterns of Administrative Performance.* Research Monograph, no. 81, 1956.

[30] Follett, *op. cit.*, pp. 245–246.

This point of view, argued so eloquently by Follett so long ago, is reinforced by the generalizations of Chester Barnard a quarter of a century after Follett's pronouncement:[31]

. . . the decision as to whether an order has authority or not lies with the persons to whom it is addressed, and does not reside in "persons of authority" or those who issue these orders . . . and . . . authority . . . rests upon the acceptance or consent of individuals.

Still another formulation of this point is based largely upon Mayo's research on the effects of interpersonal relationships upon work efficiency. Kallen concludes in these words:[32]

They [Mayo's studies] establish that the efficiency of an industrial organization follows from the assent of its personnel to the directives they receive; and that the authority of the directives is in the will of the hearer, not the purpose of the speaker. . . . When the demonstrably desirable conditions are established, on the other hand, authority becomes inward, its directives are in a functional sense self-directive, the feeling of personal dignity and worth is heightened, the esteem of one's team mates outweighs as incentive the desire for gain or the judgment of special interest; production jumps.

This fundamental principle of effective administration has profound implications for personnel work in educational institutions. For example, the fundamental purpose of personnel workers and personnel programs is not to perform a service per se but *to use a service to help students develop into full maturity.* Therefore, it is obvious that students are not passive receivers of these services; they are active participants in the services. This means that personnel work possesses a peculiar characteristic not found in many other types of enterprise. In a factory manufacturing steel beams, the raw materials are worked upon through engineering or chemical processes. But in education, of which personnel work is an integral part, something is done *with* the client as an educative experience to aid him in learning certain self-managing skills. In the real sense, therefore, as far as administration is concerned, the ultimate authority lies in the student client. Obviously, this does not mean that he is the full manager of the program. To adopt such an extreme posi-

---

[31] Barnard, *op. cit.*, pp. 163–164.

[32] Horace M. Kallen, *The Education of Free Men.* New York: Farrar, Straus & Cudahy, Inc., 1949, pp. 263–264.

tion would be as fallacious as to assume that the personnel worker is the ultimate authority. As we shall see, ours is a teamwork kind of consultation between two persons varying in interests, competencies, and involvement in the processes of maturation or development. It is this characteristic which necessitates some very drastic modifications and adaptations of business administration methods when they are applied to practices in an educational personnel program.

Our sixth fundamental of effective administration is called "coordination." This administrative function is one in which the various parts of a total enterprise are continuously dovetailed, balanced, integrated, and interrelated to produce maximum effectiveness of the program. This result is not accomplished in any mechanical way or for any extended period of time since workers change from day to day, and so do the emphases and program objectives. In our work, there is an additional dynamic force which is not found in industrial personnel programs, at least to such an extent. We refer to the annual changes in the college which are caused by graduation of seniors, the admission of freshmen, and the advancement of students toward graduation. Literally, student personnel workers face and work with a new clientele and within a newly restructured community each academic year.

Coordination of services is not a mechanical operation but something to be accomplished day after day. In some respects, coordination is at the very heart of effective administration of personnel services. Gulick says—[33]

If subdivision of work is inescapable, coordination becomes mandatory. There is, however, no one way to coordination. Experience shows that it may be achieved in two primary ways. These are:

1. By organization, that is, by interrelating the subdivisions of work by allotting them to men who are placed in a structure of authority so that the work may be coordinated by orders of superiors to subordinates, reaching from the top to the bottom of the entire enterprise.

2. By the dominance of an idea, that is, the development of intelligent singleness of purpose in the minds and wills of those who are working together as a group, so that each worker will of his own accord fit his task into the whole with skill and enthusiasm.

These two principles of coordination are not mutually exclusive, in

[33] Gulick, *op. cit.*, p. 6.

fact, no enterprise is really effective without the extensive utilization of both.

FITTING FUNCTIONS TO THE INDIVIDUAL STAFF WORKER

We turn now from a discussion of administrative functions and characteristics to the important place of the staff worker in the organization. Dimock is correct in his statement: "Good organization is made up, in part at least, of the peculiar skills of individuals, and in part of the functions to be performed." [34] Thus it is that administrators at all levels of operation seek to achieve a complex balancing of the peculiar competencies of a staff member with the peculiar requirements of a job. In developing an enterprise, administrators must answer the question: Should the organizational structure be determined first and persons found to fit it, or should the persons be found and the organizational structure built around them? To one who has worked with individuals in counseling, this question is readily resolved in favor of making the individual, the worker, the center of the organizational structure. But there are many competent administrators who operate in an opposite manner.

Increasingly, however, students of administration in industry and government have warned against the obsession for organization which is typified by the oversimplified two-dimensional charts of organizational structure. Such an oversimplified concept of organization is called "chartism," with staff assigned to individual blocks and cells. But it is also apparent that, if the objectives of the total enterprise are to be achieved, the organizational structure cannot be built solely upon the peculiar nature of the individual workers operating on the job at any particular time. That is, the purpose of the organization is not solely to further the development of the workers; it is to involve and integrate the development of the workers in achieving objectives that have been determined as institutional policy.

In this connection, Kallen contends that "the power of democratic leadership may be measured by the degree that the interest and feeling of the followers are absorbed by the action; by how far its

[34] Marshall E. Dimock, *The Executive in Action*. New York: Harper & Brothers, 1945, p. 79.

ends and means, its going and goal, are appreciated as continuously compenetrated and one."[35]

In the case of student personnel work, the goal is the stimulation of development in students; the personnel staff is a *means* to such an objective. The compenetration of goal and means is dependent upon common understanding of objectives by staff and students. And it follows that administrators need to stimulate and lead in the search for rewarding inquiry by staff as preparation for the continuous adaptation of form, structure, and function by each staff worker.

It is quite likely that in an educational institution this question would be resolved more in favor of flexibility for the individual worker than would be true in certain other kinds of enterprise. But as has been stated, there still would be structure and form, direction and definiteness in the manner in which the structure was fitted by the individual worker to his own functioning.

FUNCTIONAL GROUPING OR DEPARTMENTALIZATION

We come now to the important problem of organizing a variety of specialized functions in a total coordinated program. The organization of a diversity of functions, procedures, and operations is a necessity. As Cowley argued many years ago, not every worker can or should be expected to perform every task in a student personnel program.[36] We pointed out earlier that this calls for explicit coordination of diverse functions and workers. But it also calls for a structuring of these diverse functions, which we call "departmentalization." That is, functions and services which are similar in their basic content and emphasis are organized together in a department, bureau, or some other subdivision of the main enterprise.[37] But departmentalization of related functions raises the question: How shall these functions be grouped? Gulick has referred to the principle of unifunctioning or homogeneity in the grouping of functions

[35] Kallen, *op. cit.*, p. 277.
[36] W. H. Cowley, "The Disappearing Dean of Men," *Proceedings of the Nineteenth Annual Conference of the National Association of Deans and Advisers of Men.* Austin, Tex.: University of Texas, 1937. (Mimeographed.)
[37] *Ibid.*, p. 95.

and workers.[38] That is, the smallest subdivision of an organizational structure shall encompass homogeneous services or functions. As one moves up the hierarchy of structure, the groupings of intermediate and larger divisions of the enterprise shall retain as much homogeneity or similarity as possible. Hopf presented six principles governing such groupings of functions into structure. They are as follows:[39]

1. The organizational structure should be divided into the smallest number of levels consistent with effective distribution of authority and responsibility.

2. Subdivision of activities should proceed to the point where specific duties are commensurate with the capacities of those engaged in their performance.

3. The power of decision should be placed as closely as possible to the point where action originates.

4. Reliance should be based primarily on individual action and authority, and group action and authority should be resorted to only where clearly required for purposes of coordination.

5. Detailed information should be converted as rapidly as possible into control information as it moves upward through successive organizational levels.

6. The ultimate design of organizational structure should invariably bring to expression definite distinctions among the major levels of administrative, managerial and operative performance.

Barnard identified the following five bases on which we may build specialization of organization: place of work, time of work, persons cooperating in work, the things upon which work is performed, and the method or process used.[40]

A rereading of parts of Chapter 1 will indicate that we have applied the principle of homogeneity in the organization of student personnel work. We discussed homogeneously grouped personnel functions under the conventional categories of counseling, testing, and the like. Student personnel workers have made considerable progress in applying the principles of specialization and attendant departmentalization in organizing a program of services.

[38] Gulick, op. cit., p. 15.
[39] Harry A. Hopf, "Organization, Executive Capacity, and Progress," Advanced Management, vol. 11, no. 2, p. 40, June, 1946.
[40] Barnard, op. cit., p. 128.

STATIC BUREAUCRACY OR CONTINUOUS REORGANIZATION

Charters has contended that "improvement in a social agency in which people work with people upon social processes is a matter of chance in education." [41] Industry systematically studies its operations for reorganization when improvement is not forthcoming; to a great extent, education has been content to organize its programs, then has failed to study systematically the outcome or products to determine needed improvement.

The term "bureaucracy" has been used to describe workers and organizations in which processes and procedures, once meaningful, have been continued long after they became disassociated from improvement or from the desired objectives. In such situations, the processes of an organization have continued relatively unchanged long after they lost their usefulness in achieving the original objectives or long after these objectives were abandoned. This is an example of the tragedy of divorcing structure from policy and constant efforts to maintain the effectiveness of policy.

In contrast, the effective administrator expects continuous reorganization and change as improvements are indicated by new and relevant research or evaluation of the deficiencies of current programs. The zealous advocates of structure must be especially alert to the danger of losing sight of objectives and becoming bureaucratically efficient in maintaining an outmoded structure without major utility or purpose. The empirical and evaluative approach to organizations and structures would seem to be necessary to avoid the danger of getting into a rut. This does not mean, however, as Dimock has pointed out, that we should confuse a groove with a rut. "It is not the groove that should be prevented but the too-deep grooving which becomes a rut and eventually militates against flexibility, fresh outlook, and adaptability to change." [42] Both flexibility and adaptability are characteristic of growing organizations, that is, those which grow in importance and effectiveness with respect to changing policy and objectives. As Barnard contends, "Most

[41] W. W. Charters, "Improvement," *Educational Research Bulletin,* vol. 21, no. 4, p. 103, Apr. 15, 1942.
[42] Dimock, *op. cit.,* p. 164.

continuous organizations require repeated adoption of new purposes." [43]

THE STRUCTURE OF FORMAL ORGANIZATION

And now we turn to that aspect of administration which is more readily observed, the structure with its symbols of hierarchy, status, and authority. Every formally organized enterprise must take form, that is, it must carry on its functions in particular ways with definite assignment of authority and responsibilities. We do not refer merely to a two-dimensional chart of responsibility in relationship but rather to an integration of workers and facilities. Sears describes the formal organization as an integration of purposes, or objectives, and persons in these words:[44]

The term organization is used widely to refer to any collection of persons, materials, procedures, ideas or facts, so arranged and ordered that in each case the combination of parts makes a meaningful whole. An organization of men is an arrangement of individuals whereby each member may contribute to or participate in a joint activity, in conformity with a planned purpose and procedure, to the end that the talents and energies of all may be applied economically, effectively, and harmoniously in the activity.

Four types of formal organizational structure have been identified and described in the literature of administration: *scalar,* or the *hierarchy of authority; staff and line; spatial or geographical,* that is, centralization versus decentralization; and the *radial* plan of administration.

Scalar. "The scalar principle is the same form in organization that is sometimes called hierarchical. But to avoid all definitional variants, scalar is here preferred. . . . A scale means a series of steps, something graded. In organization it means the grading of duties, not according to different functions, for this involves another principle of organization, but according to degrees of authority and corresponding responsibility." [45]

[43] Barnard, *op. cit.*, p. 91.
[44] Sears, *op. cit.*, p. 88.
[45] James D. Mooney, *The Principles of Organization.* New York: Harper & Brothers, 1947, p. 14.

It is apparent that in any organizational structure and enterprise, individuals and jobs may be arranged in a hierarchy according to the degree of responsibility and authority possessed and exercised. Presumably this is one of the principal features of the chart concept of organization in which the president or the board of trustees is placed at the top, indicating the ultimate authority or, as Follett called it, "the illusion of final authority." The principles and practices of the scalar type of organization are so well established and so thoroughly understood, except for Follett's reversal of the hierarchy, that they need no further discussion here. So we turn to our second type of organizational structure.

Staff and Line. If the scalar concept of structure is vertical, then the staff and line concept is horizontal. That is, at any given level of authority individuals and departments may be classified as staff or line in function. There has been a great deal of confusion about this concept and Lepawsky devoted considerable space to an elaboration of the many modifications of this oversimplified concept. Contrary to some proponents, the staff and line organizations are not antagonistic nor are they alternative and rival kinds of organizations. They are rather complementary types of organizations designed for different purposes. The line organization is essentially the division of an organization according to lines of authority and responsibility from the top to the bottom and vice versa.

On the other hand, the staff organization is a division according to functions performed, usually with the main emphasis upon central functions performed by general staff for all departments. That is, functions such as production control, coordination, financial control, and similar matters are general functions performed by a central staff for all operating departments. Lepawsky stresses the complementary nature of staff and line functions as follows:[46]

While concepts like staff and line are useful organizational terms for the assignment of detailed duties and for the location of specific responsibilities, administrators can follow them too rigidly. A staff man who does not give commands to the line is ineffectual; and a line man who does not understand and exercise a modicum of staff functions is a failure. Military personnel have learned from bitter experience in World War II that the old distinctions between *staff* and *line*, the newer differentiations between *service* and *combat*, and the emerging demarcations between

[46] Lepawsky, *op. cit.*, pp. 320–321.

administration and *operation,* are too readily insisted upon. . . . In the use of these promising mechanisms of organization the major need is balance. Particularly, administrators must recognize that staff and line are coordinates, operating not in a hierarchical relation of staff over line, but on a horizontal plane of authority and responsibility under the chief executive.

Spatial Arrangements. A third type of organizational arrangement has to do with the spatial organization or what is called the "geography" of an organization. This refers to the centralization of functions in one head office as opposed to the decentralization of functions in many branch offices. The model for this type of organization is found in certain types of political divisions or jurisdictions. One hears a good deal of discussion of the merits and demerits of centralizing functions in the Federal agencies as opposed to decentralizing these functions and services in regional or state offices of the Federal government. One also hears this geographical organization discussed in connection with Federal versus state functions and rights. Lepawsky discusses this problem in terms of the advantages and disadvantages of such a geographical location of services and functions, particularly with respect to governmental agencies.[47]

The phrase "centralized control and decentralized operation" has been used by Lepawsky with respect to manufacturing and other types of commercial organizations.[48] Essentially, the problem of geography has to do with the efficiency with which functions and operations can be conducted. There seems to be a limit to the number of individuals involved in a particular operation in a particular subdivision of a general organization. When that limit is reached, a decrease in effectiveness and efficiency follows. At this point, functions and services need to be decentralized in organizational subdivisions separated geographically from a central office. This geographic distribution of functions and services follows lines of specialization: the central office retains generalized supervisory and other administrative functions; special operating services are decentralized into branch or special offices, usually with some geographic differentiation and separation. It should be pointed out that a certain amount of inefficiency caused by communication

[47] *Ibid.,* chap. 12, "The Geography of Organization."
[48] *Ibid.,* p. 376.

difficulties usually arises out of decentralization. In fact, the literature on this topic is full of admonitions that, when decentralization must take place, systematic and organized efforts to achieve coordination are called for to offset inefficiency caused by communication difficulties among geographically decentralized functions and offices.

Radial Organization. A fourth type of organizational structure is referred to as "radial," "circular," or "spherical." Barnard refers to this as circular or spherical, "with the chief executive position in the center." [49] Elsewhere in discussing types of formal organizations in connection with the topic of planning for world government, Barnard has referred to the "lateral" form of organization.[50] These terms are not identical as he uses them, yet they all stress one important point in common, namely, the character of vertical hierarchy. That is, all departments and subdivisions of an organization have similar authority and are on the same level of operational responsibility, although there may be specialization in the nature of their functions.

Tiffany uses the term "radial plan of administration" to describe a lateral structure found in Newark, New Jersey, in the Newark College of Engineering.[51] Tiffany referred to Barnard—specifically to his lecture on the planning for world government—concerning the distinction between lateral and scalar organizations. He further defined the lateral as, to use Barnard's words, "that of free agreement—by mutual understanding, by contract, or by treaty." Based upon this concept of lateral equality of authority, the New Jersey college was organized with the president, vice-president, and dean in the center of the chart, surrounded by the instructional departments. Functionally, the head of each department operates with authority and status equal to that of every other, but the president of the institution is situated in the central hub. In the meetings between the department heads and the president, the discussion and decision making are described as a process of "easy give and take." President Cullimor has this to say: "The mainspring of such an administration must be an avoidance of fiat and a dependence on

[49] Barnard, *op. cit.*, p. 112, footnote 18.
[50] Chester I. Barnard, *Organization and Management.* Cambridge, Mass.: Harvard University Press, 1949, p. 150.
[51] Earl Tiffany, "Radial Plan of Administration," *Higher Education,* vol. 4, no. 16, pp. 185–186, U. S. Office of Education, Apr. 15, 1948.

recommendation." Tiffany continued, "But after all, human beings are involved." This gives rise to the question whether, in this particular form of organization, opposing viewpoints may sometimes develop which can be resolved only by executive dicta. Doesn't that ever happen? "It never has," says President Cullimor. And if it did? "Then, as the hub, I should make the decision necessary to hold together this circle." [52]

This last significant point indicates that this radial form of organization—applied to small organizations like a college as opposed to world organizations as discussed by Barnard—operates with an equality of status and authority of all the subdivisions. But when the heads of suborganizations cannot agree, then the vertical or hierarchical authority emerges to function in making a decision binding upon the suborganizations.

These four forms of administrative structure, or organizational structure, are often thought of as being competing or as based upon opposing concepts. The last significant observation made in connection with the radial form, however, indicates that these may not be pure types in actual day-to-day functioning. Indeed, it may be possible that all four types may function on different occasions in connection with different services and at different levels of authority and operations. That is, it may well be that the hierarchical order of authority is inherent in the basic legal chartering of organizations as public corporations and institutions. It may also follow that the legal hierarchical structure of authority is always present recessively, although it may not be in effective operation on many occasions. Therefore, it may not be visible to staff or clientele who experience the available services. But with respect to legal responsibility, the hierarchical form may also be, at the same time, the dominant form of structure with respect to such matters as fiscal accountability.

On the other hand, we may well find that in student personnel work at the level of daily operations, particularly those involving highly technically trained personnel, the radial form of organization, even without a central authority figure, may be the most effective concerning technical matters in which professional competence and judgment override matters of legal and fiscal authority. In similar manner, we may find that—even within the hierarchical scalar

[52] *Ibid.*

form of organization inherent within a public corporation such as a college or university—professionally competent staff workers may function in a staff relationship with each other, thus transcending the inherent and ever-present hierarchical authority structure. Other modifications and combinations of these four structures will most likely be found in the actual day-to-day operation of any organization—particularly the educational organization wherein workers have technical and professional competence equal to, but separate from, fiscal and legal authority of the central administration and the governing board.

We should not expect, therefore, to find pure types representing all aspects of our student personnel program. And one may express some doubt that pure types exist anywhere except with respect to particular specialized functions. In other words, it may be possible, and is most likely, that any type of structure adopted must be appropriate to the type of function performed. There may well be no universal structure appropriate for every type of function performed within an organization—we should not expect to judge the adequacy of any structure except in terms of particular functions. What we call types of organizations may be not universal but particularized. We shall discuss the application of the concepts of structure to our personnel programs with this modification in mind.

THE ROLE OF THE EXECUTIVE

We have been discussing some principles of management and organizational structure as they may have relevancy to student personnel services. We now center attention upon the agents who perform administrative functions and who manage the organizational structure. In particular, we first turn to the puzzling question as to whether the administration shall be a committee or a council or some other collective administrative agency. Lepawsky generalizes thus:[53]

> At the top or executive level of any organization, whether a whole nation or an individual department, the administrative authority can be either a single individual or a plural body. . . . Primarily, the urge has been to assign a single executive who is responsible for action; but there has been a continual concession to the need for balancing different skills and representative interests.

[53] Lepawsky, *op. cit.*, pp. 241, 246.

Since this question is of the utmost importance in student personnel circles, we note first that personnel work operates within a type of institution, a school or college, in which the single-executive type of organizational structure is presently firmly established. Schools are administered by principals and superintendents, each with defined responsibilities. Colleges and universities are administered by deans and presidents, each with defined responsibilities and relationships. It may be that the seeming resolution of the problem as Lepawsky generalizes from industry has not yet fully influenced the educational enterprise. This is a real possibility since the problem of effective participation by teachers and students in the school and college administration is an ever-present, and as yet unresolved, issue.

But we shall see in our later discussion that, while we may identify a single executive at any administrative level in an educational institution, increasingly this executive functions in terms of the wishes, judgments, and viewpoint of teachers, personnel workers, and students. He does not administer, unilaterally, the wishes and judgments of the board of trustees. Such a sharing of responsible participation in the administration of educational enterprises is an important modification of the principle of unity of command, as was pointed out in a preceding section.

As Follett has indicated in discussing industrial administration, all members of an organization participate in decision making; therefore, all carry out executive functions. For convenience and at the risk of oversimplification, much of our present discussion is made in terms of a single executive agent. But we do not intend to create the impression that only the top administrator performs administrative functions. We hold that literally everyone who performs any function whatever actually performs some kind of executive work. It is true that some persons carry a heavier responsibility and more complex executive duties than do others. But, just as every member of an organization participates in policy making, so every member of an organization helps to carry out policies through the program of services. Nevertheless, our desire to emphasize the pervasiveness of executive functions should not blind us to the fact that there are specialists in management, as in every other type of function. For this reason, we shall speak of those who specialize in executive management of an organized enterprise. Perhaps the main emphasis of our concept of the role of the executive can be further described in this manner. Dimock defines his functions in simple terms as follows: "The executive does three principal things: he is a trouble shooter, a supervisor, and a promoter of the future program." [54] Contrary to the practice of the devotees of chartism or those administrators who follow in a mechanical way the rigid and formal organization in terms of responsibility and authority, the modern executive is an improviser. That is, he deals with his associates each day in a unique way, knowing full well that—while they are the same individuals they were yesterday and while the formal organization is the same—each day they all face a slightly different task, and therefore operations must be adjusted to the changing tasks. Formal organizational structure is thus used flexibly in terms of the changing task and the changing workers. In fact, the workers themselves are brought into participation in management and executive work in different ways at different times, much as they perform their own task in different ways at different times according to the nature of their assignment.

The executive specializes in the review of administrative policy and procedure and leaves to his associates the detailed operations of carrying out policies and plans. While he does not abandon his interest or responsibility for those detailed operations, he does not try to be a bottleneck through which each single and detailed decision and operation must flow. He rather develops the fine art of executive discretion and the art of administrative delegation.

Thus, as Dimock has said, "Management is not a matter of pressing a button, pulling a lever, issuing orders, scanning profit and loss statements, promulgating rules and regulations." [55] Rather, the executive works with the staff effectively in a cooperative and group-work manner, secures consent and agreement, and welds the organization into an effective team. Not the least of his major executive functions is to increase the effectiveness with which each staff member participates in the management process through planning, renewing, and evaluating the many parts of a program of services.

[54] Dimock, *op. cit.*, p. 16.
[55] *Ibid.*, p. 4.

Mayo's emphasis upon the centrality of human relationship in administration[56] is appropriate in a discussion of the executive's role in working with other workers. We like Horace Kallen's interpretation. He wrote of Mayo's studies: "They demonstrate that the administration of things is anything but independent of the government of men." We like even more Kallen's penetrating analysis of the role of each worker in decision making:[57]

But the time comes when the men and women diversely engaged in any undertaking, if they have freely discussed with one another their purpose, their ways of working, and the results they work out, find themselves in an agreement which is neither the result of a vote taken nor a compromise arranged. It is a consensus that has grown from the competitive cooperation and cooperative competition whereof free discussion consists. The process which consensus consummates is such that no participant is coerced, and each has the same liberty as the others to enter his own theory and practice in the many-way flow of ideas.

Kallen's justification for such an application of democratic consensus taking to the administrative problem of decision making follows in these words:[58]

Those who argue that such unions of the diverse are disorderly, confused and illogical are often able to prove it logically. But relationships which hold together the freely joined parts of such wholes have a tensile strength and a flexibility beside which the strictly logical and purely rational unions turn out to be weak and brittle. If such confluences of the diverse move clumsily, not all at once nor equally fast, perhaps these traits are unalienable to the democratic way, and the price of its lasting stability.

SUMMARY

We have explored the literature of public administration and industry for generalizations, principles, and points of view that may be relevant to the task of organizing and administering student personnel services in educational institutions. We believe our search has yielded profitable illustration of many puzzling issues and un-

[56] Elton Mayo, *The Human Problems of an Industrial Civilization.* Boston: Harvard University Graduate School of Business Administration, Harvard University Press, 1933, chap. 8, "The Problem of the Administrator," pp. 161–180.
[57] Kallen, *op. cit.,* p. 262.
[58] *Ibid.,* p. 13.

solved problems in our field of work. But we need to reemphasize what we have already illustrated repeatedly in our review—what we found in the literature needs to be examined carefully for possible modifications in application to the organizing of student personnel services. We shall repeatedly throw attention upon such modifications in subsequent chapters dealing with special problems of administration.

CHAPTER 3

Structure and Organization of Services

The essential character of student personnel work determines the peculiar nature of its administrative structure and organization. Student personnel work is essentially a series of interrelated technical services performed by specially trained staff and members of the faculty. Some personnel workers have been assigned—directly and explicitly, or by tradition and practice—a large measure of autonomy. This professional autonomy is not as great as that of a private practitioner, e.g., a doctor or lawyer who is responsible only to his clientele and his professional peers. Nevertheless, administratively speaking, a technical specialist employed by a college or university operates more independently of administrative review and supervision than does a worker performing clerical, custodial, or routine functions.

Some nontechnical phases of personnel work are carried on by a central executive or management staff. These central functions include report making, financial control, staff appointments, purchase of supplies, and similar general administrative functions. Other functions are only partially centralized in a headquarters; record keeping of the direct services to clients, program development, and research are examples.

One may observe at least three different types of administrative structure of services grouped according to the type of function performed. That is, we find no general or universal type of structure that fits each and every type of function and service within a college or among different divisions of a university. Representative and additional examples of organizational structures are given in the several charts included in this chapter. Comparison indicates that diversity as well as commonality characterizes student personnel services on large and small campuses.

Diversity stems from unique histories and from the differences in institutional leadership and personalities. On the one hand, we have a *centralized* administrative structure controlling certain administrative functions. This is comparable to the general structure of a college in which the head is the chief administrative officer responsible directly to a board of trustees, and with each member of the staff responsible to him. (See chart on p. 26.) In the second place, we find *partially centralized* functions and control, in which a large measure of independence or autonomy of technical functioning is delegated according to professional competence and the tasks performed. Thirdly, we find a system of *decentralized administrative* control of different services, representing an even farther extension of delegated responsibility and authority of functioning. Such decentralization, together with informal relationships and organization, is usually found on campuses with small enrollment. Conversely, on large campuses, centralization and formal organization characterize the personnel program.[1]

This third type of structure is usually found within a complex university composed of several colleges, with a highly centralized administrative program of fiscal, developmental, and physical-plant operations but with highly decentralized operations and management of instructional, research, and public service functions. (See chart on p. 70.) Within such a complex institution, we find centralized administration of such student personnel services as housing inspection and student loans, but with both centralized and decentralized functioning of such a service as counseling. The third type of structure is also found in modified form in some small institutions.

We find that the forms of administrative structure found in industry and government (scalar, staff and line, centralized versus decentralized, and radial) are extensively modified to fit the peculiarities of different types of student personnel services. In our subsequent discussion of these services, we shall note these adaptations and also the special forms of structure present in varying degrees in the case of different functions and services. We shall see that no

[1] Brumbaugh, A. J., and Ralph F. Berdie: *Student Personnel Programs in Transition.* Washington: American Council on Education, 1952.

Hendrix, Oscar R.: "A Proposed Student Personnel Organization for the University of Wyoming," Ph.D. thesis, University of Wyoming, Laramie, Wyo.. 1949.

OHIO STATE UNIVERSITY
Student Personnel Services

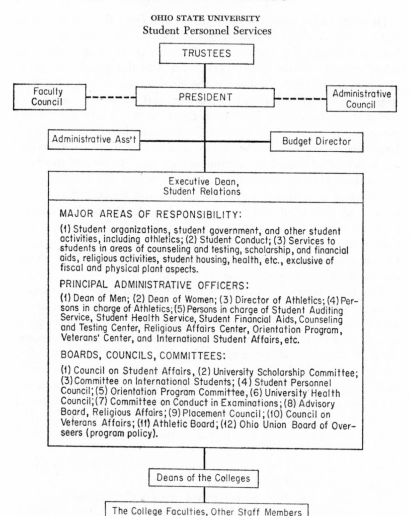

SOURCE: *Ohio State University Monthly*, Greenfield, Ohio: Greenfield Printing and Publishing Co., June 15, 1957, pp. 8–9.

one type of administrative structure will serve each and every type of service or function.

Perhaps this point is best illustrated by quoting from early recommendations for a broad-gauged personnel program in one institution. We refer to this early plan for two reasons: first, it

UNIVERSITY OF DENVER
Student Affairs

Dean

Administration and Coordination of Student Personnel Functions
Policy
Budget

Interpretation and Advisory Counseling and Discipline
Coordination of Army and Air ROTC

Associate Dean of Students
(Counselor for Women's Activities)

Advisor, sororities and women's groups
Women's Housing
Housemothers
Special Events—Women's Week, etc.

Assistant Dean of Students
(Civic Center Campus)

Administers student personnel
Counseling
Committees

ADMISSIONS AND RECORDS

Director

Administers faculty regulations governing admission
Processes admissions credentials
Assesses tuition and fees
Supplies transcripts and certifications
Prepares class schedules
Directs registration
Makes graduation checks
Edits commencement program
Prepares diplomas
Prepares statistical reports
Reports to Selective Service, Veterans Adm.
Keeps basic academic permanent records

Supervises:
Registrar
Director of Veterans Services and Recorder CCC
Admissions Evaluators

STUDENT ACTIVITIES

Coordinator

Supervises:
All student groups
Student fiscal affairs
All university student events
Manages Student Union, including food service and catering service for public
Business Management of student publications
Prepares all-university calendar
Administers scheduling procedures

Supervises:
Director of Food Services
Treasurer, All-university Student Assn.
Graduate Assistant
Catering Manager

STUDENT HEALTH SERVICES

Director

Provides medical-dental clinical service, hospitalization, and surgical benefits
Reviews health histories of new students before admission
Administers chest-hearing-vision-tests for new students
Operates First Aid Station, CCC, and Mental Hygiene Clinic
Administers health insurance program
Advises administration of mental and physical health problems

Supervises:
Psychiatrists
Physicians
Dentists
Nurses
Laboratory Technician
X-ray Technician
Assistant to Director

STUDENT COUNSELING SERVICE

Director

Provides professional counseling
Maintains confidential file on each student
Provides testing service
Supervises faculty advisement program
Provides counseling experience and training for graduate students

Supervises:
Counselors
Psychometrist

STUDENT HOUSING

Director

Supervises residence halls housing
Provides off-campus housing listings
Supervises students using university facilities, i.e., student government, and social, educational, and recreational activities
Administers applications and contracts for residence halls
Supervises housing maintenance, repairs

Supervises:
Assistant to Director
Head Residents
Resident Assistants

SOURCE: Courtesy of Dean Dan Feder, December, 1959.

reflects the influence upon college programs of early industrial personnel programs and experiences; secondly, it was and continues to be, in essential features, the general pattern found in some institutions.

In 1927 a faculty committee at the University of Minnesota recommended a general scheme for organizing the institution's total personnel program. This comprehensive plan provided for a specialized committee for policy making and program review, as well as for the decentralization of specialized services into many offices rather than their assignment to one general staff. It also provided for a radial type of organization at the level of decentralized college personnel services of both a general and a specialized character. A good deal of autonomy of functioning was delegated to the specialized personnel worker. At the same time, certain coordinating machinery was set up to make certain that independent specialists cooperated with each other when cooperation was desirable in handling the total adjustments of an individual client. The scheme recommended was as follows:[2]

In other words, personnel administration should be decentralized with certain centralized control.

If we may heed industrial experience in this field, our answer to the original question is: the classroom or laboratory instructors constitute the corps of personnel officers; they are the ones who are in constant, daily contact with the student personnel, and reliance must be placed upon them to put into practice whatever personnel policies and techniques may be developed.

In view of this consideration of the question it is suggested that the following personnel organizations be developed:

1. General University Committee on Student Personnel. (Function—initiation and correlation of personnel policies and practices.)

2. Decentralized offices of student personnel—to be organized under the direction of the dean of each college with such delegation of duties as each dean deems wise.

3. Attaching to each decentralized personnel office a committee of faculty counselors who would serve as a medium of communication between the remainder of the faculty and the dean's office and the general personnel committee.

[2] Donald G. Paterson, chairman, et al., "The Minnesota Student Personnel Program," *The Educational Record Supplement*, vol. 9, no. 7, pp. 3–4, April, 1928.

4. Special expert services to be made available as needed: such experts to be located in those offices where they can work to best advantage such as vocational adviser for women in the office of the dean of women, psychiatrist in the Student Health Service, psychologist in the department of psychology, social case worker in the department of sociology, expert on speech correction in department of speech, etc.

The general structure of services in this one institution has remained largely intact since the 1927 report was adopted, with one basic modification made in 1941. This modification called for the grouping, in a new administrative structure, of the specialized services referred to under 4 above. These specialized services and staffs are now grouped administratively as special bureaus under a centralized organization of the Office of the Dean of Students.[3] If one observes the total program of services within this university, it becomes clear that no one of the traditional types of administrative structures resembles the one observed. In fact, each of the traditional types may be found operating in one or more parts of the total program. We believe that similar observations may be made about most institutions. That is, modern student personnel services have evolved their own modified types of structure appropriate to the nature of the service and to the peculiarities of the collegiate institution in which they are performed.

Special attention is called to one aspect of the university program described above—the assignment of certain personnel functions to each and every member of the instructional staff. Every member of the instructional staff was assigned personnel functions. In addition, a special group of instructors was proposed as a counselor's committee to be attached to each dean's office and assigned still more specialized personnel functions. We believe that this part of the structure constitutes one of the most puzzling and largely unsolved problems of organization in the student personnel field. That is, while one may grant the wisdom of having all members of the instructional staff perform personnel services, one experiences many difficulties in organizing and structuring these services.

In this connection, we emphasize that personnel work is not limited to specialists by any means. Personnel work includes services performed by others in counseling, testing, housing, and other

[3] W. C. Coffey, chairman, *A Report to the President from the Committee on Administrative Reorganization*, Mar. 26, 1941. (Mimeographed.)

identified functions. For the purpose of our discussion, we shall use the term "personnel workers" to refer to the specially trained members of the staff who perform functions of a specialized technical character. When we refer to functions carried by the members of the instructional staff who usually are not professionally trained in personnel work, we shall refer to them as "faculty counselors" or by similar terms. We make this distinction to distinguish the variety of personnel services, without any implication that one type of personnel worker is any more necessary than another.

WHAT IS TO BE STRUCTURED OR ORGANIZED?

Structure or organization refers to the way in which services are organized and in which they function through the efforts of staff members. A structure is not a building composed of steel girders and brick and mortar. Rather does an administrative structure consist of the following:

1. A plan composed of explicit parts or special programs, each of which should be assigned as a responsibility to particular staff

2. Formal or readily identifiable directives assigning to a particular member of the staff responsibility and authority for performance of functions included in the general plan of program

3. One or more members of the staff who, because of special interest, training, and skills, are judged qualified to perform each function

4. Special office location visible to students where the services are to be performed

5. Such special equipment and facilities as are necessary in the performance of the functions

Three Dimensions of the Program to Be Organized

In Chapter 1 we discussed a number of administrative functions performed in the institutional program of personnel services. But the functions listed do not include all phases of the total personnel program; they refer only to those which have to do with initiating the program and maintaining its on-going development. At this point, we discuss additional parts of the total program which need to be organized.

Policy Making. The term refers to the formally and officially approved statement of the content of the institution's program. For all parts of a total program there must be authorization, by overt action or tacit approval of some authoritative body. The chief importance or utility of this formal authorization is that before money can be appropriated for an on-going program, there must be some officially adopted policy which authorizes its financial support. At no level of authority can an administrator or staff member expend the institution's money for an unauthorized program or for activities whose authorization is not implied in some officially adopted policy. In our Western culture, this firm linking between the expenditure of money and its authorization by group policy and planned approval is a most important legal responsibility, binding upon every staff member and not solely upon the top administrator. Personnel workers, largely trained in the performance of their technical tasks, are not always aware of this necessity for official authorization for the expenditure of time and money for equipment and services. They sometimes feel that the authorization for service grows naturally and implicitly out of the specialist's or the client's need for it. The difference between these two points of view—legal-administrative and technical—many times gives rise to a conflict between administrators and specialists in the educational personnel field.

Now policy making is not merely a matter of the formal approval of an over-all program or of a statement of general principles to be followed. As we stated elsewhere, administrative functions are performed at all levels of a program and in all types of programs. In like manner, we shall see that policy making is a generalized function, performed by everyone in the institution in some way or another. Only a legally authorized group may adopt an official policy binding upon the institution and every member of the staff; at the same time, every member of the staff participates in the evolution of that policy long before it is presented to the board for formal and official approval. This is one of the cardinal principles advanced by Follett regarding the democratization of modern industry and the participation by every member of an institutional staff in governing the institution.[4]

[4] Henry C. Metcalf and L. Urwick (eds.), *Dynamic Administration: The Collected Papers of Mary Parker Follett*. New York: Harper & Brothers, 1940, chaps. 2 and 3.

Policies governing programs of services are varied in complexity, scope of coverage, formality of content, manner of development, and in the peculiar ways in which they are constantly undergoing modification and revision in day-to-day functioning. One special feature of policy making in the field of student personnel work needs emphasis. For the most part, policies are not formally adopted and authorized by personnel workers themselves. Personnel workers are employees of an institution. They may participate democratically in the evolution of a policy or program, but they are not given decentralized authority to adopt a policy binding upon the institution as a whole—not without review and subsequent approval by higher authority. It is one of the special features of American education that the authority to conduct educational programs, including student personnel work, is granted by the sovereign state to public corporations known as boards of trustees. With some special exceptions, the final authority, from a legal point of view, for the approval or disapproval of the content of the institution's program resides in these boards of trustees. These boards may be, and usually are, influenced in their decision by long-standing practice and tradition and also by specific recommendations of staff members, by the students, and by the public at large. Nevertheless, the legal authority for those decisions continues to reside in the boards themselves.

These boards no longer directly administer any part of the institution's programs, yet they do govern the institution in a real sense. As noted in Chapter 2, there was a time in the history of higher education in America when these boards somewhat arbitrarily handled decision making and administrative control over the minutiae of the program—curriculum and nearly everything else.[5] In fact, sometimes not even the president of the college met with the board, which functioned in an independent manner on administrative and policy matters. Indeed, until recent decades, members of the staff, even teachers, were sometimes thought of as employees, "hired hands," who had no standing in administrative

---

For a discussion of varied methods of communication within an organization, one aspect of the making and applying of policies, see Charles E. Redfield, *Communication in Management.* Chicago: University of Chicago Press, 1953.

[5] George P. Schmidt, *The Old Time College President.* New York: Columbia University Press, 1930, pp. 43–76.

decision making.[6] But today, in most institutions of higher education and to a growing extent in secondary schools, boards of trustees and school boards have delegated a large measure of authority—even functioning autonomy—to the faculties composed of teachers and instructional administrators in the formulation and adoption of policies governing programs in the instructional field. But these same boards of trustees still retain direct supervision and authority over matters of finance, public relations, planned development and maintenance, and related matters of a noninstructional character.

Almost universally, present administrative practice delegates to faculty members jurisdiction over the development and adoption of policies governing student personnel programs. That is, the policies and program plans are not established by the student personnel staff but by the general faculties meeting in their corporate function as a legislative group regarding instructional matters. Student personnel work, therefore, is seen as a part of the institution's instructional program. This context gives our work a special character; it also gives rise to special problems of coordination between the total instructional program and personnel services.

Programs within Complex Institutions. Schools, colleges, and universities have long been structured through departmentalization of staff. That is, staff members performing similar or closely related functions are grouped together in a structure known as a department, school, division, or college. In some institutions, these departments are rather loosely organized, have a low visibility, and do not really constitute a definite administrative structure with respect to some functions and services. In other institutions, the line of authority, channels of communication, areas of jurisdiction, and the teamwork of staff members are all organized around departmental functions and structure. Throughout our subsequent discussion, we shall make special references to personnel functions modified or influenced by similar departmental structure.

We shall note that most of our personnel services are institution-wide in their scope and nature. Thus, they operate without much regard to the administrative structure of the college or division in

---

[6] J. McKeen Cattell, *University Control,* A Series of Volumes for the Promotion of Scientific Research and Educational Progress, The Science Press, New York, 1913, vol. III, p. 474.

See also Charles H. Haskins, *The Rise of Universities.* New York: Henry Holt and Company, Inc., 1923, p. 69.

which the student-client is registered for instruction. For example, the giving, scoring, and reporting of scholastic aptitude tests are not functions peculiar to or identified solely with a department of mathematics or with a college of engineering within a university. They are an institution-wide function, the results of which are used by and contribute to instructional programs. Other personnel services, such as providing housing facilities for students, are not directly related to any institutional department. Services in connection with housing of students are often not formally or explicitly related to the narrowly conceived instructional program of the institution. While it is fundamentally an educative function, it is organized with coordinate status with respect to the classroom instructional program.

There are many advantages and some disadvantageous in the departmentalization of services. If a personnel function was useful to more than one instructional or noninstructional department, it would be inefficient administration to attach a staff performing the particular personnel function to each of them. It would be economical and efficient administration if such a function were organized on an institution-wide basis with close service relationships to the various departments requiring the service. We find this type of structure appropriate in the cases of vocational guidance, psychotherapy, improvement of study skills, and the like. For example, some students from most, if not all, instructional departments can benefit from the vocational guidance service organized and functioning as an institution-wide central bureau or center.

Many other types of personnel functions need some degree of decentralization in their administrative structure and organization. In the Paterson report mentioned above, one such function is the counseling performed by members of the instructional staff. Paterson's committee recommended that attached to each college there should be a special committee of faculty members. These faculty members should be trained in counseling and able to devote a certain amount of their professional time and effort to this work. Also attached to the office of the dean of each college should be one or more specially trained personnel workers who could help the college administration utilize certain personnel services to improve the program for students.

To some readers, this scheme may appear to be a duplication of services in disregard of the principles enunciated in a preceding chapter. In small institutions, there is no question that such a complex organization would be a duplication of effort. But in a large university composed of many separate colleges, experience indicates that it is unfeasible and highly undesirable to organize all personnel functions on an institution-wide basis. For one thing, the technical services thus centrally organized would be so far removed from the point at which the students' problems are identified that the student may not be referred for specialized assistance. That is, if all types of counseling were performed only in a centralized bureau in the university and if there were no persons trained to perform some type of personnel function in dormitories, the college deans' offices, or elsewhere on the campus, some undesirable results might develop.

For instance, operating within limits of time, work load, technical competence, and difficulties of communications—the untrained workers in scattered departments might come to treat the individual student largely from an administrative and nonpersonnel point of view, administering the regulations with regard to scholastic standards with limited regard to any possible desirable modification because of the individual student's circumstances. Secondly, jurisdictional disputes might arise with an undesirable effect; students would be forced to overcome administrative obstacles in going directly to the specialized bureaus for the services they needed. A third undesirable development might arise—the ignoring of the traditional decentralized organization of American instructional programs of colleges and universities. In complex universities with intricate college organizations, boards of trustees have long delegated to the separate colleges much autonomous authority over students, especially with respect to their instructional affairs. If personnel services are to play an important part in instruction, then many, but not all, of these services must be made readily available and must be woven into the college administration and administrative practices. We shall refer to this point later because it is an important application of the principle enunciated earlier by Scott, Clothier, and Spriegel with regard to industry, namely, "that the personnel point of view shall pervade the functioning of the institution beyond the formally organized personnel program." [7]

[7] Walter D. Scott et al., *Personnel Management*. New York: McGraw-Hill Book Company, Inc., 1949, chap. 3, "The Organization and Function of a Personnel Department," pp. 23–29.

Institution-wide Specialized Services. We have referred throughout our discussion to specialized personnel services performed and organized on an institution-wide basis. In many large institutions, these services are performed by full-time, professionally trained, oriented, and experienced staff members. We shall not repeat the list of functions here. It should be noted again, however, that these services do not constitute the totality of the personnel program; there are many separate services, often more informally organized, within the separate divisions of the institution. Moreover, we repeat that the personnel point of view and certain personnel techniques should be practiced everywhere within the institution so that relationships with students are humane and influenced by current knowledge of obstacles to the development of individual students.

A large part of our discussion of administrative structure and function will pertain to these institution-wide personnel services, yet we shall digress frequently to point out special modifications and adaptations necessary to decentralize these services and functions to every part of the institution. In effect, in addition to the formally, visibly organized structures and programs, many less visible, more informally structured personnel services and functions are performed by staff members who may not hold appointments in a specially designated personnel department. Our discussion will center upon the one rather than upon the other, but this does not mean that one is more important than the other.

Types of Over-all Structure. Policies and functions do not operate without definite form; we call this form "administrative structure." We identify four types found in different institutions, and often within a single institution in some modified form. But the reader is reminded again of the diversity of structures in different institutions, a point well illustrated by the chart found in Chapter 1 and the charts given in the present chapter for State College of Washington State, Ohio State University, the University of Denver, and Florida State University.

The *unitary* structure functions at the top level, with a single administrator assigned over-all responsibility for administering, supervising, and developing specialized services which are usually departmentally organized under separate subadministrators. (See the chart of Brigham Young University in Chapter 1.)

The *dual* and parallel type of structure has been and is today characteristic of an important phase in the evolution of personnel programs in American institutions of higher education and in many secondary schools. See the chart of Occidental College on page 96. Special personnel functions and services are organized under a dean of women for women students and under a dean of men for men students. Usually there is coordination or joint effort between the two when program services involve both men and women. This occurs especially in the field of student activities which are open to and participated in by both men and women. Usually the function of discipline is also jointly handled. But other functions, such as some types of counseling, are sometimes structured along the sex lines, that is, the dean of women counseling women and the dean of men counseling men.

The *pluralistic* and autonomous structure is a third type. Here, for example, psychological testing is performed in departments of psychology or education; extracurricular activities are handled by deans of men and deans of women separately and jointly; disciplinary counseling is handled separately and jointly by deans of men and deans of women and sometimes by special faculty committees. That is, each function is departmentalized in an autonomous manner with little grouping or structural interrelatedness. Occidental College (see in Chapter 1) has some such features. See chart, p. 96.) Cowley has referred to this period in the evolution of an institution's program and has pointed out that, while departmentalization is necessary, autonomous pluralism leads to confusion and working at cross purposes.[8] In the past few decades in many institutions, decentralization usually has been coupled with some degree of administrative centralization and coordination of separate offices and services.

The fourth type of administrative structure is the *departmentalized and decentralized* type with top central administration. (See chart, p. 82.) In this type of structure, homogeneous or closely related personnel services are organized in separate departments, divisions, or bureaus, with each department having some degree of autonomy and separateness of facilities, offices, and control of program. With such decentralization of services, certain over-all ad-

[8] W. H. Cowley, "The Strategy of Coordination," *Report of the Fifteenth Annual Meeting of the ACPA*, Atlantic City, February 23–26, 1938, pp. 20–24.

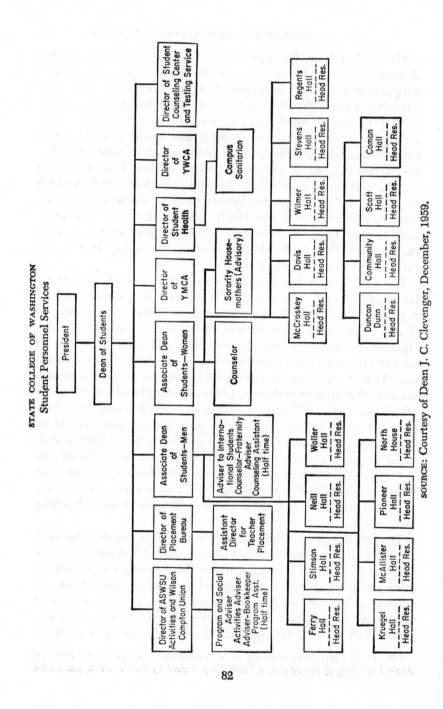

STATE COLLEGE OF WASHINGTON
Student Personnel Services

President

Dean of Students

Director of ASWSU Activities and Wilson Compton Union

Director of Placement Bureau

Associate Dean of Students—Men

Associate Dean of Students—Women

Director of YMCA

Director of Student Health

Director of YWCA

Director of Student Counseling Center and Testing Service

Program and Social Activities Adviser
Activities Adviser—Bookkeeper
Program Asst. (Half time)

Assistant Director for Teacher Placement

Adviser to International Students
Counselor—Fraternity Adviser
Counseling Assistant (Half time)

Counselor

Sorority House-mothers (Advisory)

Campus Sanitarian

Ferry Hall Head Res.

Stimson Hall Head Res.

Neill Hall Head Res.

Waller Hall Head Res.

McCroskey Hall Head Res.

Davis Hall Head Res.

Wilmer Hall Head Res.

Stevens Hall Head Res.

Regents Hall Head Res.

Kruegel Hall Head Res.

McAllister Hall Head Res.

Pioneer Hall Head Res.

North House Head Res.

Duncan Dunn Head Res.

Community Hall Head Res.

Scott Hall Head Res.

Coman Hall Head Res.

SOURCE: Courtesy of Dean J. C. Clevenger, December, 1959.

82

ministrative functions are centralized in a top administrative organization.

The functioning of such an organization at State College of Washington has been described as follows:[9]

Student government, student activities, and the entire student union operation for both program and finance are placed under the responsibility of the one man who serves as Director of ASWSU Activities and the Wilson Compton Union. Thus, instead of three operations, we have only one, and instead of competing interests between the Business Office and the Dean of Students Office, we have full responsibility within student services.

Both Art McCartan and Katy Northrup have full-time assistants who carry the titles of Counselor in the Office of the Associate Dean of Students for Men—or for Women. Dr. Martin actually serves in the traditional role of assistant dean of men, and is the administrative officer responsible for coordinating the fraternity program. He also assists with other activities of the office. Katy's full-time assistant is JoAnne Johnson, who works in terms of the traditional responsibilities of the Dean of Women's Office.

Our dormitory head residents are responsible directly to us as indicated, and we carry their salaries on our payroll. Thus, we have the opportunity to attempt to operate these halls as educational units of the institution. The Housing Office, which reports directly to the Business Manager, is responsible for maintenance and fiscal matters in housing.

Also, perhaps rather unique are the positions of Executive Director of YMCA and YWCA as part of the student personnel staff. We provide half the salary for these operations and also provide office space. We support them on the basis that they do important counseling work for us.

Our Advisor to International Students traditionally reports through our Associate Dean of Students for Men. There is really no particular reason now for this except that it is a convenient way for us to handle it.

We believe that the trend toward centralized administration early identified by Cowley[10] has been firmly established as the dominant pattern of structure and organization. While we agree with many

[9] Personal letter from J. C. Clevenger, Dean of Students, State College of Washington, Pullman, Washington, December, 1959.
[10] W. H. Cowley, "The Disappearing Dean of Men," *Proceedings of the Nineteenth Annual Conference of the National Association of Deans and Advisers of Men.* Austin, Tex.: University of Texas, p. 11. (Mimeographed.)

of the observations of Lloyd-Jones and Smith,[11] we observe that the differences between men and women students regarding needed personnel service, though substantial and real, are not such as to justify parallel and separate organizations. We believe that there should be one central administrator associated with specialized and departmentalized services provided for students. We believe each specialized service should be manned by competent men and women workers and that students should be dealt with on the basis of personal preference for a man or a woman counselor.

But we do not conclude from experience and observation that these desiderata constitute arguments justifying parallel and separate administrative organizations of the traditional deans of women and men. In fact, we hazard the prophecy that the parallel but separate type of organization will be replaced in an increasing number of large institutions. Instead, there will be administrators who function as special coordinators of the many specialized student services, supervising them but not offering them directly and separately to students as did the deans of women. We shall illustrate our point of view in discussing the organization of many other services which, because of greater volume of work and increasing technical specialization, have outgrown the older structure which provided a variety of different services by one staff member or several working in one general personnel office.

In this connection, we note that in many institutions some personnel services and programs have been physically separated from the general offices of an earlier day. These separately organized services include foreign-student advising, residences and off-campus housing, discipline, activity and student organizations, and technical counseling. Friendly contacts with students—once the principal responsibility of deans of men and women (see Dean Coulter's comments in Chapter 1)—are now the responsibility of all personnel workers and of the faculty as well.

With this general statement of our point of view about general patterns of administrative structure and organization serving as a guiding principle, we turn to a dicussion of some specific aspects.

[11] Esther Lloyd-Jones and Margaret Ruth Smith (eds.), *Student Personnel Work as Deeper Teaching*. New York: Harper & Brothers, 1954. See especially chap. I, "Changing Concepts of Student Personnel Work," and pp. 343–346.

CRITERIA FOR GROUPING OF PERSONNEL SERVICES

In an earlier chapter, we summarized experiences of industrial and public organizations concerning the way in which functions may be structurally grouped or organized. Some basic operating principles might be borrowed from these experiences if increased efficiency results from such structuring. It is evident that structures cannot be grouped together without some logic or reason inherent in the nature of the functions performed. An institution's central administration does not follow fortuitous whims and fancy in grouping into departmental structure the variety of functions and staff members. Neither should the personalities of staff members be the sole reason for grouping functions within a department. However, it should be noted in passing that, in many institutions, the criterion of the likeableness of personalities does appear to weigh heavily with some administrators in organizing and structuring personnel programs. Such instances are not documented. Nevertheless, many consultants, called upon to study an institution's total program and make recommendations for increasing its efficiency, have discovered that the personalities of the available staff seem to be the yardstick for the present structuring of the program. From following such principles of expediency, there may well arise instances of uncoordination and conflict of jurisdiction, as well as observed inefficiency in functioning of the program.[12] Personalities and their interrelationships are very important bases of administering a program; nevertheless, functions cannot always be organized effectively around presently available personalities. Additional criteria must be used in grouping or regrouping personnel functions in a new departmental structure.

Homogeneity or Functional Relatedness of Services and Functions. To secure the full benefit of specialization, functions closely related in their nature should be grouped together within the same administrative structure. For example, it would be an unwise grouping if aptitude testing for admissions were assigned to one personnel department and achievement testing for counseling uses were to be structured in an administratively independent department

[12] Brumbaugh and Berdie, *op. cit.*

within a college. While there are differences between these two kinds of testing, their interrelatedness is greater than their difference with regard to uses in counseling. In like manner, it would be inefficient to organize aptitude testing in one department and counseling of all kinds in a totally separate and independent department. Again, counseling and testing are two different personnel functions, but their interrelatedness is such as to make for enhanced efficiency in both functions by common administrative grouping. We point out, however, that it is administratively unfeasible to structure *all forms* of counseling in one department, since counseling is both a specialty and a function to be performed in some respects in every part of the institution—by teachers as well as by technically oriented counselors.

In applying the principle of unifunction, it does not follow that each and every functionally related service should be structured in the same administration, as was just pointed out in the case of counseling. In similar manner, in large institutions it is impossible, or certainly unfeasible, to organize all forms of students' recreation in one single department. To do so would mean that the music department, the department of art, the student union, and the hundreds of student organizations that carry on recreation programs would be administratively grouped together. Such a grouping, while unwieldly for departmental efficiency, might be accomplished were these recreation programs the sole function of the indicated departments. But, for example, the musical recreation programs conducted by music departments are only a part, and sometimes a minor part, of the total instructional program of the department. The same thing is true of the department of art. To group these two departments together with the student union would place the two instructional programs in a minor role and would cause many difficulties, administrative and otherwise. Thus, there are practical limitations to the application of the principle of unifunctioning; the principle must be applied in terms of the peculiarities and special features of any one institution. As is always the case, the principle should be applied with due respect to local conditions and with moderation as opposed to extreme consistency.

A second criterion has to do with a desirable application of the principle of decentralization in functioning departments. In order to decentralize services, it is necessary to structure them in sizable units that can be operated efficiently by a staff of manageable size. But to decentralize to the extent of extreme autonomy, or minute subdivisions of services, often produces conflicts of jurisdiction, separateness of function, and many other weaknesses of uncoordinated functioning. To correct these weaknesses, it is necessary to establish coordination of decentralized services and functions. We have discussed coordination in an earlier section, and we stress it here as a corrective measure for decentralization. There is homogeneity among many personnel functions. At the same time, there are many functions that are heterogeneous. This means that there must be day-to-day functioning interrelatedness among all kinds of personnel services, not merely among those similar in their fundamental nature. For example, counseling and financial services are different in content. They are therefore best organized in separate bureaus when volume of work and other factors justify such formal structuring. But many students use both services, and both must be extended to students in a coordinated and interrelated manner, if the institution's limited scholarship funds are to be wisely invested in students of the greatest scholastic and professional potentiality, for example.

The fundamental reason for coordination is found not only, or certainly not solely, in its administrative efficiency. Rather, a major argument is found in the fact that the individual client is a total personality. It is unreasonable to expect any one staff member or any group of staff members to be sufficiently expert in all phases of personality adjustment to perform all the needed services for any one student. It follows that—if the total individual is to be assisted in his personal development in an educational institution—all staff members who specialize in certain aspects of his personal development must correlate their services into a totality according to his peculiar needs.

From this, we shall develop applications in the form of correlating the many separate program services into an individualized pattern for each individual student. Because of their specialized nature, in a real sense, specialized personnel services are and will continue to be fragmented until they are coordinated at every level of performance; program operations are not being handled solely at the top administrative level. The administrator must coordinate departments and programs in his own way; each counselor who works with an individual student also coordinates and correlates, in his unique way, separate services as they are relevant to the individual student's problems.

A third criteria for the functional structuring of services has to do with the extent to which personnel programs should be organized on an institution-wide or a specialized-department basis. For example, we have referred to the question of whether counseling should be localized in a clinic or should be done, in some form, by everyone on the institution's staff, in addition. With regard to counseling and other personnel functions, a guiding principle as to the extent of centralization or decentralization should be the size and character of the enterprise and of the function itself. In a small institution, for example, it probably would make for greater economy and greater effectiveness if the loan funds were centralized in one office or committee, not decentralized among many offices and committees and staff members. In a large institution, such an extreme centralization might lead to interdivisional rivalry with regard to the equitable distribution of the funds. It might also produce such a large volume of business that a central staff would be unduly delayed in handling cases of emergency needs. In every case there is a point at which centralization delays a student in such a bottleneck that centralized services can no longer be considered efficient. In contrast, there is a point at which decentralization leads to so much confusion on the student's part about where he should go and to so much rivalry and conflict of jurisdiction that inefficiency results. As is true in the application of all other principles in the field of administration, judgments must be made from time to time as to the need for the restructuring and regrouping of functions. In our opinion, there probably is no permanent and single way in which personnel or any other functions can be universally organized and administered in any enterprise. As was discussed elsewhere, the restudy of functions and their organization is a permanent and continuing part of administration.

Perhaps we may generalize and say that personnel services, with the central emphasis upon the development of the individual pupil, should be decentralized to the extent that the personnel point of view may influence the entire institution's staff. And the use of techniques in handling individual students should become, through decentralization, so well known that the competence of the entire staff is improved.

We turn to consideration of institutional peculiarities in structuring functions. An example is found in the contrasting methods of organizing a central clinical counseling service at Ohio State University and at the University of Minnesota. Formerly at Ohio State, clinical services were provided through a three-credit course, "The Psychology of Effective Study and Individual Adjustment." In this course, staff members and graduate students in personnel work gave students counseling services concerning scholastic and personal adjustment.[13] Scholastic credit was granted for this counseling experience and service in the College of Education, located administratively within the College of Liberal Arts. There was no centralized vocational guidance clinic other than this course until the Occupational Opportunities Service was organized in 1942. This type of classroom counseling was administratively organized as part of the instructional program and was not under a dean of men, dean of women, or dean of students.

In contrast, at the University of Minnesota centralized clinical counseling was organized in 1932 as the University Testing Bureau, responsible then to an advisory committee appointed by the president.[14] Students at the University were not—and are not now—given academic credit for being counseled. However, the bureau is used for training advanced graduate students in clinical methods, graduate credit being offered in the graduate school through the Department of Psychology and the College of Education. Undoubtedly there are many complex institutional and historical and personality reasons for the two different structures of similar service in these two different institutions. We are not arguing for either type of structure; we are illustrating an important point in the adoption of any form of organization. To ignore institutional factors would be to set up obstacles and resistance to organizing effective personnel services. Thus, there is no universal type of structure, although we may summarize universal experience in terms

[13] Francis P. Robinson, *Principles and Procedures in Student Counseling.* New York: Harper & Brothers, 1950, p. 7.

[14] E. G. Williamson, "University of Minnesota Testing Bureau," *The Personnel Journal,* vol. 12, no. 6, pp. 345–355, April, 1934.

of criteria and principles which may be applied in differing ways and forms in different institutions.

AGENTS OF ADMINISTRATION

Earlier we noted the use of the word "structure" to include the staff members who perform management functions; these we call the "agents of administration." As we have pointed out, the central emphasis in a good deal of the literature on administration seems to be placed upon the top executive as the highest single staff member. In contrast, we have maintained that each member of the staff performs some administrative function. He must structure and carry out his service not in isolation from other members of the staff, but as a member of a team with whose other members he has varying degrees of working relationships and cooperation.

We observe three principal agents of administration in the student personnel program: professional workers, faculty members, and students. We shall discuss the unique role of each agent and the various ways in which these agents may be organized to perform their administrative services and functions. We shall also discuss specialized personnel services in the case of the staff and the specialists. Our reasons for including students in this discussion as agents of administration will be readily apparent when we come to that topic.

Professional Personnel Workers. In our discussion of administration, we usually think first of one person as the agent of administration. That is, the top executive of an enterprise has become well established and accepted. In student personnel work, as in other enterprises, one professional worker is usually designated as the chief administrator. As indicated previously, in some colleges two individuals are given coordinate administrative responsibilites for men and women. The chart on page 91 delineates a typical structuring of such dual administrative responsibility under a dean of students. In the chart (see p. 96) of organization for Occidental College, parallel functions for men and women are handled coordinately by a dean of men and a dean of women. Barnard has defined the functions of the top executive as "the specialized work

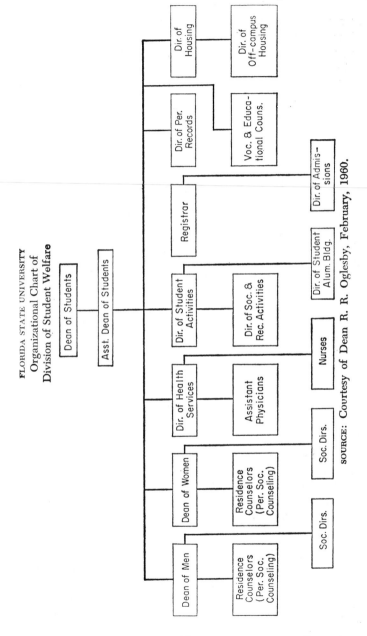

FLORIDA STATE UNIVERSITY
Organizational Chart of
Division of Student Welfare

SOURCE: Courtesy of Dean R. R. Oglesby, February, 1960.

91

of maintaining the organization in operation." [15] He goes on to state that "the essential executive functions . . . are, first, to provide the system of communication; second, to promote the securing of essential efforts; and third, to formulate and define purpose." [16]

In a formal organization, all members of the staff report on certain functions directly to the head of the enterprise, although there may be other executives between the head and the staff members in various divisions. For example, instead of reporting directly to the president of the college, a counselor may report to the head of a bureau who reports to a vice-president and through the vice-president to the president.

A discussion of the agents of administration limited to the top executive—whether it be one or two or a man or woman—does not exhaust the possibilities of the topic. As Follett has pointed out, functioning authority flows from the bottom up rather than from the top down. This generalization means that the general spirit of democracy has led to increased participation in varying degrees on the part of each staff member in program planning, policy making, and all other forms of institutional management, and in terms of particular functions. For example, in some universities members of the teaching staff participate in executive decisions concerning teachers' salaries and promotions. Nevertheless, for the most part, such administrative decisions are usually made by the top executive upon the recommendation of staff members and subexecutives. Generally, such administrative decisions do not involve such widespread participation as does program planning and evaluation. We shall see that the extent and manner of staff participation in administration is determined in part by the nature of the function under discussion.

Participation in administration concerning any function may take various forms with different members of the staff. For example, at each administrative level of operation, informal or formally structured committees of staff members may be assigned particular functions of management. Such committees may be assigned decentralized authority for preliminary consideration and even for final determination of action. Or such committees may be used

---

[15] Chester I. Barnard, *The Functions of the Executive.* Cambridge, Mass.: Harvard University Press, 1949, p. 215.

[16] *Ibid.,* p. 217.

only for preliminary discussion and identification of important elements in a situation and for the formulation of alternative recommendations to be acted upon at a higher administrative level. Assignments may be temporary—for specific purposes—or may be continuing. In some instances, a committee may be called together informally to make preliminary evaluation of a new staff member or to explore the desirability of instituting a new program project. Committees may consist of heads of departments on a permanent or rotating basis, or they may consist of heads of departments in addition to staff members serving under them.

It is our judgment that staff members should participate—provided that participation does not interfere with their technical services—in some form of management, if for no other reason than to help them communicate directly their viewpoints and their interests to others who may make decisions and policies. Moreover, such participation aids in orienting staff members to the necessity, and ways, of balancing the particular and unique interest of each with those of many other individuals and the requirements of the total enterprise. It is commonly observed that each member of the staff—left to himself—may press his interest, desires, and needs with restricted reference to balancing them with other parts of the enterprise. Quite frequently, for example, the needs of a technical staff for specialized equipment, staff additions, or for a particular kind of program must be balanced against what the community and the student clientele expect of an organization. Since no enterprise has unlimited funds, it is evident that the legitimate, but competing, needs of separate departments and individuals within departments must be weighed against each other in the wise distribution of available funds. Someone must make a judgment— an arbitrary, definitive judgment which is made after wide consultation—as to where the institution's financial resources shall be used to the best advantage of the total enterprise. In contrast, some believe that democracy implies that each member of a staff shall have equal jurisdiction over all matters—surely an impossibility if the enterprise is to go forward. Perhaps over the centuries, some considerations, such as need for going forward, have led in Western culture to development of the top executive as the decision maker who listens in Solomon fashion to the needs, considerations, and persuasive arguments of all interested parties.

But it is not solely the final and ultimate decision making which should color our thinking about the manner in which staff members may participate in administration. Even though the newest or the oldest staff member may not have final Solomon-like jurisdiction over decisions, the participation of each member is of utmost importance if the enterprise is to maintain its morale and effectiveness. Decisions cannot be made at the top without communication with the bottom and vice versa. It is a wise executive, or committee of executives, or committee of staff members who seeks consultation at all levels and from all sources before formulating recommendations and making decisions.[17]

It should be pointed out that personnel workers, although technically oriented at the graduate level of instruction and training, are sometimes relatively untrained and inexperienced in this kind of cooperative participation in management and administration. For the most part, they are trained as isolated specialists rather than as members of an administrative team; the prototype seems to be the isolated private practitioner working in a general community, rather than a member of a staff in one of many departments of an educational institution. Indeed, the beginning specialist many times is not able or disposed to participate in the over-all development of a program; he sometimes insists on arguing his own needs and their solutions with little consideration of the needs of other specialists. This behavior makes for some difficulty in developing an over-all program in which specialists must work with other specialists and nonspecialists, if there is to be interrelated effectiveness in each service.

One further point concerning the use of committees and individual staff members in administration should be made clear. Some over-zealous advocates of democracy have seemed to read into or from the concept of democracy an equality of all participants—as opposed to the need of the group's leader and his important role in helping

[17] In this connection, we read with interest and gain a description of a compulsory staff service: " . . . under this rule the abbot of a Benedictine monastery must consult the elder monks about him, even on minor matters. On matters of more vital importance he must consult everyone, even the youngest. This rule in no way abridges the line of authority of the abbot in making the final decision. He is simply prohibited from rendering any decision until the rule is obeyed." See James D. Mooney and Alan C. Reiley, *The Principles of Organization.* New York: Harper & Brothers, 1939, p. 120.

groups to arrive at decisions. We are not now discussing the executive in his capacity to make decisions; we are concerned with him as the leader of a group, who assists the group in formulating its thinking and in reaching conclusions which may not necessarily be the final decisions made in the total organization.

In many group discussions of policies and decisions, it may be effective for the committee of staff members to select its own chairman-leader. In other instances of administrative functioning, a top executive faces the necessity of changing his role to that of discussion leader of a consultation team. That is, we contend that —with regard to staff members' participation in decision making, policy making, and program planning—the head of a department, the dean of students, or any other executive plays a modified, although not independent, role. He may be perceived as exercising his decision-making authority to throttle the group's discussion so that only those conclusions acceptable to the leader-executive are reached. Such a misuse of staff participation is obviously not the most efficient way in which to secure participation and its many benefits. Rather the leader should cast aside his executive role— difficult though it may be to play an alternate one—and serve as discussion leader, drawing from the group members and helping them organize the rich experience and expressions of need which may be found at the grass-roots level of professional operation. The following chart with its alternative lines of relationship between staff and executive serving in the line relationship of authority and serving also as a staff committeeman—will illustrate our point.

We stress this manner of staff participation in administration because it permits the staff member to avoid segregating professional services to his clientele because of his participation in top level of management. For example, today one hears the complaint among some university faculty members that they are called upon to do so much committee work on dull routine matters that they have little time for direct relationships with students. In this situation, the solution involves finding better ways of tapping the rich experiences and ideas of staff for effective management of a program's day-to-day administration—without diverting their efforts from the students. Our experiences lead us to conclude that the use of staff meetings of personnel workers for exhaustive analysis of problems and for review of alternative actions and plans offers

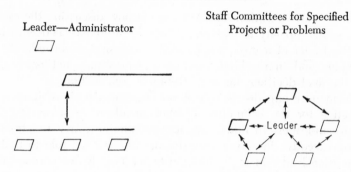

effective means of participation without weakening direct professional services to students.

Moreover, we believe that there is a second reason for centering attention upon the use of committees of staff in certain phases of administration. This concerns the enhancement of the status of those who perform day-to-day operations, sometimes perceived as dull and routine services, in contrast with what is perceived as high-level decision making. That is, the morale of the worker at the level of professional services sometimes needs to be enhanced by participation in consideration of top-level policies. Such participation usually enhances the simplest level of operations and raises it to the level of first importance. Moreover, it centers attention upon the very purpose of management—the quality of the direct service to the client. We believe that this device, and many others, should be used skillfully to maintain emphasis in administration upon the recipients of the services, the students.

We come now to the participation in administration of a second type of agent, namely, members of the faculty.

Faculty Participation. The history of faculty participation in the management of the entire educational enterprise reveals wide variation. Bogert, in discussing faculty participation in the university government, refers to four states through which this phase of education has moved.[18] He says the first stage developed in the medieval university (we assume he refers to the Italian universities

---

[18] G. G. Bogert, "Faculty Participation in American University Government," *Bulletin of the American Association of University Professors,* vol. 31, pp. 70–82, 1945.

and not the French and English) in which guilds or associations of students hired and supervised teachers. The second stage was that in which there was direct faculty control of all aspects of the institutions, a system which still exists in some forms in England. It should be noted, however, that in Germany the government through the ministry of education in each of the German provinces administered the business and financial phases of the institutions, leaving the faculty members to administer the curriculum and instructional part of the program. Bogert's third stage refers to the long-standing American practice of considering faculty members as employees in spirit and in fact.[19] As employees, members of the faculty in the colonial colleges supervised the morals of the students as well as their classroom learning and acted as proctors in dormitories. Also functioning as employees, members of the faculty did not participate in policy making or in the other decision-making functions exercised almost entirely by boards of trustees. The fourth stage Bogert refers to in these terms: "The spirit of the organization is that of a partnership of trustees, officers, and faculty, each contributing according to his own talents."[20]

One may conclude that this fourth stage has not yet been achieved in many institutions. Nevertheless, some considerable gain has been made in most. For example, in most institutions today, boards of trustees delegate almost complete authority and final jurisdiction over academic and instructional matters to the faculties and thus exercise only nominal supervision in such matters. In connection with the discussion of faculty participation at the secondary and elementary school levels, Butts made a significant generalization regarding the way in which faculty may effectively participate in management:[21]

Superintendent Arthur K. Loomis reported that the participation of the teaching staff in the formulation of policies had improved the morale of the staff and had resulted in better and wiser decisions than would otherwise have been possible. The mistake was not made of confusing policy making with executive authority. The province of the staff council was to make decisions of policy and then delegate to the

[19] *Ibid.*, p. 82.
See also Cattell, *op. cit.*
[20] Bogert, *op. cit.*
[21] R. Freeman Butts, *A Cultural History of Education.* New York: McGraw-Hill Book Company, Inc., 1947, p. 627.

proper administrative officers full authority to act and carry out the decisions.

This generalization needs to be emphasized in student personnel work, as well as in all other parts of an educational enterprise. Members of the staff should not all seek to serve as the one who carries out policy and program decision. A committee cannot administer a program, although it can profitably review and make decisions about programs. But programs are best carried out through the assignment of specific responsibilities and attendant authority to staff members competent to discharge such responsibilities in day-to-day operations.

The essential difference between using a group for policy and program making and using a single agent for carrying out the decisions made has caused confusion in some circles. The translation of a policy or program decision into its component parts, which are then assigned in an over-all teamwork balance to individuals, is an important part of effective administration. If the individual members of a policy board or faculty committee attempt to administer their policies—each with equal weight and authority in administration—serious duplication of effort and uncoordinated and conflicting administrative practices would be produced. No doubt, this is at the heart of the generalization one hears on all sides that a single executive is needed to carry out policy decisions. But again we point out that, especially in the student personnel field, it is not a single executive who carries out the program decisions but each and every staff member, each functioning in his own specialty to carry out that part of the policy and program decision which is relevant to it. In this sense, every member participates in the application of policy in the program of services to students. But this is true only of specialized personnel services and not of such administrative functions as financial transactions and employing staff members.

With regard to the personnel program, we have a special interest in faculty participation in policy and program decisions. In a real sense, an educational enterprise is manned and operated by the teaching staff. That is, the chief business of the educational enterprise is to assist the individual student to learn and to develop personally. The front-line operations of the educational enterprise take place in those situations where the individual is helped to learn directly and immediately by relationships with the teacher and with some counselor or personnel specialist. It follows then that a personnel program which is not influenced and guided and determined in large part by members of the teaching staff would be set apart from the main undertaking of the enterprise. It would indeed then be peripheral and often conflicting with the teacher's function. For this reason, the personnel program must win the support and assistance of members of the teaching staff. And this winning of support can often take place by having teachers participate in the formulation and development of plans for the personnel program.

In reaching this conclusion, we do not minimize the seriousness of the opposition from some teachers who feel that personnel work is foreign to the educational enterprise and who, therefore, present very serious obstacles to the development of a modern program. To these individuals, student personnel work is indeed peripheral to the main concept of education, which is restricted to the student-teacher relationship in classroom, conference, library, and laboratory. Even though we disagree with its substance, we must address ourselves to such a point of view since, in the final analysis, the program must become acceptable to the instructional staff if it is to permeate all the institutional practices and achieve its maximum contribution to the development of the individual student. At a later point we shall discuss some of the ways by which teachers may be aided to learn about, and to influence, the emerging personnel program. At this point, we emphasize that an important part of sound administration is incorporating classroom teachers' thinking into the development of the program in every possible way —without subjecting the program to complete blockage because of teachers whose view of education does not encompass the emerging techniques of facilitating the individual student's development through student personnel services.

Student Participation. We turn to the third type of agent participating in a broad-guaged administrative program. It is one of the peculiarities of a personnel program that the client who receives a service should also participate in certain phases of the administration and development of that service. With respect to one such service, student activities, the principle of student participation is clearly established. And few institutions deny to students the right to participate and largely to determine their own extracurricular activities. To be sure, often such a delegated form of control arises from a cynical appraisal as to the limited educational usefulness of the extracurriculum. Far too frequently, in our opinion, extracurricular activities are not taken seriously by the institution's management, trustees, or faculty except in so far as it may become a source of unfavorable publicity. And we believe that the great sources of the extracurriculum for instructional purposes are usually overshadowed by the historical tendency of the faculty to limit its educational thinking to the formal classroom curriculum.

But there is another type of student participation in management of other parts of the institution's program. We refer to the participation of students in the formulation of policies governing various aspects of the institution. Parallel with Follett's observed democratization of industry through the participation of workers at all levels in management and policy making, we also noted the growing tendency for members of the faculty to participate in formulation of management policies. In a similar manner and ever so slowly, participation by students—immature though they are in management experiences—in certain types of institutional practices is becoming increasingly visible. At first students were consulted, or permitted to express their point of view, or listened to only when some crisis arose, that is, through the use of complaint sessions. These "gripe" sessions are now well established in many institutional practices; in some institutions, top management meets regularly to hear the complaints of the students about this, that, or the other institutional practice. Slowly, however, we seem to be moving out of this limited form of participation into a more constructive and mature type of consultation about various institutional matters before policies are formulated.[22] For example, it may be that the president of the institution wishes to sound out student sentiment with respect to an increase in tuition or the development of a new curriculum. Or it may be that a dean or department head will wish to learn students' experience in the evaluation of teaching methods

[22] Williamson, E. G.: "The Dean of Students as Educator," *The Educational Record,* vol. 38, no. 3, pp. 230–240, July, 1957.

Lunn, Harry H.: *The Student's Role in College Policy Making.* Washington: American Council on Education, Commission on Student Personnel, 1956.

used by certain members of the faculty, or by all teachers. In numerous ways, this initiation of consultation taps the students' direct experience and may constitute an important form of evaluation of the institution's program. This is not to say that students' verbalized reaction to institutional practices is of itself a valid, or the only valid, kind of information necessary to effective evaluation. But the consumer's own reaction to the service which he is receiving is, in our Western culture, an important datum. We do not insist that we know better than the customer what he should like; if we do insist, we follow slow and patient methods of changing his expectations rather than ignoring his reactions.

In some institutions, systematically organized methods of communication are at hand. For example, in one college the president of the student council may sit as a regular member of the weekly meeting of the deans of the colleges and the president of the university to present the students' point of view regarding all matters discussed. Elsewhere, faculty, students, and administration form a community council which reviews all proposals for changes in programs and policy. In other institutions, the president may meet once or twice each year with selected student leaders who represent all interests and cross sections of the student body to hear what they have to say about the institution and to explore with them ideas for desirable changes. In an increasing number of institutions, students are appointed to standing committees of the faculty to review curricular matters, policies governing students, and all other matters of concern to the administration.

And we must not underestimate the contributions of student journalism to administration through news coverage and especially through expression of editorial opinions and evaluations. Unfortunately, in some institutions, some immature expressions of student reactions have caused the management of the institutions to exercise censorship and repression of such expressions of opinion. Our own experience leads us to conclude that wherever personnel workers and responsible faculty members work periodically and continuously with student leaders of journalistic enterprises to secure maturity of news content and editorial expression, this journalistic form of student participation has been most helpful in maintaining a high level of morale among the students and at the same time providing desirable and necessary insights into student life to those who make policy and program decisions.

In the light of these experiences, personnel workers themselves should be encouraged to learn to develop new forms of utilizing participation by students in the formulation and development of personnel programs. At the present time, we observe that personnel workers seem to be so technique-oriented that they tend to think of student clients as recipients rather than as participants in the processes and development of the personnel program. In contrast, we believe that the presentation of technical personnel problems of program development to responsible students will in itself, many times, reveal fundamental defects in those programs, from the students' point of view, which might hamper the development of the program if left undetected. Moreover, such presentations, with their attendant discussions, serve to enlist the sympathetic support and understanding of students in what would otherwise remain a technical mystery and which might result in a failure to stimulate some students to become self-directing in their development.

Staff and Executive Relationships. We turn now to a discussion of some special features of administration. We shall discuss three special administrative structures used to achieve unity of emphasis and coordination of program efforts: coordinating councils and boards; regular and special conferences, clinics and training institutes; and retreats with students and teachers.

Several decades ago, following the First World War with the attendant large influx of students and the necessity for developing new kinds of welfare services, most institutions experienced a rapid growth in the number and character of specialized services, many of them hitherto unknown in some American institutions. Housing bureaus, counseling bureaus, testing units, and the like proliferated within a few years. Most of these programs developed outside of the then existing offices of deans of men and deans of women, although in some institutions they were organically related from the time of initiation. But the proliferation of these new departments and programs soon led to such confusion, duplication, and uncoordination of administrative and program efforts that attempts were made to bring about some degree of unity among such great diversity. This significant development in administration is perhaps well illustrated by the following quotation from L. B. Hopkins's early survey:[23]

An administrative measure that has, I believe, a very genuine significance and will be definitely and increasingly fruitful, was the calling,
this fall, of a meeting of all those working in the field of student
welfare, the deans of schools, university administrative officers dealing
with health, athletics, and physical training, the YMCA secretary, the
ministers of the town, the registrar, and the dean of students. Such
a meeting is important because it is based on a recognition of the
unity of the field of student welfare, and the university's responsibility
to exercise leadership in providing for the direction of those forces
which determine, to a large extent, the character, general attitude, and
effectiveness of its graduates. The meeting will, I believe, be fruitful
because it will engender in those people concerned a sense of this unity,
and so lay the foundations for an increasing cooperation. The various
viewpoints here represented will all be essential to any well-rounded
program of student welfare. By this method of bringing them together
the university will, in the course of the next few years, achieve, not
a forced unification of these elements in its program, but a genuine
spontaneous cooperation. So far as I know, no such marshalling of
forces which make for physical, mental, and moral health has been
attempted, or even conceived in educational administration before.

This significant administrative marshaling of independent agencies was a step forward to be followed in many institutions by
a similar organization on a permanent and formal basis of all personnel offices and agencies. Some institutions formed coordinating
councils of a more informal nature, usually appointed by the president and consisting of almost every person in the institution who
had responsibilities for the extraclass life of students, in some
cases with the curricular problems of the institution. It was apparently the thought that if all individuals could come together, each
maintaining his own administrative autonomy, they would see the
necessity and advantage of interrelations and coordination. They
would therefore work together by referring cases to each other
when necessary and desirable; by avoiding duplication and conflict, they would unify the disparate and diverse programs. Such
a cooperative and voluntary beginning of an informal sort in many

[23] L. B. Hopkins, "Personnel Procedure in Education," *The Educational
Record Supplement,* no. 3, p. 87, October, 1926.

institutions led gradually to the development of a more formally structured centralizing of these independent offices in a new division under a dean of students. But it should be noted that this structuring and centralizing did not do away with the necessity for interdepartmental committees and councils and conferences as is discussed elsewhere in this chapter.

Conferences, Case Clinics, and Training Institutes. With or without formal administrative structuring and grouping, in any sizable institution where there is more than one personnel worker, it is necessary that the total program shall proceed with balanced stress on interrelatedness among the various specialized services. This can be achieved not by organic unity alone, but also by day-to-day conferences in an informal structure. Good institutional practice calls for innumerable conferences of different staffs whenever there is a problem common to more than one staff or one department. In later discussions on some complicated institution-wide programs, we shall see that innumerable conferences must be held in order to maintain some central emphasis and coordination of programs which involve many staff members. There is no substitute for such conferences. Written directives, memoranda, and outlines of programs are all necessary but they will not suffice unless there are frequent direct, informal communications from person to person, each representing his point of view in a total program covered by all participants from various departments.

Another special kind of conference has evolved in the field of counseling. We refer to the case conference, which may be held especially for particular types of situations or students or which may be held periodically and used in part for the training of staff members, faculty counselors, and graduate students. In these case conferences all the specialists pool their information either in person or through consultation reports so that the participants in the conference observe the total approach to all the diverse parts of the individual's life adjustments. This kind of conference is perhaps one of the most effective educational devices in teaching members of the staff, each with his own autonomous specialty, how his work and service dovetail with those of other specialists. That is, through the medium of the actual living student and his own real problem, each specialist comes to see how his work may be integrated with that of others so that the total program emphasis is correlated and coordinated within the life of the individual student. This is a form of coordination that serves as a real test of administrative effectiveness.

Retreats with Students and Teachers. A special kind of institutional structure facilitates a coordinating effect in the case of diverse and disparate departments and at the same time, enlists the support of the students. This takes the form of periodic retreats of personnel staff, students, administrators, and faculty. We refer here to the weekend retreat in which student leaders and selected staff members and personnel workers withdraw from the campus to a cabin in the mountains or elsewhere, physically separated from the distractions of the campus, to review some phases of the program and of student life in general. An agenda may be established for such a conference, limiting it to current issues besetting students or disrupting and dividing the campus; still there is an important element of spontaneity in the situation. Living together over a weekend produces a desirable quality of interpersonal and group relationship, enhanced as it always is by the students' love for recreational singing, dancing, and similar enjoyments. Such a retreat can take the form of a projective experience, releasing reactions, criticisms, and attitudes toward various phases of the university's total program, including the personnel program. Experiences would indicate that this is a most effective opportunity for testing the quality of the personnel program through a critical but sympathetic evaluation by student leaders at a time when they are thinking sincerely and naturally.

SUMMARY

Our review of some phases of the administrative structure or organization of student personnel services illustrates our point of view that generalizations made in industry and government need to be modified in adapting them to our field. We were especially aware of the character of our work which requires considerable freedom of operation by trained specialists who work directly with individual students in their life adjustments. We do not conclude from our review that we should structure our services after the model of the individual practitioner, concentrating in his private practice upon a single individual and his problems of adjustment.

Rather, we conclude that the professional personnel worker and each teacher functioning in a similar capacity should organize his efforts upon the model of a team, each of whose workers is interdependently related in a total program of assistance to each individual student as he endeavors to approximate full development through education. We especially believe that we must in student personnel work evolve our own unique structure to include the fully participating student, not a passive recipient of our services, but a unique kind of partner-learner in the functioning of each service!

CHAPTER 4

Administering the Program of Services

In Chapter 2 we reviewed the literature of administrative experiences in government and industry, searching for generalizations, suggestions, ideas, and experiences relevant to our understanding of administrative functions in student personnel work.[1] In the present chapter, we shall apply some of these generalizations to some aspects of the administration of student personnel services.[2]

We shall discuss the following administrative procedures: determination of objective; continuous program development; coordination; supervision of personnel services; selection and induction of personnel workers; staff development and in-service training; personnel problems of personnel workers; personnel workers as auxiliary instructional workers; evaluation; initiating a program; services as research stations on problems of adolescence; and maintenance of the program. We have discussed some aspects of these topics in

[1] At the risk of disrupting, with a note of sardonic wit, our serious effort to apply to our field the learning summarized in related fields of knowledge, reference is made to William James's definition of the democratic form of government administration: "William James had described democracy as a system in which you do something and then wait to see who hollers. Then you go and relieve the hollering as best you can and wait again to see who hollers as a result of your remedying the first woes." See Thomas V. Smith, *The Promise of American Politics*. Chicago: University of Chicago Press, 1936, pp. 199–200.

[2] Some very useful illustrations of administrative practices are presented in the new *Case Book—1958*, prepared and published by a committee of the National Association of Student Personnel Administrators. These cases are prepared in line with the Harvard Business School method of teaching administrative decision—presenting real situations anonymously for class discussion and evaluation of several possible decisions indicated by the nature of the situation.

previous chapters. In this chapter, we shall emphasize the functioning of administration in the day-to-day operations of a comprehensive program.

We begin our discussion by reemphasizing a familiar point. Much of the literature of administrative concepts and practices centers attention upon a particular aspect of administration. We would perhaps more clearly understand the prevailing theory derived from experiences in government and industry if we qualified the word by the modifying adjective, "central" or "top." For the most part, administration seems to be identified with the work of central executive staff, such as the president of an industrial firm or the head of a major division of an enterprise. While there is no question but that the top executive or administrator does have special functions to perform, we would be wrong to assume that in our field of endeavor only the top executive performs administrative duties. As we have stated previously, every personnel worker at every level of functioning and with every degree of specialization performs some administrative duties. We shall continually emphasize this point because it represents a true picture of the way the personnel program actually functions.

A second major emphasis will characterize our discussion of administration in student personnel work. In the literature on administration in industry and government, top management or administration is referred to as though it were divorced from direct contact with the worker, the client, or the person who receives the benefit of the service. In student personnel work, we find a different situation. Possibly this is because the personnel program is not so highly organized with so many, many parts that top management must divorce itself, in an attempt to economize effort and time, from the direct face-to-face relationship with the customer, consumer, or recipient of a service. If personnel workers constituted organization of several thousand employees dispersed over a wide geographic area, housed and performing services in different places, perhaps there would be a greater divorcement of management from direct services and therefore a greater degree of specialization in top managment. But college personnel work is performed in smaller units on campuses, with a preponderance of informal relationships among workers and students. For this and other reasons, it has thus far been possible to maintain more direct face-to-face relationships within the organization.

This is a most important feature of the administrative practice and program of personnel work. We personnel workers sometimes feel that we have become overorganized and overextended; nevertheless, every administrator and every other worker in a program does spend a significant part of his daily effort in face-to-face contact with other workers and students on a casual social basis or in a technical type of service relationship. It is true that deans of students are not as closely related in daily contact with staff as was true when college life was simpler and enrollments were smaller. Nonetheless, thus far we have not had to face the tremendous task of bridging the gap between students and top management located miles away in a special office, walled off by a multitude of workers, departments, procedures, and other conditions which have done much to dehumanize some modern industries.

Another related point bears further emphasis. In student personnel work the direct relationship between the worker and the student client cannot be decentralized further to a subprofessional worker, to an assistant or to a clerk. The essential service itself must be performed in a face-to-face relationship of a high professional level. That is, personnel work cannot be subdivided into smaller functional units of services which can then be parceled out as piecework is sometimes parceled out in highly complicated and decentralized industrial manufacturing processes. With the exception of certain supportive functions, such as testing and data collection, the service itself is performed directly by a high-level professional worker who represents the outermost decentralized functioning of the service. This is, of course, in radical contrast with the modern industrial manufacturing process in which the use of precision machinery permits greater fragmentation of a service. Student personnel work, in contrast, is a highly professional but direct face-to-face contract type of work.

It may now be seen that many modifications need to be made of the experiences of industry and government in developing administrative and organizational procedures in student personnel work.

DETERMINATION OF OBJECTIVES

In another chapter we have discussed briefly the generally accepted formulation of objectives and content of program in the field of student personnel work. These generalizations were made without reference to a particular school or institution. In applying these findings to an autonomous school or college, the broader experience must be translated into a particular program and a set of objectives peculiar to the local institution. There are no universally valid objectives for all institutions—except that the clientele of any particular institution is fairly representative of all students. But again, all sorts of modifications are necessary because of relevant local conditions.

Policy making, or the determination of program objectives, must grow out of the local institutional policies, programs, and objectives. The over-all character of an institution determines the general framework within which personnel work must operate. For example, a college which specializes in research, primarily at the graduate and upper technical levels of instruction, usually requires less of a broadly conceived counseling emphasis than does an institution which emphasizes undergraduate education, involving the solving of personal adjustment problems of transition from high school to college.

Determination of objectives is essentially a continuing exercise in answering the questions: What are we trying to do? and why? The objectives of each part of the program must be translated into the language of daily operations by staff members. Far too many objectives are worthless as controlling factors of programs because they are couched in such vague generalities that no staff member can be certain that his daily operations and daily relationships with students are achieving the objective.

Now objectives do not float out of a vacuum, nor are they permanently carved in stone. They emerge from changing human experiences. Experiences of other institutions as published or as reported in professional meetings often serve as source materials. Continuous research within the institution itself provides other new material out of which objectives may be forged. There is an additional source of objectives. One peculiar characteristic of our work, which differentiates it from some other types of programs, is that the one who receives the benefit of the service, the student client himself, determines in large measure the objectives. We have discussed this point elsewhere in terms of needed reexamination of this important source of program ideas.

The variety of services has been recognized. In addition, policies are seldom permanent. Periodic and continuous review and revision of objectives are the order of the day. Moreover, objectives are not adopted solely by legal vote of the top management or board of trustees. In most instances, everyone in the institution participates in the formulation of objectives—administrators, personnel workers, faculty, and students. Indeed, the central task in administration is to assist all members of the institution in participating effectively in continuous revision of the objectives and of the program. This is a task of first importance—to use the need for constant revision of the objectives as a means of enlisting the active participation of all members of the institution, including students, in the appraisal of the program. In this respect, the administrative process assumes major importance as a fundamental part of the program of services to the clients. That is, this part of administration—the revision of objectives—is not something apart from the program content of personnel services; it is an exercise in using administrative functions to achieve one important objective—a mature understanding of higher educational processes and objectives with respect to human development.

As was indicated above, objectives are best formulated not in vague language, but in terms of specific behavior, growth, and changes expected as a direct, or at least partial, result of the program. We shall see later that such a process lays the foundation for determining the means of evaluating the extent to which these objectives are achieved through the medium of the program.

In this connection, we have repeatedly emphasized the program's importance viewed as an integral part of the total institutional program and not as something set apart. A second most important force in determining objectives is the expectations of the immediate and wider communities in which the college operates. This means that, in some respects, some of the by-products of personnel programs become essential objectives. For example, as a result of an attempt to give more effective vocational guidance to students, the attitudes of parents toward the school—as a social enterprise supported by tax money—may be greatly improved as they realize that the school seeks to develop the best possible program of necessary educational aids for their children.

CONTINUOUS PROGRAM DEVELOPMENT

The determination of legitimate and worthwhile objectives, while crucially important as an end goal of effort, makes no fundamental difference in the lives of students unless these objectives are translated into concrete, specific programs of services. Thus, direct programs must be developed as means to achieve the adopted objectives. It becomes, therefore, a major administrative function to help organize a continuous search for effective means to the desired ends.

The relatedness and appropriateness of each program operation to the adopted objectives must be determined first by imaginative group thinking, at a later stage by experimentation and other types of evaluation. The conjuring up of means to objectives and goals for programs is a task in critical thinking—just as it is a similar task to conjure up the objectives themselves. As in the case of objectives, ideas are often discovered in the experiences of other workers in other institutions, within the institutional staff itself, and also among the students who are served by the program. Just as there are no universal objectives, except in the broadest categories, so there are no rigidly standard programs equally appropriate to all kinds of institutions. Programs must be indigenous in their development, just as objectives are necessarily adapted to local conditions.

In developing programs it is necessary to keep clearly in mind that within our field of work, programs consist essentially of competent persons performing services in face-to-face or supportive relationships with student clients. No machines or operations make up our programs in this phase of higher education; personnel work consists of services to human beings in their efforts to approximate full personal development. It follows that members of the personnel staff are the major instrumentalities, the program means, through which the program objectives are achieved. For example, a competent interviewer in a housing bureau is one program instrumentality through which the objective of hygienic and socially satisfactory housing of students is achieved. In like manner, a therapy counselor is one program instrumentality by means of which some of the objectives of mental health for students are achieved. We shall see later that the concept of staff members as program instrumentalities needs to be appraised in terms of the fact that these agents themselves have certain service needs which are comparable in some respects to the program needs of the student clientele.

One of the special and peculiar problems of administrators is to assist and stimulate staff members to keep alert to the changing character of the client and his needs and, therefore, constantly to modify direct services to the client as a means to achieve the sometimes changing end objectives. The maintenance of this open-ended professional attitude toward personnel work is still a largely unexplored field of administration, but we may find it possible to borrow some relevant experiences from other forms of enterprises.

ASSIGNMENT OF DECENTRALIZED SERVICES

In another chapter, we have argued for specialization within the field of student personnel work. Experiences in other types of enterprises indicate that no one staff member can perform more than a few of the specialized services required. In the words of Cowley—[3]

Ideally, every instructor is essentially a personnel officer, but he must depend upon specialists to perform certain personnel services for which he is untrained. In the best of all possible colleges every instructor would be individually interested in the students under his direction, but he cannot treat them concerning complex vocational problems, nor administer loans and scholarships, nor direct intelligence-testing programs, nor undertake the responsibility for a number of other personnel services.

At one stage in the early development of personnel work, there was considerable debate on the topic "The Generalist versus the Specialist." Seldom does one hear current discussion of such an either-or concept of the organization of services. There may still be institutions where economy-minded general administrators wish to make personnel specialists out of each teacher, without

[3] W. H. Cowley, *The Personnel Bibliographical Index*. Columbus, Ohio: Bureau of Educational Research, Ohio State University, 1932, p. 4.

regard to necessary technical background and competence. In general, however, we may agree that the case for specialization has been made and accepted.

Assuming the necessity for specialization and for different members of the staff to perform different services in line with their own competencies, the means of assigning and reassigning decentralized services to specialized workers becomes a major administrative problem. This assignment function should not be thought of as an arbitrary-directive type of function; it is cooperative and discussional, calling for conferences, repeated reviews, and reassignments which involve both administrators and staff workers. If personnel workers are specialists in the sense of being especially trained to perform a function, they have as great or greater knowledge of what services they are competent to perform, what services need to be performed, and what modifications of services need to be reassigned and reorganized than would a top administrator. Moreover, personnel workers are professional workers. They are therefore competent to participate in the assignment of their own functions while avoiding, of course, an autonomous position of independent functioning.

Two other special features of the assignment function of decentralized services should be mentioned. It is generally agreed that each personnel worker must assume two major responsibilities. First, he must provide adequate technical services directly to students, in line with their needs and his specialization and competence. A second related function and responsibility is equally important: each worker should coordinate his services with those of others in a particular service area and in the institution-wide program. For example, a counselor should provide special consultation services directly to student clients. In addition, he should provide consultation and advisory services to deans who make administrative decisions about individual students and to other staff members who have direct relationships with students. This form of functioning organization has been called "coordinated decentralization." [4] Such consultation and advisory relationships with other members of the institutional staff include providing personal consultation advice and also making technical records and data available for

[4] James D. Mooney and Alan C. Reiley, *The Principles of Organization.* New York: Harper & Brothers, 1939, pp. 178–179.

decision making by faculty advisers, admissions officers, academic deans, and superintendents.

In some respects, the major emphasis of current training programs for personnel workers seems to concern the first responsibility—the direct service to student clientele. Relatively less emphasis is given to the second major responsibility, consultation, in current graduate training programs. Therefore the administrator of an institutional program must give major emphasis to this function in the in-service and induction program of new staff members in order to overcome their concept of an isolated technical service given directly to student clientele. Many new counselors seem to come to an assignment expecting to work only with their student clientele—as though they were functioning as private practitioners in a city office. These new workers sometimes are not prepared to perform institutional services for the staff, but this is vitally necessary in an effectively coordinated total institutional program of services.

One other special feature of the assignment function of decentralized services should be kept in mind. Not all personnel services involve direct daily relationships with students. Some workers perform services in their offices without students—they should be assigned time to perform research or other professional activities if they are to avoid becoming specialized prematurely in a technical rut. Other personnel workers specialize in behind-the-scenes services of evaluation or data collection and seldom see the student clientele—for example, the keepers of records who usually provide services through counselors who deal directly with students. Such decentralized and specialized services are important supportive activities in the total program.

COORDINATION

We have referred to this topic in several places and here we need only emphasize its importance again. Coordination, for our purposes, may be considered the dovetailing of many separate parts into a balanced over-all program. In this sense it is a basic process in all types of administration. Coordination may be achieved within functionally related areas, such as all those services which pertain to the administration and interpretation of tests of aptitudes, interests, and scholastic achievement. Coordination is also necessary for integrating into an over-all totality such specialized and diverse functions as foreign student advising and disciplinary counseling. In the final analysis, coordination consists not of fitting static programs or services into a mosaic, but of assisting individual staff members to work together in a dynamic and complex team relationship. This is a particularly important aspect of coordination within student personnel work because of the specialized and sometimes isolated training and functioning of specialists.

As previously quoted from Gulick, coordination is achieved by organization (by interrelated subdivisions of work in a structure of authority and relationship) and by dominance of an idea. Both of these methods are highly interrelated.[5] In the field of student personnel work, we may achieve coordination by many means, all of which are highly useful in particular situations and for special purposes.[6]

One method of coordination has been described in these words:[7]

A time-honored and tested method for achieving coordination is to have one person responsible for knowing what all the others in a group are doing so that he can relate the activities of each person to the activity of the others in the group. In this way, coordination is sought through the nervous system of a single individual—probably the most effective coordinating mechanism of all. Although the group supervisor is not the only coordinating device, he is one of the most important in nearly all organizations.

In another connection, we have discussed coordination within the field of counseling in terms of the following:[8]

An assignment of functions to indicated staff members

[5] Luther Gulick, "Notes on the Theory of Organization," *Papers on the Science of Administration*. New York: Institute of Public Administration, 1937, p. 6.

[6] Williamson, E. G.: "Coordination by the Administrator," *Journal of Higher Education*, vol. 19, no. 6, pp. 301–306, June, 1948.
———: "Coordination of Student Personnel Services," *Journal of Consulting Psychology*, vol. 4, no. 6, pp. 229–233, 1940.
——— and D. G. Paterson: "Coordinating Counseling Procedures," *Journal of Higher Education*, vol. 5, no. 2, pp. 75–78, February, 1934.

[7] Herbert A Simon et al., *Public Administration*. New York: Alfred A. Knopf, Inc., 1950, pp. 130–131.

[8] Williamson, "Coordination by the Administrator," *op. cit.*, pp. 302–303.

Continuous program of informing all workers from all departments
with regard to each other's functions

Development of mutual respect for each other's specialty

Learning to look for the need to refer students to other specialists

Continuous, cooperative all-staff analysis of changing needs of clients'
services from year to year as knowledge and the surrounding dynamic
society changes

These are some of the methods of achieving coordination from
day to day. To a large extent, coordination is reduced to encouraging and assisting workers to maintain continuous acquaintance with
the specialties of the others so that there may be some erosion of
the sometimes interfering walls or moats separating the specialties.
We observe that—if there is mutual respect and up-to-date information concerning all of the special competencies—a specialist of one
kind may quickly identify a student problem which needs to be
referred to another specialist. This is, in effect, a kind of coordination
of the services themselves. It is also, of course, a kind of administrative coordination. But we place major emphasis upon the content
of the coordination rather than the mechanics themselves, which
are merely means to an end. In another connection, the use of a
modified social workers' confidential exchange as a means of acquainting each specialist with the other specialists who have served
the same individual client has been described.[9] This type of coordination is designed to minimize the effects of undesirable and
unproductive duplication of effort and also the disruption of conflicting services to the same client.

In the early days of organized personnel work following the First
World War, coordination was presented as the most pressing administrative problem in the field.[10] From present-day perspective,
it seems clear that the early concept of coordination was not an administrative one as much as it was an emphasis on casework involving the exchange of information and the interchange of facilities

[9] Williamson and Paterson, op. cit.

[10] Cowley, W. H.: "The Strategy of Coordination," Report of the Fifteenth
Annual Meeting of the American Council of Personnel Administrators,
February 23–26, 1938, Atlantic City, pp. 20–24.

Hopkins, L. B.: "Personnel Procedure in Education," The Educational Record
Supplement, vol. 7, no. 3, pp. 84 and 87, October, 1926.

Lloyd-Jones, Esther: Student Personnel Work at Northwestern University.
New York: Harper & Brothers, 1929, pp. 10–12.

among personnel workers who dealt with the same student clientele. Thus this early concept was designed to prevent undesirable duplication of effort with clients and to upgrade the quality of personnel services of different specialists by the exchange of knowledge from different fields. Hopkins spoke of coordination as making exchange information available wherever and whenever it was needed in dealing with students.[11] And Lloyd-Jones spoke of the lack of clearance and exchange of case data.[12]

In this connection, in addition to the modified social workers' confidential exchange reported in one institution, other methods have been developed to achieve coordination and are still in use. For example, Hopkins quotes Bradshaw as of 1925 and 1926[13] concerning the development of the coordinated council or committee composed of different personnel specialists in one institution. This early concept of the joint meetings of personnel workers from different services is by now well established; nearly every institution has a committee, council, or case conference of this sort which meets periodically to review all programs and to stress the interrelatedness of different services.

Two decades ago, a single individual in one institution was appointed to work on bringing about such a coordination of independent programs.[14] At that time, one of the most pressing administrative problems was to persuade independently organized and maintained services and departments to dovetail their work to eliminate duplication, to supplement each other, and otherwise to work in an institutional setting. Over the decades, separate and sometimes independent offices and departments had grown up in a Topsy-like manner, without established and structured lines of relationship. The first step in developing an institution-wide program was, therefore, centralized coordination of the services performed by separately organized departments.

A significant lesson for future program development is to be found in these early experiences. The collegiate personnel field arose out of two needs: the need for supervision of students in their

[11] Hopkins, *op. cit.*, p. 84.
[12] Lloyd-Jones, *op. cit.*, p. 12.
[13] Hopkins, *op. cit.*, p. 87.
[14] E. G. Williamson, "Minnesota's Program for the Coordination of Decentralized Student Personnel Services," *Report of the Sixteenth Annual Meeting of the American College Personnel Association*, 1939.

group life with respect to disciplinary behavior and the need for personalized attention to individual students.[15] In many, if not all, colleges and universities, these services were slowly clustered, administratively, in the separate but coordinate offices of the dean of men and the dean of women. For decades, they did yeomanly service—without benefit of the modern knowledge and techniques from the fields of psychology, education, and psychiatry. Prior to the First World War and later, members of medical staffs and psychology departments brought to campuses new knowledge and new techniques gained from war training and experiences— knowledge which was not previously available to some deans of men and deans of women. These importations initiated a period of healthy and sometimes competitive relationships between the older and the newer ways of assisting individuals with their problems.[16] Rather than wait until deans of men and deans of women could receive the modern training and retraining, the new technical services were often organized as adjuncts to departments of psychology and student health services, or were set up elsewhere on the campus, administratively separate from the then existing offices of deans. On many campuses, this type of competitive service led to undesirable results—until coordination was achieved, first by special councils, later by organic restructuring of the separate departments.

Looking back over the decades, one sees many differences in understanding of and in attitudes toward students' problems as a frequent cause of confusion and competition among persons, ideas, and programs. Some such competition is the very essence of higher education in America in that the then advanced ideas had to have an opportunity to demonstrate their usefulness. Apparently such a testing of new ideas could be done in some institutions only within separately organized structures. Some staffs were hostile to the new ideas; therefore, some institutions established new and separate organizations offering new methods in services to students. Eventually the many added departments had to be reclustered in a new organizational structure through complex and delicate administra-

[15] Eugenie A. Leonard, *The Origins of Personnel Services in American Higher Education*. Minneapolis: University of Minnesota Press, 1956.
[16] See, in Chap. 1, our previous account of this competition as perceived by Dean Coulter and Dean Goodnight.

tive operations. Perhaps this type of reorganization, arising out of the competition of new concepts and techniques, will continue in future years.

We turn now to still another special phase of coordination. In some areas of personnel work, methods are decentralized within the institution at the same time that they are being centrally organized. That is, many staff members outside of the new departments which are organized to try out new techniques later became trained and proficient in the use of those same new techniques. For example, classroom teachers became proficient in varying degrees in the use of the vocational interest test in counseling. These classroom teachers, therefore, utilized the newer counseling diagnostic techniques at the same time that specialized psychologists were employed in central counseling centers to perform the same kind of function, presumably with a higher degree of proficiency. Thus we find the decentralization of function developed along with a centralization of function. Far from being undesirable, such a stage of development is, as we shall see, a healthy sign of the general upgrading of the competency of all staff members—with consequent greater usefulness to a greater number of students. This later step represents the ideal type of decentralization of personnel function referred to long ago by Scott and Clothier and quoted earlier from Paterson's survey,[17] namely, that everyone in the institution does and should do some form of personnel work.

But it does not follow that this third stage of institutional coordination makes a specialized department unnecessary. This is a mistake made by many general educational administrators when they assume that all teachers may become sufficiently competent to perform all specialized services. It is true that one of our major objectives in student personnel work is to assist in the general upgrading of effectiveness of personal relationships between teachers and students aimed at the students' personal development. Nevertheless, it does not follow that all teachers, within the foreseeable future, will become adequately proficient in performing all or even many of these new psychological services. Our experiences thus far seem to indicate that, since the teaching profession itself is upgraded in the performance of such individualized counseling

[17] D. G. Paterson et al., "The Minnesota Student Personnel Program," *The Educational Record Supplement*, vol. 9, no. 7, April, 1928.

services, it needs all the more to be supplemented by specialists who can give longer periods of time and greater competence to the cases identified by teacher-counselors as needing such special services. It may be generalized that further development of effective personnel work reveals the need for still more of it, performed by more adequately trained workers, both teachers and other specialists.

SUPERVISION OF PERSONNEL SERVICES

In some circles, the concept of continuous daily supervision of specialists performing different services is not well accepted. That is, specialists are sometimes thought not to need administrative supervision. But the acceptance of a concept of professional autonomy leads inevitably to specialists who are in grave danger of becoming so grooved that they do not keep up with modern knowledge derived from experience and research. Such independent functioning also may become uncoordinated, with the result that the student client may suffer if some areas of need are not provided for by any one specialist.

The administrator who supervises must be provided with up-to-date information on all phases of the program which affect the workers. This calls for a continuous search for identification of what needs to be done to improve services to students. In some institutions, detailed monthly or quarterly reports of services performed and the types of clients reached are required of all workers. In others, infrequent, informal, and unscheduled spot checking is the administrative device used for supervision. In still others, a case conference in which all staff members pool their information about a particular individual provides for informal and highly acceptable supervision of specialists who desire and require a considerable amount of independence of operation. In other institutions, interdepartmental consultations with exchange of data and referral of students continually emphasize the expanding variety of desirable types of professional service.[18] And finally, continuous emphasis on the desirability of research to isolate and analyze deficiencies

[18] E. G. Williamson, "Supervised Experiences in Counselor Training Programs," *Kansas State Teachers College Bulletin,* vol. 46, no. 7, May, 1950

and effectiveness centers the staff's attention upon the upgrading of services.

SELECTION AND INDUCTION

Little has been written about the development of effective administrative practices in selecting student personnel workers. Perhaps for the most part, personnel administrators have not used personnel methods in selecting and inducting their workers, but have been content to follow the informal practices observed in the selection of faculty. Until recently, the rate of staff turnover and expansion has been so slow that there was no urgent necessity for improvement in practices. And, for the past several decades, personnel administrators, like other educational administrators, have been so busy hastily constructing programs to meet the greatly expanded enrollment that little time was available for leisurely perfecting of techniques of selection. It may be expected that this area of personnel administration will soon call for attention.

The observed practices in the selection of workers seem to be simple. When a vacancy occurs or when a new position is established by the budget, the bureau head or the dean of students usually writes to colleagues in other colleges describing the position, stating salary and prerequisites, and inviting assistance in locating qualified applicants. Sometimes communications are addressed to appointment or employment bureaus in universities that provide graduate training in this or related fields. Communications are often directed to the executive heads of professional associations and to graduate advisers of psychology and education departments having specialized courses in some phase of student personnel work.

When applicants are found, their papers are called for, including the facts of their educational and work histories, undergraduate and graduate grades and works, and recommendations from graduate professors with whom they have studied. Usually more detailed supplemental information and confidential appraisals are collected by personal communication with associates of the applicant known personally by the dean or known to be in a position to observe and appraise the applicant's personality, competence, and interpersonal relationships. In some institutions, the applicant is given tests of scholastic aptitude, vocational interest, and personality.

With such data in hand, the administrator usually begins a series of appraisal conferences which extend to those who will be associated with the applicant if he is employed, including, in many institutions, faculty members in academic fields related to the professional and academic background of the applicant. In case the position to be filled carries with it academic rank and status, the concurrence of the appropriate academic department is usually required before the appointment is made.

The few applicants who do survive these progressive selective procedures are then usually invited to interview some member of the staff who is attending professional meetings or to come to the institution with travel and incidental expenses paid by the inviting institution. In the latter case, a series of interviews and conferences provides the staff and administrator with opportunity to appraise and be appraised. This latter step is essential, since the quality of interpersonal relationships is a most important determinant of the applicant's potential effectiveness and his own personal happiness as well. Frequently administrators in central positions interview the applicant, and sometimes selected student leaders have conferences with him.

After the applicant leaves the campus, and sometimes during his visit, there follows a consensus-taking procedure. But the appointment decision is usually not based upon a simple counting majority of those polled, including students. The final selection is based upon a more penetrating and many-sided appraisal than would be possible if the administrator or a majority of the staff made the decision alone, without extensive consultation.

Such a many-phase procedure illustrates very well the principle stated several times that all members of the staff participate in administration. In this case, while the formal appointment form is signed by the head administrator, this formal signing takes place only after the widest possible consultation and review within the personnel department and often elsewhere. Our experience with this administrative practice in employing staff convinces us that only in such a way can we secure individuals whose competence extends beyond requisite professional skills to the not easily identified skills in professional teamwork operations. This use of personnel methods is, we believe, necessary in the building of an effective personnel staff.

THE LIABILITY OF STAFF FOR PERFORMANCE OF DUTIES

In the discharge of responsibility for some services, occasionally a staff member is confronted with the threat of legal action either to prevent him from exercising his delegated authority or to "punish" him for what he has already done. Such a situation may arise in connection with discipline, the suicide of a counselee, or in the cases of administrative action against a student organization, such as a fraternity. The staff member may well query what tort liability he faces in the discharge of his institutional duties and responsibilities.

In discussing this point of liability with a colleague,[19] I was referred to Davis's *Administrative Law*[20] with the interpretation that, in a state institution, such as a state university, the courts would in all likelihood hold that a counselor or other employee had no tort liability for the performance of his duties in serving student clientele.

Chapter 25, Volume III, of Davis's *Administrative Law Treatise* contains thirty-nine pages of discussion and interpretation of relevant cases in connection with Federal laws and decisions by the United States Supreme Court defining the immunity of officers. The legal principle was voiced in these words:

It is a general principle of the highest importance to the proper administration of justice that a judicial officer, in exercising the authority vested in him, shall be free to act upon his own convictions, without apprehension of personal consequences to himself.[21]

*   *   *

The purpose of the rule which exempts public officers from the harassment of private suits for damages on account of the performance of their public duties is, secondarily, for their protection, in order that its primary objective may be secured, i.e., a fearless administration of the law.[22]

[19] Prof. Robert McClure, Law School, University of Minnesota.
[20] Kenneth Culp Davis, *Administrative Law Treatise VIII*, 3 vols., rev. ed. St. Paul, Minn.: West Publishing Company, 1958, vol. 2, chap. 6.
[21] *Ibid.*, vol. 2, chap. 7, p. 508.
[22] *Ibid.*

Davis himself summarized:

In some state courts the immunity may be somewhat narrower than in the federal courts; the dictum is very common in opinions of state courts that officers exercising judicial functions are not liable in tort in absence of fraud and corruption, and yet the holdings seem generally to extend the immunity to malicious or corrupt acts.[23]

*   *   *

Tort liability is of hardly any consequence in administrative law because neither the governmental unit nor the officer is liable for wrongful acts involving discretionary functions . . . officers as well as governmental units are generally immune from liability for torts committed in the performance of discretionary acts.[24]

It would seem likely that staff workers in a public institution—perhaps in all types of institutions—would be immune from liability for the performance of their professional and administrative duties. In the absence of legal cases, the staff members should proceed with confidence in carrying out their assigned responsibilities. But each worker would be well advised to learn about the relevant laws of his own state and community.

In his 1958 three-volume revision, Davis begins his review with this summary:[25]

The central principle that takes care of the great bulk of practical problems concerning tort liability of public officers and public employees is that officers are generally immune from liability for their unintentional fault in the exercise of discretionary functions.

STAFF DEVELOPMENT AND IN-SERVICE TRAINING

As is true of selection of personnel staff, not much has been written about institutional experiences in on-the-job staff training. Our experience leads us to the conclusion that, even in the case of staff members selected by the procedures described above, the administrator must continuously work with staff to maintain their professional development. And he must employ a variety of methods. Institutional funds should be made available to encourage staff,

[23] *Ibid.*, vol. 2, chap. 8, p. 515.
[24] *Ibid.*
[25] *Ibid.*, vol. 3, chap. 26, p. 506.

perhaps on a rotational basis, to attend professional meetings and to present papers describing practices and research. Staff members should be nominated to local and national professional committees by the administrator, if they are not selected through other means. Informal staff seminars should be organized concerning new developments in each part of the program. Faculty members in related fields should be nominated to local and national professional committees by the administrator, if they are not selected through other means. Informal staff seminars should be organized concerning new developments in each part of the program. Faculty members in related fields should be invited to keep the staff abreast of technical developments. The staff should be encouraged to subscribe to professional magazines and to purchase basic and recent books for their professional libraries. And staff meetings, often cluttered with important but routine matters of management, should be devoted at least in part to exploration of new technical and professional matters.

But staff development must not be restricted to the technology underlying student personnel work. Our work takes place in a societal institution devoted to the education of youth. We are not operating within the closed orbit of technical personnel work, but within the context of an education that is broader and deeper than housing, counseling, and reading remediation. Staff development should stimulate continuous understanding by staff members of the various philosophies of higher education which compete for adoption by the faculty and central administration. And each staff member needs special development in those areas of knowledge which most personnel workers neglect in their own professional education—the humanities. There are few things to which faculty members are more sensitive than our neglect or ignorance of these historically dominant areas of higher education. From the perspective of many faculty members, we indeed appear to be technology-bound interlopers on campuses properly devoted to higher learning.[26] Perhaps this difficulty in winning acceptance from our faculty peers constitutes our most pressing problem of public relations within our several institutions.

[26] Howard Mumford Jones, "When I Was a Child," *Proceedings of the National Association of Student Personnel Administrators,* April 17–20, 1955, pp. 81–98.

Now we firmly believe that Jones's stricture is unjustified because the modern technology of student personnel work is ground in an honorable and historically established philosophy of education.[27] And we contend that our emphasis upon the full development of the individual student is, historically and philosophically, a close approximation to the American concept of education.[28] In so far as we have developed an effective program of translating that American concept into reality in the lives of individuals, to that extent we are as much legitimate American educators as are class-room teachers. Indeed we may well conclude from reading Leonard that our own educational ancestors first appeared on the American scene long before the impersonal attitudes of German universities changed concern for the whole student to a concentration upon his intellectual development. But it is small comfort to thus defend ourselves against the charge of being interlopers, since we can be called both irrelevant and academically ignorant.

We do, unfortunately, often seem to present ourselves as less than well informed about the glorious tradition of American education and less than penetrating in our understanding of the many un-resolved philosophic implications and questions involved in our practices. In other words, our preoccupation with things technical and our consequent neglect of the cultivated way of educated men may well cast us in the role of "ignorant" specialists.

Thus it is that we believe administrators bear a heavy responsi-bility for staff development in this and other neglected areas which are of interest to our faculty colleagues and long characteristic of liberally educated college graduates. We shall have more to say concerning this topic in Chapter 13.

Public Relations Problems. Reference was made above to the need for informing our faculty colleagues of the philosophic and techno-logical foundations of our program of services. Important though this effort may be, it is only one of many necessary projects. We personnel workers are viewed and evaluated by several publics—student leaders, the local chapter of the American Association of University Professors, deans of colleges, parents, the public at large,

[27] Cowley, W. H.: "The Nature of Student Personnel Work," *The Educational Record*, vol. 17, no. 2, pp. 27–29, April, 1936.
Wood, Ben D., and F. S. Beers: "The Major Strategy of Guidance," *Occupa-tions*, vol. 12, no. 8, pp. 8–12, April, 1934.
[28] Eugenie A. Leonard, *op. cit.*

and our student clientele. And as our services expand and we intensify our competition with academic and other departments for a share of limited expansion funds, we must expect that these publics will subject our work to more critical appraisal as to quality and relevancy in higher education.

Now we face a task in administration that is not adequately described as a "selling job." Creating mere understanding of what we seek to do does not intrinsically carry conviction as to its relevancy and necessity in higher education. We must seek for conviction that what we do is a necessary, not a luxurious, part of contemporary higher education. And that is a more difficult and challenging task which requires that we first understand the relevancy of our work to the objectives of colleges and universities. We argued above for increasing our understanding of the history and philosophy of education in American democracy.

Having first matured in our own understanding of our work, we then are perhaps better prepared to develop a continuing program of public relations with our colleagues and clientele. We have at hand many methods employed by other departments of our own institutions. Carefully thought out and carefully written bulletins, documents, and reports of description and explanation of programs are, of course, highly useful. Repeated feature stories in student newspapers serve to tell of our services and our research. Publications of research in technical journals are usable in reaching our faculty colleagues through the distribution of reprints. But in addition to the printed word, we may inform our publics through other media. Informal conversations at the faculty luncheon table, invitations to friendly *Kaffee Klatsches*, Christmas parties, open houses, weekend retreats, and organized staff discussions—all serve to create informal relationships that further understanding and acceptance in the educational enterprise. And Parents' Days and banquets offer opportunities to tell our story not only to our faculty colleagues, but also to our administrative superiors as well.

The means for continuous efforts at communication of our story are limited only by our own imagination and time devoted to this much neglected but essential task. Perhaps we have been so occupied with efforts to perfect our program services that we have devoted only sporadic efforts to public relations. It seems clear that in the decades ahead a larger part of effort and creativeness must be directed to this administrative responsibility.

OTHER PERSONNEL PROBLEMS OF PERSONNEL WORKERS

We have already discussed two such problems: selection of staff members and staff development. We shall mention several others briefly. Personnel workers, each within his own autonomy, were referred to previously as the instrumentalities which achieve program objectives. As is true of all other workers, care must be given to the maintenance of the desirable conditions necessary for their performance of functions. But personnel workers do not usually think of themselves as needing to upgrade their morale, improve working conditions, and stimulate their professional development. Our topic is, therefore, largely an unexplored area of administrative responsibility.

Nonetheless, we contend that it should not be assumed that personnel workers, trained in psychology, mental hygiene, and related fields of knowledge, are able to maintain the effectiveness of their services at a uniformly high level. Fluctuations in morale, efficiency, and effectiveness are observable characteristics of professional workers—as is the case with other types of educational workers. It is to be desired that experiences in this area of personnel work will soon be presented in professional literature so as to stimulate still further developments along this line. Personnel workers would do well to apply to themselves in their professional relationships the conclusions and findings discovered by industrial psychologists in research on human relations in industry. In particular, the general direction of needed exploration is characterized by Graffam in these words:[29]

At long last, it is coming to be recognized that good human relations based on recognition of personal worth and integrity of individuals, effective communication, congeniality, and participation of employees in company goals—which promote feelings of belongingness and security among the employees—are even more important factors of motivation than financial incentives and working conditions per se.

[29] Donald T. Graffam, "Brief Historical Introduction to Motivation," in Chalmers L. Stacey and Manfred F. Demartino (eds.), *Understanding Human Motivation.* Cleveland: Howard Allen, Inc., 1958, p. 8.

Campbell described briefly similar administrative responsibilities in meeting the needs of staff members of a research organization.[30] All of these administrative functions are clearly necessary for the staff of the student services program of a university or college.

Previous mention has been made of continued reeducation of staff members in the established and emerging objectives of educational institutions and in the expanding understanding of the psychology of students. Moreover, the slowly increasing knowledge of the effectiveness of services will further add to the reeducation and, therefore, to the effectiveness of personnel workers. Research, whether it be of a major type or merely the collection of some evaluative evidence, should be stimulated and encouraged by establishment of available resources, allotment of sufficient time, and also by suggestion and organization of individual staff projects.

An effective administrator will also encourage staff members in developing satisfying informal social groupings for recreation and other types of off-duty activities. In addition, staff committees should prepare systematic surveys and plan for future expansion of services. Staff members should also be involved in planning wage scales, criteria for promotion in rank and salary, systematic and special leaves of absence for research, and other aspects of professional development. As personnel staffs increase in number and in years of service, we need to follow the lead of academic departments in providing for them and their needs.

Auxiliary Instructional Workers. Personnel workers as such are not instructional workers. But they may offer important auxiliary services which will increase the effectiveness of the institution's instructional program. For example, they may provide data for increasingly accurate classification and assignment of individuals to different levels of instruction. They may motivate individuals to learn more effectively and may teach them how to read and learn more effectively. They may assist them in resolving their emotional conflicts so that the individual may devote his aptitudes more effectively to classroom learning. And in a thousand other ways these personnel workers contribute directly and indirectly to the institution's instructional objective. All of these contributions are made without any semblance of administrative authority in the field of

[30] Angus Campbell, "Administering Research Organizations," *The American Psychologist,* vol. 8, no. 6, pp. 225–230, June, 1953.

Instruction or without any attempt on the part of the personnel worker to dictate institutional instructional objectives and methods. But whenever the personnel worker has knowledge that is vital to the maximum development of the individual, that knowledge may be made available and useful to the instructors in stimulating the student's development. The administrators of programs, as well as the workers, bear heavy responsibilities to search continuously for effective ways of increasing their unique contributions to the students' educational development. This should be our most significant criterion of evaluation: What do we contribute to the educational effectiveness of the institution? And we need also to search for effective ways of making our educational roles self-evident; particularly we need to interpret and reinterpret these roles to students and faculty. This involves a continuous growth in our own understanding of the evolving meaning of education in our kind of democracy.

Evaluation. Numerous references have been made to the determination of the extent to which objectives of the personnel program are being achieved. Such evaluation may take the form of informal spot checking; it may involve systematic collection of opinions and reactions of student clients; or it may take the form of objective and controlled experimentation, using quantified criteria of changes in the behavior or self-percept of the individual student. No program can continue to develop in step with increases in related knowledge without such evaluation. It is a mark of an effective program and of effective staff work when personnel workers are interested in constant evaluations of their efforts. It should be noted, however, that systematic experimentation in many areas is not presently possible because of our present lack of effective methodology. Nevertheless, it is an important administrative function to encourage every staff member to think critically of the need and the desirability of evaluation. Out of an emphasis on professional standards may emerge increased effectiveness and more rigorous methods of evaluation.

The Initial Organization of a Program. In a sense, every program is undergoing continuous reorganization. Still, there are certain special administrative problems and functions which are peculiar to the initial stage of organization. We shall briefly mention some of these special functions in this chapter on administration.

The most important and perhaps the most difficult step in the development of the initial program is cultivating the confidence of the central administration, teachers, students, and the public at large in the personnel program itself and its workers. By all odds, the best and most permanent means of cultivating confidence is by the quality of the service performed directly and perceptibly to the students. There is nothing which instills as much confidence as experience with a successful program of assistance. For example, the elimination or reduction of tensions and anxieties associated with fear of scholastic failure is such a morale-lifting experience that confidence is automatically instilled both in the processes and the agents. Unfortunately, such quick miracles are not always possible and the counselor must look elsewhere for other confidence-developing techniques.

The selection, induction, and in-service training of new staff members is very difficult, particularly because new workers may carry over from their graduate training or previous employment ideas about the readily attained development of a program in a new situation. They forget that all programs must evolve very slowly because of the indigenous character of a campus and the need for development of confidence. Indeed, it is readily apparent that some new programs are sometimes severely handicapped for a long period of time by too rapid growth. Moreover, a new program may suffer from the psychological reaction of staff members in established departments. The history of educational reforms indicates that all new programs, and sometimes new workers, constitute some threat to the status and importance of established departments and workers. Therefore, it is advisable that new members of the staff establish courteous and friendly relationships at once to alleviate feelings of anxiety on the part of established staff members. Moreover, new staff members should be personally introduced to students, to top administration, and to teachers as a means of early incorporation into the informal social and interpersonal relationships of the institution.

We have discussed previously the normal administrative functions—assignment of duties and defining relationships of lines of cooperation and areas of specialization. Sometimes in the case of new programs, these administrative functions cannot be clearly outlined at first because the nature of the development must be the product of the unfolding of the program itself. Therefore, some original assignments of functions are rather loosely worded to provide for wide latitude of operations. Sometimes this very looseness of wording leads to uncoordinated effort and conflict. Especially important in the initial stages of program development is a clear statement— even though it may be incomplete and impermanent—of what is expected of a new worker in terms of the outcomes of his services. It should not be taken for granted that the things he will strive to achieve—as the result of his own professional training and previous experience—are necessarily the ones that are acceptable or most urgently needed in the initial stages of the development of a new program. Therefore, the administrator should spend considerable time in conferences with the worker to clarify expected outcomes, major emphases desired, and other special features basic to the strategy of the developing program.

Usually a major step preparatory to developing confidence and securing permission to develop the program is the selection of data which demonstrate the need of a program. A survey of available facilities showing deficiencies, a study of maladjustments among students, a study of students' complaints, a study of teachers' and parents' formulation of deficiencies in the program—all these are ways of collecting evidence which may convince top administration and the governing board, as well as the student body and teachers, of the need for the program. Until there is such a demonstration of need, it is not likely that money for the new program will be forthcoming in adequate amounts.

Research Stations on Problems of Adolescence. Personnel work is usually referred to as a service to individuals. Sometimes it is implied that this character and purpose are incompatible with research functions. If such an assumption were true, personnel work would be in danger of settling down into a rut of routine practice and inflexible ritual observance. On the other hand, if research is an integral part of the program of services, then changes in understanding of students' needs and adjustments will gradually and systematically produce changes in these services.[31] The length

[31] D. D. Feder, "Some Factual Backgrounds for Student Personnel Services and Functions," *Personnel-o-gram,* pp. 13–17, American College Personnel Association, 1958.

Ben Willerman, "Changing Attitudes of Fraternity Members toward Uniof the time span between discovery of new understanding and the improvement of programs is an indication of the effectiveness of administrative and professional leadership.

Personnel work has long been an integral part of higher education and has been carried on for the most part by individuals trained in the related disciplines of psychology, education, and psychiatry. For this reason, a strong research emphasis is readily observed on most campuses. That is, the individual staff member's own professional training makes it possible for him to incorporate into his practice new improvements in technique and new knowledge of student clientele. Since he is professionally up to date, he is usually also technically up to date. But if an individual begins personnel work without a related and relevant background of knowledge of human development and adjustments, of course, it is more difficult for him to remain constantly aware of the ceaseless improvements in underlying knowledge, and he is gravely in danger of falling behind both in relevant knowledge and improved techniques.

We have referred elsewhere to the way programs restructure themselves in terms of the changing knowledge underlying the personnel practice and the changing competencies of personnel workers themselves. At this point we want to emphasize that an important function of a personnel program is to continue to add to the knowledge of adolescence—not only for the sake of the contributions to the technical literature, but also to maintain staff effectiveness over the years. As a worker gets further away from his graduate training, he is more likely to become frozen in his professional practice if he does not do research or keep up with the changing disciplines related to his professional practice in

---

versity Control," *The Personnel and Guidance Journal*, vol. 37, pp. 542–550, April, 1959. See also Willerman's review of his studies as related to this research function of a personnel staff in Martin L. Snoke (ed.), *Approaches to the Study of Administration of Student Personnel Work*, University of Minnesota Student Personnel Series, no. 9, Minneapolis, 1960.

The reader may be oriented to the institutional nexus in which student personnel services function. See Lloyd S. Woodburne, *Principles of College and University Administration*. Stanford, Calif.: Stanford University Press, 1958. Chapter 11 deals with the Office of the Dean of Students, showing the dean as deputy to the president and in relation to the faculty, especially concerning organized activities.

other ways. In a real sense, we are arguing that personnel workers should be both researchers and service workers. We recognize that this double load of duty is a difficult one to carry, but it is our contention that research is one of the most important ways of maintaining professional effectiveness.

The research that we refer to usually is a by-product of an on-going service program; less frequently it is especially organized as laboratory experimentation. For example, dormitories and other types of residences have been little used for laboratory experiment or even field experiments on social interaction. However, it is evident, for example, that the roommate situation found in dormitories and other types of residences would seem to provide rich material for developing a basic understanding of interpersonal relationships. But for the most part, little attempt has been made to organize personnel programs so that the on-going program will yield data for research as an important by-product. While there may be, and undoubtedly are, many limitations in this type of field experiment as contrasted with the more precise controls possible in a laboratory, it has the virtue of being the actual living process itself, not one artificially induced during the period of an experiment.

We believe that literally every part of a personnel program may be an object of research, although the methodology and design will change from one area to another. Little is known, for instance, about the effects of financial counseling on morale, yet it is clear that colleges are enrolling an ever-increasing number of students from families of low economic status—on some vague assumption about the effectiveness of scholarship funds in inducing motivations to enroll in colleges and succeed in collegiate work. Research on self-concepts of these students may well reveal significant differences from those of other students in respect to college adjustments. The disruption and deterioration of interpersonal social controls—as evidenced in interpersonal mores and behaviors in some fraternities, dormitories, and rooming houses—would seem to offer research possibilities for better understanding of how groups are made and unmade, and how tribal-centered groups may produce the seeds of their own deterioration or strength. The many adjustments of foreign students living in residences would seem to offer opportunity for studies of the formation and modification of interracial and intercultural perspectives and attitudes. Thus we see that not only aptitude testing offers rich opportunities for research within the personnel program—so does literally every phase of the program. We contend that such research not only contributes to the maintenance of staff effectiveness, but also will continue to make significant contributions to our basic understanding of human development in educational institutions.

Maintenance of Program. We close our discussion of administrative functions with one that should need little elaboration. A program is a going concern; it must operate from day to day with maximum possible effectiveness. A program is not a static structure, nor is it something that can be initiated through the selection of a staff, then left to run itself with little or no continuous evaluation of progress and accomplishments and reformulation of means and ends. A program may be sidetracked or its original momentum may slow down to a bureaucratic crawl.[32] We need to be constantly alert to the real tendency for organized enterprises to deteriorate into self-contained and self-satisfying tribal ritual observances. Hutchins incisively satirized the "vast bureaucratic machine that goes creaking on, following the right procedure instead of seeking the right result." [33] Reisman, more insightfully, described isomorphism, the dynamic interplay of structure and function in higher education resulting from changes in subject-matter content, research in new understanding, and from institutional rivalries, intra- as well as inter-, summarizing with the comment: ". . . an institution has to change in order to remain the same." [34]

In a real sense, every effective educational program is constantly being remade day by day through modifications, improvisations, and revisions. Left to its own momentum, inevitable decline and routinizing of programs seem to parallel the inevitable aging process found in human beings—personnel workers as well as students. It is a major administrative responsibility to seek ways of avoiding, or at least postponing, such a decline in effective functioning; possibly one effective means is explicit and overt planning for

[32] Marshal E. Dimock, "The Conflict With Bureaucracy," *Administrative Vitality*. New York: Harper & Brothers, 1959.

[33] Robert M. Hutchins, "Is Democracy Possible?" *The Saturday Review*, Feb. 21, 1959, p. 17.

[34] David Reisman, *Constraint and Variety in American Education*. Lincoln, Neb.: The University of Nebraska Press, 1956, p. 31.

changes in program content and emphases.[35] For example, the periodic, fresh renewal of perception by the inevitably aging personnel staff of each new generation of students may prove to be one of the most pressing problems involved in maintaining the effectiveness of a program of services. In like manner, we also face difficulties in maintaining a program of services that is current with respect to the constantly growing relevant research presented in professional literature.

In spite of these and many other difficulties, daily maintenance of effectiveness is the highest responsibility of workers and administrators at all levels of program responsibility. In fact, it may be contended that this is the central function and responsibility of administration.

SUMMARY

We have now outlined briefly, and in only a suggestive manner, some observed aspects of the day-to-day administration of a varied program of services to students. We have emphasized that these aspects are the special responsibility of the administrators of the program. But they are also of major significance in the functioning of each worker, since he is involved in each, from the determination of objectives to the daily maintenance of currently effective personnel services. And the teamwork relationships of administrator and personnel workers in the day-to-day program is the chief responsibility of administration.

[35] Lippett, Ronald, et al.: *The Dynamics of Planned Change.* New York: Harcourt, Brace and Company, Inc., 1958.
Stoddard, George Dinsmore: "Men Are Adaptable: Are They Willing and Are They Able to Adjust to Social Change?" *The Crisis of Mankind.* Minneapolis: University of Minnesota Press, 1947, pp. 59–64.

Some Special Administrative Processes

CHAPTER 5

Administering Discipline
and Judiciary Functions

In this chapter we shall discuss a number of important aspects of the institution-wide administration of disciplinary and judiciary functions, as measures in the supervision of student behavior. In several other chapters, particularly Chapter 11, we have discussed the underlying basic issue which precipitates much discussion and tension on many campuses. We refer to the issue of whether efforts to supervise and control students' behavior are proper and justified. Some few critics contend that there is not even legal authority granted in an institution's charter to control behavior, except in the case of the limited and restricted misbehavior which actually occurs on college property.

In discussing disciplinary and judiciary functions, we should deal with the basic philosophic and policy issue of whether there should be any attempt at discipline of students. We believe that this issue is a proper one for debate, discussion, and exploration during *every* academic year. In fact, as we have argued in other chapters, we believe that this particular aspect of the institution's authority provides a basis for the annual exploration of some of the most penetrating and fundamental issues confronting citizens in a democracy, particularly citizens in an "open society." [1]

[1] Karl R. Popper, *The Open Society and Its Enemies*. Princeton, N.J.: Princeton University Press, 1950, chap. 10.

RELEVANT CONCEPTS

Three important concepts appear to us as controlling influences in the administration of discipline and in the operation of judiciary procedures: (1) *in loco parentis;* (2) fiduciary; and (3) due process. The position of the American Civil Liberties Union on the issue of legal authority and propriety of supervision of students' behavior is clearly stated in these words:[2]

The authority of the educational institution is an extension of the traditional legal authority which parents exercise over their children. Insofar as the institution is responsible for the welfare and guidance of its students, it can and must exercise reasonable control over their scholastic life and over much of their general activities. Not to do so would be to fail in the discharge of the educational function.

In support of the institution's legal authority to act *in loco parentis* Chambers[3] and Elliott and Chambers[4] have documented the legal support of that responsibility in court decisions. Bakken has also compiled, in a scholarly manner, the legal statutes and court decisions which clearly establish an educational institution's legal powers and responsibilities over students' behavior.[5] The generalization is well established that the courts will not interfere with institutional supervision unless that supervision is shown to be unreasonable. Thus legality of supervision seems well established, even though many students and some professors assert contrary opinions.

A relevant concept was presented by Seavey in characterizing

---

[2] *Academic Freedom and Civil Liberties of Students.* New York: American Civil Liberties Union, August, 1956, p. 3. (Pamphlet.)

[3] Chambers, Merritt M.: *The Colleges and the Courts: 1936–40.* New York: The Carnegie Foundation for the Advancement of Teaching, 1941.
———: *The Colleges and the Courts: 1946–50.* New York: Columbia University Press, 1952.

[4] E. C. Elliott and M. M. Chambers, *The Colleges and the Courts.* New York: The Carnegie Foundation for the Advancement of Teaching, 1936.

[5] Clarence John Bakken, *An Analysis of the Legal Basis for Operating Selected Student Personnel Services in State Tax-supported Four-year Colleges and Universities in the United States,* Ph.D. thesis, University of Denver, Denver, Colo., March, 1959. (Dean D. D. Feder, major advisor.)

as fiduciary the relationship between professors, and presumably institutions, and their students:[6]

A fiduciary is one whose function it is to act for the benefit of another as to matters relevant to the relation between them. Since schools exist primarily for the education of their students, it is obvious that professors and administrators act in a fiduciary capacity with reference to the students.

Due process is another and freely debatable concept.[7] The argument as to the manner in which the institution is to exercise its legal responsibility over students' behavior continues with much controversy. Seavey's scathing indictment of colleges, and certain courts, centers on failure of the college to adopt and follow procedures which give adequate protection to the student concerning his entitlement to fair hearings, knowledge of charges against him, and similar procedural rights established in American courts.[8]

Seavey's indictment in the case of certain student cases is clearly justified. But as to what procedures and rights are appropriate in the exercise of an institution's supervision over students' behavior and misbehavior is by no means self-evident. Seavey acknowledges that ". . . the formalities of a trial in a law court are not necessary."[9] But he did contend that ". . . a student should not have the burden of proving himself innocent."[10]

There remain many unclear questions that need careful appraisal rather than hasty appeal to trial court procedures, since students do not have rights, in the political sense, *within the institution.* Higher education is a privilege and not a right, and the institution is chartered by the state as a public institution, not as a political jurisdiction subject to ultimate control by its citizen-members, in this case the students.

---

[6] Warren A. Seavey, "Dismissal of Students: Due Process," *Harvard Law Review,* vol. 70, p. 1407, 1957.

[7] The reader will be well oriented to the due process concept as applied to the academic tenure and freedom of professors and perhaps will find some parallels with the student situation on examining Robert K. Carr, "Academic Freedom, the American Association of University Professors and the United States Supreme Court," *American Association of University Professors Bulletin,* vol. 45, pp. 5–24, March, 1959.

[8] Seavey, *op. cit.*

[9] *Ibid.,* p. 1410. See also Bakken, *op. cit.,* pp. 142–147.

[10] *Ibid.,* p. 1410.

The formulation of procedures which will protect students and at the same time permit the exercise of institutional responsibilities for their behavior is a task much in need of clear and relevant study. Indignant demands for freedom should be replaced by critical inquiry in which thoughtful students and administrators proceed—without disturbing incidents. And one basic principle should serve as a guide line: as an educational institution, *a university should be above reproach* in its fair and mature handling of student incidents and misbehavior—not because of asserted or claimed rights, but because higher education should establish procedures and precedents that are morally right and demonstrably congruent with the best traditions of liberal and democratic education. In this connection, we do not accept as adequate reform the substitution of student-manned courts for the unilateral action of the staff of the dean of students, although we agree fully with a plan for participation by thoughtful students in all disciplinary and judiciary procedures. We still like the Hawkes formulations rather than that of Preston.[11]

THE PERSISTENT PROBLEM OF STUDENT BEHAVIOR

We shall not repeat our examination of the policy question and issue in this present chapter. We are concerned with exploring certain administrative aspects under three general topics:

1. Disciplinary procedures in a program of rehabilitation

2. The development of student and faculty judiciaries, particularly in residences, as means of orderly management of misbehavior

3. The positive cultivation of desirable behavior through activities, consultation, and other relationships between organized students and the institution, such cultivation viewed as positive prevention of misbehavior

As we have indicated elsewhere, the history of organized discipline in American universities and colleges is an amazing record of *inhuman* treatment of students. On the one hand, it is more

---

[11] Hawkes, Herbert E., and Anna L. Rose Hawkes: *Through the Dean's Open Door.* New York: McGraw-Hill Book Company, Inc., 1945.

Preston, Gene R.: *Campus Justice.* Philadelphia: U.S. National Students' Association, 1957. (Mimeographed.)

characteristic of a criminal security institution, on the other, of immature, immoral, irresponsible, explosive, ungentlemanly derogation of the institution and its officers by organized students. The history of disciplinary control of students may be summed up in the phrase, "student rebellions peppered the annals of every college in America." [12] Much of this behavior and disciplinary repression of students occurred in residences or dormitories. To use Cotton Mather's phrase, "the collegiate way of living in" required students to live and to eat their meals in college-managed dormitories. The annual rioting usually focused on the quality of the food served, a theme recurring in collegiate annals with monotonous regularity.[13] But misbehavior was not confined to rioting about food; almost every kind of misbehavior seems to be chronicled in the annals of the colonial colleges.

At the risk of revealing our own inverted-value orientation and ancestral vestige of longing for *guten alten zeiten,* we rescue from forgotten and dusty tombs what is among the most exquisite social inventions of students' forms of normal misbehavior. Since repeated references are made to this form of misbehavior, it must have been a universal custom of the period. During the Revolutionary War and perhaps during the War of 1812, student militia companies were organized and stationed in some campus dormitories. Of course, ammunition was stored in the arsenal and cannon balls were normal supplies. Students must have appropriated or "liberated" some of these balls, since repeated references are made to their use in students' continued and harassing warfare with faculty proctors who sought to quell riots and maintain a studious quietude.[14] Peabody said every student room at Harvard in 1828 or thereabout had "among its *transittenda*" a cannon ball "which was heated on a cold day to warm the student." But it was also "often utilized by being rolled downstairs at such times as might

[12] Brubacher, John S., and Willis Rudy: *Higher Education in Transition.* New York: Harper & Brothers, 1958, p. 39.
Sellers, James B.: *History of the University of Alabama.* University, Ala.: University of Alabama Press, 1953, chaps. IX, X, and XV.

[13] The Harvard Butter Rebellion of 1766 was a case in point. See Samuel Batchelder, *Bits of Harvard History.* Cambridge, Mass.: Harvard University Press, 1924, p. 135.

[14] *Ibid.,* p. 256. Batchelder related that students regarded the arsenal as a "cannon-ball mine."

most nearly bisect a proctor's night-sleep." [15] Referring to Peabody's account, Batchelder described the behavior in these words:[16]

No military historian has been able to compute the number of Revolutionary eighteen and twenty-four pounders that ended their *ci-devant* martial careers by an ignominious nocturnal abstraction from their flimsy store-sheds and a precarious existence as *transittenda* in the rooms of irrepressible youth.

Presumably these cannon balls were taken by students for the purpose of adding to the radiation surface of their study fires and to warm their beds in their cold sleeping rooms. But they were also used in a "ferrous vein of humor":[17]

In practice they were invaluable for rolling along corridors or bouncing down stairs in the night watches, for dropping unexpectedly out of window by day, and for other delicious variations of the academic routine.

For these and other valid reasons, collegiate institutions were characterized as "the secret nurseries of every vice and the cages of unclean birds." [18] Strict moralistic discipline, characteristic of the colonial colleges, prevailed. The theme—the flesh is wicked— persisted, and the concept of asceticism, dominant in the pietistic church-related colleges of Europe, served as a pattern for American institutions. Faculties were employed, not so much to teach as to nurture the moral and religious development of students—and this meant correcting their habits and practices of immorality. These were definite responsibilities assigned to the teaching faculty, and the disciplinary function became a very dominant factor in the relationship between students and faculty. In later decades, when faculties were freed of the disciplinary function, they developed friendly relationships with students to replace the guerrilla-warfare pattern. Brubacher and Rudy theorized that this shift was noticeable at about the middle of the nineteenth century.[19] Hofstadter and Metzger theorize in a similar way, saying that when respon-

---

[15] Andrew P. Peabody, *Harvard Reminiscences.* Boston: Ticknor and Company, 1888, pp. 196–197.

[16] Batchelder, *op. cit.,* p. 256.

[17] *Ibid.,* p. 256.

[18] Brubacher and Rudy, *op. cit.,* p. 41.

[19] *Ibid.,* p. 39.

sibility for discipline was shifted from the faculty to the president's office about the mid-nineteenth century, the faculty reestablished cordial and friendly relationships, an important matter in the changing pattern of student life in the nineteenth century.[20]

But other factors are noted as having some causal relationship in the diminution of the widespread rebellious behavior of students. We referred elsewhere to Coulter's thesis that the general lawlessness of adult behavior in the frontier culture on the Eastern seaboard affected the climate of opinion and behavior of students.[21]

The changing pattern of teaching, from recitation to lecture, changes in the curriculum, from classics to science, and other reforms influenced by German experiences—all these affected students in their relationships with professors. Several authorities refer to the introduction of athletics and general recreation, and to the proliferation of student activities during the latter part of the nineteenth century as important in the slow shift from lawless to orderly behavior. These two general movements drained away some of the excess energy of students who earlier seemed to vent themselves in riots and misbehavior. But one cannot read the record and report that there were no riots at all after 1850. There were fewer, perhaps because students relished relief from regimentation and repression, and also experienced normal, healthy emotional reactions through organized athletics and activities. Moreover, the introduction of the concept of student participation in governing themselves during the latter part of the nineteenth century also contributed much to relieving the strain of disciplinary control. But one has only to read Lunn and Friedson's studies to see that the transformation from lawless rioting to orderliness has not yet been completed, even though one agrees with Thwing's generalization that American education is a chronicle of the "increasing

[20] Richard Hofstadter and Walter P. Metzger, "The Old Regime and the Educational Revolution," *The Development of Academic Freedom in the United States*. New York: Columbia University Press, 1955. See especially "Disorder and Deficit," pp. 303–319.

[21] E. Merton Coulter, "Between Lessons and Professors," *College Life in the Old South*. New York: The Macmillan Company, 1928.

In discussing a different aspect of education, A. Whitney Griswold generalized a similar principle of the relationship of campus to community in these words: "In our democratic scheme of things our educational system will never be able to cut its umbilical cord to the society that gave it birth." See A. Whitney Griswold, "American Education's Greatest Need," *The Saturday Review*, Mar. 14, 1959, p. 17.

orderliness of students." [22] We have indeed come a long way from the established colonial concept of the "natural depravity" of students. The attitude of colleges toward the students nearly a century ago is described by Earnest: [23]

> Insofar as the college officials had anything to do with it, the system was designed to prevent development of mature students. The elaborate rules of the early colleges were organized on the pattern of a strict prep school, and more than a little tinged with the Calvinistic doctrine of the total depravity of man.

But a different concept prevailed in an 1889 symposium, "Discipline in American Colleges," with participations by the presidents of Dartmouth, Michigan, Harvard, Cornell, Bowdoin, McGill, and California. [24] Angell of Michigan spoke of—

> . . . getting near enough to their pupils to exert a positive moral influence upon them, on appeals to their manliness, on engendering in them the spirit of right doing.

Shaler of Harvard spoke of the alternation of family and academic discipline as part of—

> . . . democratic humanization which is changing the fundamental motives of our people.

And Adams of Cornell bespoke a new attitude toward and policy about discipline, quite at variance with colonial policy, in these words:

> Perhaps the most useful rule ever promulgated in an American school was that simple one which declared that every student was required at all times to conduct himself in a manner becoming a gentleman and a scholar, and that he would be held responsible for the observance of this standard.

The measure of how far we have progressed in collegiate reformation is afforded by comparison of Earnest's characterization, and some of the others we have quoted, with that of Farnsworth in

[22] Charles Franklin Thwing, *College Administration*. New York: D. Appleton & Company, Inc., 1900, p. 113.

[23] Ernest Earnest, *Academic Procession*. Indianapolis: The Bobbs-Merrill Company, Inc., 1953, p. 45.

[24] *North American Review*, vol. 149, no. 392, p. 29, July, 1889.

his interesting and recent discussion of the role of psychiatry in collegiate education.[25]

No matter what the system of maintaining discipline may be, whether managed entirely by the faculty or in part by student government, the psychiatrist is chiefly interested in seeing that the student who is guilty of wrongdoing learns something from the subsequent corrective experience. . . . Ethical development is like intellectual development; it occurs neither suddenly nor in a vacuum. On most college discipline committees opinion is divided between those who feel that severe penalties must be applied rigorously and according to previously determined rules and another group who believed that a full understanding of the motives of the persons involved is necessary before any decision can be reached as to what should be done. The latter group cares little for punishment, but places strong emphasis on rehabilitation. The division is almost always along lines of basic attitudes toward human behavior, seldom along age lines.

THE SOCIAL OR INSTITUTIONAL CAUSES OF MISBEHAVIOR

Many interesting theories have been advanced to explain the operating causes between the modified forms of misbehavior current today, in contrast with those chronicled in the early annals of colleges. Morison stated: "As athletics increased, riots and disorder faded out." [26] Reference has been made repeatedly to the excessive pietistic and moralistic mission given to the colleges and the faculties by the founding fathers.[27] White also theorized that the greatly

[25] Dana L. Farnsworth, *Mental Health in Colleges and Universities.* Cambridge, Mass.: Harvard University Press, 1957, p. 144.

Farnsworth and Clark would have agreed on much in the handling of student discipline, even though their approaches and backgrounds were that of psychiatrist and teacher of rhetoric. Clark used his personal charm, sincerity, and wit, as well as a stern but fair sense of justice, to rehabilitate offenders in ways that would be familiar to a therapist. See Thomas Arkle Clark, *Discipline and the Derelict.* New York: The Macmillan Company, 1922.

[26] Samuel E. Morison, *Three Centuries of Harvard.* Cambridge, Mass.: Harvard University Press, 1936, p. 401.

[27] Brubacher and Rudy, *op. cit.,* chap. 3, "Early Student Life."

Earnest, *op. cit.,* p. 104.

Hofstadter, Richard, and Walter P. Metzger: *The Development of Academic Freedom in the United States.* New York: Columbia University Press, 1955, chap. II "Harvard College from Dunster to Leverett; chap. IV, "Religion, Reason, and Revolution."

Leonard, Eugenie A.: *Origins of Personnel Services in American Higher Education.* Minneapolis: University of Minnesota Press, 1956.

broadened scope of the curriculum, as well as the recreational facilities, were important factors in the change in student behavior.[28] Still another theory holds great attraction as an explanation for the increasing orderliness of student life. Morison reported the testimony of Prof. George H. Palmer, of Harvard College, saying—[29]

Of all the improvements in the College since his graduation in 1864, the friendly relation between teachers and taught was the greatest.

Kermit Fry, the noted psychiatrist, proposed still another explanation in these words:[30]

Men whose memory ranges to that time [before the First World War] find the present Yale rather sober and hard-working; the general level of industry and achievement higher, dress and manners less flamboyant. This is not to deny the merits of criticism of student apathy or student riots, or the preference for symbols of material success rather than scholarly eminence.

Farnsworth's discussion of mental hygiene of college students, especially Chapter 3, contains rich suggestions and understandings of the change in the way misbehavior is perceived and evaluated today in colleges.

Our colonial colleges may have been influenced by their European counterparts—where flogging was the principal method of control and punishment for misbehavior. But our ancestors added other forms of rigid control in an attempt to develop piety as the defense against the then current wave of rationalistic skepticism. Thus it was that evangelistic revivals on the college campus became a prevailing phenomenon in the early nineteenth century. In fact—[31]

It was considered a calamity if a class passed through its whole four years at Amherst without going through at least one revival.

In the late eighteenth and early nineteenth centuries, following the revolutions in France and America, the Eastern college cam-

---

[28] Andrew Dickson White, *Autobiography*. New York: Appleton-Century Crofts, Inc., 1917, vol. I, p. 348.

[29] Morison, *op. cit.*, p. 404.

[30] K. C. Fry, "A Psychiatrist Evaluates, in Seventy-five: A Study of a Generation in Transition," *Yale Daily News*, Anniversary number, p. 61, New Haven, 1953.

[31] Brubacher and Rudy, *op. cit.*, p. 43.

puses were swept by an intense period of revivalism, partly as a counter to the rational skepticism imported from Europe. This movement led student groups to become preoccupied with foreign missionary movements. Shortly thereafter the literary society and debating society became the centers of student interest, and the intense rivalry between the societies seems to have substituted for much of the earlier rioting. Then athletics and gymnastics were imported to the campuses "to work the devil out of the students." [32]

CHANGE IN FACULTY'S PERCEPTION OF STUDENTS

In reading the literature descriptive of student life in these decades, one is constantly reminded of the widespread practice of treating students as though they were irresponsible—with the result that students were in a constant state of warfare against professors. There was limited friendly relationship; in fact, it was not "good form" to be friendly with the faculty. Students used a special vocabulary descriptive of those who did linger after class, or otherwise violate the code of separation. The delegation and assignment to the faculty of a paternalistic system to handle petty discipline problems undoubtedly precluded friendliness. The origin of this disciplinary relationship was to be found in the Harvard College Laws of 1642, which were borrowed from the seventeenth-century English Latin schools. Almost every part of daily living was neatly regulated and the regulations were rigidly enforced for more than two centuries.[33] Indeed, it was not until 1888 that a system of faculty advisors was established in Kenyon College.

The pattern of the collegiate community continued in this fashion until the Civil War, but with a gradual introduction of recreation and athletics as substitutes for riots. Following the Civil War, everywhere one found a general relaxation of controls over students and they were left increasingly on their own outside of the classrooms. At about this time, the dormitories as a collegiate way of living were abandoned, partly because of the importation of the German concept of limited collegiate responsibility for students as one way of encouraging the development of self-discipline. In the years following the Civil War, the two concepts of college discipline

[32] *Ibid.*, p. 49.
[33] *Ibid.*, p. 51.

were sharply differentiated and widely discussed. Traditional paternalism, with its rules and controls, was contrasted with the German concept of treating students as responsible adults. In 1869, Eliot, in his inaugural address at Harvard, introduced in America the concept of students as adults. Later, the family, with its relaxed nineteenth-century discipline, was discussed by Harper as a model. Sailor introduced the term "trust-bearing" as descriptive of the type of benign relationship between faculty and students.

Peabody, in 1888, wrote of the profound change taking place in the perspective of faculty toward students' conformity to the exacting requirements of the "collegiate way of living in." This basic change in perspective toward behavior and misbehavior and ways of teaching law and order—produced by the nineteenth-century societal revolution in child rearing and family discipline— not only relaxed the faculty's control of behavior, but it also diminished students' need for and urge to misbehave. We can learn many lessons from Peabody's interpretation:[34]

Professor Channing entered college in 1804, and, as his biographer says, "was not graduated in course, as he was involved in the famous rebellion of 1807, one of the few in which the students seem, on the whole, not to have been in the wrong." I object to this statement as not broad enough. I am inclined to think that in college rebellions the students were always in the right as to principle, though injudicious in their modes of actualizing principle. There was not one of those rebellions in which the leaders were not among the foremost in their respective classes, in character no less than in scholarship. . . . There were traditional maxims and methods of college jurisprudence to which the professorial mind had become hardened, which to unsophisticated youth justly seemed at variance with natural right; and there was no form of collective protest that they could make, which was not deemed rebellious in such a sense that they were compelled either to recant, or to leave college under censure. . . . College rebellions have become impossible, because the rights of the students are now fully recognized, their sense of honor held sacred, their protests and complaints considered carefully and kindly, and their unintended wrongs relieved and remedied, even though it involve the admission of mistake, or error of judgment, on the part of the Faculty, which in earlier times would have been regarded as subversive of discipline and authority.

[34] Peabody, *op. cit.*, pp. 84–85.

THE SHIFT TO PREVENTION

At about this time there were various attempts at increased student participation in self-government in extracurricular life and behavior matters. These attempts were made in many colleges, beginning with Jefferson's famous program at the University of Virginia. Since the students were more and more left on their own outside of class, in the German pattern, riots against excessive regimentation became unnecessary. No longer, in an ever-increasing number of colleges, did the faculty seek to suppress, regulate, and control behavior and activities. Thus, student life outside of the curriculum competed with studies for the interest and attention of students—to the neglect of the latter. In time, this successful competition gave rise to the verbal, but mild, protests of teachers against the extracurriculum as a distraction from the formal classroom curriculum. And with the arrival of a new type of student in the land grant colleges—students from the lower social economic levels, with increased vocational seriousness—the riotous living of the early days abated even more, although it never entirely disappeared. Intercollegiate athletics and other forms of institutional rivalry proved, however, to be less destructive and less objectionable than did earlier rioting.

So discipline and behavior control took new forms. New emphases and points of view about effective means of behavior control substituted for earlier ones. Gradually the changing American culture influenced the modes of discipline employed on college campuses. Not only the imported German model, but the changing American frontier produced new enlightenment, as did the later Freudian search for understanding of motivations as a means of influencing the form of behavior. All these changed conditions provided for the college administrator a variety of new models for relationships between faculty and students. In the literature we find a pleading for a more relaxed and less severe form of punishment and control. Gradually the rehabilitation emphasis entered the discussions, and today it is well established as the prevailing model of relationships. This is not the place to trace the complicated process of transition from the earlier repression to the current rehabilitation philosophy of behavior control. But the reader may well determine for himself the widespread change by reading current and earlier references. To be sure, the change is never completely made, and we find today administrators and members of the faculty discipline committees who are described by Farnsworth in the following terms:[35]

. . . strict constructionists. . . . For every infraction there is a rule, together with a guide as to the proper penalty. The chief decisions center around the determination of whether or not a rule was broken and, if so, is there any clear-cut reason why the penalty should not be applied. Under such a system attention is largely given to technical or legal details, very little to reasons for the unusual behavior.

Farnsworth thus sums up the strict constructionist philosophy, which seeks—even after centuries of failure—to control student behavior by means of rules and rigid enforcement. There is no attempt to be humane in the treatment of student offenders, merely to apply with exactitude precise degrees of punishment.

This point of view is an old one, as may be seen from reading the literature on colonial punishment techniques and points of view. Today excessive and repressive and even brutal flogging has been replaced with fines and restrictions of privileges and exclusion from the university community. The actions taken have changed, but the point of view is not new.

In contrast, the essential feature of the rehabilitation emphasis in discipline and the control of behavior is the search for causes of misbehavior. The individual student is assumed to be an individual whose behavior is motivated and whose behavior is changeable if the right conditions occur. As Farnsworth said, many feel that this is a "soft" approach, and one which encourages students to misbehave because they anticipate mild forms of punishment. Speaking as a psychiatrist who has dealt with and has become involved in many student discipline cases, Farnsworth generalized in this way with regard to the possible "deterioration of moral fibre" as the result of "easy" discipline.[36]

It cannot be overemphasized that for the person who has committed some ethical indiscretion, leniency, understanding, warm friendliness, and at the same time steady pressure toward higher achievement as

[35] Farnsworth, *op. cit.*, p. 142.
[36] *Ibid.*, p. 145.

shown by firm disapproval of the wrongful act, can do a great deal for the student.

A casual reading of the record of student life shows that misbehavior, or deviant behavior, was as characteristic of the early days as virtuous behavior, if not more so. Discipline, therefore, is not something new in the collegiate world; misbehavior is as typical and characteristic of the college way of life as are textbooks and examinations and recreational activities. We do not strive for a never-never land where students are completely preoccupied with their studies; we seek, rather, better ways of mimimizing and reducing misbehavior through the patient and friendly and humane search for causes of misbehavior and for ways of eliminating these causes effectively. Excessive regulations and strict and impersonal enforcement have been attempted for so many centuries that one wonders why some college administrators repeat, in a weary fashion, the same unsuccessful attempt to eliminate deviant behavior by these means.[37]

In general, the punitive approach to discipline—a method contrasting with rehabilitation in the annals of higher education—is less effective as a means of prevention and reduction of misbehavior. The record seems to be clear on this point. Compayré has this to say:[38]

It is evident that the spirit of the Middle Ages, with its tendency to mysticism, its lack of confidence in human nature, its universal instinct of repression and restraint, was not adapted to discover, in matters of discipline, a just medium between license and extreme severity. It was decidedly toward severity that it leaned when enclosed colleges and boarding-schools came to replace the free corporations of students of earlier days. Then the rod had full sway. The rod, which was the favorite mode of discipline in convents, became the great educational instrument of colleges, "those jails full of young captives."

Recently, substitutes for excessive punishment and severity of restriction have been made. The counselor's search for causes of misbehavior has been supplemented by various improvements. Following the First World War colleges greatly increased inexpensive

[37] E. G. Williamson and John Foley, *Counseling and Discipline.* New York: McGraw-Hill Book Company, Inc., 1949, chap. 1, pp. 1–21.

[38] Gabriel Compayré, *Abelard and the Origin and Early History of Universities.* New York: Charles Scribner's Sons, 1893, p. 278.

recreational facilities for students. We have referred elsewhere to various attempts to involve students in discipline of their own behavior through student government and organized group work. These group control methods were transposed from social work and other community programs to the college campus. All were based upon a philosophy of humane assistance to misbehaving students—to help them find substitutes for misbehavior which was considered a form of error in handling social relationships, interpersonal relationships, and various societal restraints. From this viewpoint, misbehavior which produces discipline results in learning, and misbehavior is better eliminated through educational means than through excessive repression. The history of student activities, student recreation, and student government gives considerable encouragement that they may prove to be adequate substitutes for the repression and punishment so prevalent during the past centuries.

THE PSYCHOLOGY OF REHABILITATION

This is not the place for an extended discussion of the psychology of rehabilitation. But we will discuss it briefly to further illuminate the point of view which, we believe, should characterize the total campus program of behavior control. In a later section of this chapter we shall outline certain positive emphases which are designed to aid students in exercising citizenship privileges with positive and growth-furthering results. At this point we cite two sources for our thesis that attitude-perception formation is at the heart of discipline—both as self-control of behavior and as rehabilitation of misbehavior. Kurt Lewin stated a relevant point of view:[39]

Re-education influences conduct only when the new system of values and beliefs dominates the individual's perception. The acceptance of the new system is linked with the acceptance of a specific group, a particular role, a definite source of authority as new points of reference. It is basic for re-education that this linkage between acceptance of new facts or values and acceptance of certain groups or roles is very intimate and that the second frequently is a prerequisite for the first.

[39] Kurt Lewin, *Resolving Social Conflicts.* New York: Harper & Brothers, 1948, p. 68.

This explains the great difficulty of changing beliefs and values in a perceived fashion. This linkage is a main factor behind resistance to re-education, but can also be made a powerful means for successful re-education.

Hastorf and Knutson seem to provide a similar foundation for the control of behavior, by self and by the group:[40]

[Implications for Attitude Formation and Change] . . . changes in group identifications and status-strivings (acquired purposes) are essential to any relatively lasting attitudinal change. . . .

The problems of attitude change. Concentration on the problem of altering an individual's identifications, and thus many of his social purposes, would seem to be getting at both the manner in which a person perceives a situation and his attitude toward that situation.

It seems likely that all procedures, programs, and relationships obtaining between institutional staff and students should be continuously evaluated and restructured in the light of their effects upon the perceptions and attitudes of students. This is not to advocate a Gallup poll to determine attitudes on all that is attempted. It is to advocate that what is attempted, and the means, should be designed to help students perceive what is attempted as genuine and desirable, if not necessary, in the achievement of institutional and student goals that are considered relevant to higher education. In such a complex and changing climate of opinion and relationships, we believe that discipline-control (1984 Big Brother model) will come to be perceived as self-discipline (self-management)[41] and as relevant in higher education.

DISCIPLINARY COUNSELING

Discipline and counseling are two personel services most sharply separated, and usually insulated in their segregation, in the institutional personnel program. Because of the long history and current continuation of repressive disciplinary actions, counselors have

---

[40] A. H. Hastorf and A. L. Knutson, "Motivation, Perception, and Attitude Change," in Chalmers L. Stacey and Manfred F. Demartino (eds.), *Understanding Human Motivation.* Cleveland: Howard Allen, Inc., 1958, pp. 302–309.

[41] Fritz Redl and David Wineman, *Controls from Within.* Glencoe, Ill.: Free Press, 1952.

perpetually avoided any entanglement with this personnel function. Indeed, the two functions, as still found on many campuses, are sharply separated. On the one hand discipline is characterized as repressive, regulatory, and forced conformity, law-abiding, orderly, imposed, and forced control. In sharp opposition, counseling is described as growth producing, ego strengthening, self-regulating, affect integrating, confidence developing, self-initiated, and self-centered unfolding of potential.[42]

The prevalent admonition for counselors to avoid involvement in disciplinary situations has been based, in large part, upon the very oppositeness of the nature of counselors' relationships with students. That is, while the counselor is trying to produce self-initiated and self-regulated self-discipline, the disciplinarian of any school or college is, in effect, trying to regulate and impose upon the student an external restraint which is not of the individual student's own choosing. Between these two extreme concepts, there seems to be little in common, and little possibility of integration. Nevertheless, we contend that fusion is not only possible and feasible, but necessary. We have argued at length, repeatedly, that the harsh, repressive-punishment approach to control of student behavior must be replaced by a more humane effort to teach them the necessary adaptations of behavior which are imposed by their membership in organized society. Without retreating from our insistence upon the right of self-determination and the necessity of self-management, we maintain that an absolute state of attainment is impossible and, indeed, would constitute a serious undermining of the twentieth-century emphasis upon an interdependent society. We believe this to be the very heart of the controversy between discipline and counseling. What is being rejected by counselors in the concept of discipline is the attempt to completely subjugate an individual to the dictates of the group or its leaders. On the other hand, as we have repeatedly argued (see Chapter 12), the individual cannot "go it alone" without group membership and still maintain his own optimum development. We must seek some accommodation between these extreme points of view of individual autonomy and group regulation. Such a search offers us a means of abandoning discipline as harsh retribution and punishment, and then proceeding

[42] E. G. Williamson, "The Fusion of Discipline and Counseling in the Educative Process," *The Personnel and Guidance Journal*, October, 1955, p. 74.

to search for ways of helping the individual learn how to have his individuality and, at the same time, become an effective member of the group. We believe "with counseling it [discipline] can become educative, corrective, and growth producing." [43] Discipline as organized student personnel work proceeds in an orderly fashion to help the individual search for an understanding of the causes of his misbehavior and for means of achieving his personality without continued disruptive and interfering expressions of his motivations.

This is not the place to describe in great detail disciplinary counseling procedures as they have evolved in at least one university. But these procedures may be indicated in the following schematic outline: [44]

Identification of alleged disciplinary situations
Identification of students allegedly involved
Reporting of situations to the disciplinary counselors
Making of charges against the student
Case investigation
Student interviewed for counseling purposes
Appraisal of causes of incident behavior
Assessment of potentiality for rehabilitation
Tentative formulation of needed steps in rehabilitation
Comprehensive report to committee or official
A review and deliberation by committee or official
Consultation and review by committee or official with student in an
    informal face-to-face situation
Action by committee or official
Enforcement of committee action
Rehabilitation counseling as long as necessary or profitable

Thus we see that disciplinary counseling proceeds in an orderly fashion. First, there is a complaint or alleged charge of misbehavior. Then follows an orderly and friendly, but not a hasty, identification and establishment of facts. There is an orderly review and assessment of the meaning of the facts in the situation, and of the individual's potentiality. Finally an orderly agreement is reached as to what is needed to rehabilitate the individual and to maintain the integrity of the institution as an educational enterprise.

We do not argue that this type of counseling is identical with

[43] *Ibid.*, p. 75.
[44] Williamson and Foley, *op. cit.*, pp. 61–62.

that *voluntarily* sought by the individual student in dealing with his own personally identified problems. Disciplinary counseling is rather enforced and required counseling; as such, it must be viewed as different, psychologically, in terms of relationships between counselor and counselee. One other difference should be noted, namely, in this case the disciplinary counselor is perceived by the student as being, usually at the beginning at least, a threatening authority figure.[45] Therefore, it is not to be expected that the student would as readily or as completely communicate the facts about his own motivations and about the alleged incident as he would if he sought counsel voluntarily. Great patience is required on the part of the disciplinary counselor to avoid the hasty imposition of retributive punishment upon the individual, both before the facts are established and also as desirable steps to bring about the individual's relearning.

Some other special features of disciplinary counseling need exploration. It is apparent that many forms of misbehavior arise out of or are associated in some way with psychopathology. Ordinarily, the misbehaving college student may be a healthy individual who has not yet learned the ground rules of a new society or who is inclined to experiment with deviations from the accepted code of behavior. But there are a few misbehaving students, psychopathically or neurotically disorganized, who need to be referred to psychiatric service. Farnsworth has described with great clarity some of the special problems arising in such a "forced referral." [46]

The confidential nature of the psychiatrist's relationship with his patient is, of course, of special importance. Farnsworth discussed in detail how information is conveyed without violation of confidence. For example, much general information about the student and his psychological make-up may be communicated without violating the confidentialness of details. The psychiatrist has a responsibility both to his client and to the institution; he must use great care in obtaining consent, if possible, but certainly assent, if necessary for such communication. Frequently the psychiatrist can interpret the student to the administrator and to the disciplinary counselor in

---

[45] In this respect, disciplinary counseling may be studied as a special case. For an interesting analysis of this topic see Sidney I. Dean, "Treatment of the Reluctant Client," *The American Psychologist*, vol. 13, no. 11, pp. 627–630, November, 1958.

[46] Farnsworth, *op. cit.*, pp. 146–161.

such a way as to call attention to unobserved dynamics of motivation and also to unassayed potentialities of rehabilitation. Such an appraisal of basic motivations and potentialities—while difficult to carry on under forced-counseling relationships—is indispensable if discipline is to become more than retributive punishment of the old colonial-college type. Farnsworth has stated aptly, ". . . the psychiatrist is chiefly interested in seeing that the student who is guilty of wrong doing learns something from the subsequent corrective experience." [47] The maintenance of this point of view by a psychiatrist or counselor in his relationship with the disciplinary counselor, or with the administrators, may actually redress the imbalance so often caused by the righteous-indignation attitude which is so readily induced by some forms of misbehavior.

Great care must be used in referring students to counselors or psychiatrists and in receiving reports from them on the part of the disciplinary counselor. While special safeguards concerning desirable confidence are needed in disciplinary counseling, usually a straightforward discussion with students is sufficient to gain cooperation, especially since the collection of information is desired not to punish but to help them search for ways of learning something from discipline which will be satisfying and rewarding. Such a rehabilitation point of view is rather easily conveyed and communicated to most students referred for misbehavior. In the case of paranoid and disturbed individuals, extra care must be exercised to avoid violating actual confidences while searching for understanding of motivations.

Two other aspects of confidence in disciplinary counseling need exploration. Discipline records are, of course, usually confidential, and are not as readily made available to other counselors and to administrators as are ordinary personnel records. The principal justification for this extra precaution concerning records lies in the desire to bring about rehabilitation of the individual. Many times his successful rehabilitation in the community is dependent upon minimum visibility to other students. Having abandoned the old repressive-punishment approach which would make an example of misbehaving students, one searches for a cloak of low visibility which would make it possible for him to reestablish himself successfully with his peers. Certainly this would seem to be a desirable precautionary measure. But occasionally in exercising this point of view one runs into the principle of freedom of the press—in the case of the student newspaper, for example. Occasionally a student reporter desires to attend a hearing, or at least to publish some release concerning action taken in a disciplinary case. No doubt the refusal of a release is an instance of withholding of news from the press. But usually an explanation of the reasons for withholding, namely, increased rehabilitation possibilities, is sufficient to win assent.

One encounters a more complicated and difficult instance of dealing with confidential material when requests are made from government agencies for appraisals of character, loyalty, and other qualities of personality in connection with sensitive governmental positions. It is at this point that responsible officials must make a decision concerning what is in the best interests of the institution, balanced against the best rehabilitation possibilities of the individual. Recent experiences have indicated that oftentimes misbehavior which arises out of psychological disturbances may actually predispose the individual toward taking loyalty risks in sensitive governmental positions. And in respect to many private-employment situations, records of persistent and uncorrected misbehavior motivations may very well bring the individual's qualifications into question. The questions of confidentialness are difficult ones—unfortunately, no definitive formulations are available to serve as guide lines. It seems to be common practice that each such request for revealing a disciplinary record should be appraised by a responsible official in consultation with the disciplinary counselor and others as required, with major emphasis placed upon the effects of such a release upon the individual's own rehabilitation.

A disciplinary counselor, of course, as was indicated by Farnsworth in the case of the psychiatrist, carries dual responsibilities, sometimes with conflict between his two institutional roles. Of course, he must have as one major responsibility the rehabilitation of the individual when that rehabilitation is judged to be feasible and possible. On the other hand, he is employed in an institution which bears great public responsibility in its certification of competence and character—even though the latter be only implied—of students who seek employment. The fundamental ethical principle is the same, regardless of whether the employment possibility is a security-sensitive one or casual, routine employment. Nevertheless, a counselor and a placement official are understandably more concerned with placement in the sensitive positions. But careful, thoughtful, humane, and professional appraisal of the significance for the individual's future employment status and effectiveness will usually yield a sensible course of action. And not infrequently the decision is to close the incident, with or without a report that "there occurred an incident a number of years ago which we think has no significance today. And as far as we are informed, the individual student has not repeated behavior of this type. As far as we are concerned, his record is clear." [48]

The involvement of therapists in handling disciplinary cases necessarily raises a complicated question of professional ethics. This is the nagging problem of nonvoluntary counseling. In the handling of many cases of misbehavior, it is apparent that sympathetic and sincere counseling relationships are most necessary and strategic in the rehabilitation of the individual offender. Should such counseling relationships be required? At this point we are not so much discussing the initial counseling relationship with the disciplinary counselor as we are discussing the requirement that the counselee establish a therapy relationship with a counselor or a psychiatrist. We have dealt elsewhere with the question of what kind of reports such a therapist should make to the disciplinary counselor, or to the administrator who administers discipline. At this point we raise the question of whether requiring counseling is ethically justified. In our experience it is indeed justified in terms of the increased likelihood of the rehabilitation of the individual. In this sense of the desirable outcome, we believe it to be ethically sound. Nevertheless, therapy as cure punishment is, we submit, an area of our professional ethics which has not received adequate attention.

CIVIL RIGHTS AND DISCIPLINARY PROCEDURES

In the American system of laws, courts, and justice, a number of legal safeguards have been erected to protect the civil rights of an individual accused of a crime. Many of these safeguards are

---

[48] This might well serve as a guide to counselors in the release of information about many disciplinary records.

established by constitutional provision, whereas others are established by statute or by court procedures. It would be understandable for students to generalize from these legally established rights to the campus scene.[49] Thus it is that many students demand of a disciplinary counselor, or administrator, certain established rights of procedures. The accused student may demand one or more of the following:

The right to face his accuser
The right to see the written charges
The right to bring an advocate or defense counsel to any hearing
The right to cross-examine the accuser

Whether students possess any such legal rights in their capacity within an educational institution is a complicated legal question. In general, courts have been inclined to avoid interfering in the internal operations of a college unless it can be shown that the college's authority was exercised in an unreasonable manner. The college is thus left free to exercise its state-chartered authority as it judges proper in carrying out its educational mission. Establishing reasonable standards and requirements of students would appear to be within its judicial authority. Students are, after all, admitted to the status of students in the institution by virtue of the charter-authority granted by the state to the governing corporation, known as a college or university. We do not take sides on the question of whether students have legal rights in their status as students. Nevertheless, there is always a gnawing doubt as to whether the institution, being of the kind it is, is being *scrupulously* fair in safeguarding the student's welfare and privileges.

The literature of disciplinary administration reveals that frequently a procedure is used in which the one who administers discipline is serving as accuser, prosecutor, jury, and enforcement officer of action. Our general American sense of fair play would seem to justify students' feeling that no one person should be free to exercise all of these functions without a reasonable measure of external review. The American sense of fair play would also operate to grant to the individual the right for a review of a disciplinary decision by a second and unrelated agent or agency. It would seem profitable for professional personnel workers to canvass systemati-

---

[49] We will further discuss this topic in chap. 12.

cally and carefully the question of relevant civil liberties with respect to disciplinary procedures in cooperation with competent law faculties, and with such clearly established agencies as the American Civil Liberties Union. Such an orderly formulation of adequate safeguards of students' rights would seem to be more effective than facing their continuous demands for rights which have not yet been established by institutional authority. After all, there is an orderly manner of establishing rights within the institutional context. And the mere demand for rights does not serve as an adequate means for their establishment. The institution does, after all, carry legal responsibility for the maintenance of law and order among students in pursuing its societal mission of higher education. And the right of the institution to establish rules of conduct binding upon students on or off the campus would, it seems to us, be sufficient basis for the establishment of students' rights of procedures.

Clearly, an institution of higher learning should be in the vanguard of society in shielding the individual against unjust, arbitrary, capricious, and unilateral action by administrators or by committees of faculty and student members. We rather favor the careful formulation of procedures through community consensus taking which will satisfy individuals that they will be given an orderly and fair hearing in the determination of any alleged offense. We also favor the inclusion of both students and faculty on any judiciary committees which serve as juries to determine the truth or falseness of the alleged offense. Moreover, we believe that privileges are properly safeguarded when the actions or decisions of any single administrator, including the disciplinary counselor's actions, seem to the student or to his advocates, family, or associates to be in need of review. The early establishment of orderly procedures of appeal and review of a disciplinary decision seems to us to be in line with the American tradition of justice and fair play.

On the other hand, we maintain here, as elsewhere, that the institution does bear responsibility for establishing rules of conduct. We clearly advocate that students shall share joint responsibility for the establishment of these rules, and that the rules shall be periodically reviewed to keep them current with the best thinking of the collegiate community. Surely it would be a mockery of higher learning if students were not given every opportunity to establish their innocence or if allegations were assumed to be true on the basis of less-then-adequate procedures and casework, or if a disciplinary decision, once made, could not be reviewed. The practice of frequently reviewing regulations and rules governing students on every part of the campus, including dormitories, should be clearly established, with students participating as partners in their formulation, and these rules should be well publicized in bulletins and in the student newspaper. While it is desirable to avoid regression to the colonial practice of establishing minute rules and regulations governing every detail of student life, nevertheless, what are considered by the institution and the students as important and serious forms of misbehavior should be clearly included in such a list of rules. We cannot agree with those who contend that general statements and general criteria should be avoided. See Chapters 10 and 11, where we describe establishment of students' rights and responsibilities. Usually such a point is made on the grounds that general phrases and general criteria provide for wide latitude of interpretation and hence confusion.[50] Of course, there is always risk in the wide latitude of interpretation and there is often confusion in application. On the other hand, one need only review the old colonial practice to see the ineptness and bad consequences which flowed from the attempt to establish minute, detailed regulations. But whether specific or vague, every rule or regulation governing any group of men must be interpreted and applied by someone, and it is not clear how one can write so specific a rule that it is automatically applied without interpretation and confusion. In fact, we had thought that the American system of justice established court procedures for this very reason. Therefore, it seems to us that the avoidance of general criteria is not at fault, but rather the lack of orderly judicial procedures in the application and interpretation of such general criteria.

We also agree with the American Civil Liberties Union position that students should be free to criticize the college and its administrators.[51] We react with some uneasiness to vague and ill-defined reports of purported instances of action taken because student newspapers, as well as student government, allegedly criticized the ad-

[50] *Academic Freedom and Civil Liberties of Students.* New York: American Civil Liberties Union, August, 1956, p. 12. (Pamphlet.)
[51] *Ibid.,* p. 11.

ministration of a college. We think this is an abuse of administrative authority, although at the same time we contend that many students also do abuse their freedom of criticism. Nevertheless we do not feel that it is proper for students to be punished for criticism, except when the expression of that criticism exceeds the bounds of propriety, taste, and accuracy as judged not by the administrator himself, but by the disciplinary committee composed of faculty and students.

We also heartily endorse the contention of the American Civil Liberties Union concerning due process:[52]

No student should be expelled or suffer other major disciplinary action unless advised explicitly (preferably in writing) of any charges against him, accorded ample notice, and given a hearing at which he is presented with the case against him, the opportunity to have advice and to answer accusations and submit the testimony of witnesses.

We believe the burden of such a procedure is that it precludes administrators from taking arbitrary and unilateral action. While we believe that the chief administrator of an educational institution does have legal rights to take such unilateral action, we believe it should be exercised only in extreme cases, and very, very infrequently. We have contended in Chapter 12 that the involvement of student leaders of all organized groups in the disciplinary process and in control of behavior is an excellent way of decentralizing responsibility and teaching students the many lessons of responsibility. In passing, we do not agree that charges should, even preferably, be in writing. Rather we favor, as we have contended elsewhere,[53] that disciplinary procedures and hearings should be conducted in an atmosphere of informality with the committee members participating in and questioning students concerning alleged misbehavior. The introduction of the formalized courtroom procedure into college discipline would, it seems to us, make rehabilitation very difficult, and would introduce rigidity into a desirably informal inquiry.

Three other aspects of the importance of civil liberties in discipline deserve careful study: (1) using information collected in interviews—counseling and other—to incriminate students con-

[52] Ibid., p. 11.
[53] Williamson and Foley, op. cit., pp. 52–56 and 73–79.

cerning allegations of misbehavior; (2) protecting the rights of students who are uncooperative in the disciplinary relationship, refusing to answer questions or give information on the grounds that to do so would incriminate them; (3) what to do with the problem of contrition. We shall outline briefly certain aspects of these open problems in the hope that our colleagues have found satisfactory answers and will educate us, or that they will be provoked to undertake study leading to better formulations than our experience has yielded.

Concerning the first, we are aware of the danger that in seeking to reform discipline through infusing its procedures with counseling viewpoints and restructuring its procedures by incorporating counseling techniques, we may be using confidentially collected information to incriminate a student. Such an unfair procedure, of course, must be avoided in an institution of higher learning. We believe that our reform of discipline is overdue and that counseling viewpoints and techniques are the proper means to reform. But perhaps civil liberties can, at the same time, be properly safeguarded by the use of a number of procedures. Perhaps we need to adopt the practice of informing the student of the disciplinary counselor's responsibilities to the institution and that, while he wishes to be helpful to the student, he also must be mindful of his institutional responsibility for the conduct of students. Then the student may be informed that what he says and reveals may be used against him. This would scarcely be new information to the student, but it could well emphasize to him the dual role played by the disciplinary counselor. And it would avoid, or at least modify, the charge that the student had been tricked into incriminating himself through the use of friendly and disarming, or deceitful, manners and techniques.

Some students present to the disciplinary counselor a wall of resistance and are uncooperative in discussing or revealing any information about themselves in connection with the alleged misbehavior. In fact, they may aggressively assert that the university has no right even to investigate such charges. Regardless of the answer to this question of rights, the disciplinary counselor needs to be aware of the possible danger of rewriting the charges of alleged misconduct by indicting the uncooperative student for the more serious offense of failing to cooperate with a university official in the discharge of his duties. Then the student may be convicted of this new charge and given punishment.

This presents a troublesome situation for the disciplinary counselor and his administrative superiors. They are under no legal requirement to prove in open court the student's guilt. And certainly, they are expected by their superiors to prevent or reduce the incidence of misbehavior, using conviction if necessary, or at least by creating the expectation among students that misbehavior will not go unnoticed. But to convict on the basis of uncooperativeness creates the uneasy feeling that absolute power is being used in a way not congruent with the mission of a university. Faced with such a dilemma, it is understandable that the administrator, if not the disciplinary counselor, feels relief when a student acknowledges freely his involvement in alleged misbehavior. But what to do with the one who refuses to cooperate by pleading guilty? Release him from unproved charges? Or impose penalties anyway, if the circumstances seem to indicate involvement? Or transfer the case to the proper discipline committee? Or dismiss him (or her) from college on the grounds that "we don't want the kind of student who is uncooperative with the authorities in Old Siwash College"? Or convict him of conduct unbecoming a student, since students are expected to cooperate with the authorities? Should students be convicted and punished only when it can be proved that they are guilty of charges? And finally, what does proof consist of?

The third perplexing aspect of discipline is related to the second. What is the weight and role of contrition in discipline? Do the counselor, the administrator, and the discipline committee feel better, more friendly and lenient, toward a student who acknowledges involvement in an alleged misbehavior? Is a plea of guilty a valid indication of reformation? When students acknowledge involvement and say they are sorry, that they have learned their lesson, that they will never do it again—what credence should we give to such statements? Will they be more validly representative of a restructuring (reformation) of perspective and self-control if made later in the disciplinary counseling relationship? Should students be required to say they are contrite? Or should they be punished less heavily if they do say they are contrite?

A critical review of disciplinary and judicial procedures is overdue in colleges and universities. And a careful study of the issue of students' civil liberties in respect to discipline will provide a healthy ventilation of issues and problems. Many other aspects in addition to those listed above invite profitable study and examination.

JUDICIARY FUNCTIONS AND ORGANIZATIONS

Thus far in this chapter we have discussed ways of dealing with alleged misbehavior on the part of students. We have recited the dreary and miserable history of efforts to find some way of disciplining students which would prevent misbehavior, by the severity of the action. We have also spoken of the changing emphasis in discipline from repression to rehabilitation. We have reviewed the possible reform of discipline through infusion with points of view and techniques borrowed from counseling, and we have also discussed needed reforms and formulations concerning students' privileges in the area of disciplinary procedures. Thus far we have dealt largely with the individual offender, or alleged offender, in mind. Now we turn to a consideration of organized-group responsibilities and participation in the judiciary process. We prefer the term "judiciary process and procedures" to describe what roles organized students and staff play in handling individual discipline cases and also in handling discipline charges brought against organized groups of students. In Chapter 11 we described in considerable detail many of the administrative processes involved in the establishment of a policy requirement that all organized student groups assume responsibility, under certain specified and limited circumstances, for the conduct and behavior of student members. Such a requirement would parallel the traditional requirements of organized groups of students—that they maintain financial solvency, and observe the general character of the institution in the conduct of meetings and student affairs. To these responsibilities would be added a judiciary one, different from the handling of discipline cases after misbehavior occurs. This judiciary function was conceived primarily as a means of prevention or curtailing of misbehavior in the orderly operations of an organized student enterprise.

Many of the discipline cases of individuals and of groups of individuals occur in connection with programs conducted by students living in residences—fraternities, sororities, and dormitories. Sometimes the ground rules establishing what is acceptable or unacceptable behavior are established by administrators of the residences. Usually, conduct rules concerning property and facilities, noise, and housekeeping arrangements are established by dormitory directors, sometimes with a little consultation with the organized members of student government. This is not true in the case of fraternities and sororities where the members themselves agree on rules governing conduct and interpersonal relationships. We have stated repeatedly elsewhere that full partnership participation by students in the periodic review and establishment of their own rules governing their behavior should be the requirement in acceptance of responsibility for enforcement of the rules. Either the students help establish the rules and then help enforce them, or else the administrative unit must both make the rules and enforce them. The establishment of student judiciaries and courts, both within residences and on the campus as a whole, is an interesting chapter in the history of higher education. By and large, less than desirable development of effective judiciaries has been achieved in more than a century of effort, beginning with Jefferson's establishment of a student board at the University of Virginia.[54] The effort of the University of Illinois in 1869 did not succeed because of the lack of legal authority to collect fines imposed by the student court.

Despite these early failures, responsible students have increasingly and justifiably requested more responsibility in making and enforcing rules governing their affairs. And today on most large campuses, one would find a network of interrelated judiciaries, sometimes heading up in formal student government, but usually with separate and sometimes independent status. Sometimes these judiciaries are composed entirely of students and sometimes they are jointly appointed with faculty members. It is traditional now that on many campuses the head judiciary unit would consist of a faculty-student committee, appointed by the administration. Sometimes this committee has jurisdiction only over certain specified cases of serious individual misbehavior. In such cases, the disciplining of the organized groups in their misbehavior is left to

[54] Henry D. Sheldon, *Student Life and Customs*. New York: D. Appleton & Company, Inc., 1901, sec. 5, "Self-governing Associations," pp. 255–270.

a decentralized system of judiciaries which are usually not inter-related.

An adequate campus-wide judiciary system would involve the following interrelated component parts:[55]

1. Unit judiciaries in student residences and in all student organizations.

2. Student membership of the organization should agree upon their own set of rules in the residences, including fraternities and sororities, and other non-resident student organizations should adopt a generalized statement of responsibility for the conduct of individual members only in connection with group sponsored and organized and conducted programs and activities.

In the unit judiciary constitutions that should be regularly adopted by the members, and approved by the central faculty-student government group, indication should be made that certain types of "serious" university institution-wide cases should be initially handled by the unit judiciary, and then forwarded for review by the next proper higher judiciary.

In some serious instances, the mechanism for referral of student incidents and cases should be through the proper administrative channels to the central disciplinary office and from there to the over-all faculty-student judiciary.

3. In certain types of residences, usually in large domitories with several separately organized houses, an intermediate, dormitory-wide judiciary may be desired by students as a higher appeal body for judiciary decisions made at the unit level. Moreover, there may be some dormitory-wide regulations and policies which need higher review and action. In the case of fraternities and sororities, system-wide judiciaries with specified areas of jurisdiction and with judicial appeal-review responsibility should be established. Intermediary judiciaries should be established for women's dormitories, for women's rooming houses, and similarly for men. It is desirable that jurisdictions be clearly established by vote of students involved, and sometimes by all campus consensus taking. Moreover, the orderly procedures for forwarding cases for review at higher judicial levels should be spelled out in detail.

4. At all levels of the judiciary, students' procedural rights, as indicated in a previous section, should be spelled out with the approval of all students involved and on the part of the administration as well as the faculty committee.

[55] L. F. Snoxell, *Handbook on the Judiciary System.* Minneapolis: University of Minnesota, 1957. (Mimeographed.) An adaptation and modification.

5. Because of long tradition on some campuses, individual discipline cases are ultimately handled by a central office, usually in the dean of students' office, and frequently and upon appeal by a faculty-student committee appointed by the central administration. There is also sometimes a central student judiciary council, with or without faculty representation, which serves as an over-all court handling certain types of serious university-wide student cases, particularly those which have a connection with organized student groups and their affairs, or those cases appealed from lower judiciaries. The integration of these two types of university-wide judiciaries is a puzzling problem because of tradition and local conditions.

6. Associated with all of these judiciaries are several administrative and personnel offices and officers. Traditionally the dean of students has inherited from the president and the faculty major responsibility for the administration of most types of discipline, both that misbehavior occurring in the case of an individual student, or group of students, and that which occurs in connection with the events or activities sponsored and conducted by organized groups of students. First, there is a central disciplinary officer whom we have referred to as a disciplinary counselor. His assignment of responsibility may be sweeping, and he may have jurisdiction over any and all cases, serious or minor. In such cases any action he imposes as a result of his investigation should be reviewed in the first instance by his superior officer, and secondly, upon appeal, by the student involved to his superior officer and through him to the all-university discipline committee, which has jurisdiction over individual discipline. Since the disciplinary counselor is primarily concerned with rehabilitation, he usually will transfer serious cases immediately to the central judiciary, and will present the cases following his investigation, together with his recommendation for action. The actions of the central judiciary committee should be reviewable upon petition by a special appeals committee appointed by the central administration.

THE DISCIPLINARY COUNSELOR

Since so much of misbehavior occurs in connection with organized student groups and their events, it is inevitable that the members of the staff who work with organized groups would be involved in discipline. Theirs should be the responsibility for securing compliance with university officials in the conduct of student affairs and in the application of the judiciary requirement of conduct control. Such staff members, however, should not have unreviewable disciplinary powers. Rather should they refer to the proper student judiciary all instances of misbehavior reported to them, and also work with the officers of organized student groups to provide for the orderly review of alleged misbehavior on the part of organized groups. Since the dean's staff concerned with student organizations works intimately and continuously with these groups, advising them concerning judiciary responsibilities should be as normal a part of their daily task as is assisting them in maintaining financial solvency, scholastic eligibility, and other general requirements implied in official recognition of the group.

The disciplinary counselor is, in our experience, the central core of the judiciary system of the campus. We believe that he should be separately located from the dean of students, although administratively responsible as a part of such a program of personnel services. We believe that he should be free to handle individual or group cases in connection with the jurisdictions in a way which will bring about rehabilitation of groups, as well as of individuals. We believe that the staff of the disciplinary counselor should serve as adviser to, as well as participant in, the many judiciaries at a lower level of operation. The manner of his participation should be determined by local conditions and traditions. But we believe firmly in the principle of full partnership between staff members and faculty in their participation in student affairs. We do not favor the nonvoting second-class-citizen status for staff members. Nevertheless, there are many local situations in which the actual right to vote becomes entangled with the perceived desirable separation of judiciary, legislative, and executive powers. In such cases, the right to be heard in judiciary deliberations is more important than is the right to vote. And if there is to be desirable central emphasis and continuity in judiciary practices and in the application of policies and rules and regulations, then a disciplinary counselor—whatever his title—should function not as a disciplinarian in the old sense, but as a thoughtful staff member who helps students, both individually and in groups, to carry out their desirable judiciary responsibilities. Discipline, viewed as rehabilitation and as orderly judiciary procedures, we believe is a very essential part of an organized and orderly academic enterprise. And we believe that students will learn to accept a judiciary responsibility when their form of participation is regularized and well established, and when they view the desirable effects of discipline as a normal part of the educative process.

CLARIFYING EXPECTATIONS

We have argued elsewhere that rules and regulations governing students and students' conduct should be explicitly formulated, periodically reviewed, and published in some readily accessible handbook. Many universities now publish a code of behavior describing the rules and regulations students are expected to obey.[56]

Another type of clarifying statement is needed in the orientation of new students. This is a statement of the general spirit or philosophy of the institution which really expounds the point of view and the reasons underlying rules and regulations. Such a philosophy may contribute positively to the cultivation in the students of a desire to conduct themselves in a constructive and desirable way. Such a published statement would serve in many instances to create in new students the expectation that they would adopt a point of view which, in effect, would preclude, prevent, or minimize misbehavior. The positive prevention of misbehavor can, we believe, be achieved by creating a point of view and an expectancy on the part of new students that they will conduct themselves in accordance with the institution's mores. Rules and regulations unfortunately often carry negative connotations and are usually negatively oriented to prohibit some form of misbehavior. Such is our institutional practice that seldom does one read what is positively *expected* of a student. Nearly all rules contain the phrase "unbecoming a student," but seldom does one read, or hear, for that matter, a discussion of what is actually "becoming" to a student in a community of scholars. Granted, it is easier to phrase a negative prohibition of misbehavior than to state positively what is expected. Nevertheless, with so much emphasis upon rule making of a negative sort, there is a void with respect to an effective appeal to positive motivations of students.

It was with a view to filling this undesirable void that some such

[56] *Code of Student Life: 1957–1958.* Iowa City: State University of Iowa, p. 41.
Student Handbook, Bulletin of the University of Wisconsin, vol. 1956, no. 9, pp. 56–90, August, 1956.

statement as the following is suggested. Such a statement emphasizes the prevailing climate of opinion of the institution with respect to student citizenship and behavior.[57]

Good citizenship begins in one's home. For students our university
is temporarily a second home, and these examples suggest some of the
opportunities for practicing citizenship on and off the campus.

Most students entering the university have come into their national,
state, and local citizenship by birth and residence. Throughout our
country's history, men have worked to make this citizenship a precious
heritage. We enjoy a long tradition behind the fact that we are citizens.

Citizenship is real. It includes rights, duties, and opportunities.

Have you studied these rights? Every library is crowded with books
about them. We must understand our rights if we are to use them
properly. They include personal rights of life and a range of significant
liberties such as freedom of speech, and of the press. They include
economic rights of property and contract, and political rights. Each
person, moreover, is assured that there will be no interference with
his freedom to worship according to his conscience. In addition, there
are the rights of counsel, jury trial, and other safeguards to protect
individuals with "due process of law."

Alongside these rights are duties and responsibilities which every
student-citizen should study, understand, and fulfill. One is to obey the
laws and help in law enforcement. These responsibilities are basic to
our principle of living together in a democratic society. Another duty
is that of performing military service and other lawfully ordered work
in defense of the country and our liberties. A third is the duty of
meeting squarely one's share in the costs of government. A fourth is
that of taking a responsible and active part in community affairs, including, of course, the activities of our university. As part of the
privilege attendant upon academic freedom, students are expected to
act with a high-mindedness which integrates self to the well-being of
the total community.

There is a fitting relationship between these rights and duties. The
duty of obedience to law, for example, does not imply that one has
to accept every law as being desirable. There is a right of dissent that
may rise to the level of a duty when the citizen is convinced that the
prevailing law or policy is not in the public interest. To obey the law
while proposing that it be repealed or changed is one of the marks of
the public-spirited citizen. Your citizenship is lacking if you do not

[57] Adapted from "The Moccasin for New Students, 1957–58," *Bulletin of
the University of Minnesota,* vol. 60, no. 19, pp. 53–59, October, 1957.

speak out when silence might be easier, if you do not set forth your position when the majority holds another view, if you do not use your rights by thinking out loud and discussing community problems.

*   *   *

All these are part of the ideal of a liberal education and citizenship. But membership in the university community, like membership in any community, means more than privileges. It means responsibilities, too, all along the line, responsibilities for putting earnest effort into your work as a student.

One responsibility is that of preparing yourself well for your career and future life, of using these years at the university with all the integrity of mind and commitment of faith you can muster.

It is also your duty to practice unswerving honesty in and outside the classroom in all of your conduct.

Another duty is that of helping to maintain this university in its advancement of learning and search for truth.

The thinking and behavior that mark good citizenship do not come to you like a free gift, neatly wrapped and delivered. Rather you must work toward good citizenship by what you do, think, and are. You learn from parents, teachers, and pastors. You learn through study and through what you yourself do in any social group to which you belong. Through your church or synagogue you fortify your faith and commitment to values of supreme worth. Good citizenship is something you achieve through serious and continuous effort.

*   *   *

In the matter of your responsibilities in these areas, some things are expected of you in your behavior and conduct. The university expects that each student will obey the laws that the state and local authorities have made. Besides these there are certain rules and regulations the university wishes to emphasize and, of course, there are certain types of behavior which are unacceptable.

Conduct on campus, in the classrooms, and at all times should reveal your maturity, sense of responsibility, and moral standards. Courtesy to the instructors, to other students, and to the public is expected of each one of us, and a failure to show this type of responsibility is a type of conduct which is unfavorable. Each student is expected to be honest in his work. Dishonesty in assignments, examinations, or other academic work is considered a very serious offense by the faculty and other students.

The university feels that the property of the university and of other students should be respected. Theft of any kind, whether of money or other property, is unacceptable within university rules. The destruction or mutilation of books, magazines, or other library material in the university libraries is another type of conduct which is not acceptable. Equally so is damage to or destruction of the buildings or equipment of the university.

Behavior that is disturbing or disorderly reflects on the university and therefore is contrary to the best interests of the university and other students. These are some of the citizenship requirements to which each student should be alert.

The centering of the student's attention on the positive developmental behavior would seem to be in keeping with the general spirit of an educational institution.

A second positive emphasis can characterize statements for new students in college bulletins, of the entire program of personnel services. These services can be described in the *language of error*, that is, the correction of reading disabilities, the avoidance of an incorrect vocational choice, the elimination of bad study habits, and so forth. Or the description can employ the *language of positive emphasis*—cultivating new reading skills at the college level, making a wise and appropriate and satisfying vocational choice, and learning effective study habits. Sometimes our personnel services are described in such a way as to throw emphasis upon the correction of something gone wrong. But a positive emphasis upon normal development would seem to be more in keeping with our basic philosophy of student personnel work. Such positive emphasis should do much to create expectancy on the part of the students that they will proceed in a normal, orderly, and enthusiastic way in their development—intellectually, socially, and in every other respect. This climate of opinion can also create the expectancy that the institution's resources are available for friendly, effective forms of assistance in orderly, normal development. The choice of descriptive language, while a subtle point, nevertheless could contribute much to the creation of an appropriate morale. We believe that climates of opinion have much to do with avoiding certain types of misbehavior and cultivating good morale and good citizenship.

SUMMARY

Taylor sums up our point of positive emphasis in the following words:[58]

There are many things learned which are not taught, and some which cannot be unlearned. Children catch their values through the atmosphere, and are affected by courage and cynicism, love and hate, generosity and meanness, snobbery and kindness, selfishness and unselfishness. . . . Students are on the whole tolerant and liberal, and wish to do what the college expects of them in the matter of their attitudes. They will fit themselves to the social situation which the college arranges for them. Since liberal education is intentionally designed to liberalize and humanize each generation of the young, it is essential that the social situation be one congenial to liberal and democratic attitudes.

[58] Harold Taylor, *On Education and Freedom.* New York: Abelard-Schuman, Inc., Publishers, 1954, p. 21.

CHAPTER 6

Counseling Services

Counseling, as broadly conceived and defined, is the generic service of student personnel work. One reaches this conclusion after searching for unity of emphasis in the varied and diverse services subsumed under the student personnel work. This unity of emphasis emerges from the extensive literature on the subject and from a first-hand study of the organized program of services on campuses of different size and complexity.

The techniques of counseling individual students may be observed, in greatly modified form, in the individualized services for such problems as off-campus housing; granting loans and scholarships; handling discipline cases; assignment of rooms and selection of roommates in dormitories; advising on student activities and programs; helping students choose vocational objectives; selecting optional courses of study; learning to read at college rate and comprehension. Technique, function, emphasis, and method are to be found in all types of service which deal with progress toward the goals selected by students, viewed as unique individuals. Indeed, much of the early student personnel work dealt with the individual and his problems on the college scene. And student personnel work was early defined as "the individualization of mass education." Students' transitional problems—encountered as they progress from high school through college—continue to be the focus for organized services. The central concern is thus the welfare of the individual student and the maximum utilization of his capabilities.

In the older literature, the case for counseling was largely based upon and justified by the frequency of students' problems or difficulties, especially during the first year of college. The high mortality or failure rate of freshmen in large part justified the efforts of counselors and other educators to perfect means of avoiding such scholastic failures and to rehabilitate and redirect such students' efforts. Counseling thus became largely, but not exclusively, centered upon the failing students and the avoidance of failure. While we did not restrict counseling to these functions, problem centeredness was firmly associated with early counseling. Unfortunately, the association continues today in large measure.

Today we have available some studies of normal or scholastically nonfailing students which indicate that they too experience some of the problems of scholastic and emotional adjustments formerly thought to be restricted to atypical students. Studies by Murray at Harvard, Butz at Princeton, and Davie at Yale suggest that some types of emotional problems are experienced by students of apparent normalcy and high scholastic aptitude.[1] Perhaps we may soon discover that developmental problems are normal in adolescents of varying social and cultural backgrounds, and that counseling is an educational service for all youth, not only those encountering unusual difficulties in their development. In this connection we think of counseling as a set of helping techniques using as our background the generalized curve of adolescents' development.[2]

OTHER POSSIBLE GENERIC SERVICES

In tracing counseling as the generic source of personnel work, one could make a case for the uniqueness of its perspective toward students and its methods as they differ from those used in other types of educational services. Each of these services was first organized around observed problems encountered by students as they attempted transition from high school to college.

[1] Butz, Otto (ed.): *The Unsilent Generation.* New York: Rinehart & Company, Inc., 1958.
Davie, James S.: "Who Uses a College Mental Hygiene Clinic?" chap. VIII in Bryant M. Wedge (ed.), *Psychosocial Problems of College Men.* New Haven, Conn.: Yale University Press, 1958.
Murray, H. A., et al.: *Explorations in Personality.* New York: Oxford University Press, 1938.
White, Robert Winthrop: *Lives in Progress: A Study of the Natural Growth in Personality.* New York: The Dryden Press, Inc., 1952.
[2] Dale B. Harris (ed.), *The Concept of Development.* Minneapolis: University of Minnesota Press, 1957.

There are, of course, many types of services provided in any college community which deal with individual needs and problems of students. For instance, a cafeteria caters to the individual preferences and eating habits of individual students. And in this sense this service is an individualization of mass education. Indeed, there are many instances concerning which the student personnel point of view finds expression in the cafeteria's service. For this reason, many would include provision of food service in the student personnel program. But others would include in the program only those aspects of the food service which include such operations as negotiation between students and management concerning complaints about the quality and quantity of the food, rather than the management of the cafeteria itself.

SPECIAL FEATURES OF PERSONNEL SERVICES

We like to think that in our work we operate not only an individualized type of service, organized around traditional problems ranging from the choice of an occupation to the adjustment to the curriculum. But we also add a second characteristic in contrast with other types of services. We like to think that we provide *personalization* as well as *individualization* in our relationships with students. That is, we emphasize humanness in those relationships which provide services directly to an individual student. We personalize not merely because this is a customary way of satisfying students who receive services, but because of other important educational reasons. Education, viewed as the cultivation of an individual in his development of intellect, personality, and character, is necessarily a one-to-one relationship. We have long protested against impersonality in educational relationships, asserting that education must include a highly personalized relationship between teacher and learner if it is to embrace more than mechanical memorization of routine skills and information. Education, in our Western culture, is indeed a search for personalized experiences.

We must admit, of course, that it is possible—highly desirable, in fact—to personalize all of our educational services. It follows, therefore, that neither of these, individualization or personalization, is necessarily unique to personnel services. The unique features are the characteristic content problems and the combination of problem with individualization and personalization. For example, in our personnel program, we grant a loan not only because the student is financially in need, but because without this money he could not educate himself to his full capacity. And we grant the loan in such a way as to deal with his own individual problems and needs and, in a highly personalized way, to encourage him to use this money to cultivate himself as a broadly educated person. We do not grant the loan for the purpose of making money (interest-investment yield), although this is incidentally true. The real purpose of the loan, as viewed from the personnel point of view, is to invest significantly in the individual's personal development rather than in a traditional commercial operation. To be sure, there are commercial aspects of the granting of a loan, just as there are many nonpersonnel aspects of every personnel service. But personalization and individualization of individual development are essential features of student personnel services.

COUNSELING RELATIONSHIPS GENERALIZED

Counseling is a basic service in student personnel work. That is, counseling is the most common method, technique, emphasis, and function used in a variety of different services. No other service is universally applicable to all personnel work.

Secondly, there is the traditional organization of welfare services, including students' financial, clothing, food, and shelter needs. On many campuses, this is a clustering of services, organized sometimes with one title—indeed, in the early literature of student personnel work, we find the term "welfare services" frequently used.

We have referred elsewhere to a third possible generic service as a crisis service. In fact, organized student personnel service began at the University of Illinois out of a crisis. Dean Clark defined the beginning in these words: "I relieved the President of some very unpleasant duties." [3] Something went wrong with an individual student, and Dean Thomas Arkle Clark was assigned to bring about his readjustment, and peace and harmony for the university president.

[3] Thomas Arkle Clark, *Secretarial Notes on the Fourth Annual Conference of Deans and Advisers of Men,* April 20–23, 1922, p. 5.

The ability to deal with crises is a necessity for an institution in its relationships with students and with the public at large. Everyone wants crises to abate; someone has to bring about abatement; and this effort constitutes a service. True, we have been reluctant to recognize and admit that a crisis service is a normally required facility in higher education. Rather have we pretended to ourselves that there is a never-never land in which crises do not occur; if we can but survive a current crisis, then student life will henceforth move slowly and smoothly and calmly. In contrast, we would be much more realistic if we systematically and courageously faced the fact that crises are a normal accompaniment of the congregation of adolescents in a restricted community. With such a calm perspective, we might systematically and clearheadedly, and with professional acumen, effectively organize our preparation for dealing with crises.

We have argued elsewhere for the utilization of crises as the curriculum content for a type of stimulated and organized learning.[4] This perspective, no doubt, would be viewed by many as an attempt to make virtues out of a vice—even as an attempt at cultivating a vice for the purpose of extracting a virtue. Whether one agrees with our point of view or not, it is clearly evident that crises are a normal part of the collegiate scene, and have been experienced on most campuses since the day of their founding.

Still a fourth generic service alternative to counseling is heavily documented in the literature of the colonial attempt to control students. Student personnel services of that day were largely directed to the objective of *controlling behavior* or, more properly, *controlling misbehavior* through the exercise of strict supervision over all details of students' lives and through inhumane enforcement of a variety—almost an infinite variety—of regulations and rules. No doubt, some form of control service will be required in the decades ahead, as has been true in centuries past. Human beings simply do not live together in an educational-developmental operation without some kind of organized and systematized control. The college scene is no exception to the dynamic requirements of a highly organized society for a control apparatus and concept.

But the control type of service, like the crisis type of service,

---

[4] E. G. Williamson, "The Dean of Students as Educator," *The Educational Record*, vol. 38, pp. 230–240, July, 1957.

is not generic in that not every student personnel worker is involved in maintaining it. Usually crisis services, like controls, are restricted to the general administrator of the student personnel program and to his immediate assistants in charge of organized student groups. The control type of personnel service is specialized, restricted in assignment to certain members of the staff. Certainly the staff of an organized counseling service would abhor attempts to enlist their efforts in the control of certain forms of misbehavior. They wish, and properly so, to be free to establish an informal, friendly relationship with their clientele, a relationship which is the very antithesis of control and crises. Clearly their counseling services seem to be more productive of educational good and personal development if they are separated from control and crisis services and functions.

Still another alternative generic service might be considered which embraces services organized around the *needs* of students. At first glance, this would seem to be as generic as counseling. Indeed, it might appear to be the very heart of counseling itself. The counseling literature does contain many references to the necessity of providing a counseling relationship to meet the needs of students. But when we examine the content of many personnel services we find that many, many types of needs are not dealt with in some service interviews. For example, seldom does a counselor discuss the need for shelter and food. It is only when the student is emotionally disturbed about his shelter, or has some dietary deficiency, or an anxiety about his food that the counselor deals with these needs. Thus, we do not organize counseling to deal with all types and with the full range of needs, but only with certain conventional and traditional ones. In fact, we may not even have succeeded in organizing counseling around many vital needs of the individual student. Counselors have, for example, tended to shy away from *value* needs, that is, the need for value orientation and commitment of students. They have rather tended to be objective about values—for fear that they might be guilty of imposing their own or a prescribed set of values. And yet no counselor would argue seriously that a student can be without values or not oriented and committed to an explicit value system, however primitive or limited.

In similar manner, counseling traditionally does not deal with the needs of students to learn to deal with authority, except when the individual is emotionally disturbed by that authority, or unduly subdued by it. But the whole question of students' relationship with authority, with its philosophic and historical complexity, is usually not dealt with by counselors. So we see that the generic clustering of services based upon needs is not really universal, but is somewhat traditionally restricted. Nevertheless we believe that counseling, with its emphasis upon individualization and personalization—even with its restricted and traditional content concerning certain adjustment problems and needs—is probably the most universally applicable and usable core of a comprehensive program of services for students.

COUNSELING AND OTHER SERVICES

Important as are the unique characterizations of counseling with respect to individualization, personalization, and characteristic content problems, yet there are some important phases of counseling which further differentiate it from other services and which also illustrate its universal application to them. It is true, for example, that granting a loan or a scholarship to a needy student is a highly individual matter in that the service is centered upon his own financial needs—not those of a standard or minimal student, or even average student. Moreover, the student is dealt with in a personal manner, since his own financial situation, his family background, and his responsibilities are highly personal items of information. The service, as a personnel service, requires a highly personal relationship for adequate discussion of such an intimate problem. Characteristically, counseling consists of more than the face-to-face interview, the collection of information, and the summarization and interpretation of that information. All these are procedures and techniques used in almost every kind of student personnel service. But a trained counselor—in contrast with a worker trained in some other speciality—characteristically looks for certain kinds of information. He sifts out information relevant to the student's immediate problem needs, and also notes those items which refer to him as a unique individual with certain potentialities for development through educational experiences. For example, a loan officer or the staff member in charge of granting of scholarships—if trained as a professional counselor—would not only collect information about the current financial needs of a student, he would also technically appraise the individual's scholastic and educational potential and also look for signs of emotional imbalance, which may or may not be associated directly with financial needs. In contrast, a financial adviser who is not professionally trained in counseling may not be as aware of the relevant and effective ways of appraising potential, scholastic or emotional.

This is not to claim that the one would be entirely adequate and the other would be inadequate in his service to a needy student. The advantage is one of more rather than less effectiveness. At least, this is the logic for much professional training in the field of student personnel services. Perhaps the point is clear with respect to identifying the sometimes subtle indications of emotional stress and strain. Almost any worker of any background and experience is able to recognize that a student who weeps during an interview is under stress and strain. And almost every college official is competent to ask, "What are you crying about? Are you worried over your financial needs?" But it takes a somewhat more subtle counseling approach to discover that the individual is crying not over financial needs, but over anxieties concerning some other remotely related problem. Of course, a brash person, with or without training, could bluntly ask, "What are you crying about?" and no doubt this would be an adequate technique in many instances. But still, the appraisal of the answer to the blunt question sometimes requires some understanding which comes from clinical experience in dealing with people who cry for a variety of reasons, some of which they cannot discuss openly and readily—or at least not as readily as they are able to discuss their financial needs.

This is, of course, to labor an obvious point. The advantage of professional training in counseling is self-evident for those employed as counselors in an organized counseling center. But the advantage of some professional training in counseling interviewing, for example, is not as obvious to one who has not achieved some professional competence in that specialty. It is relevant to point out that all personnel workers deal with individual students concerning their problems, and that all interview students with varying degrees of effectiveness. Surely the point needs no elaboration that the complexities of students' motivations alone would justify a more sophisticated type of training beyond the experience acquired in the apprentice interviewing situation. Many subtleties which indicate the need for professional counseling are most apparent when one has had some professional experience. This is but another way of arguing that counseling as a methodology is universally usable in improving the effectiveness of every personnel service. We do not argue that all personnel workers should be professionally trained counselors. However, it would be to their advantage, in terms of effectiveness, if they experienced at least rudimentary professional training not only in interviewing, but in counseling interviewing, which includes supervised analysis of the effects of interviewing techniques of various types.

VARIETIES OF COUNSELING

Today we think of counseling as a function performed chiefly by professionally trained specialists. But many varieties preceded today's specialty, and some of them persist today. There is also a second source of varieties of counseling which originated in attempts to modify technical counseling for different kinds of relationships. These two sources provide a wide range of counseling which we shall describe briefly in this section.

Faculty Advisers

Brewer described some of the early forms of vocational guidance.[5] Williams described the system of individual faculty advisers for students, introduced in colleges about 1828.[6] Many attempts were made in many colleges during the nineteenth century to modify and soften the harsh impersonality of the colonial college, and later the German-modeled research university, through humane and personal relationships between faculty and students. As late as 1910, Slosson referred to the great weakness of American higher education as ". . . the loss of personal relationship between instructor and student."[7] Maverick reported results of an

[5] John Brewer, *History of Vocational Guidance, Origins and Early Development*. New York: Harper & Brothers, 1942.

[6] Charles Richard Williams (ed.), *Diary and Letters of Rutherford B. Hayes*. Columbus, Ohio: Ohio State Archaeological and Historical Society, 1922, vol. 1, pp. 53–54.

[7] Edwin E. Slosson, *Great American Universities*. New York: The Macmillan Company, 1910, p. 76.

investigation of various universities and colleges concerning their programs of individualizing education. He discovered that one dean of engineering had introduced in the fall of 1911 a system of mentors.[8]

The mentors have nothing whatever to do with the faculty, being a separate body and responsible to the dean. Indeed, they are the personal representatives of the dean and have to deal with the social life of the students, to advise them on all matters of whatever character may arise . . . the same as an elder brother.

Maverick also reported the establishment of a group of student advisers in 1910 at Dartmouth College.[9]

Resolved: That it be the function of the advisers to inform themselves regarding the circumstances and character of the students under their supervision, their manner of life and their college work, their antecedents, interests, and ideals. That the relation between adviser and student be regarded as friendly and confidential. That advisers meet their students at regular intervals, at the beginning of the freshman year, about once in every two weeks, once toward the end of the freshman year, and again at the end of the first and second semesters of the sophomore year for the special purpose of discussing with them the election of courses for the following semester.

In some institutions this type of advising was concentrated in the office of the dean of the college.

The reform of faculty-student relationships in the nineteenth century, substituting warm personal relationships for the prevalent cold, strict, disciplinary pattern of an earlier period, undoubtedly produced many informal faculty advisers. One established pattern of relationships with male students is exemplified by this description of Dean Jones of Yale College:[10]

When Dean Jones arrived from the West, he is said to have boasted that he could typewrite the fastest and spit the farthest of any man on the Yale faculty. He was a man's man, with a gruff manner, a warm heart, and a great liking for boys. . . . By sheer weight of personality

[8] Lewis Adams Maverick, *The Vocational Guidance of College Students.* Cambridge, Mass.: Harvard University Press, 1926, p. 21.

[9] *Ibid.,* p. 21.

[10] George Wilson Pierson, *An Educational History of Yale College, 1871– 1921.* New Haven, Conn.: Yale University Press, 1952, p. 155.

and of sound the Dean swept them all bodily along to their appointed destinations. At first you were scared stiff. Then you recognized the essential warmth of the man. The bark was much worse than the bite. He would scare you first, then punish you, then help you. Perhaps even remit the punishment, if you were trying.

In his famous 1926 survey of fourteen institutions, Hopkins provided a summary evaluation of this effort to establish warm and personal relationships through faculty advising:[11]

As far back as we have knowledge of the American college there is indication that, among the faculty members, there were certain individuals who thoroughly enjoyed personal contact with their students. These were the men also to whom the students went for counsel and advice. At later date, in many institutions, there developed the recognition of a need for more of this type of service, and it became more or less the accepted thing to formalize this service by the appointment of faculty advisers.

But Hopkins went on to characterize the work of the faculty advisers as "perfunctory." He referred to the current practice of assigning twenty to fifty students to each faculty adviser, and said that "this plan has never worked with a marked degree of success." [12] For the most part, there were not enough good advisers to make the plan work effectively. The adviser needed both a warm, personal interest in students as individuals outside the classroom and a thorough knowledge of technical requirements—courses, schedules, and credits, and the required preprofessional courses. The adviser also needed some information about occupations and vocations open to college-trained men in various specialties. In addition, the faculty adviser was usually required to carry a full teaching load. Moreover, as Hopkins pointed out, the advisers needed to know something about the technical interpretations of information about the student, much of it elicited in the personal interview, concerning interests, finances, health, habits, and attitudes. Hopkins quoted the evaluative comment of one faculty adviser in one institution as follows:[13]

[11] L. B. Hopkins, "Personnel Procedure in Education," *The Educational Record Supplement*, vol. 7, no. 3, p. 25, October, 1926.
[12] *Ibid.*
[13] *Ibid.*, p. 28.

I am convinced that the problem of giving advice must pass more and more into the hands of experts. . . . Only a specialist can give the right technical advice. I am convinced that the one who gives technical advice should also be the one who gives personal advice.

We are reminded at this point of the prophetic address of William Rainey Harper, which stressed the need for a "scientific study of the student himself . . . a general diagnosis of each student" before instruction and before he has chosen a curriculum.[14] In his speech at the inauguration of the Rev. W. H. P. Faunce as president of Brown University, October 17, 1899, Harper made this amazingly prophetic projection:[15]

This feature of the twentieth-century college education will come to be regarded as of greatest importance, and fifty years hence will prevail as widely as it is now lacking. It is the next step in the evolution of the principle of individualism, and its application will, in due time, introduce order and system into our educational work, where now only chaos is to be found.

Hopkins's evaluative remarks do indeed serve to close a period of faculty advising in which friendliness performed a much-needed improvement in faculty-student relationships. But the friendliness proved to be insufficient on two counts. In the first place, friendliness was no substitute for thorough grounding in the technical requirements of the increasingly complicated curricula of the contemporary college and university. Harper's prophetic scheme of technical diagnosis preceding instruction was presently attainable during Hopkins's time. Paterson described the importation to the college, following the First World War, of newly perfected psychological instruments for the diagnosis of scholastic and other capabilities.[16] Faculty advisers unacquainted with the newer techniques and sources of information about students and their capabilities and interests were judged inadequate for the task, and were gradually replaced in many institutions by more technically trained and oriented specialists. But faculty advising continues, necessarily,

[14] William Rainey Harper, "The Scientific Study of the Student," *The Trend in Higher Education*. Chicago: University of Chicago Press, 1905, pp. 317–326.
[15] *Ibid.*, p. 325.
[16] D. G. Paterson, "The Genesis of Modern Guidance," *The Educational Record*, vol. 19, no. 1, pp. 36–46, January, 1938.

because of the long-established requirement of "policing" the curriculum requirements for graduation through specifically granting approval following review each quarter or semester of the student's registration in courses and subjects. Only a few institutions have abandoned the credit requirement and thus the faculty advisers are not released from this policing function. Robertson recently redefined this variation of counseling, or advising, in terms reminiscent of Hopkins's description:[17]

> Furthermore, the emphasis in the advising relationship rests not on problem-solving by the adviser but in helping a student to clarify the issues, gain perspective on his difficulty, get the facts straight, and to work out alternative courses of action, but not in handing him ready-made answers. . . . Academic advising, rightly understood, is simply an extension of teaching, a conscious concern for academic and educational questions that most students have about the importance of their studies, the proper direction of their educational development, [and] the practical value of their educational objective.

Hardee has published an extensive analysis and description of counseling advising as currently organized and performed in a large number of colleges and universities. A significant number of Hopkins's criticisms of counseling as practiced three decades ago apparently have been met and improvements achieved.[18]

Counseling in Psychological Clinics

Hopkins's 1926 survey identified the current trend of gradually supplementing, and sometimes replacing, advisers with professionally oriented and trained counselors. The reformation of advising by infusion of psychological techniques, concepts, and emphases has proceeded in an orderly manner prior to and following the First World War. Counseling as an organized service in the schools had

[17] James H. Robertson, "Academic Advising in Colleges and Universities," *Association Quarterly,* vol. 32, no. 3, pp. 234, January, 1958.

Viteles organized, in 1921, a Vocational Guidance Clinic, in connection with the Psychological Clinic at the University of Pennsylvania. See Morris S. Viteles, "A Psychological Clinic for Vocational Guidance," *The Vocational Guidance Magazine,* vol. 4, pp. 78–79, Nov., 1925.

Beeley, in 1927, organized a Bureau of Student Counsel at the University of Utah. See Arthur L. Beeley, "Mental Hygiene and Counseling at the University of Utah," *Mental Health,* vol. 14, no. 4, pp. 2–13, Apr. 1, 1947.

[18] Melvene Draheim Hardee, *The Faculty in College Counseling.* New York: McGraw-Hill Book Company, Inc., 1959.

stemmed from the work of the pioneer Parsons in the Boston YMCA.[19] Parsons, a publicist, inspirational teacher, lawyer, and a self-trained counselor rather than a psychologist, developed his own personal skill and practice in assisting young adolescents to avoid vocational misplacement. For Parsons, counseling or "guidance," as he called it, was a three-step operation involving analysis of the individual, study of occupational requirements, and a comparison of the two, or counseling. In sharp contrast with the psychological frame of reference of Harper, Parsons evolved common-sense methods of analyzing individuals by means of questionnaires and interviews. Had Harper's more sophisticated psychological concept replaced that of Parsons, perhaps Paterson would not have written such a scathing indictment of the psychology underlying vocational guidance as it developed after Parsons's initiation. But Parsons's followers won out, and even today in some schools, guidance essentially consists of a set of procedures rather than a repertoire of psychological techniques. As it has been established in many states for many years, the essential psychological training of a guidance officer or counselor consisted in taking a course or two in analysis of the individual. But within the past decade, a major reform has again taken place in guidance concerning the depth of psychological sophistication now underlying counseling. Counseling is now properly called a "psychology specialty," although one may still find counselors in many schools who have had relatively little psychological training.

A more penetrating orientation and understanding of the complex and complicated field of occupational information continues to center emphasis upon Parsons's second step in guidance. The explosion of occupations and subspecializations is indeed a twentieth-century phenomenon. In a similar manner, the corresponding vocational training available today has become more complicated than it was in Parsons's day. An effective counselor, therefore, must be well informed, and as Hopkins's informer pointed out, the information requiring courses of training at the various college levels has also become increasingly complicated. Added to these complications is, of course, the great expansion of technical information and techniques involved in an analysis of the individual. To a considerable

[19] Brewer, John M.: *History of Vocational Guidance.* New York: Harper & Brothers, 1942.
Parsons, Frank: *Choosing a Vocation.* Boston: Houghton-Mifflin Company, 1909.

extent, Harper's prophetic insight has been achieved. Mere analysis of the individual has indeed become a much more complicated guidance and counseling procedure. Super perhaps best sums up the contemporary restructuring of this part of counseling.[20] That part of counseling which has to do with the choosing of a career is now thought of in terms of the theory of life patterns. Borrowing a concept from Buehler, Super has outlined a theory of vocational guidance which involves the identification of career patterns and life stages. An occupation is viewed as a way of living rather than a mere economic activity, and the cycle of the working life is described in Super's chapter titles.[21]

Adolescence as Exploration: Developing a Self-concept

The Transition from School to Work: Reality Testing

The Floundering or Trial Process: Attempting to Implement a Self-concept

The Period of Establishment: The Self-concept Modified and Implemented

The Maintenance Stage: Preserving or Being Nagged by Self-concept

The Years of Decline: Adjustment to a New Self

In Part 3 of his book, Super illustrated the change in technical depth and technological underpinnings of the analysis of the individual from the days of Parsons to the present. Currently Anne Roe has outlined a theoretical framework for research and practice of counseling in regard to identification and the development of basic interests, or needs, in work and activities.[22] Since we are not concerned here with a detailed description of contemporary counseling, but only with its role in the administration of the student per-

[20] Eysenck, H. J.: *Uses and Abuses of Psychology*. Baltimore: Penguin Books, Inc., 1953, chaps. 5, 6, 7, 8.

Rosenberg, Morris: *Occupations and Values*. Glencoe, Ill.: Free Press, 1957.

Super, Donald E.: *The Psychology of Careers*. New York: Harper & Brothers, 1957.

——— et al.: *Vocational Development: A Framework for Research*. New York: Bureau of Publications, Teachers College, Columbia University, 1957.

[21] Super, *op. cit.*, p. vii.

[22] Roe, Anne: "A Psychological Study of Eminent Psychologists and Anthropologists, and a Comparison with Biological and Physical Scientists," *Psychological Monographs*, vol. 67, no. 2 (whole no. 352), 1953.

———: *The Psychology of Occupations*. New York: John Wiley & Sons, Inc., 1956.

sonnel program, we will content ourselves with this indication of contemporary content and emphases.

In the decade immediately ahead we may confidently anticipate that recent advances in formulating general theories of personality development will provide counselors with a much-needed foundation concept.[23] Counseling may prove to be a psychological technology grounded upon a general theory of personality as it is developed within the context of interpersonal relationships interacting upon and with interests, aptitudes, aspirations, and psychological needs. In particular, Roe and Tyler are productively attacking the critical and pivotal unknown factor of the psychological problem of the origin of choice or preference.

The decade ahead may well see advances beyond the empirically derived and constructed how-to techniques of the past five decades. We now see that the founding counselors were faced with things gone wrong, a crises or a problem. They did what seemed to their common sense as needful and useful to correct and repair things gone wrong in adjustments and development. Counseling in the future may well be grounded in a productive and reassuring theory of human development which has been achieved and patterned out of selective reactions to needs. As is true of other fields of knowledge about human development, counseling would thus be subjected to critical examination of its contributions to that development. Moreover, the persistent problem of determining its effectiveness would be recast in ways productive of advances which are not now possible in our state of empiricism and technique-problem centeredness.

But one other variety of contemporary counseling needs emphasis, and that is mental hygiene.

Mental Hygiene

Parsons wrote little about emotions, at least not in a sophisticated manner. It was one of those accidents of history that the year

[23] Hall, Calvin S., and Gardner Lindzey: *Theories of Personality*. New York: John Wiley & Sons, Inc., 1957.
Harris (ed.), *op. cit.*
Maslow, A. H.: *Motivation and Personality*. New York: Harper & Brothers, 1954.
Tyler, Leona A.: "Toward a Workable Psychology of Individuality," *The American Psychologist*, vol. 14, pp. 75–81, February, 1959.

Parsons published his scheme of vocational guidance, Freud came to Clark University for his first American lecture, invited by the psychologist-president G. Stanley Hall. Had Parsons become more sophisticated in his understanding of the emerging mental hygiene movement, contemporary counseling would have become integrated more readily and sooner. But such are the accidental separateness of historical trends.

Farnsworth[24] referred to the formulation in 1910 by Stewart Patton of Princeton University of "the first specific plea for the explicit recognition of the need for personality study and development in American colleges and universities." [25]

But the great developments in mental hygiene facilities were delayed in most colleges until the postwar period, beginning 1919–1920. And then a number of psychiatrists, and sometimes clinical psychologists, were employed to deal with the emotional disturbances of students. Their published experiences revealed a wide range of emotional disturbances exhibited in the university community—almost as wide as that found in any community. Of course, there are many fewer psychotics, but those few present are perhaps more readily discernible because of the sharply defined uniqueness of their behavior in the context of normal student life. The stresses and strains of student life, however, do produce some types of anxiety states not customarily found in communities at large.

This is not the place to describe the greatly expanded psychological care and treatment of the minor neurotic manifestations of students. For our purpose, it is sufficient to indicate that facilities for the identification and care of the milder forms of neurosis are well established on many campuses today. As Farnsworth pointed out, however, there are still many sources of resistance to be found in many academic communities. Mental hygiene, it seems, is sometimes perceived as an intrusion into the college intellectual scene of the newer concept of mental and emotional disorders as an important source of behavior. In Western culture we have become so accustomed to thinking of man as essentially a rational individual

[24] Dana L. Farnsworth, *Mental Health in College and University.* Cambridge, Mass.: Harvard University Press, 1957, p. 10.

[25] J. R. Angell, "Mental Hygiene in Colleges and Universities," *Mental Hygiene,* vol. 17, pp. 543–547, October, 1933.

that our educational institutions have been erected with this one objective in central focus. Indeed, those oriented toward the European, Roman, and Greek traditions repeat the old adage that a university is the one social institution dedicated principally to intellectual activity. It is for this and other reasons—some of them quite interspersed through our culture—that the introduction of mental hygiene facilities has been delayed in colleges and universities. For one thing, the college adolescent has been thought of as highly selected, and therefore quite a normal individual, not in need of assistance such as psychotherapy. Recent studies throw much new illuminating doubt upon these assumptions.[26]

Moreover, his long history of riotous behavior has usually been explained as the result of animal spirits, severely curtailed and confined during the winter months in college dormitories, and increased in intensity by repressive discipline until it erupted in a spring riot. These two theories and other psychological folklore are, of course, nonsense when advanced as justification for inadequate counseling services, since some students do exhibit emotional disturbances of a pathological nature. In Western education we have been indeed reluctant to substitute new concepts of human motivations for our heritage from ancient Greece and Rome and to accept White-head's admonition that "knowledge is always accompanied with accessories of emotion and purpose."[27] Thus many educators have been reluctant to admit that our careful admissions procedures, based on scholastic aptitude, do not in and of themselves produce a student body homogeneous and normal in its emotional capacities.

But the recognition of the necessity of some emotional therapy —even with normal students who may be overwhelmed by the stress of an examination period or some aspect of student life—is growing perceptibly and steadily. These campus facilities are usually provided in two administrative units, a separation which produces some new problems of coordination. Psychiatrists and clinical psychologists dealing with the more complicated cases of emotional imbalance and requiring longer periods of psychotherapeutic treatment are usually properly located in the medical setting of the

[26] Butz (ed.), *op. cit.*
Murray, *op. cit.*
White, *op. cit.*
[27] Alfred North Whitehead, *Science and the Modern World.* New York: Mentor Books, The New American Library of World Literature, 1953, p. 191.

student health service. But a second type of mental hygiene facil-ity is provided in the psychological clinic manned by psychologists who function as counseling psychologists. For many decades, some difficulty was experienced in integrating medical and psychological services; no doubt, on some campuses certain difficulties may be experienced today. But the modern college or university does pro-vide facilities for mental hygiene, except for cases that are judged to be so involved and complicated and to require such extended treatment that the university concludes it is not under obligation to provide for them.

The significant point for our discussion is not so much the pro-vision of mental hygiene facilities for those who need it, or even the identification of those who need to be referred elsewhere. It rather lies in the fact that we have come to recognize that the college life, both classroom and extraclassroom, can be organized and reorganized each year so as to reduce certain tensions and con-flicts and to improve the mental health of students. But it is relevantly contended that educational institutions are educative institutions rather than hospitals. Therefore, it would be in the line of our traditional development if, after we learned to identify and deal with the pathological, we should turn our major educational efforts to the prevention of the pathological by centering emphasis upon the normal. In the case of discipline, we have indicated else-where that the recent shift from punishment to prevention—through positive emphasis on personality cultivation and develop-ment—was a natural stage in the evolution of students' out-of-class life and an integral part of the total educational enterprise. When educators recognized that some form of misbehavior was inevitable, we sought to learn ways of making misbehavior unnecessary through positive emphasis upon the quality of student life. In a somewhat similar way, colleges and universities are presently undergoing a transformation from the care of the mentally sick to the major educative function of promoting normal development as a way of alleviating some forms of mental illness. This reform may prove in the long run to be a significant turning point in Western education. Sanford's studies of the development of personality in normal college students is, we hope, the forerunner of such a major re-organization of higher education.[28]

[28] Nevitt Sanford, "Personality Development during the College Years," *Journal of Social Issues,* vol. 12, no. 4, pp. 3–70, 1956.

The opportunity for the student personnel administrator to take responsibility for and make a contribution to the reorganization of a university, with emphasis upon positive mental health, is a first-rate challenge. There are many ways of accomplishing this objective, although they must be reconstructed each year since the student population changes, and so do the dynamic folkways and social psychology of the student body. There is no need for elaborate listing of things to be done because they come readily to mind. For example, the easy acceptance of a psychiatrist and a clinical psychologist as a speaker in dormitories, fraternities, weekend retreats, and elsewhere in the student life in itself introduces students to the normalcy of concepts of mental health. This kind of education undoubtedly has great effect upon many individual students. The sheer recognition of their own emotional make-up—through the informality and casualness of the recognition itself—should do much to relieve some individuals' anxiety states, once they have experienced a stress period in their college life. The casual and matter-of-fact way in which students tell each other that they have been to see their therapist in itself is an indication of their mental health and of the acceptance of the mental hygiene point of view on the campus. Incidentally, all forms of counseling need to gain this kind of casual acceptance.

Residential Counseling

Residences have been utilized for a variety of purposes, some of them educational, others of a caretaking type.[29] We are not concerned in this discussion with the use of student housing for hygienic and health purposes, or as means of control of students' behavior. As for the use of residence to improve scholarship, we feel that considerable progress has been made in this respect, but it is largely confined thus far to improving grade-point averages rather than returning to the intellectual emphasis and content of earlier days.[30] Years ago Lowell sounded a note for needed reform

[29] Cowley, W. H.: "The History of Student Residential Housing," *School and Society,* vol. 40, no. 1040, pp. 705–712, Dec. 1, 1934.
Williamson, E. G.: "Students' Residences: Shelter or Education?" *The Personnel and Guidance Journal,* February, 1958, pp. 392–401.
[30] Strozier, Robert M.: "Educational Planning for Student Housing," *The American School and University,* vol. 23, p. 135–138, 1952.
Woolf, Maurice D., and Jean A. Woolf: "College Housing," *The Student Personnel Program.* New York: McGraw-Hill Book Company, Inc., 1953. p. 124–141.

of students' anti-intellectual mores, a note which needs to be re-soundingly struck again: "It is the ambition of every earnest teacher so to stimulate his pupils that they will discuss outside the class-room the problems he has presented to them." [31]

In addition to some emphasis on things intellectual, a considera-ble emphasis is to be noted in the literature about student housing —the use of residences for personality development, development of interpersonal skills, or learning to govern oneself in groups.[32] All of these are laudable objectives and quite necessary ones in a collegiate institution. But we are here concerned rather with the residence halls as places where students readily and easily seek to discuss, and sometimes to solve, their personal problems with their roommates, with other students in the residence, with the residence counselors, and with the management.[33] This is such a natural setting that such informal counseling is to be encouraged, provided certain conditions are met. Without these conditions, discussions of personal problems may be quite unproductive, and sometimes harmful, in that they serve to substitute for more serious types of counseling.

Of chief importance in this service is the need for trained per-sonnel.[34] All too frequently the staff members of residences are not selected with proper concern for their professional and personal qualifications to assist students with their personal adjustment prob-

[31] A. Lawrence Lowell, *At War with Academic Traditions in America.* Cambridge, Mass.: Harvard University Press, 1934, p. 39.

[32] Dowse, Eunice M., and Mary E. Harrison: "The Educational Program of the Residence Hall," *Journal of the National Association of Women Deans and Counselors,* vol. 20, no. 2, pp. 58–75, January, 1957.

Kidd, John W.: *Residence Hall Guidance.* Dubuque, Iowa: William C. Brown Company, 1956.

Orme, Rhoda: *Counseling in Residence Halls.* New York.: Bureau of Publica-tions, Teachers College, Columbia University, 1950.

———: "Counseling in Residence Halls," in Melvene D. Hardee (ed.), *Counseling and Guidance in General Education.* Yonkers, N.Y.: World Book Company, 1955.

Wilson, Edith G.: "Using Group Dynamics in the Residence Hall," *Journal of the National Association of Deans of Women,* vol. 15, no. 3, pp. 126–130, March, 1952.

[33] JoAnne Johnson, "Problems Voluntarily Taken by Students to Residence Hall Counselors," *The Personnel and Guidance Journal,* vol. 37, pp. 296–298, December, 1958.

[34] Matthew Stark, "Selection and Training of a Residence Hall Staff," *College and University Business,* vol. 20, no. 5, pp. 50–52, May, 1959.

lems. Specialization and experience in management of residences would seem to be more characteristic of managers. And far too frequently the part-time counselors, usually advanced or graduate students, are selected with the purpose of organizing activities of a recreational sort, to protect property, and to maintain orderliness. All these are necessary functions, but they are not necessarily associated with the professional insight and background necessary to help students do something constructive about their problems of studying, concentration, anxiety, loneliness, and a myriad of other adjustment problems so characteristic of some college adolescents.

Our concern is that whatever counseling concerning individuals' problems is conducted in the residences shall be of an effective quality. We do not favor employing professional counselors operating within residences, thereby decentralizing the central counseling clinic to the residences. Rather do we favor establishing systematic and continuous training-supervision programs for residence counselors, involving lectures, demonstrations, case conferences, and consultations with professional counselors from the central staff. Such a continuous professional relationship will gradually improve the understanding and use of techniques of residence counselors in handling adjustment problems of individual students. It will also alert them to the early identification of those students with serious problems which need to be referred for extended and technical assistance by professional counselors. This type of assigned relationship is a form of coordination achieved largely through the training function itself. It should be noted that orientation training at the beginning of the academic year in this sort of counseling is not sufficent. Training supervision should continue several times a month throughout the school year.

There is still a further reason for this type of involvement of the professional counselors in the supervision and training of residential counselors. The numerous informal discussions provide ample opportunity to define different counseling roles on the part of different agencies on the campus, including the residence counselors themselves. This type of definition by specific example and case proves to be a very effective means of using supervisory relationships for training purposes. Moreover, it maintains a high level of professional relationship among the various specialists, as well as with the residence counselors. In the case reference and the case discussion, as well as in staff meetings, definitions of relationships among specialists and of responsibilities of each and every staff member are continually clarified and reexamined. This procedure constitutes an administrative means of coordinating the many kinds of services with the counseling conducted in the residences. Administering the residential counseling program in this integrated fashion avoids confusion and conflict of jurisdictions; it also serves to tone up and give direction, as well as quality, to the residence counseling. Without such continuous relationships with the professional counselors, substitute forms of counseling would develop within the residences, some of which might be desirable, some detrimental to the welfare and progress of the individual students in their maturing. Our concern is that whatever counseling is done, wherever on the campus, shall be performed with high quality and with full coordination and integration with all other counseling.

The residential counselors have many other responsibilities in addition to counseling; although we are not discussing them at this point, we are not in any way lessening an emphasis upon them. They must assist student activities, especially judiciaries, and student government. They also must protect property and maintain orderliness and high morale. But, in addition, it is natural for students to turn to them as the most readily available older person with whom to discuss personal problems. It is to capitalize fully upon this natural counseling relationship that the personnel administrator needs to take steps to maintain the effectivenes of residential counseling.

Other Specialized Types of Counseling

We shall merely mention a number of these specialized developments and refer the reader elsewhere for extended discussions and descriptions. We are not here concerned with a comprehensive and descriptive treatment of all forms of counseling, but rather with certain administrative responsibilities for the total program. Anyone who has read recent literature or who has lived on a campus for any length of time knows that foreign students present very real personal and adjustment problems which require specialized techniques and knowledge.[35] We have also referred in another chapter to the growing specialization which we prefer to call

[35] *Counseling Foreign Students*, American Council on Education Studies, ser. 6, vol. 14, no. 15, Washington, September, 1950.

"disciplinary counseling." There is also a growing body of knowledge and special techniques involved in helping students from a lower-economic family background to live healthfully and effectively on the very limited funds available to them.[36] This financial counseling is related to, but not identical with, the actual granting of scholarship and loan funds. This form of counseling is concerned with how one may live on whatever money one can secure from a variety of sources. This type of counseling calls for skill in budget making and expenditure not always possessed by all counselors; in fact, many professional counselors would not think of this as part of counseling. To be sure, worries about the lack of money are accepted as the content of psychological counseling. But the actual lack of money itself would seem to be one reason why psychologically untrained financial aid officers are forced to learn something about counseling needy students.

And then, of course, there is a growing body of knowledge concerning religious counseling, or pastoral counseling,[37] as it is called. The value, moral, and philosophic conflicts expressed by college students constitute real problems, for the most part neglected by many professional counselors.[38] This specialized form of counseling may not develop into a separate, segregated counseling center, but most counselors may come to deal with this problem as a generic one, related to many, if not all, of the problem content of the varieties of counseling. And, of course, the growing speciali-

[36] Russel T. Sharpe, Chairman, et al, Committee on Student Personnel Work, *Financial Assistance for College Students,* American Council on Education Studies, ser. 6, vol. 10, no. 7, Washington, 1946.

[37] Curran, Charles A.: *Counseling in Catholic Life and Education.* New York: The Macmillan Company, 1952.
Hiltner, Seward: *Pastoral Counseling.* Nashville, Tenn.: Abingdon Press, 1949.
Lachapelle, Paul (trans., Dr. G. J. Brady): *Psychiatry for the Priest.* Westminster, Md.: The Newman Book Shop, 1945.
Liebman, Rabbi Joshua Loth (ed.): *Psychiatry and Religion.* Boston: The Beacon Press, 1948.
Oates, Wayne E.: *Religious Dimensions of Personality.* New York: Association Press, 1957.
Outler, Albert C.: *Psychotherapy and the Christian Message.* New York: Harper & Brothers, 1954.
Wise, Carroll A.: *Pastoral Counseling, Its Theory and Practice.* New York: Harper & Brothers, 1951.

[38] E. G. Williamson, "Value Orientation in Counseling," *The Personnel and Guidance Journal,* April, 1958, pp. 520–528.

zation, marriage counseling, is another important counseling area.[39]

Still another type of counseling takes place in the offices of personnel workers who advise student organizations. Because of the intimate and friendly relationship between student leaders and staff members, it would be natural that student leaders would turn to these counselors with personal problems. Many staff members in this field of specialization have little orientation to the clinical psychology of counseling. Ultimately, no doubt, this situation will be corrected, but at the present time activities advisers must perfect their own counseling technique and points of view. It is a real administrative responsibility to use staff training and supervision to upgrade the counseling background and sophistication of activities advisers so that they may identify students who need professional counseling on the one hand, and actually build some counseling emphasis and technique into their own group-related and group-oriented relationships with student leaders. We are not referring to this kind of counseling as a recruiting device for helping students select, or be assigned to, certain activities of interest to them. We are rather referring to counseling relationships which could evolve out of the natural relationships between activities advisers and student leaders.[40] Ptacek described the experience of one university in utilizing these normal relationships to assist student leaders who exhibited the need and desire for counseling, but who were reluctant to come to the regular counseling center since this meant a change of status and position for them—as they perceived their own status. Student leaders do need counseling in many, many instances, but it is not an easy problem for them to become, as they say, a "case number."

There is another area open for exploration in the development of counseling; it has to do with the use of counseling emphases and techniques in helping students select from the rich variety of opportunities in the extracurriculum experiences which will be

[39] Marriage Counseling: A Case Book. New York: Association Press, 1958.

Mudd, E. H.: The Practice of Marriage Counseling. New York: Association Press, 1951.

Skidmore, R. A., Hulda Van S. Garrett, and C. J. Skidmore: Marriage Consulting. New York: Harper & Brothers, 1956.

Vincent, C. E.: Readings in Marriage Counseling. New York: Thomas Y. Crowell Company, 1957.

[40] Paul H. Ptacek, "A University's Attempt to Counsel Student Leaders," Journal of Higher Education, vol. 28, no. 3, pp. 137–142, March, 1957.

educationally productive in their intellectual and social and emotional development. Some of this is an incidental part of general counseling, but there are many other aspects that need exploration.

Students tend to select their activities largely in terms of recreational potential rather than personal development as a counselor would perceive it. Therefore, this type of counseling requires a counselor familiar with all extracurricular activities. Obviously, he could not understand either the adjustment requirements or the potentials available to the student in the extracurriculum if he sat segregated in an isolated counseling center. This suggests that, perhaps, from an administrator's point of view, it might be highly useful if a counselor could play a dual role, serving not only as counselor of individual students but also, off duty, as an adviser to a student organization. In such a dual role there might be some inherent conflicts and contradictions, but offhand one can see many advantages to be gained. The counselor would see students behaving normally in their natural habitats and roles—sometimes quite in contrast with behavior observed in the office across the counselor's desk.

Unfortunately, at the present time there is such a differentiation between the staffs which assist with student affairs and those which counsel individual students that it is difficult to bring about effective coordination. Even the content of professional training differs markedly sometimes so that there is little communication among different types of personnel workers. For instance, if activities advisers were also trained as individual counselors, no doubt they would see many opportunities to counsel, as it were, in the informal group situation. In like manner, if counseling psychologists were trained to some degree in group-work techniques, they too could be more versatile than they are in the clinic setting.

Isolated versus Coordinated Services

We have referred elsewhere to the difficulties of bringing about a desirable coordinating relationship among specialized personnel workers. Perhaps the coordination of different counselors is the most difficult to achieve. Many counselors of the professional type are intensively trained in the individual case method and are, in a sense, professionally indoctrinated to devote themselves almost exclusively to the welfare and improvement of their clientele. They will accept information about their clientele from other sources and will accept referred individuals for specialized treatment. But many are rigid in their reluctance to divulge information they have heard their client reveal in the counseling interview. The traditions and ethics of confidence are highly sensitive professional obligations to such a trained counselor. In many instances, this would appear to be an oversensitive perception of ethics.[41]

No one can argue convincingly that the effectiveness of a counselor's assistance to his client should be sacrificed for other considerations. This is, of course, the heart of counseling. Nevertheless, as we have pointed out repeatedly, coordination is equally imperative. We contend that, instead of withdrawing into an isolated clinic devoted to self-contained development of clients, professional counselors in an academic institution have an equally important, necessary, and ethically imperative responsibility to help upgrade effectiveness of counseling performed elsewhere on the campus. This is our central thesis, and we believe that it is one of the central responsibilities of a personnel administrator. We do not believe that counseling can achieve maximum usefulness in the lives of students if the administrator permits a clinic staff to withdraw from its relationships with other counseling agencies on the campus. Indeed, we believe that counseling cannot be segregated in one clinic without losing great effectiveness. Counseling in some shape or other, effective or ineffective, good or bad, will take place in residences, in fraternities, in sororities, and in rooming houses, as well as in the offices of the faculty.

We believe also that the institutional program of counseling can be so coordinated and maintained as to preserve the necessary confidential relationship in one-to-one interviewing. At the same time, counselors can be used as instrumentalities to maintain and increase a high level of effectiveness of counseling techniques and point of view elsewhere on the campus. This objective, we believe, can be accomplished by continuous staff meetings to examine the possibilities of maintaining two types of counseling responsibilities—to individual clients and to the training-supervision of other counselors who presently may not be as sophisticated professionally as the staff of the central clinic. An objective examination

[41] *Ethical Standards of Psychologists: A Summary of Ethical Principles.* Washington: American Psychological Association, Inc., Washington, 1953, pp. 4–5.

of the proposition that both emphases can be accomplished with mutual reinforcement rather than by exclusion of one or the other is itself one of the most effective administrative devices in finding a solution to this conflict. Continuous staff discussions will lead to desirable change of attitudes and will also reveal ways of accomplishing what at first seemed impossible. This method of staff discussion is, we believe, the principal administrative device to bring desirable coordination among the different counseling centers on a campus of any complexity or size.

Special Administrative Problems and Responsibilities

We have been concerned thus far not so much with analysis and description of the specific content and technique of various kinds of counseling, but rather with identifying the administrative aspects of counseling services. While it is evident that professional counselors require supervision to maintain the quality of their counseling, we are not concerned so much with the content of what they do as counselors. In a preceding section we were engaged in identifying some of the many possible uses, adaptations, or applications of counseling technique and method and point of view in a variety of services. All of these we call "counseling services." We recognize that some of these services could and should be analyzed and described in terms of other kinds of perspectives. But in this section we shall address ourselves to certain institution-wide problems and responsibilities which apply to several, if not all, of the various types of counseling services. We shall describe five such problems and responsibilities.

The *coordination* of the variety of counseling services is as necessary as is the coordination of other personnel services. No one counseling service operates in disregard of the usefulness of another type of counseling service to a particular student. This necessary coordination takes various forms. In the first place the literature is full of illustrations of the first type, namely, *case conferences.* Various undesirable effects sometimes are produced by giving different types of counseling services, or even the same general type of counseling service, to the same individual student without clearance information and correlation of effort. For example, an emotionally disturbed student may need money from the financial office. If individual staff members there are properly alerted, they will seek either to refer the student to the mental hygiene clinic, or at least to inform the clinic about him, with the expectation that there will be coordination of effort between the different types of services. The referral of a student from one type of service to another is a well-established procedure among different types of services. It should be equally clear that this type of *referral coordination* is equally necessary among different types of counseling services as described previously in this chapter. Oftentimes all the counselors who have dealt at first hand with a student come together to pool their information and agree on their common understanding of his needs and also on what each shall do to assist in a coordinated and over-all plan.

Another important factor in coordination is clear. The systematic and continuous dovetailing of services does not occur without continuous and systematic *planning*. It is, therefore, an administrative responsibility to stimulate counselors in various services to congregate frequently, as needed, to plan systematically for the integration and coordination of their services. For example, the financial aid officer needs, through periodic conferences, to learn how he may best identify students in need of referral to the reading clinic or to the mental hygiene clinic. Techniques of identification and referral are not perfected once and for all. They require systematic evaluation, appraisal, and modification. Coordination is, therefore, a continuing responsibility of all members of the staff, and it is the administrator's responsibility to stimulate continuous review and revision of technique.

Coordination proceeds best, and most effectively, when separate staffs of the counseling services understand what each is doing. No counseling service—any more than any other type of service—continues throughout the years without change. Modification of a program requires that those outside the service who still need to use it learn about the changes introduced. This calls for frequent correspondence or joint planning sessions. For this reason, interservice orientation is a continuing administrative responsibility. The *orientation* of all new staff members is a required procedure to facilitate identification and referral of students. Since most personnel staffs are rotated periodically, such an interservice orientation program, at least of a simple sort, would seem to be required. This orientation may take the form of a joint discussion among the service staffs of the common typical problem calling for cross identification and referral. Or it may take the form of a description of the type of services provided in a particular part of the program. But any such orientation is, like coordination, a continuing required program development.

Similarly, each service undergoes modifications which arise from the *continuous incorporation of new techniques and emphases*. The technical counseling staff is constantly learning about new techniques of counseling through reading relevant literature, conducting research, or attending conferences. It would seem to be one of the necessary responsibilities of professional counselors to teach members of the student housing bureau and the financial aid office about new techniques and emphases. Counseling theory, as well as practice, undergoes improvements, we hope, as a result of experience and research. And these new improvements must be transmitted to those who are not necessarily professionally up to date. The needed stimulation and leadership would seem, therefore, to be another administrative responsibility.

And then there is the evident necessity of *research and professional development* through reading, attending conferences, and the like. The involvement of all counseling staffs in joint research programs and projects would seem to be a desirable way of stimulating continued professional development, both of those who serve the counseling clinic and those who perform counseling services elsewhere. This is especially needed by academic advisers, many of whom do not read the current literature about professional counseling and therefore may not have the benefit of current techniques and emphases. Frequent local one-day conferences can be held for counselors, academic as well as professional, covering contemporary points of view, emphases, and technique. And research can be conducted by many types of counselors, who contribute not only counseling data but fresh points of view, in addition to those contributed by professional counselors themselves.

Another administrative responsibility involves stimulating *continuous search for improvement* in counseling techniques throughout the institution. Sometimes this task is a delicate one because certain staff members may not wish to be stimulated to improve their counseling effectiveness. For instance, some academic advisers may be satisfied with their interviewing procedures. And the residential staff may feel that they have sufficient understanding of the handling of emotional disturbances and that they do not need continuously to seek for improvement. Delicate task or not, it becomes a matter of administrative concern when the counseling relationships conducted in one part of an institution—say in the athletic department concerning athletes who are scholastically deficient—are at variance with the counseling techniques used in the counseling center. A similar concern arises when the methods of emotional conditioning used in a fraternity initiation may drive an initiate to the student health service for physical and psychiatric relief of tension. In such instances it becomes a matter of administrative concern that there shall be some upgrading of sophisticated understanding that merely increasing pressure on some students does not necessarily produce scholastic improvement or emotional maturity. In like manner, it becomes a matter of concern that sophomore pledge trainers in charge of initiation shall not repeat the mistakes of the past century—at least not all of them in one semester—with respect to the old, outmoded psychological theory that the only efficient way of achieving manhood is by learning to withstand the psychological and physical pressures and strains invented by ingenious sophomores.

Interstaff coordination and stimulation of professional development, leading to an improvement in counseling technique, calls for high strategy and delicate management. Difficult as the leadership task may be, the personnel staff cannot be satisfied unless there is some leveling of counseling effectiveness and some lessening of the shocking disparity between current and outmoded techniques. Winning the acceptance of the professional counseling staff as the source—an effective and useful source—of keeping up to date in learning all that is known about effective counseling technique is a continuing task in administrative leadership.

Sometimes better understanding of each other's specialties—and therefore of each other's usefulness in dealing with individual clients—would be achieved within the limits of available time if specialists were to *exchange functions*. For example, a clinic counselor could profitably spend some time with a disciplinary counselor, reading his cases, doing some of his initial interviewing, and registering some of the complaints and allegations of misbehavior.

In like manner, a therapist could serve in an activities center, advising student leaders as they plan an organized program. This type of interchange of function has, of course, great limitations because of the need in each function for some specialized knowledge and skill. But in the marginal aspects of each specialization, such an exchange would seem to yield understanding as well as ability to identify students to be referred to the other specialist. Moreover, such an interchange would create more sympathetic understanding of each other's problems and difficulties and provide for cross-fertilization of ideas from one field of knowledge to another. Such special *coordination through interchange* requires encouragement and reward. *Joint research projects* in which counselors and group workers join together in solving problems of dormitory living, group therapy, and the like sometimes produce increased coordination of effort of separate specialized workers. The possibilities of these types of coordination are unlimited.

SUMMARY

In this chapter we have reviewed briefly several important extensions and modifications of counseling, since that specialized service has been adopted to a variety of service relationships with students. Without attenuating the traditional specialization of counseling as it is practiced by counseling psychologists in centers, we identified many adaptations of emphasis, contact problems, and techniques observable in other student personnel services, including faculty academic advising, vocational guidance, mental hygiene counseling, a variety of other forms of counseling, religious counseling, and activity advising.

For the administrator and staff of student personnel services, a central problem is to maintain effective coordination of diverse counseling efforts so that individual students profit from the most effective utilization of available resources of the institution. Such utilization requires not only good intentions to cooperate, but continuous knowledge of available specialties and the habit of exchanging knowledge and services. The creation and maintenance of habits of this type of coordination and cooperation are challenging opportunities for administrative leadership. Seminars, case conferences, joint research projects, friendly and informal personal relationships are but a few of the many available means of coordinating diverse counseling services so that students may benefit from the most effective techniques known to some specialist of the total staff.

CHAPTER 7

The Staff as Consultants to Student Organizations

The innumerable and diverse activities sponsored and conducted by student organizations are fully characteristic and representative of the American collegiate way of living.[1] And the *voluntary charac-ter* of these activities is well established in the history of higher education. They constitute the free, off-duty life of students. Not only an outlet for energy and interest, they also serve an exploratory function with respect to vocational careers, hobbies, and leisure activities. They also serve to balance work and recuperation from the resulting fatigue and boredom. Indeed, one often hears repeated the admonition of many decades standing: First do your studies, then go into activities. In such a sequence, activities seem to in-dicate that motivations may not be adequately exploited and utilized in the classroom and laboratory.

These activities also reflect the established proclivity of all Amer-icans to organize voluntary organizations around common interests and causes. They have long characterized American culture. In-deed, over a century ago these voluntary associations were noted by the perceptive French visitor Tocqueville in the following words: "Americans of all ages, all conditions, and all dispositions constantly form associations."[2] He identified the dynamics of these

---

[1] What we say about relationships with formally organized groups of students pertains also and equally to informal groups unorganized as to name and charter.

[2] Alexis de Tocqueville, *The Republic of the United States of America.* New York: J. & H. G. Langley, 1840, part the second, chap. V, p. 106.

associations as "the art of pursuing in common the object of their common desires." [3]

Lerner argued recently that the "associative impulse is strong in American life" [4] and that this enables us to avoid the excesses of state worship and societal individualism. In support of his argument, he referred to Max Weber's characterization of American "voluntary associations" as "bridging the transition between the closed hierarchical society of the Old World and the fragmented individualization of the New World and he [Weber] saw how crucial a social function these groupings performed in American life." [5]

In these days of derision of "togetherness," we need to exercise balanced judgment in reappraising both individualism and the universal "associative impulse." There are many residual values and virtues to be had in our practice of joining voluntary associations. And it needs to be reasserted that not all members of any group have become standardized parts of the whole. Our culture is indeed richer in depth as the result of our "open society," [6] which permits and encourages the association of our citizens in numerous clubs and associations, bound together by common interests and aspirations to accomplish both personal and societal improvement and betterment.

There are several implications for the student personnel worker in the view of activities as reflections of the typically American voluntary offduty organized associations. To students, the extracurriculum is perceived as their own area of autonomy, belonging to them and not properly subject to supervision by the authorities of an institution. Habitually, the assertion of autonomy is a bone of contention between students and the administration because of the oversimplified assumption that institutional authority is and should be confined to actions taking place on the physical premises of a university. (We deal with the question of the authority of an institution to regulate student affairs on or off campus in Chapter 12; our conclusions need not be stated here.)

[3] *Ibid.*, p. 107.
[4] Max Lerner, *America as a Civilization*. New York: Simon and Schuster, Inc., 1947, p. 630.
[5] *Ibid.*, p. 630.
[6] Karl R. Popper, *The Open Society and Its Enemies*. Princeton, N.J.: Princeton University Press, 1950, p. 169.

Apart from the question of authority to supervise, it is often contended in discussions of the extracurriculum that students learn most readily when they are left alone to regulate their own affairs. This is, of course, an appealing argument based in part upon Dewey's principle of learning by doing. By participating in supervising themselves, it is contended, students learn best the responsibilities of adulthood. While this principle of learning is sound, nevertheless, it is often quoted as justification for acts of irresponsibility as well as those indicative of maturity. Similar pleas for students' freedoms have been made periodically over the centuries with respect to learning in the formal curriculum. We believe that the principle is equally relevant with respect to learning in both curriculum and extracurriculum. Two decades ago Coffman rejected this claim for the pedagogical effectiveness of reorganizing the school so that the "pupil discovers his own needs and then . . . the school gives him what he wants." [7] Coffman also looked upon "the student activities as one of the most liberalizing of the educational forces of the university." But he definitely did not believe in basing either curriculum or extracurriculum completely and solely upon the "passing show" that may vagariously attract the student's "unstable" and superficial interests and attention.[8] In Chapter 12 we shall argue similarly in our discussion of the relationship of students to the authority of an institution of higher education with respect to all aspects of their maturity and learning.

A discussion of one more point will round out our study of this feature of the extracurriculum—its relationships with the institution's authority structure. It is not entirely within the power of an institution to establish a "no limits" rule with regard to its supervision of extracurricular activities (see Chapter 12). While institutions do differ with respect to the tightness of their supervision— from one of oppression to one of indifference—nevertheless, every institution is sensitive to some activities which bring unfavorable publicity, such as destructive behavior of students in moments of relaxation following football games in the autumn or dormitory raids in the spring. In such extreme circumstances, nearly every

---

[7] Lotus Delta Coffman, *Freedom through Education*. Minneapolis: University of Minnesota Press, 1939, p. 15.

[8] *Ibid.*

institution seeks to establish some degree of supervision over some kinds of extracurricular activities.

Still another implication often found in the literature is that in the extracurriculum the student should devote his time to casual and relaxing freedom to do as his natural whim moves him. Closely allied to this claim is the point that useful enthusiasm is possible only when adults are absent and when students are thus able to react naturally. Such a Rousseauan generalization perhaps springs from memories of unpleasant and stifling experiences with adults. But one need not conclude that all adults are thought of as oppressing, and we need not model our extracurriculum either as an entirely self-operated, permissive autonomy or as a protective barrier against oppressive administrators. Other models may be more fruitful.

We also need to examine the implied assumption of the extracurriculum that students are free to join or not join and that those who do not join are uninterested. A thoughtful examination will reveal that student leaders use the same compelling advertising pressures as are found in any community and many of the students who do not join are made to feel inadequate. Moreover, this claim leaves unsolved what to do with those who desire or need to join a certain activity but cannot do so for many personal reasons. Every personnel worker has observed the tragedy of the ineffective student who needs the very experiences which his inadequacy denies to him or for which he is disqualified because of the voluntary election of members to organizations.

We have introduced our discussion of staff in their relationships with student activities by briefly identifying a number of important and relevant characteristics and assumptions of those activities. These characteristics serve to define the relationships of the student personnel worker to those activities. And this is the subject of our chapter, the nature of the responsibilities and functions performed by student personnel workers with respect to the students' extracurricular activities.

SOME GAINS ACHIEVED THROUGH ACTIVITIES

In American higher institutions, we are accustomed to the faculty's traditionally derogatory attitude toward the extracurriculum as essentially anti-intellectual; in consequence, we sometimes forget that, in many ways, it is but a campus expression of a basic component of American culture. As such, it has its virtues, even though its essentially off-duty character may make of it a force opposed to the faculty's desire—that students concentrate all energies upon things intellectual. A number of American commentators on our culture have appraised certain advantageous features of American voluntary associations; we may think in parallel terms of the extracurricular activities of students. Grace Coyle identified a number of these.[9] She spoke of the voluntary associations as yielding certain essential advantages in a democratic society. They include opportunities for social contacts and relationships. Our often impersonal mass industries seem to produce the kind of frustrated personalities which require "freshening" through personalized relationships in neighborhood environments and through membership in voluntary associations.[10]

Coyle also referred to American leisure activities as desirable for the free expression of culture interests. For identifying another gain achieved through activities and associations, she referred to the desirable "creation of decentralized foci of power which develops around conflicting interests." In contrast with cultures in which there is monolithic concentration of authority, in America we distribute authority and power—at least the power of public influence and opinion—through the actions and pressures of a multitude of organizations. We need to note carefully that many of these organizations not only pressure for selfish group interests, but they also help promote the general welfare through charitable projects involving voluntary off-duty contributions of time and effort, as well as money. Thus, in nongovernmental and extralegal activities, much human betterment and improvement is achieved by voluntary organizations.

When viewed in the light of parallel structure and content, the organized activities of students are not irrelevant to the broad mission of a societal institution such as a university. While they may sometimes encourage anti-intellectualism or at least non-

[9] Grace Longwell Coyle, *Group Experience and Democratic Values.* New York: Women's Press, 1948.

[10] See also exposition of this social philosophy in Elton Mayo, *The Social Problems of an Industrial Civilization.* Boston: Harvard University Bureau of Business Research, 1945.

intellectual interests and activities (see Chapter 13), such a deplorable situation provides us with a challenge to see whether we can infuse intellectual content into these voluntary activities without stultifying them and rigidifying them into ritual observances.

THE STAFF AND ACTIVITIES

In other chapters we have discussed two principal roles of the student personnel worker: (1) maintaining for student clientele professional services, such as counseling and financial assistance; and (2) administering these services with regard to such management functions as selecting and employing staff members, upgrading professional training, integrating professional services with the total educational program in relationships with student clientele, and similar functions. In this present chapter we turn to another significant role of the staff, especially the administrative members, in their staff-leadership relationships with organized groups, fraternities, student government councils, dormitory councils, political action groups, religious organizations, and others.

We shall not discuss the use of techniques of leadership or management of small groups by either staff or student leaders of groups. We have illustrated the use of many such techniques in the chapters describing institutional case-incidents concerning judiciary functions, academic freedom, consultation, and other student issues. Moreover, the ever-growing repertoire of group-dynamics techniques is adequately described by other authors and need not be duplicated here.[11]

We digress from our thesis to justify going beyond traditional techniques of group dynamics to explore new roles of staff members. We conclude that much of the discussion of the dynamics of small groups begins with three assumptions:

1. Most or a majority of the members are of good will, being motivated to help the group accomplish commonly defined tasks,

[11] Cartwright, Dorwin, and Alvin Zander (eds.): *Group Dynamics.* Evanston, Ill.: Row, Peterson & Company, 1953.

Hare, A. Paul, Edgar F. Borgata, and Robert E. Bales (eds.): *Small Groups.* New York: Alfred A. Knopf, Inc., 1955.

Hoffmann, Randall W., and Robert Plutchik: *Small-group Discussion in Orientation and Teaching.* New York: G. P. Putnam's Sons, 1959.

Laird, Donald A., and Eleanor C. Laird: *The New Psychology for Leadership.* New York: McGraw-Hill Book Company, Inc., 1956.

then to proceed to learn cooperative relationships in the group endeavor.

2. For the most part, the group contains within itself resources of motivations, skills, ideas, and competence sufficient to accomplish its adopted objectives. The task is to organize for accomplishing these objectives.

3. Whatever objectives the group adopts as its own are sufficient for the group's program of activities. The wider institutional context of the group is not as relevant as is the group's perception of those relationships and of its own internal motivations and interests.

There are numerous instances, it seems to us, in which these conditions are such that the organized group activity can proceed according to the best understanding of group dynamics. But our experiences in student personnel work in an educational institution lead us to reexamine these assumptions with respect to many organized student activities. We begin our operations as a staff—in some instances and some situations—at a prior point of relationship to the group. We consider the needs of some members, the many nonparticipating students who need group experience, who lack skills in organizing as well as content thought of by the group or accepted by it as an organization program. The institutional context of many of these activities requires, in the interest of the nonmember students as well as the institution, that there be some supervision in the background, at least. A relevant example is discussed later; in this instance, we seek to make a convincing case for persuading and assisting students in reforming the extracurriculum by increasing its contribution to the intellectual development of students (see Chapter 13). One need not emphasize that many of these voluntary activities exist at a low level of intellectual content; surely, after decades of such functioning, it would not be thought an improper, unfair intrusion for a member of the personnel staff to intervene in the voluntary activity to change its content by persuading students of the virtue of such a change. In a second example, we have illustrated some of the techniques used to persuade students to substitute judiciary responsibility for traditional irresponsibility in the extracurricular activities (see Chapter 11). These two examples illustrate what we mean by starting our discussion at a prior point of assumption with respect to the motivations and *expertise* of the groups. We are not arguing that only staff members have good ideas for programs or that only staff members can supervise group activities effectively. In the case of the conduct-control situation, we were attempting to persuade students to *help* the institution "police" its own student activities; this serves as an illustration of the integration of functions that our experience has led us to favor.

We proceed to examine in this chapter some special roles, responsibilities, and opportunities of the student personnel staff in connection with students as members of organized groups. We will be concerned not so much with the traditional role of group adviser as with ways in which the staff may properly (we will define the word) display, introduce, and suggest new content, emphases, and objectives for the group to review as possible additions to or substitutions in the organized programs and activities. As the group reviews and decides what to do, what is the proper role of the staff? What new emphases and objectives may need to be introduced for group consideration and possible adoption? This is the topic for our discussion.

THE STAFF MEMBER AS CONSULTANT-LEADER

Each member of the staff may properly emphasize, suggest, and demonstrate ways of action to be considered by student leaders in the conduct of a group or organization in his *staff-leadership capacity*.[12] The content of this staff-leadership role consists of suggesting, for students' review, relevant objectives, purposes, and program content which supplement the things planned by groups and their leaders as the groups' organized programs of activities.

We conclude from our experiences that the staff may properly play an active role in its relationship with student organizations and with their elected leaders, both in planning organizational activities and in conducting their affairs. We believe this active role as a

[12] McGregor et al., have described the comparable *staff* (not *line*) relationship played by technical consultants (psychologists and others) in industrial organizations who, in this case, concentrated upon the assignment of aiding top management and executives to create and "maintain healthy human relationships" in the organization. McGregor et al., "The Consultant Role and Organizational Leadership: Improving Human Relations in Industry," *Journal of Social Issues*, vol. 4, no. 3, 1948.

consultant has been understressed, even obscured, by overemphasis upon the traditional passive role of adult group advisers. We shall limit this chapter to an exploration of the staff's role in serving as technical consultants to student organizations which maintain voluntary membership. In other chapters we have stressed a second staff responsibility, namely, administrative review of students' organizational programs. These two duties, often conflicting as they do, will be appraised in their relationships, one with the other.

The concept of dynamic leadership, as a responsibility of staff members, is not restricted to administrators of the personnel program. Moreover, the staff's role is not limited to the traditional administrative responsibility of supervising the group to the end that the institution's public relations or other interests are undamaged and its regulations fully observed by the group. It is, or course, clear that some staff workers must, in the nature of university administration, carry responsibility for helping student organizations conduct the kinds of programs which are clearly congruent with the nature of the educational enterprise. Nevertheless, this policing function need not, in any serious way, interfere with the discharge of other functions that are advisory and educational in content and emphasis.

And staff members who serve in the capacity of advisers to student organizations should, we believe, feel free to make suggestions as to program emphases and content. The staff may also suggest new content of public relations programs in behalf of the university or of the student body at large. They may also suggest improvements in the conduct of student meetings and new ways of financing programs and similar important matters.

Personnel specialists in general—not only those trained in group activities—have available many worthwhile and helpful suggestions which they can transmit to student organizations in a leadership capacity and relationship. For example, specialists in charge of loans and scholarships may profitably suggest to student leaders that projects be adopted for collecting or earning money for scholarships as part of the organization's democratic-leadership responsibility to students and to the institution. Similarly, those in charge of discipline should give leadership to student government in fraternities, dormitories, and other organizations to assist students in discharging each group's democratic responsibility for the behavior control of its own members in the interest of the group, as well as of the institution (see Chapter 11). And residential counselors should cultivate the teaching role of stimulating free and open discussion of the sensitive and controversial issues which divide the campus from time to time, *including* annual orderly review of dormitory charges and costs.

These are but a few illustrations of the many rich opportunities for leadership by student personnel workers in their relationships with individual student leaders and with organized groups. In no way does the exercise of this leadership responsibility deprive students and their leaders of responsibility for final selection of the program to be conducted by the organization. Rather do these staff members serve as resource persons to identify—from their own experiences with student clientele—many worthwhile things which could be considered and perhaps adopted by the group as its own program. The choice is that of the group, but the staff member, in his capacity as teacher, may profitably and legitimately suggest many possible things for review by the organization.

We have argued consistently in opposition to the assignment of a passive, advisory role to the staff in its relationship with organized student enterprises. We readily grant that the purpose of the institution is to help each and every student develop self-control from within himself as an individual and through his responsible group membership. But we contend that self-management can develop also through relationships with the staff, which exercises a leadership role in respect to such matters. This is not even to argue that all students must become members of some group if they are to develop a measure of self-discipline and control. Worthwhile learning can and does take place with minimal assistance from teachers of any type. Rather are we arguing that a richness of possible development through group membership shall be so clearly evident to students that many of them will be faced with possible choices which they then may or may not accept. If they do choose to accept group membership, then their development and integration as individuals in effective roles would seem to be a rich opportunity for effective leadership-teaching by the personnel staff. In other chapters we have explored the opportunities for staff relationships, or counseling, with individual students—

apart from any group membership. We are here concerned with different types of learning through associations and relationships between students and the staff members who serve as consultants to organized student groups.

TO ADVISE OR SUPERVISE?

The student personnel worker may be called upon to play one or more of several roles in his relationship with organized student groups:

1. He may be asked to advise *when asked* by students regarding their own voluntary activities.

2. He may serve as a *joint partner* with students concerning programs and activities which are both voluntary student activities and also an organized part of the university's program. For example, certain features and phases of organized orientation are both student and university activities. We have also referred to other joint activities, such as judiciary functions, supervision of finances of student organizations, and others—all functions in which the university's role and interest require close supervision.

3. He may serve as a *consultant* in determining what suggestions and reactions students may have to the institution's own programs, such as the establishment of costs and rates for dormitory occupancy.

4. He may serve a *leadership* role, suggesting and urging adoption of new objectives by an organization.

5. He may serve as a *technical consultant,* having *expertise* superior to that possessed by students and helpful in improving programs geared to their own objectives and achieved through their own activities.

Historically, the faculty adviser has played a passive role except when students' activities and programs brought disrepute to the institution or in some other way were objectionable and non-acceptable; in such case, the role of *supervisor* was adopted. Most of us tend to consider the passive role of the adviser as the best role in terms of the voluntary nature of students' activities. But this is not necessarily true, especially in those instances in which staff has technical competence usable to help the group improve the quality and effectiveness of its program, both for the institution's objectives and for benefit and the satisfaction of individual members.

All forms of leadership relationships with organized groups of students involve a variety of techniques of relationships. Some day we may be sufficiently wise to identify the particular techniques and relationships usable in each separate type of relationship. On the other hand, perhaps situations and relationships do not occur neatly categorized as to the type of project and program. Or perhaps techniques are interchangeable and transferable and relationships may be structured in other categories than types of programs. That is, relationships may be structured in terms of the nature of the relationships between staff member and student rather than in terms of the type of program sponsored. Because of age differences and differences in technique and technical background and *expertise*, it may be that the relationship which we call "adviser" actually has served to mask the hidden authority of the faculty adviser. McGregor[13] analyzed the role of the staff consultant in a commercial organization, largely concentrating on the psychological needs of the managers in their work capacities.[14] McGregor indicated how the psychologist, serving as a technical consultant on problems of human relationships, could play a staff role in improving these relationships. Since student personnel workers are essentially educators with respect to the development of students in their full personality and capacity, perhaps we need to rethink and reexamine the nature of our relationships to organized student groups and especially to student leaders of these groups. We seem to be reluctant to discuss overtly the psychology of student leaders, even though it has been clearly established that they have peculiar types of student problems of relationships and personal development.[15] Grace Coyle has discussed another, but related, role of the staff in the voluntary student organizations—the role of the executive secretary who helps the group crystallize its objectives and plan to meet them through program techniques.[16]

[13] *Ibid.*
[14] *Ibid.*
[15] Paul Ptacek, "A University's Attempt to Counsel Student Leaders," *Journal of Higher Education*, vol. 28, no. 3, pp. 137–142, March, 1957. Reprinted.
[16] Coyle, *op. cit.*, p. 154.

DIFFICULTIES IN INTEGRATING ROLES

It is clear that the attempted integration of supervisory and advisory roles is often confusing and sometimes productive of conflict. Students do not always readily perceive which "uniform" the staff member is wearing in a particular situation—that of policeman or friend—if we may borrow the students' own characterizations of their perception of these two roles.

The question arises: How may relationships of staff to the student organizations be organized? On the one hand, advisory relationships, defined as voluntary, may be separated from supervisory and clearly labeled. When pressed too far, this form of relationship would segregate in the office of one or two staff members the unpleasant supervisory policing functions and would leave other staff members free to develop a voluntary relationship which could be severed at the will of the students and which would be purely advisory. Such a possible segregation proceeds on the assumption that voluntary advice is incongruent with policing and with the judicious use of administrative authority. Almost universally, the use of authority is thought of as always triggering resistance in students, fearful of authority figures, who demand the right to make mistakes —at whatever cost to the institution and individuals involved.

On the other hand, the advisory and supervisory relationships may be integrated in some form in the same staff, even at the risk of confusing the two roles in many instances and of triggering resistance. We have argued for similar integration with respect to individual misbehavior and disciplinary counseling (see Chapter 5).

Concerning the integration of supervisory and advisory relationships, our argument proceeds from the same assumption; one objective of an educational institution is to teach a more mature concept of authority as a substitute for the adolescent's resistance to it, his fear of its being necessarily evil and unreasonable. We repeat Coyle's relevant admonition that "all adolescents must come to terms with authority." [17]

Such an attempt at integration, while difficult, does avoid the evils of segregation of authority symbols and also avoids the associa-

[17] *Ibid.*, p. 120.

tion of the concept of authority with unpleasant negation of what students want to do. Moreover, the integration of the two roles may serve to prevent the occurrence of arbitrary and repressive authority which is viewed as always saying "no" to everything students want to do. And such an attempt at integration avoids the popularity of the glad-hand type of relationship, expressed in the admonition from some faculty members, "Let students do what they want to do. Be democratic, say 'yes'. Be the servant of the students. Give advice only when asked." Now the segregation of the glad-hand type of relationship may be satisfactory to some individuals, but it always leaves to someone else the disagreeable task of saying "no" when "no" must be said in the institution's own interest and in the interest sometimes of the individual student. Moreover, we have made the case elsewhere that adults are necessary to learning of some kind and that, as a teacher, a staff member may serve an important role in helping the student learn to live with authority and to find freedom within authority, and at the same time he may improve a program in the interests of the students, as well as the institution. The concept of *partnership in learning* requires integration of the two relationships with students and a comparable status of authority for each of the partners. We therefore believe that it is a more mature concept of the administration of student personnel work for the regulatory and supervisory functions—inevitably a requirement of the institution—to be combined with the advisory relationship of a helpful partner.

A large measure of integration of roles may be achieved through straightforward, honest explanations of which role is being played and why. This will avoid confusion and build a staff member's confidence and sense of justification in adopting a particular role. We also favor a continuous educational program of explanation of of authority for each of the partners. We therefore believe that it is not at all an easy or popular task to remind students that supervision is necessary, but the point can be stated in such a way as to win their respect and some acceptance and recognition. Moreover, such straightforward explanations continuously remind the students that we are sympathetic with them and that, through our empathy, we modify our supervisory role so as to make it more permissive. And, finally, integrating roles may be demonstrated perceptibly by justi-

THE STAFF AS CONSULTANTS TO STUDENT ORGANIZATIONS   227

fied exceptions to the rules when enforcement would be unfair and severe to individuals or to groups.

In some instances, such a practice of exceptions in application of rules will be characterized as vacillating and confusing because students will receive variable decisions from period to period. We are reminded that sometimes students seem to require rigid consistency in the enforcement of supervisory rules. In certain circumstances, they may not favor or desire modification of rules, even when it would be unjust and unfair and too severe to enforce the rules in a rigid manner. They seem to fear variability more than consistency. Even at the risk of such immature desire for rigidity in established limits, one can still discuss with students the necessity for some authority and supervisory apparatus, since the need for them is amply demonstrated whenever the institution's sensitive spots are disturbed by students. Therefore, it is better, we conclude, to illustrate and demonstrate a benign and judiciously modifiable authority rather than one that is stubborn and easily and unpredictably provoked.

PROGRAM REVIEW AS A PROCEDURE
OF STAFF RELATIONSHIPS

EXHIBIT A

UNIVERSITY OF MINNESOTA
Office of the Dean of Students
Student Activities Bureau

October 2, 1957

MEMORANDUM

TO: Mary Pearson

FROM: Paul A. Bloland

SUBJECT: A Program in Advising Small Groups

The staff of the Student Activities Bureau has been traditionally organized in area assignments. The over 300 groups have been pulled together in more or less functional groups according to common characteristics, i.e., political and social action groups, recreation and hobby groups, and assigned to the staff of professional advisers. Each of these advisers carried one or two major areas of responsibility, such as the academic fraternities, All-University Congress, etc., to which he devoted much of his advising attention. He was also assigned a miscellaneous number of the small special interest groups.

Until several years ago, no systematic attempt was made to maintain any sort of liaison with these groups. About two years ago, however, the so-called "Program Review" technique was developed and each member of the staff was asked to try to have at least one annual such formal contact with each of the groups in his area.

In evaluating the technique, we found that it did result in more contacts with these small groups by members of our staff although it still fell short of the complete coverage goal we had set for ourselves. These contacts were perceived by students as being positive and helpful and resulted in further consultation of our office by the student leader involved. We found also that it was very difficult for a staff member to carry one or two major area assignments and still find the time for program reviews not perceived by them to be related to these assignments.

Because we felt that it was important for these small groups to receive some attention, a special assignment was established by the Director with the approval of the Dean of Students. It was decided to assign one person to establish a program involving these groups. This program would include some experimentation with various techniques while providing a Bureau contact with all of these groups.

The detailed group assignment will probably include the following categories of organizations: scholarship and achievement groups, some college boards, departmental and professional, music and fine arts groups, recreational and hobby groups. These groups have been characterized in the past by minimal contacts with the Student Activities Bureau, a limited understanding of their responsibilities as recognized student groups, stereotyped programs with few new ideas or emphases, a strong academic or professional interest, financing problems, and membership problems.

The adviser in this new area would have the following duties:

1. To hold at least one formal program review before Spring quarter with each of the groups listed under her area assignment.
2. To experiment with and evaluate the program review technique.
3. To set up procedures on scheduling, recording of content, evaluation, use of forms, content of the reviews, etc.
4. To investigate the use of the conference-type program review with several groups included at one time.
5. To consider the need for sponsoring SAB conferences on small-group problems. Leaders from a number of groups might be invited to discuss mutual problems. They might all be from one interest area such as hobby groups, recreational groups, etc.
6. To investigate the possibility of using student assistants to advise these groups. See the *Personnel and Guidance Journal* for October 1956.
7. To consider how the interest card might be used to form new special interest groups.
8. To explore ways of working with the various college boards and of attempting to establish some liaison between special interest groups in a particular college and the respective college board.
9. To maintain tabulation sheets and complete records on the various aspects

of the program. I would like to have all documents come to me, including the write-ups of the program reviews.

Other ideas may suggest themselves and certain of these ideas will prove to be unfeasible, but I think that we can learn a lot about the technique and these groups this year.

As soon as the staff assignments are arranged, you should begin to transfer the folder for these groups to your office so that you can begin to go through them and refile them. In the meantime, you should begin to learn about the program review, sitting in on some and doing some under supervision.

The program is to be worked out under the direct supervision of Dr. Johnson with Judy Harris assisting when her duties permit.

The staff charged with responsibility in activities faces periodically a problem in maintaining relationships with some student leaders and with some student organizations. One wishes to make oneself so useful that students will come and ask for help in developing their programs and in conducting them. But occasionally a student officer will vaunt his independence and emphasize the voluntary nature of his organization by systematically, rather than absentmindedly, avoiding such professional advice. Shall the staff member invite the student in for an interview and shall this be done regularly and systematically?

The arguments for and against invited relationships are many and relevant. Nevertheless, the staff has two options: (1) waiting for incidents; or (2) systematizing relationships on the assumption that peaceful, nonincident relationships of a friendly and helpful nature will prevent or reduce the severity and disruptive nature of incidents, or permit more constructive and effective recovery of orderliness and educational good when unpreventable incidents do occur (see Chapters 8, 10, and 12).

Our experience with both types of situation leads us to favor a systematic program review at least once a year with student leaders of all organizations. Such a systematic interview can be a friendly one and need not arouse resistance. Moreover, a systematic schedule of interviews keeps the staff alert to developments on a large, complex campus. On a small campus, a staff member usually knows all that goes on of an organized character; this is not true of an increasing number of large institutions. Therefore, periodic interviews involving program review of a general character has many advantages over the episodic-incident review of a program failure or program mistake. In the first place, the practice establishes the *normalcy* of the relationship itself. By and large, students come to do the things that are expected of them in an educational institution, without becoming abject institutional company men. Also, the twentieth-century concept of seeking professional advice on personal problems and those of one's organization is as much a part of our democratic way of life as is voting for our leaders. The periodic review also avoids defining the relationship solely in terms of conflict and incidents, with the attendant tensions and the risk of developing a tradition of feuding with the administration. It is true that many students and some staff members will see no relevancy in a program review when nothing has gone wrong. But this attitude in itself illustrates the regrettable time-place binding of the staff's relationship with an incident. In an educational institution, the happy relationships are to be desired not only as a quality of human relationship, but also in the effort to avoid incidents through the normalcy of program planning.

In program reviews, held systematically, there is an opportunity to suggest new emphases in building program traditions, and sometimes the staff members may suggest more effective ways of achieving a program objective of a student organization. Most student leaders like to collect all sorts of suggestions and therefore voluntarily seek ideas from many sources. There is no reason why the personnel staff should not serve as such a resource, along with faculty advisers of the same organization.

Moreover, the periodic review makes policing a more happy relationship between helpful friends and thereby avoids the tension of the feud with adults to which some adolescents are prone. When the supervisor of activities must intervene, he does it then on a friendly basis which makes action and discussion possible.

Perhaps the most significant usefulness of the periodic review is that it establishes the normalcy of the use of *expertise* in program development and therefore serves to substitute for the traditional autonomy of the extracurriculum. Just as many new student leaders each year invent new program ideas, so, in similar way, may staff members serve as inventors or as sources of communication of ideas from other campuses, at least.

By means of Exhibits A and B, we illustrate one university's use of the staff as one means of strengthening the integration of diverse student organizations into the university community. This

EXHIBIT B

STUDENT ACTIVITIES BUREAU
PROGRAM REVIEW CHECKLIST

(°—check our records before interview)

Group_____

Members_____Nat. Affil._____

(Interview participants)

1. Review *staff functions, adviser's role, services* (financial, publications, leadership training, etc.):

2. *Program content evaluation* (identify particularly for educational-intellectual content):

    Problems:

3. Social Service: Present projects.

    Participation in projects of other groups.

    ° Possible projects.

    Approval of off-campus solicitation of funds. Reporting *all* projects.

4. *Social-recreational Program:* Extent?

    Registration procedure. Possible improvement.

°5. *Possible all-campus programs of interest:*

6. *Scholastic eligibility of members:* Explain policy relating to this group, need for advance check, exception procedure.

°7. *Organization's Finances:* Balance_____Date last transaction_____
    How raise money?
    How spend it?

°8. *Verify officers names and addresses, faculty adviser.* Any members on scholastic probation?

°9. *Office and phone of officers:*

°10. *Required records missing:* Membership and officer list, constitution, official recognition, financial supervision, other_____

11. *Constitution:* Need revision?   Revised without SCSA review?

12. *Approvals:* Explain (social, off-campus, special program, film, publicity, rooms, speakers, public address apparatus, other_____)
    Any not using?

13. *Other items:*

Follow-up letter?_____Ticklers?_____Date:_ _____Adviser:_____)

is *not* a policing relationship but is supplementary to the special and often restricted interests of faculty advisers. The staff serves on the one hand to bring them back into the total student community through suggesting some relevant projects and at the same time to strengthen their preserved relationships with the university as a whole. Students as well as faculty often become highly departmentalized and compartmentalized in their specialized education. We believe that such narrow specialization is, if pursued too narrowly, as educationally unsound in the extracurriculum as it is in the formal curriculum.

Exhibit A. Memorandum outlining the objectives and procedures used in annual program reviews with small groups, usually those whose membership clusters around the common interest of major or vocational studies, avocation, or political-action motivation.

Exhibit B. The interview form used as a guide in structuring, loosely, the conference.

Exhibit C. The dictated report of such an annual program review, this one with an art honorary (scholastic) organization.

EXHIBIT C

UNIVERSITY OF MINNESOTA
Office of the Dean of Students
Student Activities Bureau

MEMORANDUM

TO: Files

FROM: Elinor McGrew, Student Activities Bureau Adviser

SUBJECT: Conference with Shirlee Clark, president of Delta Phi Delta, and Glenn Janson, corresponding secretary

Program Review for Delta Phi Delta, Art Honorary

Membership: The group has about 30 members at present. During any quarter of their junior year, art students who have attained a "B" average in art and have an over-all 1.5 academic average may be nominated by faculty members or by other students for membership in Delta Phi Delta. At present there are about 30 members in the group. The feeling of the group is that this late selection is unfortunate and that the rapid turnover of membership is detrimental to the group. They are subject to national rulings, however, and, while the point has been discussed in national sessions, there is no indication the restriction will be relaxed. (Members pay dues of $1.00 per quarter. Of their $15.00 initiation dues, $3.00 goes to the local group—the remainder covers cost of the pin and dues to national.)

Purpose: Membership in the organization is an honor that represents recognition nationally since the group does function actively nationally. The two members with whom I consulted felt that the group provided a "sense of belonging" to its members—people who are usually quite highly individualistic and seldom joiners. They said that the meetings (held 3 Tuesday evenings per month) are primarily social. They handle general business, but are not highly structured. They have two faculty advisers, Dr. Reid Hastie and Mrs. Jo Rollins, who work closely with the group.

There is also an alumni chapter of Delta Phi Delta composed of about 60 members in the Twin City area. This group is active. There is some interchange between the groups, but they function independently.

Projects: Annually during Spring quarter the group has sponsored an *art show* to exhibit work done by members at the Rainbow Cafe. This spring they showed Mrs. Rollins's work. This has always been successful. They mentioned plans to bring the show to campus (Northrup or the Union).

They also sponsor a *Studio Tour* during Spring quarter. Open houses are scheduled from 2–6 PM at studios of Twin Cities artists (this year on May 5th). Tickets costing $1.00 are on sale at downtown ticket offices and are sold by faculty and alums. Money earned from this project goes into a scholarship fund that is publicized and administered by the group. This was a $75.00 scholarship to cover costs of materials and supplies last year. (I suggested coordinating this selection with the Bureau of Loans and Scholarships—thus centralizing such programs and providing an opportunity for having the scholarship listed in the Cap and Gown Day Bulletin).

A third project the group had was a *sale of original Christmas Cards.* This last year, arrangements were made, but the project was not completed. In the past it has been a successful program.

We discussed the relationship of the group to the rest of the campus. Traditionally, the group has functioned internally in an area isolated from the campus. I raised the point of their being in an ideal position to contribute specialized information to the campus at large—suggesting at least one social service project yearly—perhaps in addition to their scholarship program. Their decision to bring their art show to the campus will contribute in this area. Before leaving, they did comment that they had never thought of the University in terms of a community concept. They had never considered giving anything to the campus as a group or as individuals. This is an area they will explore. They indicated that the conference was very informative to them.

CONTENT AND EMPHASES IN THE
STAFF-CONSULTANT ROLE

In the present chapter we wish to accomplish two objectives: (1) to expound the point that an active leadership-teaching role of staff members is congruent with the social philosophy underlying students' voluntary activities; and (2) to mention briefly certain content of that teaching role which may need to be emphasized by the staff. Having made the first point in preceding paragraphs, we now turn to the second. We will review a number of emphases, often underemphasized in some extracurricular activities, which seem to us to be appropriate content of the educational role of the staff adviser to student organizations. We believe, as the result of our own experiences and those of other administrators in other institutions, that it is both our opportunity as advisers to students and our responsibility as educators to assist students in learning to build these and other emphases into their free and voluntary organized activities.

When Students Fail to Discharge Responsibilities

We have referred frequently to a phrase, "the right to make our own mistakes," to indicate a point of view of considerable significance and widespread adoption. In a teaching institution, of course, we anticipate that students will make errors in their learning; in a sense, one can argue that making errors is a prerequisite to learning, since learning is the elimination of errors. A student enterprise which does not run the risk of error is unknown. As long as students are in activities, there will be risks of error and errors, some of which may prove to be embarrassing or even harmful to the institution. A compulsion for security would lead an administrator to wish for a studentless campus, thereby avoiding all such possibility of error. Short of such a psychotic state of isolation from students, one must be content with a loosely defined zone of permitted and anticipated error. And this is, of course, an ever-changing zone, since it reflects and is determined by the expectations of many segments of the faculty, parents, and general public.

In determining the risks that are to be anticipated and permitted in student affairs, one has constantly to remind oneself that the institution is a hardy and vigorous one and can indeed survive many shocks. One also repeats the dictum that the education of students proceeds always with certain risks. All one can do is to minimize them, not hope to eliminate them. By extension of this reasoning, we are led to make efforts as a staff to educate students concerning the risks of error and failure as a step in avoiding them. This is a teaching function comparable in content and emphasis to the classroom teacher's identification of errors habitually made by students in their examinations. The teacher directs his efforts and emphases to the correction of these anticipated errors. In like manner, in the extracurriculum students can be taught to anticipate error and failure and to make some efforts at self-control in avoiding them. Generally we think of this kind of warning and alerting only in terms of bad publicity which follows dormitory raids, carousals, and other forms of highly visible and highly audible behavior. But there are other risks and other failures which have institutional significance, as well as consequences for students themselves. For example, in one institution, failure of a student effort to collect money for charitable purposes may well produce criticism from the community and thereby sensitize the institution's staff to the need for avoiding this mistake another year. The institution's community standing is, in part, determined by the amount of money students raise for charitable purposes, especially in those community drives which enlist the efforts of all citizens. Should a staff member sit idly by and permit such a failure? The answer will vary, of course, from institution to institution and from situation to situation; for the most part, effective teaching efforts will serve to minimize the risks of such mistakes. There comes a point, however, at which the staff member must make up his mind whether the program must be manned by staff to replace students who have neglected their obligations or have shown lack of the *expertise* required to put on an effective program. At this point, determination must be made as to whether it is profitable for the students to make the mistake and whether the institution can bear the cost. In the case of a charity drive with reverberations in the community, the staff may have to step in and, in part, make it a staff drive. In other instances, the failure of a program provides the staff with a seminar topic to teach methods of avoiding such failures. Variability in reactions to anticipated failure of a student activity or program would seem to be a better operating principle than rigid adherence to students' freedom to make mistakes on the one hand, or to the staff member's compulsive obligation to supervise students' programs.

Some Borrowed Methods of Change in Relationship

Repeatedly we have referred to the conflict type of relationship between individual student and the institution (see Chapter 5). Later we shall discuss a similar type of relationship involving organized groups (see Chapter 11). We will also discuss one aspect of this relationship, the authority of the institution, a development which has a troublesome and confused history (see Chapter 12). In the present section we wish to explore some ways of easing and transforming the conflict relationship into a more harmonious and constructive one. We contend that such efforts at transformation are basic responsibilities of the staff—all members of the student personnel staff—and are not restricted either to those who administer discipline or to those who advise and supervise organized students and their activities.

We can profit, in our exploration of peace-making techniques, from the findings of social psychology. For instance, in discussing the learnings of psychology relevant to statesmanship and international conflict and crises, Blake reviewed many experimentally derived methods of resolving intergroup disputes and conflicts. He named four ways of terminating such conflict:[18]

1. Isolate the groups and eliminate contact between them.
2. Unite them into one group, even if it means cracking their heads together.
3. Join the contest, let the more powerful annihilate the weaker.
4. Maintain the identify of each group and through functional relations seek resolution by interaction, discussion and decision.

If we substitute the words "administration" and "students," or "fraternities" and "student government," for the word "intergroup," then some illuminating generalizations may be made and some helpful "ways of relieving differences between contending groups" may be derived. To be sure, the administration may not wish or be able to perceive itself as a contending group. But it is certainly thus perceived by faculty and students. Indeed, it would be more precise to describe it perceived as an entrenched and aggressive group! And students, emboldened by charismatic certainty like the youthful St. George battling the wicked dragon, may also experience reluctance in compromising with a less than complete routing of the entrenched administration.

If these impedimenta can be cast aside or avoided adroitly, then social psychology has much to suggest in the way of staff techniques

[18] Robert R. Blake, "Psychology and the Crises of Statesmanship," *The American Psychologist,* vol. 14, pp. 87–94, February, 1959.

to be employed in the development of effective working relationships. In later sections we discussed similar points in terms of "normal" relationships of staff. These staff members do not usually carry administrative powers and therefore they are not perceived as a contending group.

In our present discussion the intergroup conflict occurs because the administration is perceived as making the rules and restrictions which bind and limit freedom of students. It is the administration that must be overpowered if rules are to be cast out—hence the conflict situation and the relevancy of social psychology. While Blake was discussing organized states and groups of equivalent status, we do not distort his findings by applying them to the conflict situation sometimes associated with rule making and enforcing in universities. Blake generalized as follows:[19]

. . . the most appropriate way found was that of confronting contending groups with a common problem which could be resolved only through their joint efforts. Once a superordinate goal was accepted as a challenge by high status members of both sides then mutual efforts by individuals . . . became more common. Contending groups started to pull together, and contacts between members turned to positive purposes instead of serving as occasions for accusations and mutual invective.

Blake goes on, referring to research by Sherif, to identify two conditions necessary to the success of the use of a superordinate goal: a desire by all parties to seek a solution; and an agreement on a single definition of the problem developed by both sides, apart from stated preferred solutions. Willerman has described an experiment of such use of superordinate goals in which fraternities, feuding with a university about conduct autonomy, after prolonged "gripe" sessions, shifted their perception of those relationships and joined in the evolution of a joint judiciary partnership.[20]

Blake also referred to still another method of resolving conflict which has relevancy for our situation. This is to adapt therapeutic techniques to the problem of relationships between groups. The unit of therapy becomes, in Blake's terms, the "competing groups in relationships with one another."

[19] *Ibid.*, p. 92.
[20] Ben Willerman, "Changing Attitudes of Fraternity Members toward University Control," *The Personnel and Guidance Journal,* vol. 37, pp. 542–550, April, 1959.

Again some reluctance may be experienced on the part of both students and administration in perceiving themselves in terms of therapy, especially if either group maintains the rigid feeling of righteous certainty that motivates crusading reformers or entrenched defenders of law and order. But if such obstacles can be overcome, then modified therapy can contribute to resolving conflicts of ideas and dissipating attendant emotions. All in all, we believe that these generalizations from an adjacent academic department will prove useful in reconstructing the perennial conflict of structure and function, administration and students, to meaningful learning of ways of resolving conflicts appropriate in an institution of higher learning. In several chapters of this book which give accounts of incidents illustrative of administrative techniques, the reader can readily identify those points at which some student editor, student leader, central administrator, or member of the student personnel staff effectively won allegiance to a superordinate goal, thereby recasting the conflict feud into the "equivalency of war" in ways that William James would have understood and applauded.

An Educative Concept of Group Leadership

Kallen has given us a description which serves to guide our thinking of democratic leadership in a group of free men:[21]

When different individualities join together freely on equal terms, when the consequent group accepts, appreciates and takes the fullest possible account of the personality of each of its members so that everyone's place and function in the team play of the whole expresses his character and powers, changing as those alter, this society is free.

If the staff worker serves effectively to present to the student group, and especially to its leaders, this concept of the societal and educational role of the group with respect to its individual members' development, that in itself will be a worthwhile leadership contribution to the group of students. In this connection it is obvious that students are citizens; as such, they are entitled to all the rights of our democracy. And yet it is equally true that the purpose of a college is not limited to the enjoyment of rights. The

---

[21] Horace Kallen, *The Education of Free Men.* New York: Farrar, Straus & Cudahy, Inc. 1949, p. 257.

THE STAFF AS CONSULTANTS TO STUDENT ORGANIZATIONS

college is engaged in another, but not antagonistic, mission, which
Pusey of Harvard has stated in these terms:[22]

> The teacher's special job is to nurture in young people the desire to
> extend themselves, and to help them, with their minds and wills, to
> grow beyond competence into full humanity.

In our American colleges, democratic leadership, both on the
part of members of the staff and student leaders themselves, serves
the mission of aiding young students to grow into full humanity
*as fully responsive members of an interdependent and humane
society.* There are rich possibilities for development in this concept.
The group's opportunity to explore its capacity to help its
members develop into full humanity is a challenge to redirect its
program and to make it more effective. Because of his own maturity
and his rich experiences derived from years of working with other
groups, the staff member can play a significant role in teaching
students and their leaders as they achieve deeper and broader
understanding of full humanity as the objective of group membership within an institution of higher education. This is the theme
of our Chapter 13 with respect to the intellectual aspect of full
humanity.

The Group's Objectives

The above general statement of the fundamental utility of an
organized group of students may be translated into these three
more specific objectives:

1. To produce an output of organized group teamwork. That is,
to initiate the planning of a program, to make plans, then to do
something as a group through integrated efforts of members acting
as a team under the group's plan of operations.

2. To maintain and strengthen the group as a group. That is, to
promote highly satisfying interpersonal working relationships among
members, to arbitrate disputes, to encourage the efforts of all
members, and to stimulate interdependence among them.

3. To give status and satisfaction to the group's members through
that membership and through assigned roles and responsibilities.

---

[22] Nathan M. Pusey, "The Exploding World of Education," *Fortune*, September, 1955, p. 204.

That is, to exploit the group's activities for the sake of the development of the individual members.

This third objective is much less evident in the workings and the results of some groups than are the first two. But we believe that Karl Pearson's dictum about the state is equally relevant to the task of all voluntary, organized student groups: "The first demand of the state upon the individual is not for self-sacrifice, but for self-development." [23]

The Strategy of Participation of Apathetic Students

In order that each member of a group may develop his full potentiality through participating in the group's activities, it is first necessary to teach each member the desirable habit of participation. Participation is not merely joining a miscellany of busy-body projects. Participation is active membership, which means involvement in projects which require and result from a consensus of varied opinions and wishes and which represent a group decision, not the opinion of any one member or group of members. The democratic way of life, which we believe to be one of the fundamental objectives of all student organizations, is not only a system of beliefs, *it is a cluster of habits acquired through active participation.*[24]

Participation, as Aristotle foresaw long ago, is the *sine qua non* of democratic behavior. The democratic ideal does not impose upon its adherents the necessity of agreement. . . . But it is precisely because democracy admits of difference and disagreement that it requires participation. Participation in arriving at decisions is the method through which citizens of democracies learn the democratic way of life.

The essential part of our concept of participation is not merely one of organizing worthwhile activities. *It is rather one of actively joining in the consensus-taking process by means of which the group arrives at its common objectives and common programs to achieve those objectives.* This is an educational concept of the usefulness of student groups and organizations. In stressing this concept of the group's objectives, the staff worker plays a significant

[23] Karl Pearson, *The Grammar of Science.* London: A. and C. Black, Ltd., 1892, p. 28.

[24] T. V. Smith and Eduard C. Lindeman, *The Democratic Way of Life.* New York: Mentor Books, The New American Library of World Literature, 1951, p. 149.

educative role in his relationships with organized groups of students. For these reasons, thoughtful and effective relationships with groups and their leaders offer the staff worker rich opportunities to cultivate students' skill in democratic participation in group life. And personnel workers, like student leaders of groups, should keep attention centered upon this particular use of the group's program of activities for self-development.

The Dangers of Participation

This assay of the significance of student personnel work leads us to a critical review of the role of the individual member within the group. Our strong emphasis upon the desirability of democratic participation in the group may appear to some to be an undermining of individuality through forced, or at least induced and persuaded, conformity to the group. To be sure, it is true, as Murphy points out, that "one literally 'loses' oneself in the group—not just in the crowd, but in the disciplined, highly integrated, military, or industrial, or religious, or artistic, or scientific unit." [25] Lewin has pointed out that "in German culture 'loyalty' is typically identified with 'obedience.' They do not see any other alternative to efficient group organization based on obedience but an atmosphere of laissez-faire and inefficiency based on individualistic freedom." [26]

These forms of group participation which induce, persuade, or even compel the individual to accept an obligation of absolute obedience to the group and conformity in every respect to its dictates—such conditions of membership are, of course, the very antithesis of what we seek to develop through membership in American student organizations. No doubt many students, immature, or insecure about their own adequacy and status, do pose an ever-present danger of induced, abject conformity, regardless of what may be the fundamental aspirations of either the staff members or the student leaders. Currently, we are conscious of the grave dangers of too much conformity. Indeed, we may even pose the problem of the undesirability, if not immorality, of certain types and degrees of conformity that are achieved through group membership.

[25] Gardner Murphy, *Personality*. New York: Harper & Brothers, 1947, p. 921.
[26] Kurt Lewin, *Resolving Social Conflicts*. New York: Harper & Brothers, 1948, p. 51.

Whyte has made us conscious of the ever-present dangers that intrude upon the individual through some types of membership in some types of organizations.[27] But even Whyte, upon closer reading, does not condemn membership in organizations in any wholesale fashion. He does point to the inherent risks and dangers of accepting the notion that the organization is a transcendental, monolithic, predatory agent for standardizing its members beyond their power to control. And no doubt, these are ever-present dangers which must be constantly avoided. Nevertheless, this appraisal of the possible ill effects of group membership does not spell out the full potential of membership in most student organizations in an educational institution. There are advantages as well as risks to be had through membership in groups. Without membership in groups, man would not have achieved his present culture and civilization. Indeed, we believe that it is when man joins together with others that he achieves many things that would not be achieved in individual, atomistic isolation. We shall stress the opposite of danger by stressing the potential of group membership for the development of the individual member. Linton has this to say:[28]

. . . to belong to a society is to sacrifice some measure of individual liberty, no matter how slight the restraints which the society consciously imposes. The so-called free societies are not really free. They are merely those societies which encourage their members to express their individuality along a few minor and socially acceptable lines. At the same time they condition their members to abide by innumerable rules and regulations, doing this so subtly and completely that these members are largely unconscious that the rules exist. If a society has done its work of shaping the individual properly, he is no more conscious of most of the restrictions it has imposed than he is of the restraints which his habitual clothing imposes on his movements.

If one can but accept Linton's anthropological evaluations of the relationship between a group and its members and then adopt Pearson's view of the first demand upon society as being the self-development of its members, then one can be reassured that membership in any group need not erase essential individuality.

[27] William H. Whyte, *The Organization Man.* New York: Simon and Schuster, Inc., 1956.
[28] Ralph Linton, *The Cultural Background of Personality.* New York: D. Appleton-Century Company, Inc., 1945, p. 17.

Indeed, one may then go on to assert, as Will Herberg does, that ". . . the human self emerges only in community and has no real existence apart from it. The self is not prior to society, but coeval with it." [29] Such a doctrine should give us assurance that in aiding individuals to develop individuality through membership in groups, we personnel workers are indeed serving a significant educative or developmental function. And our task then becomes one of serving as consultants to the group and its leadership in the realization of this objective for each of its members.

Freedom to Participate

We turn to another aspect of dynamic leadership in student organizations and groups. Should individual members of the college be free to participate or not to participate in any group activities or in a group's activities? This is a basic question facing all student leaders and student personnel workers. Every member of the staff, particularly those who counsel individual students, is continuously and acutely aware of the very large number of students who wish to participate but who are inhibited because of limited and inadequate skill, low confidence, and a feeling of inability to make the required initial step. On the one hand, if we were able to organize student life so that all students were effectively persuaded, or cajoled, or pressured to participate, then we risk weakening the organized group by the dead weight of those who passively fail to learn the democratic way of playing an active membership role. On the other hand, individualistic freedom on the part of group members often weakens the organized group and fails to teach many members the democratic responsibility each must carry for the whole enterprise. With regard to this issue, we hold with Coyle that ". . . *each individual should be encouraged to develop his powers to the fullest and we believe he should freely devote those powers to the social good by full participation in the society in which he lives.*" [30] Coyle has stated the strategic and societal importance of participation by each member of a group, saying that this is one way, perhaps one of the many necessary ways, open to him to achieve his full potentiality. It is true that democratic

[29] Will Herberg, "Freud, Religion, and Social Reality," *Commentary*, vol. 23, no. 1, p. 281, March, 1957.
[30] Coyle, *op. cit.*, p. 67.

habits cannot effectively be imposed upon an individual; he must learn through voluntary and self-chosen responsible participation. Nevertheless, especially in an educational institution, we face the fact that such important learning does not occur if a student chooses to remain inactive with respect to any or all organized or informal activities.

The basic question therefore must be faced by each group and by its leaders: How is each member encouraged and influenced to learn through active participation? This dictum applies equally in the case of students who choose to remain unaffiliated with any organized group. It must be acknowledged that in a democracy we cannot use autocratic ways of enforcing participation. But, paradoxically, neither can we afford the dead weight of inactive members sitting on the sidelines, learning little of the lessons of democracy, and contributing but little, if anything, to the group's enterprises. This is especially true if one views the college as a societal instrumentality for the preparation of adults for citizenship responsibility. Whatever the student leaders may think of this dilemma in an organized program, the student personnel workers should, we believe, take the position that they hope that the program will be of sufficient merit to interest each potential member so that he will be persuaded that it is to his benefit to join in the group's activities. Should he not so decide, we cannot coerce him, however much we may need his contribution and whatever substitute efforts we must make to overcome the handicap of his negligence of group responsibilities.

The Exercise of the Right of Dissent

We turn to still another question bearing upon leadership roles of staff members and student leaders. Is it desirable to enroll or continue dissenters as members in the group? How does one deal with minority opinion? Should the group seek to formulate an *official orthodoxy* binding upon its members? How shall we maintain the solidarity of a concentrated group opinion or point of view without imposing an official orthodoxy which oppresses individual opinion?

We seek an answer to these questions vital to a group's unity and integrity by appraising what would happen if the group were homogeneous with respect to any particular issue or question. Lewin says—[31]

Only through practical experience can one learn that peculiar demo-cratic combination of conduct which includes responsibility toward the group, ability to recognize differences of opinion without considering the other person a criminal, and readiness to accept criticism in a matter of fact way while offering criticism with sensitivity for the other person's feeling.

This necessary lesson in democratic living, how to deal with a variety of conflicting opinions, can be learned *only* when dis-senters are given full voice. Sometimes this means that the leader or the staff member needs to suggest the staging of an actual round-table discussion during which diverse points of view are presented to the group. It is especially a serious responsibility of the leader to represent and to cultivate all elements of opinion in the group, and not to stack the cards against a particular point of view, though he may himself favor the opposite one. In this connection, we note the conclusion that ". . . the group with the trained leader is superior in the quality of its thinking because the leader helps the group make effective use of minority opinions." [32]

We find not only operational but also philosophical justification for using our leadership influence as personnel workers in the en-couragement of minority opinion. In support of this function, the philosopher Kallen stated a basic reason for leading the group in its treatment of those who hold minority views, a reason diffi-cult for many to accept. Many members and some staff are willing to tolerate differences of opinions, but Kallen says we must do more:[33]

In that [democratic] insight difference, otherness, is not the same as wrong and evil; the unlike is equally good and right *as* unlike and *because* unlike. The free man's role, in free society, is to understand and to respect the unlike, to achieve a sympathetic realization of what he is and how he works, and to arrange ways of cooperation, to liquidate moods of sufferance.

[31] Lewin, *op. cit.,* p. 52.
[32] Cartwright and Zander (eds.), *op. cit.,* p. 548.
[33] Kallen, *op. cit.,* p. 23.

Wolpert, another of philosophic turn of mind, justifies minority opinions in still another way, as a way of testing truth:[34]

> But the shortest distance to education is still the circuitous route of doubt and error, of wonder and conflict, of struggle in the arena of ideas where all things are to be proved, and the good held fast. Men who will one day govern themselves must first learn to think for themselves. Independent minds can neither be hammered nor drilled into shape—they must grow.

With such ideational leadership, staff members can devote themselves with confidence to a more active role in group decision making. The passive acceptance of majority opinion does not exhaust the educational leadership roles of either staff members or student group leaders. The majority opinion is not always right, and it is our teaching responsibility to assist the group in appraising the merits of ideas and suggestions, regardless of their source, but particularly when they originate with minority members. This is, of course, not an easy teaching role.

The Abuse of the Right to Dissent

No doubt every staff member, if not every student leader, while granting this basic principle of the need, as well as the right, of the dissenter to have a voice in group decisions, nevertheless recalls instances in which this privilege was much abused. As is true of all other basic principles, moderation must be used in maintaining the right of the dissenter to speak. It is equally apparent, so it seems to us, that dissenters must learn—and this is a staff leadership responsibility—effective ways of exercising their right to dissent. While the literature of student personnel work and student government is filled with suggestions as to how leaders of the majority opinion may be trained, one finds a dearth of information as to how dissenters may be trained to operate as effective and constructive members of groups. And this suggests a much needed exploration if we are to gain from the dissenter the kind of worthwhile contribution which Kallen and others suggest is possible.

[34] Stanley A. Wolpert, "The Meaning of Academic Freedom," *Student Government Bulletin*, vol. 2, no. 6, p. 5, U.S. National Student Association, Philadelphia, March, 1954.

Decision Making within the Group

We turn to a related aspect of the problem of dynamic leadership: How does a group arrive at decisions? We believe that one of the most profound tests of democratically operated group activities is the way in which it makes its decisions—through dictation by a few members or through consensus-taking discussions in which each member contributes his ideas through the give and take of free discussion. In such consensus taking, as Kallen calls it, no one is coerced, and each has an equal privilege—unfortunately, however, not usually equal preparation or competence—to express his opinion and judgment. This is not voting by *Robert's Rules of Order;* it is rather a circular discussion, or circular communication, in which all, except the overly timid, collaborate as free persons. This is the way in which those governed (the members) give their free consent to their leaders—through exercise of the art of conferring as a group of equal, participating members. But it should be noted that, while each has equal opportunity to participate, this concept *does not require* that we think that each has equal potential to make equally valuable and equally effective contributions to the group discussion.

We should note that a single group or organization operating within a total community cannot be democratic in its consensus taking unless some such philosophy pervades the entire organization. As Lewin asserts—[35]

The experiments in training of democratic leaders, for instance, a foreman in a factory, indicate strongly that it does not suffice to have the subleaders who deal with the small face-to-face groups trained in democratic procedures. If the power above them, such as the management of the factory, does not understand and does not apply democratic procedures, either a revolution occurs or the effect of democratic leadership in the lower brackets will quickly fade. This is not surprising because cultural patterns are social atmospheres which cannot be handed out bit by bit.

Thus it is that problem solving and decision making in any student organization is, in very large part, a function and a tradition of the entire college, in which faculty and administration need to

[35] Lewin, *op. cit.,* pp. 39–40.

operate perceptibly on the same principles as those the students follow. There cannot be rigid autocracy in the classroom or the president's office, and at the same time the practice of problem-solving, democratic consensus taking in student organizations. Some marked degree of generality of democratic participation must operate in most, if not all, parts of the institution. Otherwise, disruptive reform movements become organized to extend a single pattern of operation to all institutional processes. This is not to argue for uniformity of procedures but for a dominant *Zeitgeist* associated with preponderance of community-wide discussion of issues which affect the community as a whole, that is, free discussion prior to decision making by the proper agency.

Now problem solving and decision making in a student group are also functions of the members themselves, their motivations, and habitual modes of operation. If the dominant members, or the dominant leaders, or the staff member serving as adviser have a great hunger for power and need to run things, then they will seek to dictate the answers to problems, and the group will have little opportunity for problem-solving and decision-making experiences. It should be noted from experience that there are about as many power grabbers among student leaders as there are among student personnel workers, faculty workers, and administrators. In some circles it seems to be assumed that students are democratically "pure" in their motivations, whereas personnel workers are suspect. But scarcely a year passes on most campuses but what some power-hungry student captures, sometimes with his associates, an organized group so that he may have an apparatus for his messianic manipulations. The discovery of effective ways of dealing with such situations, as a member of the staff, is much needed. Such individuals are unlikely to accept the suggestion that they present themselves voluntarily for therapy counseling. As a matter of fact, they have in many instances gained control of a group as a substitute for therapy. Nevertheless, the staff member who is working with student leaders needs to utilize modified therapeutic counseling methods in dealing with many student leaders within the context of group operations and relationships. Student leaders are by no means free from the need for counseling, but they often experience difficulties in establishing counseling relationships.[36]

[36] Ptacek, *op. cit.*

Improving Participation in Group Processes and Activities

Continuing our discussion of decision making and problem solving, many staff members have observed the difficulties of the immature and insecure member who avoids responsibility for decision making by asking the student leaders, or the staff members, to make decisions for him or at least to signal how he should vote in group decisions. While this dependency is very gratifying to the ego of a staff member, he needs to recognize the basic motivation of this student and to search for ways of encouraging him in his timid effort to face and accept responsibility. Moreover, the staff member also needs to point out such individual students to the student leaders themselves. They, like the staff members, may be flattered by being found useful through dependency, and may thereby deprive the student members of much-needed, but unsought, opportunities to accept and discharge responsibility. But student leaders and staff both need experience in teaching these timid members effectively, and giving them personal attention which will encourage them to begin the process of learning how to be effective and satisfying group members. And very frequently, out of such individual assistance come constructive and effective suggestions for the group's own enterprise. We do not hold that natural leaders, who have previously acquired self-sufficiency and security, necessarily have a monopoly on good ideas for the group's programs. Rather have we found that many timid and shy individuals can, if properly encouraged, suggest even better ideas than those of the leaders and the staff member.

We are advocating that both student leader and staff member working with the student leader be deeply committed to Whitehead's concept of education, that "the students are alive, and the purpose of education is to stimulate and guide their self-development." [37] In fact, we contend that in college this is *the* purpose of all group activities.

Effective Group Rule Making

The development and adoption of the group's own rules and procedures can be made into problem-solving tasks. That is, the con-

[37] Alfred North Whitehead, *The Aims of Education and Other Essays.* New York: The Macmillan Company, 1927, p. v.

sensus-taking procedures necessary for democratic adoption of rules and procedures may be organized so that each and every member is not only permitted to state his point of view and opinion, but also is positively encouraged to take part in the free give-and-take review and evaluation of alternative opinions and possible actions. In some instances, the leader should hold off final action and consensus taking until there has been such expression by all members. Indeed, it is often quite encouraging to the silent members to be specifically singled out, and their opinions solicited. Often new ideas are originated by these silent students. And certainly, in most instances, ideas of better quality emerge from the public testing of all suggestions. This is democratic decision making at its best.

In this connection, it seems to us that the slavish following of *Robert's Rules of Order* in the conduct of student meetings often enables a minority to silence a majority, or at least to curtail the public testing of ideas through the free enquiry of discussion and examination. We rather favor the informal give-and-take discussion preceding formal action, with the latter often taken merely for the record, after the group has arrived at its own consensus. Too often are discussions of a productive nature curtailed by parliamentary procedures, with the result that decisions are hasty improvisations, later to be changed, or incomplete reviews of relevant information and alternative possible courses of action.

Coordination of Group Effort

Still another important ingredient of democratic decision making stems from the capacity of the group for coordinated effort. This, in turn, is related to the respect of each member for the others and for the objectives of the group. Good decisions grow out of such respect. And respect requires that much time be devoted generously to the welfare, concern, and interest of each member of the group. We may often ride, often roughshod, over individuals who may not concur with the majority opinion, but in so doing, our forced decision will undermine the group itself and lead to its dissolution.

We conclude that democratic problem solving requires that some way be found for each member of the group to play some role in decision making and in carrying out decisions. These roles may be an assignment to explore a possible action or decision, to review relevant experience and evidence, to take a particular part in discussion, or to evaluate and summarize a discussion. These and other roles may be rotated among members to bring all into the group's processes. And this rotation is a desirable way of distributing functional leadership roles among members, thereby enhancing the learning of each. While some roles must be fixed on certain occasions, most leadership roles may be rotated on other occasions. The staff member's role is often to suggest to the group's leaders possible assignments to neglected and inactive members.

The Summing-up Procedure

We come to a final step in group decision making. A bulletin of the United States National Student Association (USNSA) contained a description of the postcouncil evaluation or postmortem session. This often takes place after adjournment of the formal meeting, sometimes in the same room and sometimes "informally down at the local college hang-out." [38] It is referred to as an "expected final order of business." [39] Such a postmortem gives to each member an opportunity to make additional comments, some not thought of previously, some evaluative in character. The procedure relaxes tension and makes easier for some the transition from the role of antagonists to sociable fellow students.

In other situations it is proposed that the president surrender the floor to each member who has one minute to "get it off his chest." Whatever the form, all procedures should be rotated frequently so that they may not become deadened ritualistic observance, and some kind of evaluation process would seem to be a desirable way of closing the decision-making functions of student groups. Similar, but more elaborate, reviews of accomplishment customarily close a school year of group program activities, perhaps in a weekend retreat away from the campus. The staff adviser may also properly serve as a consultant who reviews the year's activities objectively and critically, pointing out both weaknesses and strengths with suggested steps for another year.

Orienting Student Leaders to Their Group Responsibilities

This brings us to a brief review of the task of the group's student leader. We are searching for the important functions which are performed by a staff member in his role as adviser and assistant

[38] *Student Government Bulletin*, vol. 4, no. 2, p. 27, U.S. National Student Association, Philadelphia, November, 1955.
[39] *Ibid.*, p. 27.

to groups and to group leaders in carrying on group functions, activities, and programs. But what we shall say has application also to every member of the student personnel staff.

Sometimes the group's adviser needs to introduce the concept of leadership as determined by the group itself. It is a commonplace generalization in the literature of administration that a leader cannot act with maximum effectiveness unless he has won the assent of his followers. Follett says—[40]

The best leader does not ask people to serve him, but the common end. . . . The best leader has not followers, but men and women working with him. . . . We want to arouse not the attitudes of obedience, but the attitudes of cooperation, and we cannot do that effectively unless we are working for a common purpose understood and defined as such.

That is, orders to be effective must flow up from the grass roots to the top. To state it in another way, those who carry out orders or plans or consensus decisions do so most enthusiastically when they play a role in consenting and in planning the action. Actually, orders or conclusions may originate anywhere, top or bottom or in between. The point of origination is not the significant one; it is important that every member should play some self-perceived and significant role in the formulation and acceptance of the conclusion. This does not mean that everybody votes with equal power to make the decision; it means that the effective leader finds some way of bringing everyone into decision making.

Unlike some elected student leaders of groups, the leader is limited in his freedom to determine his own role and function. In a real sense, the leader of a group is its executive secretary: "The unique behavior of leaders is concerned with (a) analyzing the situation and (b) initiating action required." [41]

We may define the learned role of student group leaders in another way:[42]

Leadership is viewed as the performance of those acts which help the group achieve its objectives. Such acts may be termed *group*

[40] Henry C. Metcalf and L. Urwick (eds.), *Dynamic Administration: The Collected Papers of Mary Parker Follett*. New York: Harper & Brothers, 1942, p. 262.
[41] Cartwright and Zander, *op. cit.*, p. 547.
[42] *Ibid.*, p. 538.

functions. More specifically, then, leadership consists of such actions by group members as those which aid in setting group goals, moving the group toward its goals, improving the quality of the interactions among the members, building the cohesiveness of the group, or making resources available to the group. In principle, leadership may be performed by one or many members of the group.

To some it seems evident that in democratically conducted groups, every member plays some kind of leadership role. Such a dictum leads some to conclude that the best group is one in which everyone is a leader and there is no single leader. But we believe with Strang—[43]

Democracy does not imply lack of leadership. The group leader cannot simply turn students loose to work out their own salvation. They need resources in the form of expert information and questions which direct their attention to points of view which they should consider. . . . Nor does democracy imply lack of discipline. The most rigorous disciplinarian is not a person, but a life situation.

While it may be true that the functions of leadership are best handled when widely shared among members, this does not mean that there should be no leader as such. The essential point to be made in considering the functions of a group's leader is not that everyone should be considered a leader of equal stature, but rather that the group shall retain control of assignment of leadership functions. This is truly the essence of democratic procedures. Unfortunately, it should be noted that sometimes among students the factor of popularity is a more qualifying criterion for a particular function than is competence. Such a superficial basis for selection of leaders creates problems of unity and effectiveness for the group and for the staff adviser. In such cases, the adviser needs to search for effective ways of helping the group to learn discriminating means of identifying leadership competencies through appraisal techniques which may resemble those used by counselors in relationships with students.

SUMMARY

We close this discussion of staff consulting functions by pointing to one most essential additional responsibility of both the group

[43] Ruth Strang, *Group Activities in College and Secondary School.* New York: Harper & Brothers, 1941, p. 89.

leader and of the staff adviser. We refer to the need to help members of the group not only to identify their perceptibly visible needs of importance to them, but also to consider and to adopt new, higher, and broader objectives for the group. This type of leadership is most significant, particularly in an educational institution dedicated to liberalizing, and thus broadening, the horizon of individual students by adding to the clarity and depth of their perception of the role of an educated man in a society of free men. We know of no better expression of this type of leadership than that of Chalmers:[44]

Often I have asked graduate students and instructors to try to say in a sentence what America is. Usually I hear the reply, "It is the rule of the majority." It is, of course, no such thing. The unhampered rule of the majority is tyranny. America is the rule of the majority tempered by justice, and the peculiar responsibility of education is to make it possible for people to define, to seek, and to achieve that most elusive thing, justice, in the seemingly new situations which constantly confront that old-timer, human nature. It is also the job of the schools to bring it about that people unfalteringly sense that this is the most important enterprise of responsible manhood.

[44] Gordon Keith Chalmers, "Education and America's Need," *The Educational Record*, vol. 34, no. 3, p. 238, July, 1953.

PART THREE

New Services and Policies: Illustrative Cases

CHAPTER 8

Making Rules and Policies

Each time a staff member takes, directs, authorizes, or approves an action, a financial expenditure, the use of equipment, a service to students, or the use of staff time for some activity, he is acting by virtue of or in terms of a written or unwritten, explicit or implicit, general or specific policy, rule, or authorization adopted by some source of authority. Such is the orderly procedure followed in complex organizations.

We shall see that such authorizations of professional activities range widely in specificity. We cite, by way of an example of simplicity, this detailed regulation adopted to achieve the orderly maintenance of a neat campus:[1]

All signs, posters, announcements, and other publicity material must be confined to the bulletin boards and the other officially recognized University channels of publicity and their display must be approved by an officer of the University appointed by the President.

At perhaps an opposite extreme in complexity and generality, we cite the following example of a policy which endorses and approves in principle a generalized statement of permission and intention:[2]

The University of Minnesota has long been committed to the use of its full resources for the development of leadership and responsible citizenship in its students. In the midst of an ever broadening program of research and public service, this commitment to the instruction of youth remains a central objective.

[1] *Minutes of the Board of Regents, University of Minnesota,* Oct. 19, 1935.
[2] *Minutes of the Board of Regents, University of Minnesota,* May 11, 1951.

Over the years the experiences of the administration and staff working with students have demonstrated that responsible leadership can be developed by students. Moreover, consulting and sharing with students the background of University affairs and problems have served to develop a deeper loyalty to the University and have yielded continued high morale. It is also apparent that the co-operation of student organizations, such as the All-University Student Congress, has contributed significantly in the effective functioning of many projects and activities sponsored by the University itself.

Such co-operative relationships are not easily attained for many reasons, among which faulty communication is of major significance. Experience indicates that a university functions best when mutual understanding and respect prevail among its many members, both staff and students. Indeed a major administrative need of any complex university involves the facilitation of more complete communication. In this undertaking more than negative avoidance of misunderstanding and friction is at stake. The development of positive and responsible leadership and citizenship is the goal to be attained.

It is therefore desirable that all members of the University endeavor to maintain cordial, friendly, and co-operative relationships between members of the staff on the one hand and responsible student leaders on the other.

Without implying that the ultimate authority for responsible decisions rests elsewhere than in the Board of Regents itself, by provisions of its basic charter, the Regents look with favor upon all efforts that are designed to improve the consultation, communications, and relationships between staff members and responsible student leaders. This statement is adopted to the end that encouragement may be given both to staff members and to student leaders in their joint efforts to further the welfare and services of the University as an agency of the state.

The broad range of types of authorization is further complicated by the dynamic interplay of many forces on the campus which produce continuous changes both in the form of application and the substance of these authorizations. On a similar point Barnard generalizes that "most continuous organizations require repeated adoption of new purposes."[3] We are not here concerned with categorizing the many forms of rules and policies but with certain essential phases of the complex processes involved in initial formu-

[3] Chester A. Barnard, *The Functions of the Executive*. Cambridge, Mass.: Harvard University Press, 1948, p. 91.

lation and continuous reformulation of objectives adopted as policies. Since the dynamic student life necessitates continuous changes
in the content and form of personnel services, we center our discussion upon administrative activities involved in making rules and
policies. We will note that some policies serve as general support
and background for specific activities influencing or even determining day-to-day behavior of staff and students. Other policies
refer to specific and restricted aspects of student affairs. In the
present discussion, we shall not make distinctions between these
two kinds of authorization, one broad and general in scope, the
other specific and narrow in content.

Many workers in personnel programs perform technical services
for students with little consciousness of the bearing of policies upon
their work. For example, counselors and therapists interview students with but little involvement in interpretation of policies and
rules. But those who requisition loans and scholarships must operate within officially defined requirements of interest rates, terms of
repayment, and limits of indebtedness. Housing inspectors exercise
delegated trustees' powers to determine the hygienic, safety, and
moral conditions under which students may live on or off campus.
And activity advisers confer with organizational leaders of programs with due regard to required standards of taste, educational
relevance, and public relations potential. Thus it is that policies
and rules bear in varied ways upon the operations of a program
of services to students. And it is clear that some degree of clarity
of understanding of these guiding-policy influences, dynamically
changeable as they are, is highly important in the functioning of
these services. We believe, therefore, that it is important in the
improvement of administration that such clarity be sought. And
this task we shall attempt in this chapter.

In Chapters 3 and 4 we discussed briefly some aspects of the
process of formulating rules and policies governing student personnel services. We stated that many rules and regulations are unwritten, habitual, or traditional procedures rather than explicit
statements describing or indicating some authorized activity. We
also mentioned that the basic authority to make policies governing
some services has been delegated by boards of trustees to faculties as legislative agencies. We noted also that many rules and
policies, while unwritten, are nevertheless operative through speci-

fied budget allowances assigned by the central administration to the support of one program or service rather than another. In the present chapter, we shall identify other administrative procedures involved in rule and policy making and also illustrate these points through a number of incidents and experiences.

Perhaps we may adequately sum up our observations of the origin of rules and policies in terms of a loosely drawn thesis. This thesis would direct attention to three conditions out of which policies and rules are developed:

1. Students' incidents lead to formulation of new or to revised policies or rules prohibiting some form of behavior.

2. Some policies establishing privileges and rights are modeled after forms established in communities of adult citizens.

3. Some policies establish professional services on the basis of demonstrated needs to prevent or alleviate difficulties and problems currently experienced by students.

First, we would hold that many explicit governing policies are adopted by official committees or boards or administrators only after incidents and accidents in students' behavior, individual and group, have developed unchartered or unanticipated forms. That is, students continuously invent new forms of behavior and activities not defined by, prohibited by, or even anticipated by framers of existing rules and policies. Some such new behavior proves to be unacceptable to whatever agency of the college is delegated the responsibility for determining acceptability—an individual administrator, a committee of students, or any other organized authority. In many instances, the authority is, in effect, the entire institution and the process of defining rules and policies governing behavior takes the form of community-wide establishment of mores, customs, traditions, and other guide lines of behavior.

The appropriate authority agency determines which of the new inventions seem to be unacceptable and then initiates rule-making or policy-making behavior patterns. That is, the incident, or invention, may initiate exploration, formal or informal, organized or unorganized, of the nature of the incident, its causes, its public relations consequences, both within and outside the institution, and many other descriptive and evaluative aspects. In some instances, the rule-making behavior may be initiated within the context of an indignant reaction from the president of the institution, communicated directly to the dean of students with the instruction: "Can't we stop that kind of incident!" If the dean of students translates these instructions into a "stop" order, he, of course, anticipates but may fail to prevent repetition of the newly invented behavior.

In most institutions today, more than one individual must become indignant or find the new behavior unacceptable before there can be widespread acceptance of a rule prohibiting such behavior. That is, the mere formulation of a rule of prohibition does not in any way automatically initiate widespread acceptance of the rule. It follows that rule making must be preceded, or at least paralleled, by efforts to win widespread acceptance of prohibition. And widespread acceptance must be preceded by widespread agreement that the invented behavior is, in fact, unacceptable from several of many points of view—welfare of the college, decency standards, students' welfare, or other. Once there is widespread agreement as to the undesirability of the form of behavior, then rule making and policy making can proceed explicitly and with extensive student and staff participation.

Perhaps most workers would agree that the formulation of a rule by one authority, even though it be a dean of students, is not sufficient today on most campuses. One dean stated the point in these words: ". . . the disciplinary procedures have been so democratized that they must rest upon the approval and confidence of the student body. This means that all rules are subject to constraint, discussion and revision. . . ." [4]

Well-nigh universally is it contended among student leaders that there should be widespread discussion of possible rules considered as alternatives to be weighed, compared, and contrasted. And this sort of consensus-taking process requires time, sometimes months or even years, before there is widespread agreement and, therefore, widespread acceptance. This important point concerning the making of policy through consensus taking is eloquently advocated by Kallen in these words: [5]

[4] Everett Hunt, "The Dean and the Psychiatrist," *Bulletin of the Association of American University Professors,* vol. 39, no. 1, p. 29, 1953.

[5] Horace M. Kallen, *The Education of Free Men.* New York: Farrar, Straus & Cudahy, Inc., 1949, pp. 12–13.

But the time comes when the men and women diversely engaged in any undertaking, if they have freely discussed with one another their purpose, their ways of working and the results they work out, find themselves in an agreement which is neither the result of a vote taken nor a compromise arranged. It is a consensus that has grown from the competitive cooperation and cooperative competition whereof free discussion consists. The process which consensus consummates is such that no participant is coerced, and each has the same liberty as the others to enter his own theory and practice in the many-way flow of ideas.

In addition to desirable widespread acceptance, we believe that a rule or policy prohibiting some forms of behavior is usually best and most easily enforced when the conditions or forms under which behavior is permitted, or prohibited, are spelled out in some detail. The argument for such detail stems from students' apprehension that the enforcing authority agency may take advantage of vagueness and generality of wording to distort and even to overextend a policy or rule to a degree inconsistent with our Western mores of fairness and reasonableness. In other words, an administrator of services must be ever cognizant of a prevalent and intense motivation among some students and faculty to restrain and restrict the actions of an authority agency within explicit delegation, grants, or recognition of authority in specific situations. We do not argue for or completely agree with such a restriction on an administrative agency charged with application of a policy or rule to a situation or incident. We rather call attention to the ever-present influence of such a vector force in the application of the policy or rule.

Thus far we have mentioned only the making of those rules and policies which seek to prohibit defined disruptive and unacceptable behavior. Unfortunately, a reading of the history of rule making in colleges would lead one to the conclusion that most rules have been made perhaps in the heat of righteous indignation and were designed to prohibit some form of defined misbehavior. Such an interpretation has been documented in the following references to which the reader is referred, with the suggestion that a careful study will, perhaps, dispose him to a reluctance to continue the disgraceful tradition of overemphasis on negation and prohibition in collegiate rule making:

Anonymous: *A Collection of College Words and Customs*. Cambridge, Mass.: John Bartlett, 1851. (Revised and enlarged ed., 1856; 2d ed., B. F. Hall, 1956.)

Coulter, E. Merton: *College Life in the Old South*. New York: The Macmillan Company, 1928.

Haskins, Charles H.: *The Rise of Universities*. New York: Peter Smith, 1940.

Schmidt, George P.: *The Old Time College President*. New York: Columbia University Press, 1930.

Sheldon, Henry D.: *Student Life and Customs*. New York: D. Appleton and Company, Inc., 1901.

Williamson, E. G., and J. D. Foley: *Counseling and Discipline*. New York: McGraw-Hill Book Company, Inc., 1949.

Students of today in their extracurricular life and in their residences desire to know what they *can* do and not merely what they *cannot* do. And one would conjecture that more benefits would stem from efforts to define positive guide lines.

Promoting certain kinds of desired behavior among students is the second point in our loose thesis about rule-making behavior. It may very well be, for example, that students or others will generalize from their observation of the practice of civil liberties in the community surrounding the college and will desire to establish on the campus certain civil liberties. An example is found in a recent statement of the American Civil Liberties Union:[6]

Human progress and democracy depend upon the free contest of ideas. This is as true on the campus as in the community at large. . . .

Freedom of Expression. The student government, student organizations and the students generally should be free, without penalty, to discuss, pass resolutions upon, and take other lawful action respecting any matter which directly or indirectly concerns them or affects them as construed in the widest sense, within the bounds of common decency. Such an area of student criticism should include the nature of the curriculum, extent of elective versus required courses, and the content of required courses.

It may also well be that, as we have indicated elsewhere, students will desire to develop for themselves positive policies in the campus community, defining their proper voice in the management of the

[6] *Academic Freedom and Civil Liberties of Students.* New York: American Civil Liberties Union, August, 1956, p. 11.

institution. This is somewhat parallel to the attempt in industry to define the role of workers in management.[7] Moreover, students may generalize on their own status in the college from their observations of attempts by organized professors to play a role in the determination of university decisions and policies. Such discoveries of new forms of desired behavior will be followed by attempts to establish similar or identical forms of behavior among students. These efforts are sometimes described as establishing the "rights" of students.

Frequently these efforts are perceived as defensive tactics to protect students' rights from "stubborn administrative autocracy."[8] In some cases, these defensive tactics arise out of the feeling that ". . . the interest of the college administration is fundamentally opposed to the students' interest."[9] Under such psychological handicaps, administrators and trustees are placed at a great disadvantage in their own active participation in constructing positive policies. Of course, it may properly be contended that the history of oppression of rights and privileges of students is almost as unsavory as the parallel chronicle in the case of professors.[10] Nevertheless, one is justified in asserting that in many institutions students' rights and privileges have been expanded and strengthened by administrators working in close community relationships with students.[11]

Whatever the motivations and the roles of administrators and students, this second source of rules and policies is readily identified as a positive means of establishing and defining more securely the acceptable roles of students in the college community. Lunn states this point in these words:[12]

Where student participation in college government is alive and vital there is an acceptance of the fact that the college is a community.

[7] E. G. Williamson, "The Need for Consultation between Students and Administration," *College and University*, April, 1951, pp. 323–329.

[8] Burgess Johnson, *Campus versus Classroom*. New York: Ives Washburn, Inc., 1946, p. 71.

[9] Eliot Friedson, *Student Government, Student Leaders, and the American College*. Philadelphia: U.S. National Student Association, 1955, p. 36.

[10] Richard Hofstadter and Walter P. Metzger, *The Development of Academic Freedom in the United States*. New York: Columbia University Press, 1955.

[11] Harry H. Lunn, *The Student's Role in College Policy-making*. Washington: American Council on Education, 1957.

[12] *Ibid.*, p. 4.

Students, faculty members, administrators, and trustees are all members of this community. The college, as a community, can reach its objectives only if there is a growing sense of common goals and an opportunity and a willingness on the part of all to accept personal responsibility in achieving them.

Such origination differs markedly from the first source of origination in that it is not dependent upon the initiation of disruptive incidents and misbehavior. Rather does it take its character from a positive effort to secure for students what seems to be desirable behavior in keeping with the basic educative mission of the institution.

Our thesis also embraces a third source of policy governing student personnel services more directly. That is, only certain parts of services (e.g., disciplinary counseling and administration) are involved in the application of rules and policies to students' misbehavior and in the definition and establishment of their rights and privileges in the college community (e.g., student government, activities center, and faculty-student committees). The overwhelming part of the program is rather oriented to a different kind of supporting policy. Most technical personnel services are authorized by a resolution of trustees or faculty which declares it to be the policy of the institution to bring to bear upon students' problems the best technical knowledge available in the institution. For example, the granting of a loan to a needy student is not a matter of protecting or defining his civil or academic rights, but one of helping him secure the needed financial underpinning so that he can profit from instructional opportunities. Similarly, counseling services are not derived from protection of a civil right or prevention of a misbehavior, although they may be related as symptoms to therapy. Generally, counseling is rather a positive effort to help the student profit, to the limit of his capacities, from the educational opportunities provided in the institution.

We shall find that this third kind of policy is sometimes not explicitly formulated in actions of faculty or trustees; it is implicit in the assignment of budgetary and personnel resources to perform a technical service. In such instances, the president often makes unwritten policy by assigning money or staff to a service. It is true, of course, that for purposes of public enlightenment, faculty members or trustees or the president may issue a general statement endorsing the need for counseling or for loan services or for housing inspection. In a sense, this is a statement of intention to develop some form of assistance to students. Such a statement is usually worded in a manner quite different from the statement of rules and policies governing behavior or defining rights and privileges of students. Most such policies establishing personnel services emphasize the desirability of helping students achieve optimally from their educational experiences and, in effect, they describe the principal features of such services. An example is contained in the following statement:[13]

RECOMMENDATIONS

A recent and extensive survey of the many phases of the University's total program of counseling provides the background for certain recommendations designed to strengthen that program in preparation for the post-war period. These recommendations deal only with major problems of a general nature. Variations and adaptations should be made, when desirable, within the several colleges. Major attention is given in this report to those phases of counseling which are most directly related to instruction.

In the judgment of the Senate Committee on Education, the changes outlined in the following recommendations should be adopted as guiding principles in preparing for the post-war period. These recommendations call for the gradual strengthening of those parts of the present counseling programs which, during the past two decades, have demonstrated their effectiveness.

1. In each college of the University, especially those enrolling undergraduate students, a small number of especially qualified teachers should be appointed to serve as special counselors to students regarding scholastic progress, selection of courses, registration and personal adjustment problems. These counselors would be expected to provide the nucleus of the college's counseling services to students, especially freshmen and sophomores. But other teachers should continue to counsel students as a normal part of their teaching responsibilities. . . .

*   *   *

3. In each college the dean should assume or should delegate responsibility for general supervision of all phases of the college's student

[13] *Minutes of the Senate, University of Minnesota,* May 18, 1944, pp. 6–9.

personnel program including admissions, advanced standing, transfer of credits, student's scholastic work, registration, advising and counseling.

*   *   *

The relationship between college counselors and University personnel officers should be supplementary and not competitive since the welfare of students cannot be the exclusive jurisdiction of any one group. Frequent conferences, consultations, exchange of personnel information, and detailed reports of services to individual students should be the means through which the policy of co-operative responsibility finds expression. Members of one group should use the services of the other to make more certain that each student received the best available assistance in exploiting his opportunities within the University.

For the most part, student personnel workers are more informed about and more accustomed to this third type of policy making than they are with respect to the first two. Exceptions to this generalization would include deans of students who have much to do with misbehavior and with rights, especially the controversy over rights, and in addition carry responsibility for the establishment and maintenance of technical services. In contrast, the technical staff which provides these services are trained in and accustomed to dealing with the technical maintenance of a service rather than with policy and budgetary considerations. Perhaps such factors operate to produce the current practice of implicit and unwritten policies governing technical services in contrast with the other two sources of different kinds of policies and rules.

PUBLIC RELATIONS AND POLICY MAKING

The anticipated or experienced reaction of the public is a frequently mentioned factor, allegedly causally related to the making of decisions, the restraint of some students' activities, and the making of some policies, rules, and regulations. No comprehensive and definitive study has been made or reported of the weight which public reactions, real or anticipated, actually play in the relationship of the university's administration and students' activities and affairs. In the absence of such studies, we have hypothesized elsewhere that the public as a source of criticism and pressures is an actual and effective determinant of administrative action and policy formulation. Friedson commented that college administrators (deans of students) seek to suppress, "tone down," and "manipulate" students' activities in an attempt to placate critical alumni who possess wealth to donate if and when they are content with the college's operations.[14] Similarly, a public or state university is caught in the cross fire of conflicting and opposing determination of citizens who contend that, being taxpayers, they possess the right to dictate what the institution should or should not do, permit, or suppress, both in the classroom and in the extra-curriculum.[15]

Now it is clear that the charters of private and public institutions do not reserve any such rights of dictation to taxpayers or to donors of any kind. Nevertheless, the very complexity of institutional decision making is such as to make inevitable some attentive appraisal, pre- or post-, at least selectively, to some of the varied vector forces that bear upon the institution from groups or individuals within and from those on the outside. Even an act of rejection of an external attempt to dictate the content of the curriculum through the threatened withholding of financial gifts is in itself a negative definition of the influence of selective public opinion upon the internal activity of a college.[16] We have referred elsewhere to Coffman's early effort to free a state university from improper exploitation by partisan advocates of conflicting political, economic, and ideational, as well as commercial, demands upon

[14] Friedson, *op. cit.*, pp. 43–45.

[15] Reisman has identified some of these intramural and extramural pressures in colleges and, more in detail, in public schools. See David Reisman, *Constraint and Variety in American Education*. Lincoln, Neb.: University of Nebraska Press, 1956, pp. 32–33, 110–113. See especially "The Intellectual Veto Groups," pp. 53–106.

[16] See Grenville Clark's magnificent refusal to accede to the demand and attempt to curb the activities of professors on and off the campus and the threat to withhold gifts from Harvard. Mr. Clark wrote to Mr. Ober, the objector, that ". . . Harvard cannot be influenced at all to depart from her basic tradition of freedom by any fear that gifts will be withheld." See Grenville Clark and James Bryant Conant, "Freedom at Harvard," in Howard Mumford Jones (ed.), *Primer of Freedom*. Cambridge, Mass.: Harvard University Press, 1949, p. 17.

students.[17] Gray recounted a classical pressure campaign by a fundamentalist religious leader to prohibit the teaching of evolution.[18]

Perhaps the reader needs to be convinced of the ever-present danger of the wrecking and restricting shackles of some pressure groups to be found within the publics to which the institution is expected to conform and accede. A definitive history of both the defense against and the yielding to these disruptive forces is now available for all to read and be convinced that vigilance is required.[19] Parenthetically, it does not follow, as some apprehensive students and faculty seem to have universally generalized, that all external pressure groups are to be feared and resisted. Nor does it follow that all administrators have yielded to corrupting forces. Coffman is an example of a strong leader who resisted improper public pressure groups.[20] His desire to win favorable public relations did not prevent him from selectively accepting some and rejecting other critics judged to be improper in the educational enterprise.

In this cursory appraisal of public relations as an important force in the making of decisions and policies, we have thus far made our points by employing the example of institutional and classroom affairs. Now we wish to generalize our points to the extracurriculum and to student affairs and behavior. The behavior of students is a case in point. Sex, alcohol, honesty, decorum, tobacco, noisy rowdyism, courtesy in relations with adults—these and many other modal forms of behavior often incite citizens of the community, even members of the faculty to efforts at reform.[21] Perhaps as many adults are motivated to shield the young from corruption in moral behavior as are those who feel compelled to protect tender

[17] Lotus Delta Coffman, "The Exploitation of Youth," *The Educational Record*, January, 1936, p. 105.

[18] James Gray, "Struggles for Integrity," *The University of Minnesota, 1851–1951*. Minneapolis: University of Minnesota Press, 1951, pp. 293–307.

[19] Hofstadter and Metzger, *op. cit.*

[20] Coffman, *op. cit.*
Gray, *op. cit.*

[21] The story of colonial traditional concern for behavior, morality, and religiosity has been summarized. See E. G. Williamson and John Foley, *Counseling and Discipline*. New York: McGraw-Hill Book Company, Inc., 1947. See also Eugenie A. Leonard, *Origins of Student Personnel Work*. Minneapolis: University of Minnesota Press, 1956.

youth from corruption by radical and un-American ideational doctrines.[22]

It is, of course, true that our present academic mores are such as to sanctify and approve efforts at protection of academic self-determination—in contrast with support of efforts at reform and regulation of moral and behavior freedom. Indeed, our American history of higher education is, to a significant extent, a dramatic effort to cast aside the colonial college commitment to moral and religious instruction and character formation. In the nineteenth century, the faculty, thus freed of the disruptive and anti-intellectual efforts at discipline of riotous and rioting student life, turned to concern for the intellectual cultivation of students. At this time, American society was itself settling down into civilized ways of living that replaced the riotous immorality of the frontier days. And perhaps this true condition was one of the basic factors operating in the eager and widespread efforts at abandonment of the colonial pattern and the fervent incorporation of the Germanic pattern of student-faculty partnership in the pursuit of *Wissenschaftlehre* rather than moral rectitude and religious perfection.[23]

The shift from Puritan-Protestant to Germanic mores and behavior standards proceeded slowly and unevenly over the nineteenth and early twentieth centuries. And the shift from one to the other has by no means been universal or even completed.[24] Indeed, in few communities has the public ever fully consented to the abandonment of morality preoccupation for intellectual development as the major concern of higher education. In fact, the public is often sharply divided on the relevancy of these two objectives of American higher education. The mediation of such conflicting public pressure groups constitutes a controversial climate of opinion in which to make decisions and policies which set guide lines for student affairs.

Elsewhere we shall discuss some other aspects of this evaluation

---

[22] The story of Vice-president Coolidge's 1921 crusade against "Enemies of the Republic" among the students has been told. See Ernest Earnest, *Academic Procession*. Indianapolis: The Bobbs-Merrill Company, Inc., pp. 261–266.

[23] Hofstadter and Metzger, *op. cit.*, chap. VIII, "The German Influence." Leonard, *op. cit.*

[24] For an account of the persistence of concern for morality and religious development among other instructional patterns, see Schmidt, *op. cit.*

of public relations as one of many forces determining policies. We covered the topic in this chapter because to ignore the many publics seeking to dictate policies and rules and decisions would be to ignore the actual and full climate of opinion which bears continuously upon policy making. We agree with Friedson's generalization about the sensitivity of deans of students forced to mediate between influential alumni-donors and energetic students. But our experience indicates that these are only two of the many publics which seek to and should, to some extent and in some situations, play dominant roles in formulation of rules and policies.

POLICY AND AUTHORIZATION OF PROGRAMS

We have discussed the origination and special characteristics of the three different kinds of rules and policies which bear upon the program. Let us turn to a related and perhaps more basic aspect. We refer to the source of authority determining the objectives and content of programs. The question of authority to establish services is, of course, a policy question; we have elsewhere pointed to the fact that traditionally, in general terms, the authority of the faculty is determining on most campuses. We also pointed out that, in the case of many parts of the program, the source of authority was operative in the budget-making and fund-assignment acts rather than in the formal voting of the faculty on the establishment of each and every service. That is, one would find on most campuses parts of a total program established by explicit policies and statements of support adopted by faculty as a whole or by committees. But in many parts of the program, one would find no explicit statement of policy authorizing and supporting the expenditure of money for a particular program and for the support of staff.

We should not conclude that the personnel program is the only one that proceeds in such a peculiar state of unwritten authorization. No doubt, in every part of a campus one would find many programs, conducted by staff members and involving expenditures of money, that have not been clearly and explicitly voted upon by faculty, or trustees, or even authorized by the administration in detail. Usually a college operates somewhat casually, and the authority for programs is often established by extension of a more generalized statement of powers and authorization. Sometimes authorization is implied in the appointment of staff members with titles sufficiently broad to support an elaboration of existing or new activities and responsibilities.

ALTERNATE SOURCES OF AUTHORITY

We turn to a related aspect of the problem of authority agencies. In the final analysis, who does determine policies and rules? What agency decides that one service rather than another is to be developed or expanded? Since trustees are the ultimate legal repository of authority by charter, should all authorizations, rules, and policies be adopted in some form by the board? Is there one single ultimate source of authorization of programs when there are conflicting and competing policies, wishes, influences, and orders? To which authority does a dean of students turn? Shall the trustees impose their ideas of what is best regarding the discussion or advocacy by students of current political points of view? Shall fraternity national officers and local alumni specify the governing policy regarding selective membership standards? May nonuniversity political pressure groups use student activities for purposes of exploiting the institution's status in the community to further a cause? Shall students be required to conform in behavior to dominant and prevailing community standards regarding drinking, sex, decorum, and the like? Shall the faculty's belief in the principle of freedom of expression in the classroom be applied, without restriction, to students' out-of-class political activities? Who shall determine the direction, the rate of development, and the objectives of a program? These are basic issues faced each day by every administrator—from whom shall he take his orders?

One might go on and on and frame other questions about the source of authority involved in the functioning of many other parts of a college program. As deans well know, it is not so very difficult to answer such questions regarding noncontroversial technical programs. For example, with regard to the use of aptitude tests, psychologists decide what tests meet technical standards of excellence. Indeed, we employ these staff members to determine the objectives and content of their own programs. Also, with regard to health services, competent doctors determine the nature of their own medical services. With regard to any number of technical services, there is no ambiguity of authority. Thus, we employ experts and turn over to them almost complete autonomy with regard to both objectives and content of services. But some aspects of student life raise serious questions, and often controversy, as to which of several authorities shall determine policy, rules, and programs. And there are no simple answers to such questions. That is, not only do the college president and the faculty give orders to personnel workers; parents, alumni, students, and others often constitute firm and aggressive alternative sources of influence and pressure, and often decision making, concerning content, emphases, techniques, and rate of increase in student personnel programs.

While agreeing that these varied sources of authority constitute relevant influences, there is a possible resolution, it seems to us, of what is sometimes a confusing situation. Such a resolution may take this form: our own staff's evolving understanding of the changing educational needs of students shall carry weight in determining the character and content of our program. Indeed, we believe that this should be the central, but not the sole, source of authority determining the character of our services. And all other influences are of significance as forces which set some outer limits within which we are able to improvise and assist in the educational development of students.

By way of summarizing this one point, ambiguity of authority, we list the identifiable alternative sources of authority that bear, in general, on those who operate the program of services for students. In a subsequent section we shall trace out in some detail the combined and coordinated operation of these sources of authority in specific program situations, problems, and crises.

Some Illustrative Sources of Authority
Influence Which Determines Operations of the Program

Heads of organized services:
    Deans of students, men and women
    Head counselors
    Residence heads
Organized alumni of fraternities and alumnae of sororities:
    District officers
    Chapter advisers
    National executives and boards

Organized owners or renters of rooming houses

College deans

College trustees

Parents of students

Faculty—as a whole and those on committees dealing with aspects of students' problems

Regional and national associations of personnel workers—influential through adopted statements regarding standards and content of technical services

Volunteer citizens' associations interested in politics, civil liberties, and political activities and programs

We illustrate our point about the varied agencies involved in policy establishment by the following tabulation of policies published in one institution's current policy manual:[25]

Agency	Number of policies approved by the agency
President of University	1
Board of Regents	8
Senate (University faculty)	10
Senate Committee on Student Affairs	35
Senate Committee on Education	1
Office of the Dean of Students	2
Conference of University Officers	2
Administrative Committee of Senate	2

POLICIES IN THE MAKING

Now we turn our attention to the identification of some highly fluid and dynamic processes involved in the making and revising of policies and related rules and procedure. In the absence of experimental studies, we shall identify processes through actual instances of conflicting authorities involved in the search for consensus in one university community. There were varied, diverse, intense, and often stubbornly held points of view on issues of vital concern to students, faculty, central administration, and to the several publics at large. We shall see that policy making is in itself a most important administrative and program responsibility; indeed, we

[25] *Policy Manual for Student Organizations.* Minneapolis: Student Activities Bureau, Office of the Dean of Students, University of Minnesota, 1956.

contend that it can be one of the most productive program events concerning the administration of student personnel services viewed as means of furthering the education of students. This possibility is especially true of those policy-making experiences which are associated with controversy about basic educational and value issues. We have argued and illustrated this point elsewhere.[26]

Documents describing a number of policy-making incidents in this and later chapters were taken selectively from the files of our own university. We would have gladly used incidents from other campuses, but unfortunately none are available in sufficient detail to make them useful in illustrating policy-making processes. In many instances workers are so personally involved in controversy and so many of the steps and facets of the controversy are so highly confidential, that often documentation is not readily available for publication. Nevertheless, it is clear that, if these very complex and most important processes of policy making are ever to be understood, and therefore more appropriately exploited in professional training, as well as in policy-making itself, more monographic studies of similar incidents are needed in the literature of our work. We therefore utilize these incidents from our own institution in the hope that we can encourage coworkers to publish their own experiences.

The following instance illustrates the generalization that the search for consensus in the making of policy often requires years of efforts and frequently involves revision of earlier consensuses. In these situations, no doubt, some kind of policies and rules could have been adopted in less time by sacrificing some of the educational gains resulting from involving many individuals in the controversy and in drafting successive approximations of policy statement. In stressing these educational gains from prolonged community discussion, we are reminded of our favorite educational philosophy, which holds that the vigorous and organized pursuit of truth is often more rewarding to the learner than is its attainment. Such a philosophy often consoles those who must wait out the storm of controversy until the calm of rationality makes possible mature policy formation.

[26] E. G. Williamson, "The Dean of Students as Educator," *The Educational Record*, July, 1957, pp. 230–240.

STUDENTS' PROGRAMS AND OFF-CAMPUS AUDIENCES

The following experience in policy making centers attention on efforts to formulate a policy giving students wide latitude in their educational activities, at the same time affording consideration of the central administration's responsibility for maintenance of the educational integrity of the university. It is evident that any acceptable policy dealing with such a complex issue must be the result of conflicting points of view about the essential core of academic freedom. Such a resultant policy should also accommodate diverse judgments, sincerely and intensely held, about the proper conduct of university affairs. The reader will observe that the methods used in formulating a policy about such a complex issue actually produced much learning among students, not only about the issues, but also about the complex process of community consensus taking. We believe that the stimulation of such learning is an essential part of the student personnel program. Perhaps one may even contend that the production of such learning is of far more significance in our community of scholars than is the product of the controversy—a formulated policy.

In October, 1951, the publicity (student) chairman of the University Young Republicans' Club issued the following announcement:[27]

> To whom it may concern: We have invited Senator McCarthy to speak here, not because we wish to back his recent actions, as on a whole our club opposes them, but instead because one of our University Young Republicans Club's goals is to bring the students closer to politics and government. . . .

In a subsequent resolution on November 6, the executive committee of the club had this to say:[28]

> We, the University of Minnesota Republican Club Executive Board, feel that it is the duty of this State University, sponsored and financed by the people of this state, to follow policies which will extend education to all citizens of this state. We are strongly opposed to the adminis-

[27] University of Minnesota Republican Club Announcement, October, 1951. (Mimeograph stencil in files of the Student Activities Bureau.)
[28] Minutes of the Senate Committee on Student Affairs, Nov. 21, 1951.

tration's policy of forbidding the broadcast of speeches made by persons, sponsored by a University group, for educational purposes.

These resolutions followed an expression by the Dean of Students of some doubt that the University Young Republicans' Club had been originally chartered by the university for the purpose of educating the people of the state. Had the club intended to bring Senator McCarthy here as part of a student-sponsored event for a student audience, it was asserted, the program would have been permitted under established policies.[29] These policies established wide freedoms to student organizations with regard to campus events and activities. But the club had, before approaching the administration, established some tentative arrangements with local radio and television stations to ensure off-campus coverage of the Senator's speech.

This position, taken by the administration, that a student organization bore no responsibility for and had been given no privilege of extending its activities to the state, precipitated a vigorous and prolonged controversy which finally issued in the adoption of a new policy extending privileges granted to student organizations. Numerous editorials in the student newspapers, letters to the editor, adopted resolutions, and other expressions of opposition to the administration's position—all of these educational activities helped to make the controversy a very lively learning experience. The All-University Student Congress joined in with resolutions criticizing the administration for curtailment of freedom of speech and other freedoms. Members of the faculty also voiced opposition to any restriction on the right of student organizations to bring speakers of their own choice to the campus. In time, the original issue— the lack of any clear statement of privileges granted to student organizations to extend their programs off the campus to nonstudent audiences—became identified with the general problem of freedom of thinking, academic freedom, freedom of speech, and many related issues. And, as is usual in complex and tense controversies experienced by most campuses at some time or other, many other critics of the university joined in the controversy. For example, the Dean of Students received the following letters:

[29] *Basic University Policy Concerning Student Organizations and Their Activities, Policy Manual for Student Organizations.* Minneapolis: Office of the Dean of Students, University of Minnesota, 1956, pp. 14–17.

It must be a little embarrassing to you to receive the publicity you are getting in connection with Senator McCarthy's proposed speech.

I do not know what the regulations are at the University of Minnesota but it seems everytime one of the native sons appears over there, there is no trouble about getting it broadcast.

Do you realize that the University belongs to the citizens of the state, who pay the taxes, and perhaps many of them feel that Senator McCarthy is an able man? I am one of the many in this country who thinks he has done a real job and I hope he will be accorded some of the favors you have given to others.[30]

Dear Sir:

The attempts by you and other *left-wingers* at the University to keep people from hearing McCarthy is *backfiring*.

People are saying, "Why is D. Williamson afraid of McCarthy?" I know![31]

The *Minnesota Daily* editorialized in these words:[32]

No one involved in this situation (excepting possibly Dean of Students E. G. Williamson who was out of town) has any knowledge of a University policy prohibiting broadcasts sponsored by student groups. But if student groups want consistent treatment in the future, this dispute must be settled on a policy level. If no policy exists, one must be written.

Thus the controversy, within two or three weeks, had developed into a complex of many issues involving freedom of speech suppression, censorship of news, discrimination against Republicans, favoritism for liberal speakers, McCarthy himself as the issue, and many others. And to make the controversy more educationally profitable to students, a professor of philosophy began to give a "course" for students to teach them how to listen to McCarthy if and when he did come to the campus. The student organization Students for Democratic Action also initiated such a listening course. These events led to an editorial by the *Minnesota Daily* pinpointing the issue much more precisely and contributing to the possibility that a resolution could be achieved.[33]

[30] Personal letter from an alumnus, Nov. 23, 1951.
[31] Personal letter from an anonymous citizen, Dec. 5, 1951.
[32] The *Minnesota Daily*, Nov. 16, 1951. Editorial.
[33] The *Minnesota Daily*, Nov. 20, 1951. Editorial.

Why does the University administration not want to broadcast from campus a speech by Senator Joseph McCarthy?

Why did the President of Ohio State University deny a Quaker the right to speak on that campus?

Why was the editor of the University of Chicago's student newspaper removed after he had been an individual sponsor of a community youth rally?

Every case involving freedom of speech must be judged individually; freedom is not always a black and white issue. But in the three actions mentioned above there probably lies a single motivating reason—fear of public pressure.

College administrators fear to be associated in any way with controversial figures, either radical or reactionary. They recognize that there exists among the people an unusual state of mind, one not wholly in accord with democratic principles. . . .

If the University allows a broadcast of Senator McCarthy's speech, there will be public pressure on the University. One can sympathize with the administrator who doesn't want his university to become a center of heated controversy. . . .

Controversy can be avoided by disallowing the McCarthy broadcast. But that actually would be a compromise as with principle. Will the educational community follow the public, or will it lead?

By this time issues and their interrelations were becoming clearly perceptible to the university community, partly through the editorials of the student newspaper and partly by means of free discussion in faculty and student committees and in the meetings of the All-University Student Congress. Subcommittees of the Senate Committee on Student Affairs and committees of the congress were at work drafting an acceptable statement of policy which would reconcile the identified opposing forces, namely, the university's perceived interests in its relationship with the state's citizenry and students' interest in the widest possible freedom of expression on the campus.

At stake was another orienting value system—the university's educational mission of teaching students how to deal rationally with controversial issues and with controversial personalities. Thoughtful students, faculty, and administrators were at work between committee sessions searching for ways of strengthening these basic values. Gradually consensus began to appear, in the form of suggested resolutions stating basic policies. A committee of the All-University Student Congress proposed the following three "recommendations for an ideal University policy":[34]

1. That the University policy regarding off-campus broadcasts be clarified, preferably in writing, so student groups can determine in advance whether certain speakers will be approved.

2. The present policy "no one is allowed to broadcast" be changed to "everyone is allowed to broadcast."

3. That if any speaker is not permitted to broadcast, the administration must give a written reply to the sponsoring student group stating the reasons for disapproval.

This resolution was approved by the congress but it was not subsequently endorsed by the Senate Committee on Student Affairs. Nevertheless, considerable progress had been made in policy making and, as is usually true, much rewriting was required to reconcile conflicting points of view conscientiously held and also to safeguard the many values and positions of the various segments of a university community. The encouraging sign was that after weeks of acrimonious and often vituperative controversy, orderly consensus-taking efforts were emerging with a search for a written policy to replace the unproductive controversy.

Under date of November 21, 1951, a carefully prepared report of factual findings and recommendations adopted by the All-University Student Congress was presented to the Senate Committee on Student Affairs. After arguing that the Dean of Students, under the present written policy, did not possess authority to deny an organization's request for broadcast of a speaker, the report went on:[35]

First, Congress urges a written clarification of the policy of approval of broadcasts and speakers. We feel that justice and fairness to all can only be accomplished by a definite statement of policy. We realize the matter is necessarily vague, but we think a lot can be done by indicating what factors will be considered as weighing on the decision. Not only will this promote equitable treatment of all groups, but will also provide a means by which a group can determine in advance who

[34] *Resolution adopted by the All-University Student Congress, Minutes,* Nov. 20, 1951.

[35] *All-University Congress Report to the Senate Committee on Student Affairs,* Nov. 21, 1951. Attached to *Minutes of the Senate Committee on Student Affairs,* Nov. 21, 1951. (Mimeographed.)

will be acceptable as a speaker and broadcast material. Thus, no commitments would be made and later have to be canceled at possible financial loss to the student group. The committee regrets that there have been inconsistencies in the past. . . .

Congress, therefore, urges you to approve the broadcasting of the speech of Senator Joseph McCarthy, or in any event, urges a reconsideration of the decision, and re-examination of the policy.

We are especially heartened at the cooperation of the administration in this matter. We realize that at many schools we would not be allowed to be here. Instead, we were actually encouraged to look into the matter. We trust the administration will respect our opinion as we respect theirs.

Finally, four months after the precipitating incident, the request for an auditorium from which to broadcast Senator McCarthy's speech, the Senate Committee on Student Affairs adopted the following resolution, an addition to the 1946 *Basic University Policy Concerning Student Organizations and Their Activities:*[36]

The foregoing activities, affairs, and programs shall be directed primarily to the University community and to students, and may not be extended by student organizations, using any means including any medium of communication, beyond that community without the guidance and approval of the Student Activities Bureau. Any such extension of activities, affairs, and programs, beyond the University community shall be an incidental part of the organization's total program and shall be consistent with the furtherance of students' educational objectives as defined in the Basic University Policy Concerning Student Organizations and Their Activities approved by the University Senate, October 31, 1946. . . .

The Committee wishes to point out the following features of the policy in order that it may be more adequately discussed by the Senate Committee on Student Affairs and other organizations who may wish to make comments:

1. This entire provision applies to recognized student organizations only, i.e., student-controlled.

2. The "extension" referred to applies only to the extension by student organizations. News coverage by established news organizations is not to be considered an extension by a student organization, since neither the Student Activities Bureau nor the Senate Committee on

[36] *Minutes of the Senate Committee on Student Affairs,* Feb. 1, 1952. An attached report.

Student Affairs has any jurisdiction over any non-student news agency, either within or without the University.

3. The Committee wishes to point out that individual students who wish to reach non-University audiences primarily, are free to affiliate as individuals with any non-University groups and reach their objectives through this group, without reflection upon the University. By so limiting the audience to University community members, the committee hopes that there will be no objections to the presentation of any material to the students, thus broadening the exchange of ideas among students.

4. The Student Activities Bureau was designated as the approving and guiding body for activities extending beyond the University community because it has the facilities and provides an opportunity for appeal from decisions through established channels.

5. The recommended policy is designed to fit with the Basic University Policy Concerning Student Organizations and Their Activities in terms of parallel phrasing and supplementation.

SUMMARY

Thus we see that much good came out of the controversy, although it was clear from the beginning that adoption of a new written policy was not the initial issue. Frequently in student personnel work, unanticipated gains do come out of controversy—if only members of the staff working with faculty and student leaders are sufficiently wise and adroit in directing and guiding controversy toward such goals. Upon reading this abbreviated account of the making of a basic policy governing student organizations, the reader may raise the question: Could not the policy have been written without the controversy? The answer is, obviously, "yes," but usually in the busy and congested daily lives of students and staff workers there is little available time and little imaginative motivation to conjure up all the possible policies that one could think of. We refer to our thesis, stated earlier in this chapter, that one almost comes to anticipate that policies will be written largely when controversy and conflict indicate the need for such policies, or when a deficiency in established policies is perceived. That is, the on-going dynamic student life may bring to public attention the need for a policy or for a change in existing policies. In this sense, policy making follows the discovery of the need for a policy, usually through conflict and controversy. Surely the history of the forging of human rights in Western culture is replete with similar illustrations of some social and educational good issuing from controversy.

One could well conjure up many models of a more perfect society in which wise philosopher-kings have thought out, without aid of controversy and conflict, those wise policies which would obviate or even prevent controversy. But we mortals do not live in a state governed by a philosopher-king. And in our own state of affairs, much argument can be made for the utilization of controversy for educational purposes.[37] This is not necessarily to argue that controversy ought to be initiated and generated with such products in mind. But, fortunately, every community of scholars possesses sufficient differences of opinions, freely and aggressively expressed, that one does not ever want for controversy to exploit for learning by students and by the entire university community. If student personnel workers can but bring themselves to perceive such opportunities for stimulating learning in the center of controversy, if they can further steel themselves to the criticism and even vituperation which is sometimes their lot, then much good can be had from this dynamic, volatile, often unpredictable, usually initially uncontrollable curriculum within the extracurriculum. Edman's dictum may well serve as a productive guide line in this type of policy making: ". . . not only covenants openly arrived at in foreign affairs, but also common interests or private interests publicly aired and understood are necessities in democratic practice."[38]

[37] Williamson, "The Dean of Students as Educator," *op. cit.*

[38] Irwin Edman, *Fountainheads of Freedom.* New York: Reynal & Hitchcock, Inc., 1941, p. 172.

The appealing and dialectically opposite search for stable and enduring "certainty" of individuality is appraised under an intriguing title. See Allen Wheelis, *The Quest for Identity.* New York: W. W. Norton & Company, Inc., 1958.

CHAPTER 9

Maintaining Students' Academic Freedoms

In this chapter we will discuss a topic seldom included in the literature of student personnel work. Even then, it is usually in justification of administrative restrictions imposed upon radical students who make trouble by criticizing regents or presidents, by publishing radical editorials, or by insisting upon their right to invite any speaker of their choice to the campus—preferably a notorious Communist who will be most critical of our American way of life. Our review of these academic freedoms for students will be productive of thoughtful reaction rather than choleric resistance if we first identify certain assumptions that serve as guide lines in our development of this part of the program of services to students. Believing that academic freedom is a special case of freedom in general, we begin by identifying a concept of freedom. While this concept was first used in a political context, nevertheless, it is congenial and relevant to the social philosophy given expression in and through a community of scholars. "Freedom . . . means expression of individuality, or self-expression. . . . A person is free to the extent that he has the capacity, the opportunity, and the incentive to give expression to what is in him and to develop his potentialities." [1]

Bay defined a "right," a much-used term in students' relationships with university officials, in these words: "A 'right' . . . means a demand for a specific sphere of freedom around one or more speci-

[1] Christian Bay, *The Structure of Freedom.* Stanford, Calif.: Stanford University Press, 1958, p. 15.

fic individuals."[2] But he further quoted Plamenatz's concept of right, which again possesses and emphasizes human development as of the essence, and which again relates his thinking of rights in the political context as clearly relevant to our review of educational services to students in their development of individuality. Just as the purpose of society is to exist and operate for the benefit of all its citizens, just so does a university exist and operate for the full development of its scholars—both faculty and students. "A right is a power which a creature ought to possess, either because its exercise by him is itself good or else because it is a means to what is good, and in the exercise of which all rational beings ought to protect him."[3]

To round out this relevant concept of freedom, we quote again from Bay:[4]

A society is free, in the total sense of freedom, to the extent that its members have the capacity, opportunity, and incentive to develop the principles of their own individual consciousness and to be faithful to them above all other considerations, even if this at times should place them severely at odds with the state and with public opinion. This is to me the most plausible practical meaning of the widely accepted theory that the state should exist for the benefit of the individuals rather than the other way round.

Later we shall explore one implication of Bay's concept of freedom in the case of an organized enterprise such as a university, in which individuals must join together—thus modifying their individual freedom—in order to accomplish together that which cannot be attained separately and alone. But for the present, we emphasize the philosophic point or value orientation that the community of scholars, like a political jurisdiction, exists to further the development of its members.

In our review of students' freedoms and rights, we will emphasize the development of individuality, in its highest form and dimension, as the supporting reason for the establishment and maintenance of those freedoms and rights. And we shall seek to demonstrate the significant role of personnel workers in the maintenance of students'

[2] Ibid., p. 6, footnote 7.
[3] Ibid., p. 6, footnote 7. See also John P. Plamenatz, Consent, Freedom and Political Obligation. London: Oxford University Press, 1938, p. 89.
[4] Bay, op. cit., p. 387.

freedoms. It is clear from the record that, like some presidents and academic deans, some deans of students have suppressed some students' freedoms.[5] The record also is replete with instances of the opposite. We hope to quote the record in such a way as to redress the current imbalance in interpretation.

Academic freedom, as we understand it today, originated in German universities of the nineteenth century.[6] In founding Berlin University in 1809, Humboldt, Minister of Education, established academic freedom as a necessary condition in the new type of university dedicated to research as a basic method of advancing intellectual development, as well as a method of discovering new knowledge.[7] The new freedom was twofold in its scope and coverage, and was indicated by the key words, *Lernfreiheit* and *Lehrfreiheit*, freedom of learning by students and freedom of teaching by professors. Teachers were free to examine any kind of evidence related to any problem, topic, issue, or concept and also free to report their findings in lectures and publications. They enjoyed full freedom of teaching and freedom of inquiry.[8] Indeed, this freedom of inquiry was indispensable as a condition of teaching in a university. Academic freedom was ". . . the atmosphere of consent that surrounded the whole process of research and instruction." [9]

Parallel with freedom for the professor to inquire and to *profess* the results of his inquiry, German university students enjoyed freedom of learning. Students were ". . . free to roam from place to place, sampling academic wares; . . . they were free to determine the choice and sequence of courses, and were responsible to no one for regular attendance; . . . they lived in private quarters and controlled their private lives." [10] Paulsen wrote that the "freedom

[5] The reader will find documented instances and cases in Reginald H. Green and Elnora H. Coleman, *The Students' Stake in Academic and Educational Freedom.* Philadelphia: U.S. National Student Association, March, 1959. (Mimeographed.)

[6] Richard Hofstadter and Walter P. Metzger, "The German Influence," *The Development of Academic Freedom in the United States.* New York: Columbia University Press, 1955.

[7] Friedrich Paulsen, *The German Universities and University Study.* New York: Longmans, Green & Co., Inc., 1906, p. 75.

[8] For a fresh restatement of teachers' academic freedom, see Max Frank, "The Meanings of Academic Freedom," *American Association of University Professors Bulletin,* vol. 43, no. 3, pp. 498–506, September, 1957.

[9] Hofstadter and Metzger, *op. cit.,* p. 387.

[10] *Ibid.,* p. 386.

from outward compulsion is therefore the symbol of student days, the much-vaunted academic freedom." [11]

Paulsen, the German scholar, was perhaps the most eloquent of recent advocates of freedom for students. He said of the student, ". . . there is no exertion of official influence, hardly so much as advice is given him; and he is at liberty to choose to attend no lectures and to do no work." [12] The translator of Paulsen's book, Edward Delavan Perry, added this delightful footnote: "In some universities he must at least enter his name for a certain minimum number of lectures per week." [13]

Transposing the German Experience

In transposing the Germanic concept of academic freedom to American colonial-type colleges and to the state universities founded during the middle and later decades of the nineteenth century, American educators did not include all types of freedom for our students, as we shall note in a moment.

After 1900, we are told, only one American educator included students' freedoms in his analysis of academic freedom. In 1907, Charles W. Eliot referred to the "freedom to choose his studies, to refuse to attend chapel, to compete on even terms for scholarship, and to choose his own friends." [14]

The trend away from students' freedom reached a high point in 1940 when Nicholas Murray Butler, retired president of Columbia University and trained in a German university, asserted that ". . . for those who are *in statu pupillari* the phrase academic freedom has no meaning whatsoever. That phrase relates solely to freedom of thought and inquiry and to freedom of teaching on the part of accomplished scholars.[15]

[11] Paulsen, *op. cit.*, p. 265.
[12] Friedrich Paulsen, *German Universities*. New York: The Macmillan Company, 1895, p. 201.
[13] *Ibid.*
[14] Charles W. Eliot, "Academic Freedom," *Science*, vol. 26, July 5, 1907.
[15] Nicholas Murray Butler, "The True Function of a University in this World Crisis," *Vital Speeches*, vol. 7, no. 1, p. 12, Oct. 15, 1940. In an earlier speech, Butler had made no mention of students in a discussion of *Lehrfreiheit* and its development in German universities as a characteristic of universities in America. See Nicholas Murray Butler, "Academic Freedom in a Changing World," *The Obligation of Universities to the Social Order*. New York: New York University Press, 1933, pp. 466–473.

Perhaps Butler's denial of students' freedom was but a symptom of the current prewar hysteria. Whatever its significance, it served effectively to highlight the American *selective adaptation* of Germanic freedom to university life.[16] American students were not given much of *Lernfreiheit* except for Eliot's importation of freedom from classroom attendance.

Reasons for this selective importation are not entirely clear. Metzger contended that problems arising in the administrative structure of American universities, with lay boards of trustees, absorbed the attention of American theorists. Faced with the task of adorning, democratizing, and protecting the academic job, they lost sight of the goal of *Lehrfreiheit*. The focus of academic freedom in this country became primarily institutional, not educational.[17]

Certainly the failure to import *Lernfreiheit* was not because American students had not enjoyed academic freedom in German universities. Indeed, the record does show clearly that they—most of them professors or at least of graduate school status—enjoyed the delightful freedoms they themselves experienced in German universities. In spite of their enjoyable experiences, they established few similar freedoms for American undergraduate students.

Hofstadter and Metzger spell out a possible explanation in their analysis of the German experiences of some American educators. They point out that most American students going to Germany for study were young men suddenly projected into a more permissive culture.[18]

. . . we can assume that it would be an American in whom the asceticism of Calvin and the prudishness of Victoria were deeply and ineradicably ingrained who would resist the blandishments of the carefree German Sabbath, the *Kneipe* in the afternoon, and perhaps an innocent, initiating love affair. . . . To an unmeasurable degree, the German university's reputation rested on the remembrance of freedoms enjoyed that were not in any narrow sense academic. Needless to say, this did not diminish its reputation.

---

[16] Walter P. Metzger, "The German Contribution to the American Theory of Academic Freedom," *American Association of University Professors Bulletin,* vol. 41, no. 2, pp. 214–230, Summer, 1955.

[17] *Ibid.*

[18] Hofstadter and Metzger, *op. cit.,* p. 393.

We digress to make a significant point, a correction of an early interpretation of the German influence on American higher education. Often that influence has been characterized as seeming to establish impersonality as the prevailing relationship of professors with students. Moreover, this has been appraised as the origin of American abandonment of colonial concern for students, pietistic and individualistic as it was in large measure, and the shifting to students of responsibility for their out-of-class affairs. For instance, Tappan of Michigan, after his advanced education in Germany, turned his dormitories into classrooms and forced students to live in private homes.[19]

It seems likely that such an American reaction to German education was just that, a selective and modified transposition,[20] because the relationship of American students, mature and advanced in age and education, with German professors was far from impersonal.[21] Hall, Hart, and Thwing have described in detail their highly personal and friendly experiences with professors, their families, and with German students.[22]

We need to revise our earlier assignment of the word "impersonalism" to the functioning of German universities. Perhaps Americans studying in German universities misinterpreted the freeing of

[19] Charles M. Perry, *Henry Philip Tappan*. Ann Arbor, Mich.: University of Michigan Press, 1933, p. 232. See also W. H. Cowley, "The History of Student Residential Housing," *School and Society*, vol. 40, Dec. 1 and Dec. 8, 1934 pp. 705–712, 758–764.

[20] See Hofstadter and Metzger, *op. cit.*, chap. 8, for an elaboration of this thesis.

[21] W. H. Cowley, "The University in the United States of America," part I, in Edward Bradby (ed.), *"The University outside Europe*. London: Oxford University Press, 1939, pp. 58–59. Although Cowley used the word "impersonalism," he did not himself misinterpret the German pattern as one of impersonal relationships. Possibly he was referring to our own misinterpretation in *How to Counsel Students* (pp. 1–7). The term was used to describe a relationship opposite to Borden P. Bowne's "personalism," a term used to describe his concept of the relationship between a believer and the universe. See Borden P. Bowne, *Personalism*. Boston: Houghton Mifflin Company, 1908.

[22] Hall, G. Stanley: *Life and Confessions of a Psychologist*. New York: D. Appleton & Company, Inc., 1923, chap. 5, "Germany: Antioch College and Europe Again."

Hart, James Morgan: *German Universities: A Narrative of Personal Experience*. New York: G. P. Putnam's Sons, 1878, pp. 274–275.

Thwing, Charles Franklin: *The American and German University: One Hundred Years of History*. New York: The Macmillan Company, 1928, chaps. 1–3.

German professors from concern for students' personal problems in order to concentrate upon *Wissenschaftlehre*. Whatever the facts, American educators and personnel workers did indeed forge new relationships in the late decades of the past century to substitute for the colonial pattern and in so doing, they quoted the German pattern as *the* desirable one. We carried forward this interpretation of the German pattern as justification, or rationalization, for a "sink or swim" indifference for American students until the second decade of this century, when new forces caused us to establish a new program of concern for students and their personal problems.

George Williams has restored to the current literature the familiar phrase "sink or swim" that has too long denoted this indifferent attitude toward students.[23]

Just last week the Dean of Sciences of a university with almost 20,000 students told me: "When we hire young fellows and assistants, we ask ourselves only one question: Is the young man capable of going ahead and doing good research as a graduate student? We don't give a damn about his teaching ability. We let the students sink or swim; it's their affair, not ours."

Surely this philosophy of education was constructed in America out of twentieth-century debasing of higher education according to the impersonal model of production-line manufacturing. The German scholars would be shocked at such dehumanizing of the relationship between students and teachers. Not even the myopic and "mole-like" European philologist, so caustically described by Nietzsche,[24] held such an impersonal valuation of students. This "sink or swim" philosophy of education is a tragic departure from the centuries-old tradition of Western education; it is *not* an extension of that tradition. Such educators, not personnel workers, are the real interlopers and intruders in liberal education as we have seen it develop since the twelfth century. Our task, then, becomes a necessity—to humanize as well as individualize education for students. Fortunately, many scientists share our concern for the individual student. Sir William Osler, distinguished medical teacher, expressed a humanized valuation of students in these

[23] George Williams, *Some of My Best Friends Are Professors*. New York: Abelard-Schuman, Inc., Publishers, 1958, p. 98.
[24] Frau Foerster-Nietzsche (trans. by Anthony M. Ludovici): *The Life of Nietzsche*, vol. 1. New York: Sturgis and Walton Company, 1912, pp. 183–184.

words: "When a simple earnest spirit animates a college, there is no appreciable interval between the teacher and the taught—both are in the same class, the one a little more advanced than the other." [25]

We return from our digression about German importations to the reason for the failure of Americans to return with academic freedoms for students, only with those for professors.

Under the prevailing American societal and collegiate conditions, it would have been unlikely that faculties or trustees would formally vote to follow the German tradition of official and institutional neutrality and indifference toward student behavior and affairs outside of the classroom. Indeed relevant to our thesis is the observation that, until the middle of the nineteenth century, American college students were regarded as ". . . morally deficient or immature. . . . The college in America could not be a market place of ideas so long as it regarded its students as both gullible and perverse." [26] Such a point of view was an outgrowth of denominational educators' attempts to rally "Christian piety and humanistic study against the skeptical rationalism of the Enlightenment." [27] The relative immaturity in age and behavior of American students, faculty preoccupation with problems of disruptive and riotous student behavior and discipline, traditional denominational fervor and piety, crushing financial poverty—these and other conditions in the American college during the late eighteenth and early nineteenth centuries in a real sense precluded the granting to our students of the much-vaunted academic freedom so firmly established in Germanic culture and tradition.

Limitations of the German Experience

We have examined the German concept of students' freedom because some proponents of efforts to formulate an American policy refer to the prototype of German universities before the First World War as support for their advocacy. Now, in reviewing the German experiences, one is indeed impressed with the record of intellectual and personal maturity achieved by some German stu-

[25] A. C. Spectorsky (ed.), *The College Years*. New York: Hawthorn Books, Inc., 1958, p. 380.

[26] Hofstadter and Metzger, *op. cit.*, pp. 282–283.

[27] *Ibid.*, p. 277.

dents under conditions of complete autonomy and self-responsibility. But there is another side of the coin which bears inspection.

There are several restrictions in application indicated in the lessons to be learned from the German experience. Hadley of Yale referred long ago to the moral excesses often resulting from this freedom of the individual and rejected this freedom as a model for American students.[28] Undoubtedly these excesses were part of the price paid in "risking boys to gain men," to use Rousseau's words. Some American educators might be willing to take such risks, but they must first win acceptance by the public trustees and parents. At this point we begin to identify the persistence of tradition and the influence extended from the colonial college and, indeed, from later Puritan culture.

Perhaps the acceptance of academic freedom would be more readily forthcoming if the gains to be realized had been clearly and convincingly demonstrated by experiences with some younger American students. An American educator of the past century might have agreed that American students should be granted some of the German type of freedom, but effective leadership and clear demonstrations were needed to persuade more than a few college leaders to move in the direction of greater freedom for students. Even today we need to appraise both the risks to be taken and the gains to be attained by allowing certain types of academic freedom for students. The mere blind imitation of the German model is not necessarily appropriate in the realization of American objectives.

A second and more important guide line is available for evaluating the German experiment in academic autonomy and freedom. The fundamental strategy of academic freedom for students is lost in many discussions of that freedom as formulated in German universities more than a century ago. The purpose of that freedom, as conceived by German professors, was to develop men, independent in thought and purpose, fully conscious of their own moral and social responsibility. *Responsibility, not license, was the purpose of German academic freedom.* "Only in the midst of freedom, however, can one learn what use to make of freedom, how to

[28] Arthur T. Hadley, "Academic Freedom in Theory and Practice," *The Atlantic Monthly*, vol. 91, pp. 152–160, 334–344, February–March, 1903.

commune with oneself and govern oneself." [29] Paulsen quoted Von Sybel with respect to the strategic philosophy justifying academic freedom for students:[30]

We cannot estimate highly enough the advantage accruing from the tendency of our universities, in their innermost nature, toward the complete emancipation of a man's spirit. In the preliminary school authority rules the entire man, as it must of necessity do; and later, the practice of a profession, and with it authority again, claims considerable portions of our life. But every cultured man on German soil must and shall have at least one period in his life when the organs of authority, when even nation, state, and teacher demand of him, as the highest of all commandments, that he shall be spiritually free.

Thus we note that the early advocates of academic freedom passionately contended that freedom was a solemn requirement and requisite of *male* maturity. Such a method of achieving maturity needs to be critically appraised to determine its relevancy to the needs and objectives of American education. We are not suggesting that male, or even female, maturity is less desirable and necessary in America today than it was in Germany. But surely Lilge's appraisal of German higher education and its ineffectiveness during the Hitler *Zeit* justify a critical reappraisal of German attitudes before we transpose them to our own institutions.[31] It is possible that we may have improved upon the much-vaunted academic freedom which is so frequently distorted in transposition as an attitude and policy of indifference, sink or swim, toward the maturity learning of students within and outside of the classroom.

In making such a critical appraisal, we clearly see that there were risks involved in throwing an individual upon his own resources if he were to become an independent, fully self-reliant man. Such risks are indeed readily acknowledged as inherent in the development of men of all sorts and conditions. In justification of the German formula of maturity, Paulsen quoted Rousseau to the effect that "we must risk boys if we would gain men." [32] But, as

---

[29] Paulsen, *German Universities, op. cit.,* p. 207.
[30] *Ibid.,* pp. 209–210.
[31] Frederic Lilge, *The Abuse of Learning.* New York: The Macmillan Company, 1948.
[32] Paulsen, *German Universities, op. cit.,* p. 209.

counterpoint, in our efforts to transpose the German concept of academic freedom to American students, we must not ignore or underestimate the influence in the last century of higher education in the
men's colleges on the Eastern seaboard. No such moral or intellectual risks were permitted within these American colonial colleges.
Rather did the faculties seek to prevent the risks of immorality
and impiety through rigid and suppressive control of behavior.
At few points do we find such striking contrasts in two national
philosophies of education—German and colonial American. And
it could well be that a thorough examination of both of these
models will prove each to be less than fully effective in the present-
day society, with its emphasis upon freedom to be achieved through
interdependence within a corporate state.[33]

A third guide line in our appraisal is the overlooked point that
not every student in the German university of a century ago was
considered competent, qualified, or eligible for such complete
freedom to become himself without external and adult restraint.
Paulsen concluded that no infallible way has yet been found to
make all students reasonable, industrious, and virtuous. Then he
said, "Let it be admitted that our system is unsuitable for twenty
or thirty out of every hundred who are not capable of freedom and
never learn to use it aright." [34]

We would do well to approach our task of redefining students'
freedoms with awareness of Paulsen's dictum. Perhaps we may
discover that the American concept of unique individuality holds
true not only for aptitudes for work, but also for aptitudes for responsible use of freedom. This is not to anticipate that some
students should be denied freedoms. Rather it is to suggest that
perhaps we will conclude, after exercising our academic freedom
to investigate freedom of inquiry as a necessary condition of
effective education, that students must learn, through vigorous
effort, effective ways of using or exercising their freedom. Such a
conclusion would not be a startlingly new discovery—that freedom
is less than an automatically acquired absolute as a universal way
of life and that we need to devote perhaps our lifetimes to learning
effective uses of freedom. Even staunch friends of freedom agreed

[33] William O. Stanley, "Freedom and Education in a Corporate Society,"
Educational Theory, vol. 7, no. 1, January, 1957.
[34] Paulsen, *German Universities and University Study, op. cit.,* p. 296.

that "youth's right to dissent should not be mistaken for right to mutiny or rowdyism." [35]

An additional guide line, in our appraisal of the German model of students' freedoms, is the firm assertion of German educators that freedom from outer compulsion and restraint was not given merely to do as he please. Freedom must rather be used to gain full stature of maturity; it is, indeed, *the* necessary condition, so Paulsen argued, for full development of the individual. Thus it follows that a most serious responsibility is correlated with and prerequisite to academic freedom. Paulsen argued in this way:[36]

Responsibility is the correlate of this freedom. The less of external compulsion there is, the more imperative is the duty of self-control. Whoever confounds freedom with license misunderstands its meaning; it is given to the individual not that he may do as he pleases, but that he may learn to govern himself.

Transposing to the American Scene

In turning from German to American student life, one may comment in passing that the correlate of responsibility seems to receive little emphasis and attention in current discussions of students' freedoms. Rather are contemporary discussions largely centered on efforts to win freedom from external restraint,[37] freedom from administrative supervision, freedom from this or that imposition.[38] Seldom does one hear discussion of what use the student shall make of his freedom from restraint, except to enjoy freedom from adult supervision. This is indeed a far cry from Paulsen's concept of the imperative use of freedom in the development of self-

[35] Max Black et al., "Faculty-Trustee Relations," *American Association of University Professors Bulletin*, vol. 42, no. 4, p. 622, 1956.

[36] Paulsen, *German Universities and University Study, op. cit.*, p. 266.

[37] Latham used the term "freedom from restraint" in appraising recent actions of the U.S. Supreme Court as "an unsleeping effort to repel interference with the maximum autonomy that can be reposed in the individual—especially interference by the government." See Earl Latham, "The Supreme Court's Crusade for Freedom," *Commentary*, p. 108, August, 1959.

[38] *Academic Freedom*. New York: American Civil Liberties Union, Committee on Academic Freedom, 1959.

Friedson, Eliot: *Student Government, Student Leaders and the American College*. Philadelphia: U.S. National Student Association, 1955.

MacIver, Robert M.: *Academic Freedom in Our Time*. New York: Columbia University Press, 1955.

responsibility and maturity. But one may hazard the hope that the contemporary emphasis on efforts to win freedoms from external, i.e., administrative, restraint will, in due course, be followed by sober and mature recognition of the correlative responsibility to make wise use of these freedoms gained, including the use of freedom to respond maturely to external criticisms and even to unreasonable attacks upon the internal workings of the academic enterprise.[39]

An exhaustive analysis of recent (1955) faculty apprehensions and pressures about freedom to teach and freedom of political belief and conduct is reported by Paul F. Lazarsfeld and Wagner Thielens, Jr., in *The Academic Mind: Social Scientists in a Time of Crisis.*[40] The facts reported are deeply disquieting. Nonetheless, one need not agree with Hacker that "when universities are directed largely by the professors . . . academic freedom in America and academic prestige will have a much better chance of being secure in and outside of 'difficult years.'"[41]

In this connection, one might profitably view the problem of academic freedom for our students in the light of the psychologists' identification of the college adolescent's struggle for separation of his identify from his family, which first takes the form of fighting against perceived parental intrusion upon one's individuality. This stage of maturity is then usually followed by a sober use of the freedom gained for more self-responsibility. This would seem to be a sound general schema of students' progression from freshman to senior year in college. Indeed, if such gains are realized by students, then any controversy or conflict over academic freedoms would be well justified as necessary and perhaps minimal conditions which are required in the maturing process itself.

Finally, in appraising the relevancy of the German experience in constructing conditions favorable to our own freedom of inquiry, we need to consider some significant differences in the two types of

[39] George Z. F. Bereday, "The Freedom to Attack the University," *The Journal of Higher Education,* January, 1956, pp. 8–10. See also Zachariah Chafee, Jr., "The Freedom to Think," *The Blessings of Liberty.* Philadelphia: J. B. Lippincott Company, 1956.

[40] Published by Free Press, Glencoe, Ill., 1958. See chap. 8, "Impaired Relations with Students."

[41] Louis M. Hacker, "Academic Freedom in the 'Difficult Years,'" *Civil Liberties,* no. 67, February, 1959.

universities. In the Germany of a century and more ago, college preparatory and general education courses were turned over to the *gymnasium* (high school), leaving the university free for advanced inquiry and instruction. Residential facilities were abandoned or decreased relatively, and the student largely was left to shift for himself. The admission age of university students was raised. These changed conditions related to the new societal responsibility assigned to the universities, to help reconstruct German culture through *Wissenschaft*. All of these differences combined to liberate ". . . the German professor from most parental responsibilities. There was less danger, where the student-teacher relation was an *entente cordiale* and not a forced alliance, that the presence of students would spoil the inspiration of searchers. There was a greater chance, in the freer devotion of mind to mind, for the habit of discipleship to be reborn."[42]

If such results could but be obtained in American universities, then surely we would be rewarded in our efforts to forge forms of academic freedom appropriate to our American society. In a real sense, we interpret the mission of student personnel workers to be joining with student leaders and academic colleagues in such a quest.

THE AMERICAN CAMPUS

Some college campuses continue to reveal the dominating influence of the colonial college with its tradition of restrictions on students' affairs.[43] In these institutions, the German model seems to have exerted but little influence, especially with regard to freedom of inquiry with respect to controversial issues. Perhaps the early American tradition of restriction of discussion to noncontroversial topics was too firmly ingrained to be modified by the German influences. To evaluate the full force of our own early tradition, we recall for the reader two incidents occurring long ago. They seem to have their counterparts in Friedson's report of his recent investigation. In 1832, the Jefferson [*sic*] Society of the University of Virginia sponsored a student oration on Jefferson's birthday concerning the abolition of slavery, quoting

[42] Hofstadter and Metzger, *op. cit.*, p. 370.
[43] Friedson, *op. cit.*

in support the opinions of Washington and Jefferson. The faculty was disturbed and resolved that ". . . because the university was supported by all parties, it was unwise to bring up such a controversial topic. Hereafter, they ruled, there should be no oration on any distracting question of state or national policy nor on any point of theological dispute." [44]

A second illustration of the American attitude toward freedom of speech for students occurred at about the same time. In 1833, an antislavery society was formed at Lane Theological Seminary, Cincinnati. After some debates by students, one of whom was the son of an ex-slave, the trustees disbanded the club with this *obiter dictum*: ". . . education must be completed before the young are fitted to engage in the collisions of active life [and thus] no associations of Societies among the students ought to be allowed in [the] Seminary except such as have for their immediate object improvement in the prescribed course of studies." [45]

Now with these two ancient examples before us, we select one from the period following the First World War. It will illustrate, not prove, our point that the persistent restrictive tradition of the colonial college is a possible explanation of the difficulty of forging appropriate forms of academic freedom in America. Our discussion will, we hope, serve to emphasize some of the difficulties facing administrators who carry some partial responsibility for maintaining academic freedom. Between the early incidents and those of the 1920 period, the controversy over academic freedom was largely one between trustees and faculty. [46] The climax of that controversy was reached in the famous Wisconsin pronouncement which we quote in the next chapter.

In 1921, Vice-president Calvin Coolidge wrote a series of articles for the *Delineator* entitled "Enemies of the Republic." He cited the report in the *Vassar Miscellany News* of a student who had attended a Senate committee hearing. Concerning this hearing, she said she was "quite impressed by the Soviet ambassador" and "struck by his moderation and intelligence compared to the narrowness of

[44] Ernest Earnest, *Academic Procession*. Indianapolis: The Bobbs-Merrill Company, Inc., 1953, p. 85.
[45] *Ibid.*, p. 85.
[46] Hofstadter and Metzger, *op. cit.*

some of the committee." [47] Coolidge also quoted from a *Radcliffe News* report on a speech before a socialist club containing this statement: "Every society must have a state, and we must not stop with the United States of America, but go on and achieve the United States of the world."[48]

Earnest continued with his analysis of the controversy over issues and personalities in the colleges during this period. He refers to the prevalent practice of organizing procedures whereby some students reported on the content of professors' lectures. He quotes Harry Haldeman, founder of the Better America Federation of America: "Through the children of the best families throughout the land, who are attending universities, we are having students of radical tendencies watched. We are receiving reports of what is going on both as to students and teachers that uphold radical doctrines and views." [49]

It is perhaps unnecessary to refer further to records of the prevailing climate of opinion. Free speech was suspect in a time of frantic search for defense against the invasion by "true believers" who threatened the Republic's foundations and citizens' freedoms.[50] And it seemed at times—as was the case thirty years later in the crusade of Senator McCarthy—that we must lose our civil liberties in our very effort to save them.

That this was an early period of danger from external forces is clear three decades later. Our colleges had been invaded by repressive forces, and another invasion was to be made a decade later.[51] And our sincere but hysterical defense was to repress discussion and insulate students from controversial and radical ideas foreign to our culture. We hysterically ignored the lessons of history about repression of freedoms, and we later were to question whether the great German tradition of academic freedom had proved

[47] Earnest, *op. cit.*, p. 260.
[48] *Ibid.*
[49] *Ibid.*, p. 261.
[50] Not all educators were silent in this decade. See "A Student's Right to Hear: A Presidential Defense," *American Association of University Professors Bulletin*, vol. 44, no. 4, pp. 764–768, December, 1958. A letter written in 1921 by President Hopkins of Dartmouth in response to an attack by an alumnus against a campus speaker.
[51] Lotus Delta Coffman, "The Exploitation of Youth," *The Educational Record*, vol. 17, no. 1, pp. 95–105, 1936.

effective in defense of the German culture.[52] That there were real grounds for our fears of invasion was clear two decades later, when the revealed record showed clearly that some of our students had been ideationally seduced with lies and false ideals.

We now conclude that we need constantly to continue our search for sound ideas. But perhaps we have now learned that even a century of effort to repress foreign ideas is inadequate for sifting and winnowing the kernels of truth from the chaff of untruth. A critical appraisal of the current college scene will indicate that we have not yet reached a conclusion concerning effective ways of conducting our inquiries in search for truth. Our colleges and universities must continue their search for methods of inquiry which will yield at least partial understanding of the great issues that divide our society.

FREEDOM OF INQUIRY TODAY

Perhaps it is not unduly optimistic to conclude that today, whatever tomorrow may bring, the climate of opinion on some campuses is shifting from the colonial pattern of regimentation of behavior and early nineteenth-century repression of radical thinking to a current American approximation of the German freedom of inquiry and learning. At the least, the colonial, often bigoted, evangelical fervor has been largely replaced by concern for students' intellectual development and habits of critical inquiry in expanding areas of man's understanding.

Thus it is that today many college campuses both reflect and respond to the community's controversies and inquiries concerning freedoms and liberties. In this present discussion, we are not so much involved with the merits and dimensions of a particular current controversy. We are rather concerned with the role of the student personnel worker, especially the dean of students, in helping to maintain conditions which make for serious and free discussion and inquiry about such issues.

The scene is not cause for smug contentment. On many fronts, academic freedom among students is being challenged and criticized. We find that, currently, some admissions practices are sub-

[52] Lilge, *op. cit.*

jected to scrutiny with regard to possible discrimination on the basis of race and religion. And private housing quarters are likewise investigated concerning discriminatory practices based on race and religion. Indeed, the very question of the freedom of the student to live where he wishes, without the university's supervision concerning moral conditions, sanitary and safety conditions, and supervised social affairs, is a lively issue on many campuses. For instance, in May of 1958, students at Cornell University, long an established citadel for academic freedom for professors, revolted against ". . . a proposed tightening of rules that now permit undergraduate girls to attend unchaperoned house parties in off-campus rooming houses. . . . According to some non-fraternity students, any ban on their house parties would constitute discrimination." [53]

To continue, the asserted right of fraternities to determine their own membership standards, including discrimination based on race and religion, has led to their demands for an autonomy which is said to be based upon the constitutional right to select one's own friends in voluntary associations.[54]

In its 1957 meeting, the National Interfraternity Council heard a report from its special committee on autonomy: "It was unanimously agreed [by the committee] that the 1953 resolution on autonomy was authoritative and correct."

The 1953 resolution was as follows:[55]

Whereas the national fraternity system has over the years made notable contributions to the educational programs of colleges and universities of the United States and Canada, and

Whereas the National Interfraternity Conference earnestly desires that these contributions shall be continued and if possible expanded, and

Whereas such contributions have been made possible largely as the result of the character of membership of fraternities, especially with regard to unity of purpose and compatibility of interest, and

Whereas anything that tends to dissipate that unity of purpose and compatibility of interest weakens the fraternity,

[53] *New York Times*, May 23, 1958. A second story on June 8 quoted the student council president as saying that students' resentment was directed more against the nonconsultative methods by means of which various restrictions were imposed than against the restrictions themselves.

[54] *National Interfraternity Conference Yearbook*, Forty-ninth Annual Meeting, New York, 1958.

[55] *Ibid.*, p. 50.

BE IT RESOLVED:

1. That in the opinion of the National Interfraternity Conference each member fraternity should have the right to adopt qualifications for membership applicable to all its chapters free from any interference or restriction by any non-member;

2. That any attempt to restrict or regulate the right of a fraternity to choose its own membership from among students of good moral and scholastic standing in any college or university in which it has a chapter is an interference in the fundamental principle of free association;

3. That in accordance with such principles the National Interfraternity Conference declares itself in favor of fraternity autonomy with respect to fraternity membership.

The American Civil Liberties Union, under date of August, 1956, issued a statement on academic freedom and civil liberties of students. According to this pronouncement, a student should be privileged—[56]

. . . to participate in the total work of the educational institution. . . . to express his own views as an individual; should ". . . live under a government of law, created, where appropriate, by joint action,"

Students should be permitted to organize their own student government:

. . . should be free to organize and join associations for educational, political, social, religious, cultural, and other lawful purposes.

They should not be required to file a list of members but should be free to use rooms and other facilities as far as the primary use for educational purposes permits.

A student organization should be free to choose its own faculty adviser.

. . . college administrators face the difficult responsibility of measuring the degree of freedom that students enjoy. They also have responsibility for defending this freedom against hostile and open irresponsible forces in the outside community; . . . it should be the proper responsibility of schools and colleges to encourage students to meet, to organize, to speak and to listen, to participate in independent activity for political, religious, social and recreational purposes. . . .

They should be free to organize their forums and to publish their student newspaper, free to determine their own news and editorial policies.

[56] *Academic Freedom and Civil Liberties of Students.* New York: American Civil Liberties Union, August, 1956

FREEDOM FROM ADMINISTRATORS

On many campuses the cause of academic freedom for students takes the form of efforts to free students from supervision by administrators. Clearly, to many students, the issue is not restricted to their freedom of inquiry and expression of ideologies; rather it involves the critical questioning of the institution's right to impose restrictions of any type upon them. We turn to an examination of this aspect of the academic-freedom issue. We propose to examine the claimed justifications for such restraints. In the very organization of an educational institution in American culture, one does find historical precedent, if not justification, for rules and regulations governing students in their out-of-class life, both organized and individual. Elsewhere we have reviewed many of these ancient rules and regulations in connection with the problem of collegiate discipline.[57] And earlier we quoted Hofstadter and Metzger, who referred to characterizations of the students a century ago as immature and essentially incapable of moral and self-responsibility.[58] But historical precedent scarcely justifies continuance of many rules of the past. Indeed, we doubt that many students ever were so morally depraved as to justify all of the rules and regulations found in the ancient annals of some institutions.[59] But we contend that rules and regulations are requisite to many institutions. We conclude that the real issue centers on methods used in the maintenance of orderliness and upon the reasonableness of the procedures used.

WHOSE RESPONSIBILITY IS ACADEMIC FREEDOM?

Academic freedom and civil liberties for students involve the dean of students and the staff which supervises activities and organizations. This involvement of the dean of students has historical

[57] E. G. Williamson and John D. Foley, *Counseling and Discipline.* McGraw-Hill Book Company, Inc., New York, 1949.

[58] Hofstadter and Metzger, *op. cit.,* pp. 282–283.

[59] To buttress this point, we suggest that the reader consult E. Merton Coulter, *College Life in the Old South.* New York: The Macmillan Company, 1928.

roots in the gradual shifting of responsibility for student affairs from the trustees to the president,[60] to the faculty, and then to the agents of the president. In many instances in the early colonial colleges, the trustees supervised some student affairs, especially those involving disciplining students for riotous behavior. Gradually this duty was transferred to the faculty, then to the president, and finally to the president's assistant, currently called "dean of students." One cannot but be depressed by reading the history of efforts to control behavior. Student behavior was riotous; scarcely a school year passed without one riot. In describing student life of this early period, Hofstadter and Metzger generalized in these words: ". . . a semester unmarred by expulsions was memorable in college annals; a chapel that escaped vandalism enjoyed a most unnatural quiet. The chief instrument of student aggression—the firecracker—was a part of standard student equipment; the ivied halls would shake to the reverberations of explosions." [61] To counteract this depressing story of American student life, one should turn to Thwing's stimulating documentation of the gradual, but painfully slow, transition from lawlessness on the campus to some semblance of civilized behavior.[62]

But the long history of repression of student behavior has left its rigid and heavy legacy on many campuses. For instance, there persist on many campuses inflexible mores of fighting administrative and faculty authority. We must concede, in justification of such mores, that the record reveals many, many instances of brutal repression and violation of civil liberties of students. Nevertheless, the continuing atmosphere of conflict between students and any agency of authority is a challenge to our efforts at reform. Not the least of the undesirable effects of such a tradition of conflict is the resulting difficulty of perceiving and evaluating the issue of academic freedom as anything more than organized and persistent guerrilla warfare between the institution and organized student groups.

There are, of course, other important phases of the issue of stu-

[60] George P. Schmidt, The Old Time College President. New York: Columbia University Press, 1930.
[61] Hofstadter and Metzger, op. cit., p. 307.
[62] Charles Franklin Thwing, A History of Higher Education in America. New York: D. Appleton & Company, Inc., 1906.

dents' academic freedom. The German tradition emphasized the conditions necessary for intellectual activity in terms of freedom to explore and investigate any problem or question which might occur to either student or faculty. This was an institutional atmosphere of assent and consent. Unfortunately, in American institutions, particularly those under public support, this is a freedom but little understood by the public at large as necessary in academic progression, and it is a freedom constantly interrupted by advocates of one dogma or another. In a recent newsletter, the Division of Higher Education of the Congregational Christian Churches answered the question: Who threatens academic freedom?

Freedom, it was contended, ought to include the often-denied right of a student "to comment on the nature of the education to which he is subjected . . . influences nearer home which historically have limited freedoms in our colleges and universities." The requirement by faculty for "blind obedience and conformity and an outward show of respect and deference" is mentioned. Also included are the administration's demands for endorsement of *faits accompli,* and trustees who "look upon the president as an errand boy—and faculty members as economic failures who should not meddle in important matters." All of these are indicted as interference with academic freedom. Finally, the public is indicted for application of "the theory that the schools belong to the people. . . ." This leads to attempts to determine academic policy through majority vote "or by the nuisance value of minority pressure groups. . . ." [63]

Such a proprietary attitude of taxpayers and trustees seriously restricts our colleges. Friedson identified the fear of public criticism, related to financial support, as a prime motivation behind efforts to control and restrict students' freedoms and activities.[64] No doubt, many restrictions of students' academic freedom have been justified on the grounds that the public, especially donors or legislators, would demand them. This is perhaps as true in the case of private institutions supported by private philanthropy as it is in the case of public institutions supported by legislative

[63] *Newsletter No. 68,* p. 1, Division of Higher Education and the AMA Board of Home Missions, Congregational Christian Churches, Chicago, March, 1958.
[64] Friedson, *op. cit.,* pp. 44–45.

appropriations.[65] The fear of public criticism has, no doubt, been used and overused by both administrators and some faculty members. On the other hand, liberally oriented faculty and students sometimes seem to contend that such fears are not fully justified and should be, or can be, ignored. Perhaps one can, indeed, discover many instances of unnecessary anxiety states in some administrators. Nonetheless, serious students should heed Henry's generalization, based upon years of administrative dealing with problems of public accountability: ". . . in a democratic society, public attitudes toward issues affecting the course of the institutions of that society are an essential part of the climate in which administrative decisions are to be made." [66]

To continue our review of conditions leading to restrictions on students, we may identify still another reason for these restrictions— the eagerness of some administrators to manage student affairs. No doubt, many overeager deans, and sometimes faculty advisers, do use their managerial authority and their backlog of experience to deprive students of some learning opportunities. But let us look at this phenomenon from another equally valid and relevant perspective. For some strange reason, the tradition has evolved that this form of usurpation of students' rights to make their own mistakes seems to be a more serious offense when committed in the extracurriculum than in the classroom. When a teacher does all the discussing in the classroom and, in fact, dominates discussion, it appears to be an acceptable, even if unpopular, practice. But when an administrator, especially a dean of students, contributes ideas and participates in management of student affairs, it sometimes appears to be a violation of academic freedom in the extracurriculum. To one who views the extracurriculum as a part of the total educational program, it would seem that an administrator has a significant teaching function which cannot be achieved by playing a passive role. But, of course, dominance is never desirable or necessary in playing that role. Good teaching is good teaching, whether it be in the extracurriculum or in the curriculum, and a

<hr/>

[65] See Hofstadter and Metzger, *op. cit.*, for the record of repression of faculty in both types of institutions.

[66] David D. Henry, "Public Attitudes on Academic Freedom, Politics and Tenure," *Bulletin of the Association of American Colleges*, vol. 36, no. 3, p. 351, Fall, 1950.

dominating teacher in either area does violate, perhaps not academic freedom, but at least students' learning opportunities.

Still another identifiable and more promising condition making for student liberties is the recent tendency to create more active and responsible functions and roles for students in institutional policy making.[67] To some extent this is a tremendous change in the passive role of the student over the centuries, since he was too long the object of instruction. The long history of efforts to cultivate a more active participating role in the learning process has been clearly traced.[68] The many attempts to define the student's active role in his own affairs outside the classroom have been equally well documented.[69]

We note that regimentation has occurred in the extracurriculum as well as in the classroom. But there is one essential difference. The student could not often revolt in the classroom, so he vented his frustrations in unrestrained living and in organized riots in the dormitory and the extracurriculum. Perhaps as a consequence, there developed in the extracurriculum a dominant tradition of autonomy, in part encouraged by the faculty's preoccupation with intellectual learning alone. And it became traditional that there was some inherent right in the student's desire to manage his own affairs outside the classroom. Such a tradition often ran counter to the accountability and responsibility carried by the administrator—usually the president, and later his dean of students—for disruptive behavior outside of the classroom. These and many other factors seem to have led to attempts to curb some free play of students, as well as to indignant resistance against these unfair intrusions into this area of students' rights.

[67] Harry H. Lunn, *The Student's Role in College Policy-making.* Washington: American Council on Education, 1957. See also the many publications of the U.S. National Student Association.

[68] William Boyd, *The History of Western Education*, 4th ed. London: A. & C. Black, Ltd., 1947.

[69] Haskins, Charles H.: *The Rise of Universities.* New York: Peter Smith, 1940, part III, pp. 79–126.

Rait, R. S.: *Life in the Medieval University.* Cambridge, Mass.: Harvard University Press, 1912.

Rashdall, Hastings: *The Universities of Europe in the Middle Ages,* 3 vols. New York: Oxford University Press, 1895.

Sheldon, Henry D.: *Student Life and Customs.* New York: D. Appleton & Company, Inc., 1901.

THE DEAN OF STUDENTS AND ACADEMIC FREEDOM

Having noted these identifiable trends and currents which are often working at cross-purposes, we turn now to an evaluation of the role of the dean of students in the maintenance of academic freedom and civil liberties among students. On the one hand, he is expected to maintain order and decency and to prevent riotous living and riots. On the other hand, he is expected to respect the basic civil liberties of students, to avoid harsh repression of and interference with freedom of thought, and to respect the relevant and legitimate privacy of behavior of students, both on and off campus. In the midst of his often conflicting roles, the dean of students also has an opportunity to assist students in organizing the extracurriculum so that it can contribute to the total intellectual development of the students, as well as to their personal and emotional and social maturity.[70]

As an educator he must respect a certain amount of autonomy in the extracurriculum, as well as in the privacy of student life. Nevertheless, he must clearly stop short of acknowledging complete autonomy in student-managed affairs because of justified institutional responsibilities for some types of student affairs and behavior. The annual exploration and redefinition of the areas of concern and autonomy in student affairs is itself but one of the many changing dynamic tasks of student leaders, working cooperatively with the administration and the faculty.

The dean of students as an administrator is one central official who, in the name of the president, the trustees, and sometimes the faculty, must approve or disapprove some organized programs and activities. Understandably, he is often viewed as the one who not only makes the rules but also enforces them in student affairs. Many dean of students have unwisely neglected to develop procedures in which their judicial, legislative, and executive functions are shared with student and faculty committees. Too frequently, the dean of students as administrator has operated within the anonymity and secrecy of his own office; he has not often vol-

[70] E. G. Williamson, "The Dean of Students as Educator," *The Educational Record*, July, 1957, pp. 230–240.

untarily subjected his roles and functions to public scrutiny. Consequently, in such cases, he has appeared to be arbitrary and beyond public accountability. More recently the tradition of public accountability and public review of administrative functions has been evolving, especially with regard to matters which involve wide freedom of discussion of controversial issues.[71]

With respect to such a sensitive matter as civil liberties, especially in view of the unsavory history and some current practices, it is clear that unilateral administrative action by any central administrator is not an appropriate method of operation. And the dean of students should be the first to recognize that civil liberties and some other aspects of present-day student affairs are indeed a shared community responsibility.

IN OPPOSITION TO STUDENT ISOLATION FROM AND INDEPENDENCE OF INSTITUTIONAL RESPONSIBILITES

Sometimes discussion of academic freedom for students leads to advocacy of oversimplified and absolutistic solutions. Until some judicious practices were introduced on campuses, absolutistic repression of student behavior and student liberties was given thorough trial. Its gradual, but too-long-delayed, abandonment was followed by a reactive attempt to define the administration out of the sphere of responsibility for student behavior and affairs. This was the age in which students, with some administrative and faculty support, sought for an area of complete independence and autonomy.[72] It was advocated by some that the institution turn over to the students the management of their own affairs and leave them to their own devices, assuming no responsibility for what they did outside of the classroom. In support of such independence of

[71] *Ibid.* See also E. G. Williamson and B. J. Borreson, "Learning to Resolve Social Conflicts," *The Educational Record,* January, 1950, pp. 26–38.

[72] While MacIver uses the modifier "relative," it seems clear that he is advocating autonomy with but few restrictions and, as indicated elsewhere, these few have to do with morality of students' behavior. In discussing academic freedom and democratic government he says, ". . . it [academic freedom] means the relative autonomy of student groups and student organizations in the conduct of their own extracurricular and extramural activities. . . ." MacIver, *op. cit.,* p. 208.

action, some advocates referred to academic freedom in European universities, especially in German universities—a model we have evaluated at some length. And, in further support of autonomy, an analogy was frequently drawn between the free enterprise in ideas on a campus and the free discussion of Hyde Park or Pershing Square.

A contrasting point of view originates in the field of political science. In his thoughtful appraisal of human freedom as a social institution, Bay concluded that—[73]

No society can give full freedom to all individuals or, indeed, even to one individual. The price of social cooperation in the service of joint needs is acceptance of restraints; even a mere physical co-existence in the same society requires some restraints. Moreover, there are conflicts within every individual too. He must keep some goals and impulses in check if he wants to promote or express others. I have already referred to the observation that men are apt to have short-term desires as well as long-term ideas of what is desirable. No person in any society can achieve maturity without experiencing conflicts of this and other kinds and thus sensing at times the necessity of restraining some of his impulses and desires.

Such aspirations, while not new to the academic scene, do raise very pertinent questions, most of which have not been fully answered or resolved. It will perhaps give point to our subsequent case study in Chapter 10 if we state some of the questions suggested by a thoughtful and serious review of the proposal for independence in student affairs:

Are there no outer limits in academic freedom for students?

To what extent does the public, or do the several publics, have any rights to criticize and to influence student rights and privileges and behavior?

Is absolute freedom from external restraints desirable or possible? [74]

Are restraints ever justifiable in terms of their effects upon the maturing of the individual student?

[73] Bay, *op. cit.*, pp. 15–16.

[74] The author heard President Pusey declare at the Harvard commencement in June, 1958, while conferring degrees upon candidates in the Law School, "You are qualified to apply those wise restraints that make men free."

Does a college or university have any right to protect its "good name" from undesirable behavior by its students?[75]

Is a campus open to any use by any citizen or by any students for any purpose, political, moral, social, religious, etc.?[76]

Does freedom of inquiry operate without any restraints or restrictions or forms of assistance in the direction of the end goal of identification of truth?

Are all students equally eligible and competent in the exercise of freedom of inquiry?

Is freedom of inquiry identical with freedom of behavior?

Is any supporting societal or institutional mechanism or apparatus required in the maintenance of freedom of inquiry?

Does the college administration have any significant contribution to make to the maintenance of academic freedom?

Is academic freedom appropriate and necessary to the faculty, but inappropriate and unnecessary for the administration?

Can freedom of inquiry be segregated, or must it be equally free for all components of a campus, including administration, students, and faculty?

What is the role of students in the maintenance of the conditions necessary for freedom of inquiry?

What appropriate procedures of public accountability are necessary in the maintenance of academic freedom by any agent or agents?

What appeal procedures concerning decisions by faculty or

[75] After framing this query, we came across a concession on this point from an unexpected source. Robert M. MacIver, clearly no advocate of administrative autonomy, conceded that "the institution must, of course, safeguard itself against any direct association of its name with any student behavior that is out of accord with its honor or its dignity and may properly intervene when any activity conducted under its aegis is seriously offensive on moral grounds." See MacIver, op. cit., p. 209.

[76] We recalled at this point the wise words of a former president who vigorously protested the defamation and exploitation of his university and his students by often ruthless reform-movement leaders determined to use the university for propaganda for one cause or another: "If youth are not to be exploited unduly by special leaders in the name of politics, religion, or social or political theories—then a way must be found to make them self-reliant and independent in thought and action." See Lotus Delta Coffman, "The Exploitation of Youth," The Educational Record, January, 1936, p. 105.

administration are necessary in the maintenance of academic freedom?

Credos. These questions are obviously biased, and our bias will now be clearly identified for appraisal by the reader. We believe that the contention that freedom is self-regulating and does not require any form of institutionalization, for example, is sheer nonsense. Even Hyde Park and Pershing Square must be maintained by some agents as public institutions so that free individuals may use them for free expression of personal opinion. Moreover, we contend that the history of academic freedom among students contains many instances of the maintenance and defense of that freedom by administrators, as well as by students and faculty. We believe that the literature of this topic is unrepresentatively full of sometimes over-hasty generalizations based upon some clearly identified administrative repressions of freedom. On the other hand, we agree that many administrators exercise their veto power in an arbitrary and capricious manner. We also agree that there are many nervous trustees and presidents and deans of students who act too hastily in taking charge of student affairs in anticipation of public criticism—which sometimes does not occur. We would also admit to a bias that the deans of students should be more aggressive in helping to establish new freedoms, rather than in merely rigidly applying more restrictions. We heartily join in advocating the aggressive reduction of "stifling paternalism" by college authorities and governing boards over student activities.[77] We also agree heartily that the college is committed to "progressive withdrawal of its authority" over students and their affairs.[78] If education is essentially a self-motivated striving for maturity through learning experiences in the curriculum and the extra-curriculum, then the gradual and seldom completed substitution of self-regulation or self-management for external supervision of these learning experiences makes sense in every educational enterprise. To continue to treat all adolescents as if they were irresponsible children, of course, is educational nonsense. But we need to remind ourselves of Paulsen's conclusion that not every student is always at a stage of maturity which makes him eligible for

[77] *Academic Freedom and Civil Liberties of Students.* New York: American Civil Liberties Union, August, 1956, p. 4.

[78] *Ibid.,* p. 3.

complete self-regulation. Taylor made a cogent observation: to be free in the making of independent choices, the "free person must know a great deal" and must "learn how to correct [his judgment] through further experience." [79]

We are also impressed with Stanley's analysis of the concept of freedom in our current corporate society, as opposed to the early concept which evolved in a society organized in much simpler fashion.[80] Stanley reminded us that the early framers of the concept of political and economic freedom ". . . lived in a time in which men, with considerable justification, regarded arbitrary governments as the chief enemy of human freedom." [81] Accordingly, they constructed elaborate safeguards to protect both the individual and his property against legal interference or violence. Thus they set historical forms in man's search for freedom *from* rather than *within* government:[82]

> The exclusion of means from the definition of freedom as the absence of governmental restraint was the product of historical circumstance and class interest rather than of any theoretical consideration.

We need to remind ourselves of the historical origin of the controversy over freedom in man's struggle for lessening of governmental restraints upon his liberty. Hutchins said that "civil liberties [are] those rights historically carved out against governmental interference with private life." [83] Some students and faculty seem to generalize from the oppressive actions of despotic kings and dictators of past centuries to college administrators—as though there were no discernible differences in context or behavior and that all those who possessed and exercised power were identically motivated and equally to be resisted and even feared. Perhaps rational examination of the relevancy of such a generalization is sometimes in order.

[79] Harold Taylor, *On Education and Freedom.* New York: Abelard-Schuman, Inc., Publishers, 1954, p. 45.
[80] Stanley, *op. cit.*
[81] *Ibid.,* p. 7. This story of the struggle to protect individuals against exploitive government and industry is documented. See Irwin Edman, *Fountainheads of Freedom.* New York: Reynal & Hitchcock, Inc., 1941.
[82] *Ibid.,* p. 7.
[83] Robert M. Hutchins, "Is Democracy Possible?" *The Saturday Review,* Feb. 21, 1959, p. 16.

Stanley continued his analysis with this generalization:[84]

Freedom in the human sense is an attribute of culture. . . . Stripped of these products of society, he is not a free man but a helpless wretch. . . . But they also exact a price-submission to the norms of knowledge and the rules of skill. Similarly, various types of human organization and cooperation both expand the ambit of freedom and exact their price. . . . No society, however free, is exempt from restraints and no society, however tyrannical, is without its freedoms.

To return to our main point in extending Stanley's generalizations: we believe that the absence of external restraint in an organized society is neither possible nor will the mere absence necessarily, in and of itself, produce a desirable stage of maturity in a college student. We hold to the point of view that in an educational institution, certain kinds of restraints not only should be minimal as they bear upon the individual student, but also these very restraints should be organized explicitly for the purpose of furthering the student's maturity. The purpose of education is to stimulate the students' striving for maturity—not freedom from restraint, but freedom within restraint.

We believe that Riesman stated the essential crux of the controversy in these words, defining man's freedom to choose the form of his restraints:

The autonomous are those who . . . are capable of conforming to the behavioral norms of their society . . . but are free to choose whether to conform or not.[85]

And we believe that one measure of maturity is the willingness to accept the consequences of such choices.

Two decades ago, Lynd summarized this concept of freedom *within* restraint in words that are fully relevant to today's query:[86]

We are today living through the end of that phase of our cultural history which was dominated by the conditions of individual liberty.

[84] Stanley, *op. cit.*, p. 7.

[85] David Reisman, *The Lonely Crowd: A Study of the Changing American Character*. New York: Anchor Books, 1950, p. 278.

[86] Robert S. Lynd, *Knowledge for What?* Princeton, N.J.: Princeton University Press, 1940, p. 87.

Heavily laden with institutions developed to that end, we are re-luctantly moving into a new phase in which we must somehow manage to rewrite our institutions in terms of organized community of purpose.

We have repeatedly emphasized the thesis that, in parallel manner, many college adolescents experience a difficult and some-times chaotic *Sturm und Drang*—rewriting their personal institu-tions in a search for identity of self, separate and distinct from childhood, and from family, to some extent. For these students, the central core of the academic-freedom issue frequently is cen-tered in the restless search for new, more satisfying, and more pro-ductive relationships with authority figures. As many students of college age seek to separate themselves and their identity from parental and home restraints and relationships, they "make the period of adolescence a crucial stage of psychological transition involving ego problems." [87] Changes brought about by sexual ma-turity, body development, changes in economic roles and social status—these are some of the psychological field forces which impinge upon the individual in his relationships and come to focus largely upon relationships within the family. In most cases of development from childhood to adolescence and from adolescence to adulthood, the transition is made by the individual with a mini-mum of psychological conflict, either internally repressed or ex-ternally exploded in relationships in the family and outside. The normalcy of the transition indicates that there is no universalized period of *Sturm und Drang* characterized by the catch phrase "adolescent revolt" or, as Dean Hunt phrased the stage, "The de-pendence-independence struggle of adolescents." [88] Indeed, at least one study indicates a typically increasing and improving parent-child relationship throughout the entire teen-age period.[89] The relationship of the child to the parent and of the adolescent to the

---

[87] A. H. Hastorf and A. L. Knutson, "Motivation, Perception, and Attitude Changes," in Chalmers L. Stacey and Manfred F. Demartino (eds.), *Under-standing Human Motivation*. Cleveland: Howard Allen, Inc., 1958, sec. 31, p. 308.

[88] Everett Hunt, "The Dean and the Psychiatrist," *Bulletin of the American Association of University Professors*, vol. 39, no. 1, p. 33, 1953.

[89] Dale B. Harris and Sing Chu Tseng, "Children's Attitudes toward Peers and Parents as Revealed by Sentence Completions," *Child Development*, vol. 28, no. 4, pp. 401–411, December, 1957.

parent is a highly individual matter, depending upon the particular family and its experiences.[90]

But in some revolting adolescents, particularly adolescents of the college age, there comes a clearer, but still distorted, perception associated with newly discovered political concepts of freedom from restraint, particularly that restraint imposed by adults, who are thereby perceived as authoritarian, repressing, and therefore legitimate targets for resistance and revolt. Some students, no doubt, have indeed experienced repressive adults who imposed authority and restraint. These students may very well, in their endeavor to separate themselves and their identity from authority restraints, overgeneralize about harsh and repressive adults. And they may thus overgeneralize, sometimes coming to the conclusion that all authority personalities are harsh and repressive and undemocratic and therefore may justifiably be resisted. Such an overgeneralization can be readily identified by a second party, but this identification does not always teach such a student the need to examine critically his own overgeneralization. And since the dean of students is the one who says "no," just as a harsh parent has previously been the one who says "no," so the dean of students may come to be identified in the student's reaction-conflict relationships with repressive and parental authority. And to quote the phrase "*in loco parentis*" to such a student is, of course, to reinforce his overgeneralized conclusion that all adults band together to repress adolescents. Fortunately, in only a very few cases does an overgeneralization proceed to these extremities. But when such an overgeneralizing adolescent captures a leadership position or status of authority and power—such as the president of student government, a dormitory, or a fraternity, or the editorship of a student publication—then the dean of students is in serious difficulty, and so is the entire institution. And such a student proceeds—as does a dean of students or any other administrator who has absolute power—to use that power as an extension and expression of his own psy-

[90] Henry, Nelson B. (ed.): "Adolescence." *The Forty-third Yearbook of the National Society for the Study of Education,* part 1, Chicago: National Society for the Study of Education, 1944, chaps. 11, 12, 13.

Landis, Paul H.: *Adolescence and Youth.* New York: McGraw-Hill Book Company, Inc., 1952, chaps. 7 and 13.

Malm, Marguerite, and Olis G. Jamison: *Adolescence.* New York: McGraw-Hill Book Company, Inc., 1952, chap. 12.

chological universe of notions, concepts, motivations, causes, and other factors determining his behavior and his relationships with others. It is, indeed, of limited comfort when such a charismatic[91] student leader controls a campus or some vital organization, to generalize on research results, saying that he is "atypical" of adolescents in general. And it is equally true that such an *obiter dictum* applies forcibly in the case of an atypical dean of students, faculty member, or other administrator. The "true believer" leader is dangerous in any status and at any age.[92]

One could argue from our analysis of students' reaction to authority that the establishment of autonomy might be expected to resolve the problem conflict. But we rather prefer Coyle's dictum, ". . . the need to come to terms with authority."[93] All students must live with and under some higher authority in school and later in their occupation and community. It follows that they must forge some kind of relationship with authority figures in ways that are productive of individual development. In connection with this point of preparation for adult relationships with authority figures, we believe that the Germanic atomistic-autonomy concept is, at least in American colleges, societally and psychologically irresponsible because it fails to produce the kind of democratic sense of social responsibility that we identify with citizenship in American culture. Atomistic autonomy was never fully possible in organized society and is not characteristic of our present culture.[94]

Metaphorically, freedom in its essence is the acceptance of the chains which suit you and for which you are suited, and of the harness in which you pull towards an end chosen and valued by yourself, and not

[91]Gerth, H. H., and C. Wright Mills (trans. and eds.): *From Max Weber: Essays in Sociology.* New York: Oxford University Press, 1946, p. 295.

Weber, Max: *The Theory of Social and Economic Organization.* London: William Hodge and Company, Ltd., 1947, p. 329.

[92]Hoffer, Eric: *The True Believer.* New York: Mentor Books, The New American Library of Word Literature, 1958.

Popper, Karl R.: *The Open Society and Its Enemies.* Princeton, N.J.: Princeton University Press, 1950. A reading of this work will enlighten us as to the pervasiveness in Western culture of intellectual corruption by Plato, Hegel, and Marx, who seductively argue the philosophy of totalitarianism.

[93] Grace Longwell Coyle, *Group Experiences and Democratic Values.* New York: Woman's Press, 1948, p. 120.

[94] Bronislaw Malinowski, *Freedom and Civilization.* New York: Roy Publishers, 1944, p. 242.

imposed. It is not, and never can be, the absence of restrictions, obligations of law, and of duty. In this form it becomes the extreme despotism of an African chief, or of an Oriental despot.

Fromm stated this same concept of the relationship between society and its members in terms of *required* social character:[95]

> In order that any society may function well, its members must acquire the kind of character which makes them *want* to act in the way they *have* to act as members of the society or of a special class within it. They have to *desire* what objectively is *necessary* for them to do. *Outer force* is to be replaced by *inner compulsion* and by the particular kind of human energy which is channeled into character traits.

Somehow or other, every individual must face the profound problem of becoming himself in his full potentiality and at the same time interacting with other maturing selves. This is the paradox *freedom through restrictions* of American culture and, indeed, of all organized human society. We need to rethink the implications of Kirk's dictum: ". . . liberty, prescriptive freedom as we Americans know it, cannot endure without order." [96]

We conclude that, rather than continuing guerrilla warfare with students, it would be better if we could find ways of helping the adolescent to search for some manner of accommodation of conflicting forces and for resolution of these forces—some accommodation which does not sacrifice the individual's unique individuality, but which furthers his own development. Revision is needed of the query concerning freedom for students, as faced by deans of students: How can desirable freedoms be achieved by students *within* the authority-governed structure of the college? The question should be: What form of functioning relationship between students and administrators will accomplish the maturity of students and the continuing vigor of the institution in aiding all students to achieve their maturity?

We believe that freedom and responsibility are issues which continuously require examination and reexamination to determine possible and desirable reformulations necessary in the freedom of all

[95] Erich Fromm, "Individual and Social Origins of Neurosis," *American Sociological Review*, no. 9, 1944, p. 381.

[96] Russell Kirk, "Conditions of Freedom," *The Commonweal*, vol. 63, no. 15, p. 372, Jan. 13, 1956. See also Russell Kirk, *Academic Freedom*. Chicago: Henry Regnery Company, 1955.

individuals. We also believe that students should be assisted in examining their relationships with authority as a *central* learning in their college days. And lastly, we also believe that all extra-curricular activities and programs can be organized to provide rich opportunities for this kind of learning in our democratic society and within our community of scholars.

AN INSTITUTIONAL CASE IN POINT

We have devoted much space to an analysis and evaluation of some important factors bearing upon the role of student personnel workers in controversy about academic freedom. Such a lengthy analysis serves to establish this role as being of major importance in the total program of services. To some of our colleagues, no doubt, we have extended our concept beyond the traditional personnel functions. Nevertheless, we contend that this is but one of many important personnel functions needed in present-day student life.

We turn now, in Chapter 10, to a relatively simple case situation. However, it is a stubbornly persistent one, and it illustrates both the complexity of the search for effective freedoms and the mixed conditions and difficulties confronting those who organize such a search. This situation is, of course, related to only one of many aspects of academic freedom for students. It is, however, one of the most controversial issues and very strong personal feelings are held and expressed concerning it. And it is, we believe, very close to the central core of the issue of all forms of freedom—the establishment and maintenance of wide latitude in inquiry and learning by students.

CHAPTER 10

The Speaker Policy and Academic Freedom

Perhaps most colleges and universities in America have experienced at some time or other, and usually annually, controversy and conflict of opinion over the question: Shall the campus be open to all speakers invited by student organizations to address the organization's membership or the student body at large? Liberally oriented faculty members have long contended that any prior restriction before the event was an abridgement of academic freedom. Almost universally, they advocate a policy similar to the one adopted in 1894 by the Board of Regents of Wisconsin in the midst of violent controversy over freedom of teaching in the classroom:[1]

Whatever may be the limitations which trammel inquiry elsewhere we believe the great State University of Wisconsin should ever encourage that continual and fearless sifting and winnowing by which alone the truth can be found.

[1] Theodore Herfurth, *Sifting and Winnowing: A Chapter in the History of Academic Freedom at the University of Wisconsin.* Madison, Wis.: University of Wisconsin Press, 1949, p. 11. This monograph tells of the dramatic effort of the class of 1910, of which the author's wife was a member, to memorialize the famous 1894 incident in the struggle for academic freedom. The author's story is a classic in the continuing struggle.

The metaphor of winnowing wheat from chaff was early used by Charles W. Eliot in his 1869 inaugural address, "Educational Reform." He used these words: "The winnowing breeze of freedom must blow through all its [university] chambers." See David Andrew Weaver (ed.), *Builders of American Universities,* vol. I. Alton, Ill.: Shurtleff College Press, 1950, p. 36.

While few boards of trustees have formally adopted such a position, yet many individuals and organizations continue to demand that a "no restriction" policy should be the established order.[2] In contrast, many administrators, some faculty members, and a few student leaders hold with Henry[3] that the university community should be selective in extending its permission to outsiders, even though invited, to address student groups:

. . . the institution reserves the right to determine what shall be the setting for an educational event, to decide when a given event serves an educational purpose and whether or not the participants in that event fulfill the educational standards established by the institution . . . a student as a citizen has the right to hear a speaker of his choice; students *as a group* do not have the right in the name of and under the auspices of the university to arrange for speakers of their choice except through the framework of institutional purposes and responsibilities.

Gildersleeve asserted a similar point of view toward students' rights:[4]

. . . fired by enthusiasm for democracy, some of the more radical students in many colleges began to think of the college as a political unit and of themselves as citizens, entitled, according to the proper democratic process, to determine the conduct of the affairs of the institution by majority vote of the student body or some specialized organizations like political clubs. This was especially likely to arise in the cases of invitations that some students wanted to extend to highly sensational speakers from outside to come and use the college campus as a sounding board. Then any interference by the administration or faculty would be condemned as a violation of that right to "freedom of speech" guaranteed to American citizens by our Constitution . . . now I have always been perfectly sure that in a college no such rights existed for students as students. The only right a student has *as a student* is the

---

[2] As a preface to our discussion of the Minnesota experience, we point out that the University of Wisconsin presently requires registration of guest speakers and has spelled out requirements and privileges of organization in *Objectives, Policies, and Regulations Concerning the Presentation of Guest Speakers from off Campus by Student Organizations,* which was adopted by the Committee on Student Life and Interests, June 10, 1954, and Nov. 11, 1954.

[3] David D. Henry, "Public Attitudes on Academic Freedom, Politics and Tenure," *Bulletin of the Association of American Colleges,* vol. 36, no. 3, pp. 352–353, October, 1950.

[4] V. C. Gildersleeve, "The Abuse of Democracy," *The Saturday Review,* Nov. 24, 1956, p. 36.

right to receive the best possible education that the college can give. (He retains, of course, his political rights as a citizen of the state.)

The dean of students is usually delegated responsibility for supervising this type of student activity; in that role he immediately becomes the center of controversy among differing advocates of academic freedom for students. On the one hand, he may be importuned to approve without review all requests for permission to invite a speaker to the campus, or he may be expected to face the contention that he has no right to review and approve. On the other hand, he may be expected by trustees and president to maintain some degree of selectivity of such programs. It should be noted that this freedom issue is not one of official invitation to a nonuniversity speaker; the issue centers on the right of student organizations, chartered by the college, to enjoy complete freedom in this respect.

AN ILLUSTRATIVE CASE OF POLICY FORMULATION AND REFORMULATION

In the present chapter we are concerned with identification, and description, of techniques and procedures employed by deans and personnel workers, especially in the attempted transformation of controversy and conflict over a claimed right to the writing and community adoption of a policy governing students and the administration. In reading this partial record of an institutional case, the reader must often interpolate or extrapolate actions that were taking place behind the public scene.

In the University of Minnesota, to select one institution in which records are available, the first written formulation of an administrative policy concerning this phase of student life is found in the *Minutes of the Senate Committee on Student Affairs* of January 9, 1936. (This group was composed of faculty and students.) The minutes contain the following statement:[5]

[5] *Minutes of the Senate Committee on Student Affairs*, Jan. 9, 1936. Perhaps the formulation of this regulatory policy was not unrelated to the invasion of the campus by political-reform forces, as reported in the same year by Lotus Delta Coffman, president of the University of Minnesota. See Lotus Delta Coffman, "The Exploitation of Youth," *The Educational Record*, January. 1936, pp. 95–105.

In regard to speakers at student meetings. Many of the organizations are desirous of bringing speakers to the campus at various times—sometimes local speakers, sometimes speakers from outside of the cities [presumably Minneapolis and St. Paul]. There is at present an understanding in the President's Office that the names of all local speakers are to be approved in the Office of the Dean of Student Affairs before arrangements are completed for bringing them here, and that all speakers brought from outside [probably outside the state] should be approved by the President and invited by him as guests of the University.

As far as the record indicates, the latter provision that the President should approve and invite the speakers as guests was not put into operation. But in the years following 1936, the *Minnesota Daily*, a student newspaper, published stories about the never-ending guerrilla warfare between the student liberal groups and faculty members and the Office of the Dean of Student Affairs concerning the application of the 1936 directive to requests for approval of speakers. Some speakers were not approved because they or their sponsoring organization were allegedly advocating communistic doctrine and armed overthrow of the United States government. In some academic years, committees of faculty and students attempted to resolve the controversial issues by means of a new formulation of policy to be adopted by the faculty senate. Also, from time to time the administrative requirement was criticized on the floor of the senate and numerous editorials in the student newspaper kept the issue alive, which was appropriate in an institution of higher learning, since the issue was a basic one with regard to student rights and privileges.

Selections from the available records will serve to identify the form in which the controversy was developing during the decade and a half 1936 to 1951. The reader is cautioned to retain awareness of the tendency to "downtown quarterback" such controversial records and to overdramatize the "hero" and condemn the "evil one." Our own purpose is not to laud or condemn, but only to learn from the record so that, when our turn comes to administer controversies, we shall be wise in exercising our own *expertise* gained from reading the records of our professional predecessors. We seek to learn effective functions for an administrator, not to judge the right or wrong of these conflicts. In the light of our personal experiences, we incline to a sympathetic and empathetic reading of these early records concerning a basic issue that continues to divide many a campus.

Gathering in dimly-lighted Gopher Hall a block from the 14th Avenue gates last night after they had been denied the privilege of meeting "as an organization" in the Union's "discussion room" yesterday, about 30 members of the University Communist Club listened to a speech by a former University of Kansas student, now a worker in the Communist party.

The fact that the speaker, Kenneth Born, who discussed issues before students in the 1936 campaign, was "off-campus" was the principal reason the Communists were not allowed to gather in the Union. In refusing them permission to meet Dean Nicholson issued this statement yesterday:

"The Union discussion room may be used for discussion of anything of interest to students, Communism not barred. The Communist Club, as a club of the University, has no privileges, but those individuals interested in the communist faith can, the same as any other students, reserve this room for discussion purposes.

"All discussion meetings are open to every student in the University. The room is not to be used for the purpose of hearing outside speakers."

The Communists had scheduled a meeting for yesterday noon there as a "discussion group," but were prevented from hearing Born at that time by the University regulation.

*   *   *

About five or six persons attended the meeting yesterday, he said. Printed dodgers advertising the meeting last night were distributed about the campus Monday by the University branch of the Young Communists league.

The small mimeographed leaflets declared that Dean Nicholson's "latest decree barring the Communist club from using the so-called 'Union Square' room . . . is one of the manifestations of reaction that paves the road to the stark oppression of fascism." [6]

*   *   *

The weekend tempest anent Clarence Hathaway, the Marxist Club, and the Student Affairs Office demonstrates beyond dispute the necessity for an immediate and thorough clarification of University regulations and policies governing the rights and privileges of campus organizations. The present difficulties might have been entirely avoided had such a clear, definite delineation of policy been available.

*   *   *

[6] The *Minnesota Daily*, Oct. 6, 1936, pp. 1–2.

The questions of interpretation and of fact which have arisen cannot be properly solved so long as there exist no concrete, specific rules whereby such matters may be solved before, not after, a storm breaks. These storms have broken before and there is no guarantee that the present one will not be succeeded by more.

It is a matter of immediate moment that the Student Affairs Office lay down in black and white an unequivocal set of rules of procedure, and with these rules as precise a statement as possible of the policy underlying the regulations. To do so is no more than a common-sense step toward better comprehension on the part of all concerned, and a considerable guarantee that confusions such as exist today will not be repeated.[7]

There were letters to the editor:[8]

. . . The University has the opportunity to become the greatest example of progressive education along liberal lines. Now is the time for the student body to take a stand against the rigid ways of the reactionaries and to come out for liberalism. The Marxist club situation offers this chance. We must not stop until Dean Nicholson's policies are repudiated by the administration. . . . (Helen Johnson)

*   *   *

. . . Is Dean Nicholson one of those who believes so devoutly in his own opinion as eternal truth that he can with clear conscience say, "Truth should be heard and this is truth; but error we cannot let run riot in the land."

A fundamental concept of a university is freedom for all opinions and ideas and a free choice between them. Dean Nicholson's policy of growing discrimination stultifies that idea. (Philip Monypenny)

Editorials discussed the subject:[9]

E. E. Nicholson, dean of student affairs, has issued an edict prohibiting "all" discussion of political problems before *certain* campus groups by outside speakers until after the forthcoming election.

The edict came Wednesday when Dean Nicholson announced he had decided Clarence Hathaway, who was to address the Marxist club on "The 1938 Elections," must either change his topic or postpone his talk until the forthcoming election.

At the same time no disapproval was voiced over a talk by Stafford King before the Stassen-for-governor club in which King endorsed Stassen's candidacy for the Minnesota governorship.

[7] The *Minnesota Daily,* Oct. 11, 1938, p. 2.
[8] The *Minnesota Daily,* Oct. 11, 1938, p. 2.
[9] The *Minnesota Daily,* Oct. 8, 1938, p. 2. Editorial.

Dean Nicholson's explanation of why King could discuss the political campaign and Hathaway couldn't goes something like this:

The Marxist club is recognized officially as a study group, and any address dealing with a political campaign is out of order; *but* the Stassen club is organzied as a political group, therefore having open approval to hear political discussions by anyone at any time they please.

The absurdity in the explanation is obvious, and one might speculate as to the motives which prompted it.

*   *   *

Our defense of the right of a Communist to speak is not (as opponents to freedom of speech and academic freedom will rush to announce) an endorsement of Communist principles. But we insist, regardless of our own political sympathy, that a Communist, as well as a Republican or Farmer-Laborite, shall be granted equal privileges to express their views on the campus.

It would seem, from protests already being drafted by student and faculty groups, that Dean Nicholson, target of similar protests in the past, has placed himself in another unenviable position. Approval of one speaker and disapproval of another is outright discrimination, and the dean has little grounds upon which to base his ruling.

Dean Nicholson's statement follows:[10]

Facts relating to the published statements appearing in the papers:
That Mr. Hathaway had been refused permission to speak on the University Campus.
Mr. Hathaway has not been refused such permission.

On October fourth I received a list of proposed speakers to appear before the Marxist club from Mr. Charles Sandler, chairman of the Marxist club—all talks bearing on or related to Marxism.

To me the most interesting of the topics was "The Elections of 1938." This topic suggested to me an analysis of the 1938 elections.

I asked Mr. Sandler to come in to see me. Mr. Sandler and myself were agreed in our interpretation of the topic.

I suggested that this talk could be given to a greater advantage following elections. Mr. Sandler suggested changing the topic, a decision left open so Mr. Sandler might make contact with Mr. Hathaway, I supposed by letter or telegram.

Later Mr. Sandler came in and stated that he had called on Mr.

[10] The *Minnesota Daily*, Oct. 11, 1938, p. 1.

Hathaway, who it had happened was in town. Mr. Hathaway suggested that he would be willing to change his subject or talk later on the subject submitted as he expected to be in this territory later on.

Mr. Sandler and myself were agreed that the original subject would have a more general interest following the election, and decided to ask Mr. Hathaway to come to the campus later on.

At this time we cleared the date originally assigned, moving the other speakers up one date, leaving formal approval of date for Mr. Hathaway until a definite date could be assigned.

At no time was the barring of Mr. Hathaway mentioned or suggested. Referring to the permission given the "Stassen-for-Governor Club." This is a regularly recognized political club. Such clubs are allowed to serve their purpose by having political talks. Any recognized political group may have the same privilege.

The Marxist club is not a political club by the terms of its constitution.

Edward E. Nicholson
Dean of Student Affairs

Fortunately or unfortunately, during the decade 1930 to 1940, there were few instances in which a negative decision was issued by the Office of the Dean of Student Affairs with respect to an organization's petition to extend an invitation to a nonuniversity speaker. The absence of such denials of the privilege of bringing speakers to the campus served to avoid open rupture, although this was not the intention of such decisions. But the McCarthy incident of 1951–1952 (see Chapter 8) once more brought out the fact that students operated within an administrative procedure based upon administrative policy, a secondary source of irritation to some students and faculty. Although the guerrilla warfare terminated with the beginning of the Second World War, the controversy resumed following the cessation of hostilities.

In 1946, a formal charter spelling out the rights, privileges, and responsibilities of organized student groups was adopted by the faculty senate.[11] This charter (the university's first comprehensive written charter) formally granted to organized student groups the privilege of conducting a variety of enterprises and

[11] *Policy Manual for Student Organizations.* Minneapolis: Student Activities Bureau Office of the Dean of Students, University of Minnesota, 1956.

activities, including bringing speakers of their choice to the campus. But the 1936 order for review of speakers by the Office of the Dean of Students was not rescinded. It should be noted that the 1936 statement indicated that the procedure had been established by presidential directive rather than by policy adopted by the faculty senate. This mode of adoption indicated clearly that the central administration of that day considered this to be an administrative matter, to be determined by directive rather than by the adoption of faculty policy.

Thus the two sides of the controversy seemed to be administrative practices on the one hand, and faculty-student points of view on the other. The students, for the most part, seemed to accept the necessity of securing approval, but there were complaints against the procedural requirements. On numerous occasions, the matter came before the Senate Committee on Student Affairs for review. For example, on November 21, 1951, the Senate Committee on Student Affairs heard a request to change its policy so that only registration, not approval, would be required of organizations which invited nonuniversity speakers to address their meetings. After the hearing, the committee voted to reaffirm the 1936 policy.[12]

A NEW CONTROVERSY

The dynamic student affairs centered around other and less controversial issues for some years. Then came the famous Sobell incident in which a request to invite Mrs. Sobell to the campus was referred to the Senate Committee on Student Affairs before a decision was made. Upon recommendation of the committee, Mrs. Sobell was permitted to come to the campus. At that time the Dean of Students requested that the senate committee establish a subcommittee to consider revision of the policy and practice.[13]

Soon thereafter, the Office of the Dean of Students issued a summary report indicating that only three requests for speakers had

[12] *Minutes of the Senate Committee on Student Affairs,* Nov. 21, 1951. At this time the committee apparently believed that it was within its power to amend or approve the 1936 directive. Later a closer reading of the record established the fact that the subject of the directive was within the president's jurisdiction.

[13] *Minutes of the Senate Committee on Student Affairs,* Dec. 7, 1954.

been denied within a period of years. The *Minnesota Daily* reported the following:[14]

Student organizations requested permission for 184 speakers to talk at their activities last year, and all were approved under the University speaker policy.

This report was given Friday by Dean of Students E. G. Williamson before the Senate Committee on Student Affairs (SCSA).

"Since I became dean in 1941, I can remember only three people being refused permission to speak on campus," said Dean Williamson yesterday. "They were Grace Carlson, Senator McCarthy, and, most recently, Paul Robeson."

It was reported that in some cases the Dean of Students had voluntarily gone to the faculty committee on student affairs for advice about approval or disapproval prior to administrative decision.

The report apparently stimulated two members of the faculty to present to the Senate Committee on Student Affairs a memorandum of objections to the practice involving review and approval by the Dean of Students. This memorandum served to underline an essential faculty opposition to participation by any administrator, especially a dean of students, in the performance of any academic function. The following paragraph states this point of view:[15]

There are some even more fundamental objections to a veto policy enforced by the Dean of Students. If the choice of speakers is to be determined by their educational value, and if there is to be a veto power, we must ask why the Dean of Students should be in a better position to decide the suitability of a speaker than the faculty adviser of the group concerned. For this a faculty member has a better knowledge of the special interests of the group, and he is, furthermore, perfectly free to consult with his colleagues or even with the Dean of Students if he feels that he needs assistance in deciding whether a particular speaker would be advisable; and he could be directly responsible to the Senate. We are entirely opposed to any veto—by faculty or administration—but if there must be one, then we suggest that it

[14] The *Minnesota Daily*, Nov. 5, 1957. Report by E. G. Williamson to the Senate Committee on Student Affairs.

[15] Mulford Sibley, professor of political science, and Michael Scriver, instructor in philosophy, *Memorandum to Members of the Senate Committee on Student Affairs*, January, 1955.

should be exercised by the faculty, who are presumably the best judges of "educational value."

A committee of faculty and students, a subcommittee of the Senate Committee on Student Affairs, subsequently labored faithfully and tirelessly for months; later, they brought in for consideration several proposals involving radical changes in procedures. For example, under the date of May 25, 1955, the subcommittee reported to the senate committee the following recommended changes in procedures:[16]

Therefore in particular reference to the sponsorship of off-campus speakers by student organizations, the Senate Committee on Student Affairs establishes the following policy:

1. Student organizations may bring to campus speakers of their choice upon carrying out the responsibilities outlined below.

2. The student organization shall plan its program in accordance with the educational purposes of the University.

3. A representative of the student organization shall advise in person the Student Activities Bureau concerning the name and qualifications of the speaker; the subject of the talk; the nature of the meeting (i.e., for members only, open to the community, etc.); whether there will be an admissions charge or solicitation; the time, date and place of the meeting. The organization will initiate registration on procedures as far in advance of the event as possible. This registration must be completed a minimum of three working days prior to the event.

The qualification of a speaker and the nature of the program shall be correctly represented by the group in advising with the Student Activities Bureau and in the advance publicity.

4. Instances of failure to carry out the above responsibilities shall be subject to disciplinary action except that speakers may be enjoined in advance *only* in accordance with number 5.

5. Student organizations may be enjoined in advance from bringing a speaker to the campus when a charge by the Office of the Dean of Students of non-conformity with University policy is upheld after review by the All-University Judiciary Council or by the Senate Committee on Student Affairs. When such charges are brought by the Dean of Students the meeting may not be held until such review takes place.

6. Failure to abide by existing public laws on the part of guest speakers shall be interpreted as a responsibility of the sponsoring group.

[16] *Minutes of the Senate Committee on Student Affairs,* May 25, 1955. No action was taken by the committee.

7. This statement supplements existing University policies and *supersedes* only the Speaker Approval Policy established by the Senate Committee on Student Affairs on January 9, 1936 and reaffirmed on November 21, 1951.

Following submission of the tentative recommendations of May 6 and their publication in the student *Minnesota Daily*, word was received from the central administration that it desired to be consulted on such an important policy decision. Conferences were held with the result that the subcommittee changed its report. The chairman of the subcommittee stated to the *Minnesota Daily* on June 24:[17]

"The May 25 draft, one of several sub-committee drafts," said William F. Maloney, Assistant Dean of Medical Sciences and Chairman of the SCSA Sub-committee on Speaker Approval, "was submitted erroneously to the SCSA before the sub-committee consulted administrative officials on the matter.

"On the basis of our consultation with the administration the subcommittee decided that the May 25 draft would be unrealistic in view of the present administrative feelings on this matter," he said.

In the *Minnesota Daily*, writing a letter to the editor under date of June 24, 1955, an instructor in philosophy had this to say:[18]

I think it should be made clear that one more attempt to provide workable principles of free speech and student self-government on this campus has been frustrated in the usual way. . . .

I have some idea of how hard that sub-committee worked in gathering evidence and formulating a new and more liberal set of principles, and I share the sense of disillusion and distaste which some of them felt when it finally became clear that the administration "felt itself unable to agree that the suggestions made were realistic. . . ."

But the administration was apparently unwilling to accept a policy whose only substantial innovation was the obligation to make public their reasons for refusing permission if this ever occurred. This is one way of making it easy for authoritarian pressure groups in the community to influence speaker policy.

There is, however, another argument against the present policy which renders irrelevant all the statistics about how many applications

[17] The *Minnesota Daily*, June 24, 1955.
[18] Michael Scriven, "Speaker Policy Aired," The *Minnesota Daily*, June 24, 1955. A letter to the editor by an instructor of philosophy at the university.

have been granted and how few refused. For a refusal goes on record as such only when the officers of the society concerned insist on a public showdown, and ignore the suggestions, warnings, and admonitions of the SAB at their compulsory consultation.

How often in these days will students be willing to make this sort of a name for themselves—one which will not only dog them here but also jeopardize their later job opportunities? What should perturb us is the indirect effect of this type of regulation on students contemplating asking various speakers. "Mightn't the SAB raise difficulties over this one? Wouldn't someone a little less controversial be better?" they ask themselves.

That's known as student responsibility without rights. . . .

Earlier, at its meeting on June 10, 1955, the senate committee had adopted a statement which restated the 1936 directive and noted that administration of policies, rules, and regulations had been assigned by the central administration to the Student Activities Bureau. Then the statement continued with these words:[19]

. . . further, that the Senate Committee on Student Affairs affirms that portion of the Basic University Policy Concerning Student Organizations and their activities as established in 1946, which sets forth the principle that actions of the Office of the Dean of Students are reviewable by the Senate Committee on Student Affairs. . . .

Then the subcommittee read into the minutes of June 10, 1955, the following principles, meant ". . . to be of aid in future considerations and the further evolution of policy regarding sponsorship of outside speakers by student organizations." [20]

1. Student groups should make their own choice of off-campus speakers.

2. Programs involving off-campus speakers should be registered in an official University office.

3. Consultation with the Student Activities Bureau is desirable when groups are planning meetings to be addressed by off-campus speakers in order that the organization's educational objectives may be better fulfilled.

4. Judgment after the fact as to the appropriateness of the speaker who was sponsored by the student organization should be made by the

[19] *Minutes of the Senate Committee on Student Affairs,* June 10, 1955.
[20] *Ibid.*

Senate Committee on Student Affairs on the basis of the fulfillment of the purposes of the group in terms of its educational objectives and the educational responsibilities of the University.

5. In any given instance, certain administrative factors might exist of which the group making such judgment would not normally have knowledge and which should be considered in judging appropriateness of the speaker's choice. A satisfactory method of acquainting them of these factors should be devised.

Thus the matter rested until the following Fall term of the collegiate year. On the date of November 8, the *Minnesota Daily* continued the controversy with an editorial entitled "Anyone Should Be Allowed to Speak on This Campus."

The new *Minnesota Daily* editor added one more reason to the constantly increasing number voiced against the speaker policy:[21]

We are showing lack of faith in the intelligence and maturity of University students and citizens of Minnesota by continuing the present speaker policy.

Denial of permission to speak implies that the University cannot understand a free and unrestricted exchange of ideas.

The editor also quoted from the so-called "Harvard Speakers' Policy" described in the *Harvard Alumni Bulletin* of March 12, 1949, over the signature of Dean Wilbur J. Bender. The following paragraphs appear:[22]

. . . we have confidence in the maturity and intelligence of our Harvard students. We have confidence in the strength of our free and dynamic American democracy.

There is no danger from an open Communist which is half so great as the danger from those who would destroy freedom in the name of freedom. . . . If Harvard students can be corrupted by an Eisler, Harvard College had better shut down as an educational institution.

On December 2, a story appeared in the student newspaper concerning a report drafted by a committee and, it was said, presented to the Minnesota Chapter of the American Association of University

[21] The *Minnesota Daily*, Nov. 8, 1955.
[22] The *Minnesota Daily*, Nov. 8, 1955. See also the original source, Wilbur J. Bender, "Freedom in the College: A Policy," in Howard Mumford Jones (ed.), *Primer of Intellectual Freedom*. Cambridge, Mass.: Harvard University Press, 1949, pp. 2–4.

Professors. Contained in this draft were the following relevant paragraphs:[23]

A University must . . . be hospitable to an infinite variety of skills and viewpoints, relying upon open competition among them as the surest safeguard of truth.

Its whole spirit requires investigation, criticism, and presentation of ideas in an atmosphere of freedom and mutual confidence. This is the real meaning of "academic" freedom. . . .

As scholars and teachers of scholars, we feel that this position would be inconsistent with any practices which have the effect, whether intentional or unintentional, of inhibiting the invitation to this campus of speakers judged to be of interest by the group responsible for the invitation.

Much discussion continued while the subcommittee attempted further redrafting of an acceptable statement embracing the significant points which had, by now, emerged in the complex and prolonged community consensus taking. The reader may readily identify many phrases and sentences in the following adopted policy which had previously emerged at various times during the preceding years of full exercise of freedom of discussion. On February 10, 1956, the Senate Committee on Student Affairs adopted the following policy, subsequently approved on March 8 by the senate:[24]

POLICY ON SPEAKERS BROUGHT TO THE CAMPUS BY STUDENT ORGANIZATIONS

The Senate Committee on Student Affairs maintains that an essential part of the education of each student is the availability of diverse viewpoints expressed by speakers engaged by student organizations. To limit opportunities to hear various viewpoints would be inconsistent with the educational responsibility of the University. A necessary complement to the classroom is the opportunity to review and discuss opinions of speakers representing varying attitudes concerning human affairs.

The committee believes that all departments of the University, including the Senate Committee on Student Affairs, should seek to encourage

[23] Pauline Bjerke, "Campus AAUP Group Drafts Speaker Policy Resolution," The *Minnesota Daily,* Dec. 2, 1955.

An inspection of the existing chapter minutes indicates that there is no record of action by the Minnesota chapter.

[24] *Minutes of the Senate Committee on Student Affairs,* Feb. 10, 1956. *Senate Minutes,* Mar. 8, 1956.

and assist student organizations in furthering opportunities to hear the widest range of viewpoints held and advocated regarding issues that divide our society.

Consistent with the 1946 Basic Policy Concerning Student Organizations and their Activities, the following policy shall be adopted:

1. Recognizing that the responsibility for administering policies, regulations, and for general supervision over student activities has been assigned by the central administration to the Office of the Dean of Students, student organizations, in planning an event involving an off-campus speaker, shall consult with and inform the Student Activities Bureau of the name and qualifications of the speaker, the subject of his remarks, and the time, date, place, and nature of the meeting. In each case a request for approval should be made a minimum of three working days prior to the event.

2. In the event of a decision adverse to the request of the organization for approval of the program planned, submitted in accord with number 1 above, the Dean of Students shall promptly inform the Senate Committee on Student Affairs which will meet as quickly as possible in a public hearing to uphold or reverse the decision.

3. Further, when such a decision is upheld or reversed by the Senate Committee on Student Affairs, its decision may be appealed in accordance with the established appeal procedure.

4. The Office of the Dean of Students will report annually to the Senate Committee on Student Affairs concerning the implementation of this policy, including a summary of off-campus speaker activity with a description of the procedures used and the problems encountered in administrating this policy. Upon request, the Senate Committee on Student Affairs may serve as a consultative body for the Office of the Dean of Students on any problem involved in the application of the policy at any time during the year.

5. The principles embodied in the preamble shall serve as a guide in the application of this policy. These principles imply that approval should be withheld from a speaker only if it can be clearly judged his presentation would serve no educational purpose or if the presentation would violate the laws of the State of Minnesota or of the United States.

6. The Senate Committee on Student Affairs recommends that the President authorize the Dean of Students to adopt the procedures outlined in numbers 2, 4 and 5 above.

One might have plaintively expected that the controversy would end with the above policy. But such an assumption would not be based upon realistic understanding of the dynamic diversity of opinion, continuously and freely voiced in a free university community. Indeed, we had heard only from the advocates of a liberal point of view, and now the big guns on the right were wheeled into line.

On February 17, 1956, the student newspaper reported that—

Herbert Aptheker, a member of the United States Communist Party since 1939, will speak on the "Negro's Future" at 11:30 a.m. today in the Union Main Ballroom.[25]

The request of the student group for permission to bring Aptheker to the campus was approved. The *Minnesota Daily* quoted:[26]

It is gratifying that a speaker of this nature is allowed to come here. The University has often been criticized for allowing Leftist speakers to appear either because of their seemingly extreme views or because it is felt that students are not able to distinguish between propaganda and the truth.

Adherents to the first case are decreasing but those that believe in the second view still have support.

University students are capable of distinguishing between fact and fantasy and the *Daily* hopes that they will take Aptheker's speech as an opportunity to demonstrate this.

The *Daily* thus spoke confidently—but without prophetic insight. A state-wide storm broke about the shoulders of the university [*sic*] administrators as a result of this announcement that an openly avowed Communist would be permitted to speak before students. Protests came from off the campus and the Ramsey County Women's Republican Club presented a vigorous demand to the governor in these words:[27]

. . . it seems incredible that a tax-supported state institution of learning should even countenance the presence of an avowed Communist as a speaker at a student assembly. As taxpayers we vigorously protest any sanction of known Communists as speakers at the University of Minnesota or any other tax-supported educational institution. . . .

[25] The *Minnesota Daily*, Feb. 17, 1956.
[26] The *Minnesota Daily*, Feb. 16, 1956. Editorial.
[27] The *Minnesota Daily*, Mar. 27, 1956.

The *Redwood Falls Gazette,* on February 23, editorialized as follows:[28]

On Friday, February 17, at the University of Minnesota, I saw a most disheartening enactment of today's most touted virtue—broadmindedness.

Unwittingly or not, the All-University Congress student forum committee obligingly served the Commuinst cause and put into effect two recent edicts of the Communist party; one, that communists except certain key members are to work openly; the second "build Reuther, bust Meany. . . ."

I cannot believe that self-sacrificing parents would agree to having young minds and souls exposed to the upside-down world of Marxist ideology as expounded by those members of the Communist party whose premise is false and whose goal is to destroy free institutions and our America.

A PERTINENT DIGRESSIONAL REMARK

While we certainly agree with the above critics that students need to be continuously alerted to the subtle and overt perversions of truth by Communists and other "true believers," [29] yet we are periodically reminded of the urgent necessity for academic freedom, both within the classroom and in student affairs. Carl Becker's closely reasoned statement of the educational necessity for and the political justification of free and open instruction of youth in our democracy should be read by both those who advocate and those who fear academic freedom in universities.[30]

. . . If we cannot justify freedom of the mind, and therefore freedom of learning and teaching, by saying that it is a God-given imprescriptible

[28] The *Redwood Falls Gazette* (Minn.), Feb. 23, 1956.
One wonders about the editor's appraisal of Bender's statement of the justification, at Harvard, of permitting students to hear such ideology expounded on the campus as a serious part of the education of youth. See Jones (ed.), *op. cit.*
[29] Eric Hoffer, *The True Believer.* New York: Mentor Books, The New American Library of World Literature, 1958.
The right and the left, Plato, Hegel, and Marx, have been devastatingly appraised. See Karl R. Popper, *The Open Society and Its Enemies.* Princeton, N.J.: Princeton University Press, 1950.
[30] Carl L. Becker, *Freedom and Responsibility in the American Way of Life.* New York: Vantage Books, 1955, p. 57.

right, we can at least justify it by saying that the impulse to know what is true is an inherent human trait, that it has been the principal source of whatever happiness and ordered life man has been able to achieve, and that it is his only hope for a life better ordered and a happiness more general and more secure.

In a moment of discouragement, we might be appalled at the disparity between Becker's insight and the Ramsey County Women's Republican Club's expression of a philosophy of education. And we might relish some sense of comradeship in an age-long uphill struggle in Becker's reminder—[31]

. . . the community always holds the cup of hemlock, in one form or another, in reserve for those who teach too ardently or conspicuously facts or doctrines that are commonly regarded as a menace to the social order.

But such morbid reactions are readily dissipated by Harold Taylor's optimistic appraisal of the long-range gains derived from the controversy of competing ideas:[32]

. . . our greatest strength as a country lies in the fact that we have diversity of opinion and diversity of people. We can absorb and use ideas of all kinds, provided we keep ourselves in a situation in which every idea can have public expression. What has given this country's thought its vitality in the past is the continual struggle of men and women to gain acceptance for their own views, and the continual push of a variety of minority opinions. What marks our history from that of other countries is the way in which we have been able to avoid an orthodoxy, to remain open-minded and flexible, to absorb radical ideas into the flow of social process, and to put them to work when they were needed.

THE CONTROVERSY CONTINUES

The storm continued unabated for many months, without any public attempt on the part of university officials to answer the critics.

Following the gradual abatement of the controversy, on May 25, 1956, the *Minnesota Daily* quoted the incoming student congress

---

[31] *Ibid.*, pp. 64–65.

[32] Harold Taylor, *On Education and Freedom.* New York: Abelard-Schuman, Inc., Publishers, 1954, p. 244.

president, Harold Bakken, and vice-president Jim Greeno, to the following effect:[33]

They don't expect the problem of speaker policy to be brought up again next year, that they will not worry about a "paper policy" and that student government can more profitably spend its time in other areas. Discouraging statement indeed. More discouraging yet is that Bakken does not favor a nonrestrictive speaker policy. Bakken and Greeno are quite right when they say that the University has had wide diversity in speakers this year. But the fact remains that no matter how much diversity, there is still machinery in operation with which to prevent off-campus speakers from coming to campus.

A LAST (SIC) STEP IN POLICY FORMULATION

It finally became clear that perhaps the controversy over the so-called "Speaker Policy" had been exhausted as a curriculum for stimulating student learning. And, to tidy up administrative procedures, President Morrill, under date of May 1, 1956, wrote a letter to this effect:[34]

Recently in going through the printed minutes of the meeting of the Senate on March 8, 1956, I re-read the report of the Committee on Student Affairs pertaining to speaker approval policy.

Having considered this report, the Senate recommended that the President authorize the Dean of Students to adopt the procedures outlined in numbers 2, 4, and 5 above. I do not find on checking my file, that I ever formally notified Dean Williamson's office that I do wish him to proceed in conformity with the procedures established by the report. This letter constitutes such notification.

SUMMARY

And now, at long last, a new policy was in effect, one concerning which there was still intense feeling and dissatisfaction, but which represented one more of many never-ending educational attempts to find a stable (sic) resolution of the opposing, contradictory, and conflicting forces of the university community and the state community at large. In the extended search for such a stable resolution,

[33] The *Minnesota Daily*, May 25, 1956. Editorial.
[34] Letter from President J. L. Morrill to Assistant Dean Martin L. Snoke, May 1, 1956.

much had been learned by each member of the community who followed the controversy and participated in it. But it would be a foolish dean of students who expected that this would be the final policy. A wise one would, rather, anticipate with some relief, as well as some regret, that future generations of students would need, repeatedly, to reexamine basic issues and conflicting forces, and thus continue the search for new and stable resolutions of these forces. Thus is policy made and remade in an educational institution. And thus also are students' freedoms maintained in furthering their individual maturity by means of the extracurriculum.

CHAPTER 11

Balancing Rights with Responsibilities

In preceding chapters we reported our experiences in policy making centered on building new rights or extending established ones, especially those involved in learning to evaluate a variety of opinions about controversial issues and personalities. As experiments in forging civil liberties for students, they had the full support and enthusiasm of faculty and students.

We turn now to another experiment in policy working which received little such support and enthusiasm. In fact, this third incident aroused widespread resistance among students and little enthusiasm in many faculty members. It is a relevant digression to comment here on the mores observed in a community of scholars: efforts to forge and safeguard students' liberties and freedoms received much support, while our experiment in responsible control of behavior was upheld by few faculty and student leaders. We need not argue that both civil liberties and self-responsibility for behavior are necessary in a community of scholars. We proceeded in the following experiment on the assumption that liberty of any kind cannot exist in an uncontrolled, or irresponsibly controlled, community of students. We further operated on the strong conviction that students themselves should function as full partners —not independently or separately—with university officials and faculty in formulating, adopting, and executing responsible management of their own behavior, individually and collectively. We turn to such an experiment in policy and program making.

First we shall sketch the relevant background of our problem issue. Frederick Lewis Allen has described in graphic terms the chaotic lawlessness in student behavior found on many campuses following the First World War—parallel to the lawlessness and chaos found in American society at large.[1] During this postwar period, American society underwent fundamental changes in mores and morals, especially with regard to dress, speech, intoxication, sexual behavior, and personal honesty.[2] And the behavior standards of students were greatly influenced by those of citizens at large. Many of the old university and college sanctions and prohibitions—established for the most part by faculty regulations, policies, and rules, or rules made by the dean of men and dean of women—were weakened, if not entirely discarded. The story of this change in student behavior has not yet been adequately described, but anyone who lived through it recognized that it was truly revolutionary in character.

Coffman has told of another revolution on the campus, describing the radical political groups which sought to exploit youth and invade campuses through various political reform movements in the Depression years of the 1930s.[3] They were a powerful force in the upheaval in and reformation of higher education and the morals and mores of students. The situation on campuses was, of course, paralleled by the radically changing American economy and political scene in the surrounding communities.

[1] Frederick Lewis Allen, *Only Yesterday.* New York: Harper & Brothers, 1931; Bantam Books, 1946.

Further illumination of this explosive period comes through a campus-interview survey of students' opinions about the problems, conflicts, and dynamics of students of that decade. See R. H. Edwards, J. M. Artman, and Galen M. Fisher, *Undergraduates: A Study of Morale in Twenty-three American Colleges and Universities.* Garden City, New York: Doubleday, Doran & Company, Inc., 1928.

[2] This revolution is described in detailed summary. See Max Lerner, *America as a Civilization.* New York: Simon and Schuster, Inc., 1957. Note especially "Manners, Taste and Fashion," pp. 639–650; "Varieties of American Character," pp. 650–666; "Morals in Revolution," pp. 666–677; "Society and Sexual Expression," pp. 677–688; "Life Goals and the Pursuit of Happiness," pp. 688–699.

See also Charles A. Beard and Mary R. Beard, *The Rise of American Civilization,* rev. ed. New York: The Macmillan Company, 1933, chap. 25, "The Gilded Age."

Note Harvey Wish, *Society and Thought in Modern America.* New York: Longmans, Green & Co., Inc., 1952, chap. 20, "The 'Lost Generation' and Henry L. Mencken."

[3] Lotus Delta Coffman, "Exploitation of Youth," *The Educational Record,* January, 1936, pp. 95–105.

We are not here concerned with the character of that revolution, or with the subsequent radical changes in behavior prevalent on campuses. Rather, we are interested in recalling for the reader the background of the 1920s and the subsequent influences of the Depression. Such background will serve to illustrate our thesis that the basic policies governing students can be and need to be changed from rules unilaterally made and enforced by the administration. What is needed is the joint establishment of policies, accepted by university officials and responsible student groups, which center some (but not all) of the responsibility for securing student compliance squarely upon the shoulders of the student leaders themselves. We shall trace the various steps and processes involved in securing student leaders' acceptance of their responsibility for what may be called the judiciary function of student organizations. We contend that such a judiciary responsibility should involve efforts by student leaders working with organization members to secure compliance with the college regulations governing student organizations. But these regulations should be formulated by the organizational leaders *in cooperation* with institutional officials and committees.

With such policy development, student organizations, in exercising their privilege of operating as organizations, would also accept responsibility for compliance with democratically adopted regulations. The securing of compliance would call for the exercise of a judiciary function. This additional function would be added to other traditional responsibilities, including financial solvency; the conduct of programs in such a way as to bring credit rather than discredit to the college; maintenance of at least minimally acceptable scholarship standards among organization members; and others. Some student organizations also conduct welfare and charitable projects within their membership and on the campus.[4] They also conduct other programs which contribute something positive to the welfare of the college as a whole. Some organizations also carry out programs designed to cultivate loyalty to the institution in return for what it has done for the organizations

[4] E. G. Williamson et al., "Learning Habits of Charitable Giving through the Extracurriculum," *Educational and Psychological Measurement,* vol. 2, no. 1, pp. 103–120, Spring, 1951.

and their members. Our essential point is that such a judiciary function is established with organizations of students as an accepted responsibility of members.

The following story is a brief synopsis of some of the important steps involved in securing acceptance by student organizations of their responsibility for their members' conduct concerning policies and rules governing student behavior. A good many of the difficulties in conduct and behavior have often arisen in college residences, but all student organizations—in the conduct of any programs or activities—are included in the judiciary responsibility. The tradition of independent and autonomous behavior in connection with organization-conducted events and affairs has been most clearly established in residential student organizations. Nevertheless all organizations conduct some recreational and other programs which often produce behavior unbecoming in students and in violation of college-established regulations and standards. We shall review some of the conflicting events and tortured interpretations that were by-products of the slow development and acceptance of the judiciary function as a responsibility inherent in the organization's relationships with its members and with the college which sponsors it and makes its functioning possible.

ORIGINATION AMONG FRATERNITIES

For reasons that will be apparent, our discussion begins with the early development of judiciary responsibilities among fraternities. An early formal action establishing group responsibility among fraternities was taken by the Board of Regents on March 22, 1910, in accepting a constitution of the newly formed Interfraternity Council.[5] The formulation of the constitution followed the recommendation of a committee appointed by the Regents to investigate the fraternity system at Minnesota and nearby universities. The circumstances leading to the appointment of this committee have been described as follows:[6]

[5] *Minutes of the Board of Regents,* Mar. 22, 1910.
[6] The paragraphs shown are the contents of an unsigned memorandum found in the files of E. E. Nicholson, Dean of Student Affairs, possibly prepared by him, and dated Apr. 8, 1938.

ORGANIZATION OF THE INTERFRATERNITY COUNCIL AT THE
UNIVERSITY OF MINNESOTA

The formal organization of the Interfraternity Council took a period of from two to three years, beginning in about 1907 or 1908. Difficulties were met, since extreme jealousy existed between the various groups, and no committee seemingly gave satisfaction.

In the late spring of 1909, Professor E. E. Nicholson, of Chemistry, informally met Governor Lind, who had just returned from a trip through the state and was quite worried about the attitude of various sections toward fraternities at the University of Minnesota. He was thinking of going before the Legislature in the fall and asking that fraternities be abolished at Minnesota.

Professor Nicholson suggested that the Board of Regents appoint a committee of faculty and students to investigate the situation at Minnesota and other surrounding institutions. To Professor Nicholson's surprise, Governor Lind agreed and such steps were taken in the fall. . . .

They visited a number of institutions, the report of which is attached. This report was accepted on October 26, 1909, by the Board of Regents. A constitution was drawn, agreed to very shortly, and formally accepted by the Board of Regents on March 22, 1910.

A search of the Regents' files failed to disclose the committee report as indicated in this memorandum, but the following was entered in the minutes of the executive committee on September 28, 1909:

Voted an appropriation of $180 to defray expenses of Professor Nicholson and two students, to visit other institutions and collect information concerning College Fraternities.

The constitution as adopted was contained in the Regents' minutes of March 22, 1910. The action taken was recorded in these words:[7]

The Academic Fraternities at the University of Minnesota presented the following constitution which they are willing to adopt, providing the Board of Regents will insure the permanency and stability of the Interfraternity Council by guaranteeing the enforcement of such rules of the Council as may be approved by the Board of Regents, alike, upon all Academic Fraternities in the University of Minnesota. The Board voted to approve this agreement, the following is the constitution, approved.

[7] *Minutes of the Board of Regents*, Mar. 22, 1910.

The approved constitution, granting independent powers, contains the following definition of these powers:[8]

Section 1. Legislative. The Council shall have power to regulate all Interfraternity matters.

Section 2. Disciplinary. The Council shall have power to enforce its own rules. The Council shall also have power to exercise such authority as may be granted it by the Board of Regents.

But these wide powers were apparently restricted in practice to matters of rushing, pledging, and initiation of members. For example, the bylaws adopted on March 13, 1924, and amended February 18, 1926, are concerned with defining eligibility for initiation, rushing, pledging, and with stating the penalties for violations.[9] It is likely that the preamble clause, "We . . . who are competing with one another for members," referred to the basic purpose in founding the Council—to regulate and restrain undesirable methods of membership recruitment. At any rate, the Council continued for years to concern itself, in its relations with individual chapters, with regulating rushing and pledging of members. Few other controls over chapters were referred to in the Council's minutes and we may conclude that it exercised few, if any, other powers over its member fraternities. On May 20, 1941, a new constitution was approved by the Senate Committee on Student Affairs, rather than by the Board of Regents as heretofore.[10] The new constitution contained a new clause, ". . . its enforcement guaranteed by the Dean of Students." [11] The new constitution contained the following definition of powers:[12]

The Council shall have power: to conduct such Interfraternity affairs and/or matters as do not conflict with University policies and regulations and are not vested in other individuals or bodies.

[8] *Constitution and Bylaws of the Interfraternity Council,* Art. III. Minneapolis: University of Minnesota. Approved by the Board of Regents, June 19, 1924. (Printed Pamphlet.)

[9] *Bylaws of the Interfraternity Council.* Minneapolis: University of Minnesota. In effect September, 1926. (Printed Pamphlet.)

[10] *Minutes of the Senate Committee on Student Affairs,* May 20, 1941.

[11] *Preamble of Organization.* Minneapolis: Interfraternity Council, University of Minnesota, 1941. (Mimeographed.)

[12] *Constitution of the Interfraternity Council of the University of Minnesota,* 1941, Art. II, sec. I.

But once more the council's powers were restricted, in practice, to supervision of rushing, pledging, and initiating members. And it was not until 1945 that a new wording appeared in the constitution.

Until the close of the Second World War, the responsibility for enforcing university standards, policies, and rules concerning the conduct of individual students and organized groups rested in the Offices of the Dean of Student Affairs and the Dean of Women, combined in 1941 into the Office of the Dean of Students. Staff members in these offices were responsible for working with student leaders in conducting their organizational affairs acceptably—to the public at large and the university community. In the normal course of events, individual cases of misbehavior were brought to a committee on student discipline. But misbehavior which grew out of or was associated with organized student affairs conducted by recognized student organizations was either handled within the organization or by the Dean of Student Affairs or the Dean of Women. These university officials acted individually as judiciaries; they investigated, enforced policies, and took action against individuals and groups judged guilty of misbehavior as they had defined it.

A NEW FRATERNITY COURT

In the year 1944, there arose within the membership of the Interfraternity Council a desire to take some responsible part in the judicial function. "The president introduced the idea of an Interfraternity Court. It was decided that a mimeographed plan of the court would be sent to all fraternities." [13] The minutes of the council meeting of November 29, 1944, contained this item: "It was also moved that the Interfraternity Court plan, with the above additions, be submitted to Dean Williamson for approval. Motion seconded and carried."

On March 1, 1945, the Senate Committee on Student Affairs adopted a new constitution which established a new Interfraternity Court in these words: [14]

[13] *Interfraternity Council Meeting Minutes,* Oct. 25, 1944.
[14] *Constitution of the Academic Interfraternity Council,* Art. VI, sec. 1, 1945. Theron Johnson, director of the Student Activities Bureau, was elected by the Council as first president of the Court.

There is hereby created a Fraternity Court which shall adjudicate disputes between, and hear and determine complaints and charges of alleged violations of Interfraternity and University rules and regulations made against, various social and academic fraternities. The court shall make judgments, impose penalties where warranted and assume such other duties and functions, and exercise such other powers, as the Interfraternity Council by this Constitution and any amendments thereto, by its by-laws, or by any duly adopted resolutions at its meetings, may from time to time provide and prescribe. The court in its actions shall at all times strive to further the best interests of the fraternities and the fraternity system as a whole.

But even with these sweeping and new powers, the court continued with hearings on facetious charges of violations of rushing and pledging rules. For example, our files contain this minute of court action:[15]

On February 20, 1945, Sigma Alpha Epsilon Fraternity appeared before the Fraternity Court to answer charges brought to it. This charge concerned the initiation of Jack Hedlund. The true name of Jack Hedlund which appeared in the papers is Jack Schlukebier. This name is legally being changed to Jack Hedlund, therefore no violation was involved. His eligibility has been checked and was in order. Case dismissed.

But some serious hearings were held by the court concerning violation of social-control regulations. Considerable progress was evidenced in the following records of court action:[16]

DECISION OF THE FRATERNITY COURT IN THE CASE
OF PHI GAMMA DELTA, DEFENDANT:

On Tuesday, April 17, 1945, and Thursday, April 26, 1945, Phi Gamma Delta Fraternity appeared before the Fraternity Court to answer charges brought by the Executive Committee of the Interfraternity Council. These charges concerned an alleged unregistered party held in the chapter house at 1601 University Avenue Southeast on Friday, March 2, 1945, alleged to have extended beyond the time limits prescribed by the University.

Statements made by representatives of Phi Gamma Delta indicated that the party began at approximately 2:00 p.m. and that the group

---

[15] *Minutes of the Interfraternity Court,* Mar. 1, 1945.
[16] *Minutes of the Interfraternity Court,* May 1, 1945.

had dispersed by 6:00 p.m. Phi Gamma Delta stated that the party had not lasted into the evening. Members of Phi Gamma Delta living in the chapter house stated that, although there had been about 30 persons present in the house during the afternoon, and although there had been beer in the house during the afternoon, the party had definitely broken up and did not continue into the evening.

Other witnesses appearing before the Court corroborated the existence of the party in the afternoon and the presence of beer. Witnesses also stated that they saw two girls on the 16th Avenue boulevard adjacent to the Phi Gamma Delta house, and that two men left the front steps of the house to enter a car with the two girls. The time of the incident was stated to be approximately 1:30 a.m. Further testimony indicated that at approximately 12:45 a.m. girls were seen in the living room of the Phi Gamma Delta house.

In defense of the preceding testimony, representatives of Phi Gamma Delta stated that a possibility existed that the persons seen at 12:45 a.m. and 1:30 a.m. were interlopers, and had no connection with Phi Gamma Delta.

The Court was not impressed with this possibility. . . .

The Court finds Phi Gamma Delta guilty of the charges as alleged—guilty in a technical sense, in that the party was not registered and that University regulations were disregarded;—and also guilty of a violation in spirit of the ideals and community program of the fraternity system as a whole.

In accordance with the decision, the Court suspends chapter social privileges of Phi Gamma Delta for a period of thirty days, beginning May 1, 1945. In addition, a fine of $50 is imposed. This fine stands suspended, upon the condition that Phi Gamma Delta is not adjudged guilty by this Court of any succeeding violations, of any nature, before January 1, 1946. In the event that Phi Gamma Delta is declared guilty of a future charge before the specified date, the $50 fine will be levied in addition to any other penalty applied by the Court at that time.

BOB RYDHOLM
May 1, 1945

The 1945 change in wording of the constitution led to much improvement, even though it left the dean of students and the fraternity adviser with too much responsibility for dealing with behavior arising in connection with group-sponsored events. Each academic year several such events were reported and they were dealt with by action of the staff and by the Interfraternity Court, which imposed penalties and deprived the groups of privileges.

NEW POWERS AND RESPONSIBILITIES

But relief finally appeared. Near the close of the year 1952, at a meeting of the old and new members of the executive committees of the Interfraternity Council, the outgoing president requested that some day the council be given added responsibility for judiciary functions. This was the initial disclosure of a willingness to develop a substitute for the traditional "cops and robbers" or guerrilla warfare–type of relationship with university officials. This significant change in the relationship is documented in the following record:[17]

Summary report by Jim Wetherbee: Jim stressed long range planning for the new officers. Disciplinary progress is one of the main advances made this year. Good job, Jim!

A related and supporting comment appeared in a staff summary of the year's record:[18]

1952—Jim Wetherbee
1. Immediate cooperation.
2. Constitution passed. . . .
8. More power, more effective voice for students, work with the Dean of Students in a working relationship.

With the encouragement of the staff, the 1952 executive committee drafted a new judiciary plan which was subsequently adopted by the Interfraternity Council itself in a new constitution. The new duties and powers of the council embraced strong and explicit regulations of social affairs, discipline, and other matters, in addition to rushing, pledging, and initiation. The new provision was worded as follows:[19]

B. The Interfraternity Council shall establish and secure compliance with policies for the direction and control of Interfraternity relationships, such as rushing, pledging, initiation, scholarship, athletic contests, dis-

[17] *Interfraternity Council Meeting Minutes,* Apr. 30, 1952. Jim Wetherbee was president during part of the academic year 1951–1952, having replaced B. O. Patty, who had resigned.
[18] *Analysis of IFC—Past, Present, and Future.* Minneapolis: Student Activities Bureau, University of Minnesota, 1954. A staff memorandum. (Mimeographed.)
[19] *Constitution of the Interfraternity Council of the University of Minnesota,* sec. 3. Approved by the Senate Committee on Student Affairs, Feb. 29, 1952.

cipline, social affairs, finance and all other problems of concern to more than one fraternity chapter.

These improvements in "paper" responsibility were not validated until after a series of time-consuming but highly influential grassroots meetings[20] between staff advisers and the executive committee concerning responsibility of the chapter for standards of behavior and other related issues. The following Fall quarter, the staff and executive committee met at length with the full membership of each chapter and made clear the university's stake in judiciaries. Perhaps these meetings were far more productive in improving relationships than was any other action taken. After much discussion and consultation, the following resolution was adopted by the council:[21]

After careful consideration and discussion by and in the individual chapters, the IFC does hereby reaffirm its approval of and pledges its cooperation in carrying out Section 3 of the By-laws passed by the IFC in 1944.

Section 3 defined the obligations of chapters and the council, including the following statements of policy:[22]

3. That the fraternity shall promote conduct consistent with good morals and good taste. . . .
7. That the Interfraternity Council shall undertake the enforcement of the above policies and use all competent sources of advice in deciding the specific policies in regard to the above mentioned points.

During the academic year of 1952–1953, the executive and judiciary committees of the council met frequently with the staff of the Student Activities Bureau concerning matters of policy and program. During this year, the judiciary committee held hearings on some serious incidents, taking very firm and severe actions against chapters judged in violation of regulations and conduct standards. The available records will reveal a basic and strategic change in judiciary practices and leadership at this point. Despite, or possibly

[20] I am informed that these were then referred to as the "Pine Tavern Techniques," after the commercial name of the luncheon establishment in which many such meetings were held. The use of such techniques are highly recommended to our colleagues in other institutions where appropriate.
[21] *Interfraternity Council Minutes,* Nov. 19, 1952.
[22] Quoted in a letter to the dean of students from Burt Cohen, president of the Interfraternity Council, Dec. 2, 1952.

because of, the fact that two implicated chapters had members in the judiciary court, the actions taken against the chapters were more severe than any taken during preceding periods for similar offenses. Thus the fraternity system came to the realization that the new judiciary function was not a "paper dragon" but a real and strong exercise of mature responsibility for the enforcement of democratically adopted rules of conduct.

In a memorandum, the director of the Student Activities Bureau reviewed progress in these words:[23]

The Interfraternity Council is currently preparing an evaluation of the quarter's operation of their new judiciary plan. The last Executive Committee meeting was devoted to this evaluation and an informal discussion of a new slate of officers for 1953–54.

On the basis of the discussion and from the data we have, the following seem to be reasonable conclusions:

1. Since the plan was instituted, the number of registered social functions has doubled over a year ago. This increase is not the result of special house parties, but seems to be a function of the IFC's insistence upon registration of social activity. . . .

2. The number of incidents arising in groups included within the plan has been almost nil. . . .

3. The present Executive Committee is well aware of the imperative need for indoctrinating new chapter officers. Time consuming as it may be, another round robin similar to that conducted this fall is probably in order.

And thus there gradually emerged a clearly defined, widely perceived, and accepted partnership between the Interfraternity Council and the university. This partnership involved joint responsibility for defining desired standards of conduct and affairs and joint efforts at enforcement through the judiciary committee of the council. The new relationship involved frequent consultation with the full membership of individual chapters meeting in off-the-record discussion of a wide range of fraternity problems and relationships.[24] After many attempts at formulating a statement during the summer months of 1952, the *Memorandum on Social Regulations* was later

[23] B. J. Borreson, *Staff Memorandum*, Apr. 7, 1953.

[24] Ben Willerman, "Changing the Attitudes of Fraternity Members toward University Control," *The Personnel and Guidance Journal*, vol. 37, pp. 542–550, April, 1959.

adopted, specifying the desired types and conditions of social affairs and stating—[25]

IV. Violations. Any infractions of these rules, any other University social regulations, any state or municipal laws; any damage to private or public property or any actions adversely affecting public opinion shall be referred to the Interfraternity Council Judiciary Chairman and shall be acted upon by the Interfraternity Council Judiciary Committee. The Interfraternity Council Judiciary Committee shall be the interpreter of the intent of these regulations and of the intent of the chapter charged with violating this agreement.

The full acceptance of partnership in judiciary responsibility by the council and by most chapters proved to be very satisfactory to member fraternities, to the Interfraternity Council, and to the Office of the Dean of Students, which represented the university. As might be expected, leaders of the council experienced a greater sense of personal involvement, since they had drafted the judiciary plan and were, in effect, helping to make the ground rules and standards by which behavior was judged and evaluated. Moreover, the fraternities' own leaders sat with majority voting privileges in the meetings of the judiciary which heard charges and evidence, evaluated situations, and arrived at judiciary decisions. Disciplinary actions therefore could no longer be viewed as unilateral, arbitrary, capricious, or repressive actions taken by university agencies. Widespread participation was thus linked with widespread acceptance of responsibility for conduct of individual members and groups and for conduct affecting the interests of the host institution.

Members of the judiciary soon learned that, because they took dual perspective and responsibility (fraternity and university), they were sometimes subjected to the criticisms formerly directed at university officials—they were called "harsh," "repressive," "unfair," and even "antifraternity" in their perspective. But gradually the fraternity system as a whole learned to respect members of the judiciary and the executive committee of the Interfraternity Council which supported the judiciary. Moreover, the number of incidents decreased markedly, since the fraternity members did not wish to be associated, either as chapters or as a system, with unfavorable publicity. The judiciary function now had become a shared responsibility between fraternities and university, and responsibility for avoidance of unacceptable behavior, as mutually defined, became widely accepted among fraternity leaders. This is not the place to describe in detail the thousands of man-hours that went into this reform of the judicial function in fraternity chapters. But this needs to be emphasized: almost daily communications continued each year until there was, at both grass-roots and leadership levels, clear understanding that some kind of judiciary function, performed by someone, was inevitable and that it would be preferable to have the function shared by fraternity and university officials. Parenthetically, even now (1960), each year the story of the judiciary function is communicated directly by the executive committee of the council, accompanied by a staff member, to each chapter in full chapter meeting. In our experience, such periodic, frank, uninhibited, off-the-record discussions of behavior problems and judiciary responsibilities seem to be required for maintaining shared responsibility for behavior. In this way, each new generation is oriented to and indoctrinated with the significance of the judiciary function so that it will not fall into disuse, disregard, disrespect, and nonobservance.

EXTENDING THE ADVANTAGES OF STUDENT JUDICIARIES

All in all, the experience was so satisfying—both to fraternities and to the university—that efforts soon were made to extend some modification of this plan of shared judiciary responsibility to other organizations. The story that follows describes such an extension and the eventual adoption of a new policy governing organizations.

At its meeting on February 16, 1954, the Senate Committee on Student Affairs (then eleven faculty members, two alumni, and fourteen students) tentatively approved the first draft of a policy which "would clarify and extend the responsibility of student organizations for the conduct of the members at group-sponsored activities and functions." [26]

The committee minutes of that date contain the following account of the discussion and action: [27]

[26] B. J. Borreson, secretary. *Memorandum to the Presidents of All Student Organizations, Attached to Minutes of the Senate Committee on Student Affairs,* Mar. 2, 1954.

[27] *Minutes of the Senate Committee on Student Affairs,* Feb. 16, 1954.

PROPOSED POLICY FOR EXTENDING THE RESPONSIBILITIES
OF STUDENT GROUPS IN THE CONTROL AND DISCIPLINING
OF THEIR OWN MEMBERS

Gordy Smith reported that late last fall quarter it occurred to members of the IFC Executive Committee to ask themselves what right they had to assume responsibility for disciplining their member groups. After investigation, they could discover no statement of policy placing the responsibility for group conduct and behavior upon the organizations. This present tentative draft of policy is designed to spell out responsibilities which are only implied in the existing "Basic University Policy Concerning Student Organizations and Their Activities." IFC would like the Committee to circulate a tentative draft among all student organizations, asking for their comments.

*   *   *

MOTION 31

It was moved and seconded that the tentative draft of clarification of the basic policy be approved for routing through regular consultative procedures; comments and suggestions to be returned to the Committee by April 15.

Motion 31 was passed.

*   *   *

The letter going out to all the organizations with the tentative draft is to state that a request for discussion of any points of the proposed policy can be made at any time.

DEMOCRATIC COMMUNITY CONSENSUS TAKING

As was the customary practice, the committee instructed its secretary to send copies to the presidents of all student organizations, asking for their reactions and comments.[28] In the covering

---

[28] This practice of consultation, also discussed in chap. 12, is, in many respects, a parallel development of practices evolving in industrial organizations.

Robert Tannenbaum and F. Massarik, "Participation by Subordinates in the Managerial Decision-making Process." Berkeley, Calif.: Institute of Industrial Relations, University of California, 1950. (Reprint #14.)

Chris Argyris, "Organizational Leadership and Participative Management," *Journal of Business,* vol. 28, pp. 1–7, 1955.

letter, the secretary of the committee introduced the proposed judiciary plan with these words:[29]

Back in 1946, the faculty Senate, upon recommendation of its Senate Committee on Student Affairs, adopted a comprehensive statement of the privileges and responsibilities of recognized student organizations at the University of Minnesota. A copy of this policy is enclosed.

In the years before 1946, a whole body of specific rules and regulations had been adopted to meet specific problems. The Basic University Policy Concerning Student Organizations and Their Activities was an attempt to establish a general philosophy—one might even say a constitution—governing the relations between student organizations and the University. As a "constitution" its provisions were necessarily general.

A letter of explanation was also sent to the residential counselors and house mothers of all residential student organizations, including fraternities, sororities, dormitories, and large rooming houses. The desire was to inform the residential counselors, graduate students, and advanced technical students, to assist them in exploring and analyzing this proposed policy so as to stimulate the widest possible understanding of it and thereby to reveal any weaknesses or strengths in it.

From the standpoint of the university, it should be noted that sharing judiciary functions and maintaining acceptable standards of conduct in connection with student events was a most important and desirable quality in student affairs. Experiences of the two decades, 1920–1930 and 1930–1940, readily came to mind as indicative of the kind of lawless, disruptive, and antagonistic behavior which resulted from minimum assumption of responsibility by the organizations on the the one hand, and the inevitable unilateral policing of student events and affairs by university officials on the other hand. Any degree of sharing which the student organizations could be persuaded to accept would be positive gain from the standpoint of the university. Moreover, it was the staff's experience —as tested with fraternities—that better student programs and affairs generally result when preoccupation with misbehavior by group members is eliminated. That is, we thought we saw positive

[29] B. J. Borreson, secretary. *Memorandum to the Presidents of All Student Organizations, Attached to Minutes of the Senate Committee on Student Affairs,* Mar. 2, 1954.

gains in the better-quality programs resulting from a strengthening of the judiciary function in the student groups. We thought it by no means a mere coincidence that—parallel with our increased strengthening of judiciary functions within the fraternity system as a whole—there was a marked increase in the chapters' response to opportunities to conduct charitable projects or to participate in the university's charitable projects. Since sororities and fraternities have long been one of the major sources of charitable projects on this campus, we credited the fraternity system along with the religious organizations for the current marked increase in charitable giving.[30]

Such conclusions were not reached by the university staff alone. Many student leaders arrived at similar conclusions and we took no steps except after much consultation with them and with the senate committee. There was by no means universal demand for student participation in the judiciary function. However, the prevailing sentiment among many leaders and organizations was strong enough to suggest that our experiment with fraternities would gain similar benefits for other groups by strengthening desirable relationships and programs.

The reactions that followed justified this conclusion. On March 23, 1954, Betty Shippee of the Student Activities Bureau reported on the written replies received to that date from various organizations to B. J. Borreson, the director, giving the membership's initial reactions to the proposed new judiciary plan. We quote some of these reactions below because they illustrate the magnitude of the educational program facing the staff. Almost every conceivable interpretation and misinterpretation, as well as distortion, of the meaning and implications of the policy are to be found in these comments. Also, one may identify in them the concepts of some groups and individual students concerning the nature of their relationship with the host university. Moreover, one gleans some inkling of the conceptions of freedom and responsibility in our democracy held by some of these individuals. One might well experience a feeling of despair that so little is understood about the implications of an organization operating within a university.

[30] Williamson et al., *op. cit.*

Sometimes one might conclude that some members of these student organizations believe that freedom entails no responsibility except to gratify one's desires—with limited personal responsibility for the maintenance of the university as an educational institution.

AN OPPORTUNITY FOR STUDENTS' EDUCATION

Truly, the Student Activities Bureau faced a tremendous educational challenge. We saw that the judiciary plan was really a magnificent opportunity to stimulate student groups to think more clearly and penetratingly about their relationships with the university and the concept of freedom and responsibility—thus perhaps gaining clearer understanding of the age-old philosophic problem of the rights of the individual in association with other individuals and with corporate groups. Perhaps this educational campaign was to be far more significant than the adoption of a new policy. Indeed, the stimulation of student groups to think through the meaning of such a policy each year by reviewing its content might well prove to be a basic educational function performed by the staff of the Student Activities Bureau. And it might be that in succeeding generations we would be able to contribute to the individual's understanding of the meaning of citizenship in a university within a democratic state. If such proved to be our opportunity, then we indeed owed a great debt of gratitude to the retiring president of the Interfraternity Council in 1950, who first suggested shared judiciary functions and initiated the request for such responsibility.

Controversy makes good news. And the shared judiciary policy, which came to be known among students as the "Conduct Control Policy," proved to be no exception for the student newspaper. In editorial comments, in news stories, and in letters to the editor, the *Minnesota Daily* was exceedingly helpful in stimulating students to think carefully about the meaning of this proposed judiciary plan. The responses were very interesting—some of them missing the point, some of them confusing points, and many of them making valid criticisms of the early draft of the plan. We quote some excerpts from these letters below, to illustrate again how widespread communication and participation in the formulating of a policy can have beneficial educational results for some students.[31]

Under the date of April 22, 1954, the secretary of the Senate Committee on Student Affairs reported to the chairman as follows:

Number of groups solicited through the first mailing 350
Number of groups sent reminder request for reply 330
Total replies received 75
    No comment 21
    Favorable 39
    Favorable with reservations 9
    Unfavorable 6

The secretary also reported the following categorization of replies:

Statements ambiguous 10
Definition of terms needed 3
Does not clarify 6
Can be interpreted to mean greater policing power for university 6
Self-regulation reports to SAB contradictory 6
Question extent to which a group should bind itself to answer for any individual's action 4

In Support of the Proposed Policy

The House Council of Comstock Hall wishes to inform you that it endorses both of the resolutions presented by you—one, the joint resolution of the Senate Committee on Student Affairs and the All-University Congress and second, the policy clarifying and extending the responsibility of student organizations for the conduct of members in group-sponsored activities and functions.

       o   o   o

We have no particular suggestions. The comments were generally in favor of the tentative draft. Personally, I will do my best to see that the listed responsibilities are adhered to by this chapter.

       o   o   o

The Chapter feels that the policy clarifying and extending the responsibility of student organizations for the conduct of its members in activities is an excellent idea.

[31] *Memorandum*, attached to *Minutes of the Senate Committee on Student Affairs*, Apr. 22, 1954.

Our chapter having had an incident regarding the responsibility of the chapter for its members last fall, feel that making the whole chapter responsible is the only practical way of handling such. We also feel it will make the chapters and organizations more conscious of existing laws and regulations.

*   *   *

In reply to the tentative draft as proposed by the SCSA:

I think leaving more responsibility with the organization is good. It gives an organization a chance to see if it can really conduct itself the way a college organization should.

I also back up the University in helping to maintain student organizations.

*   *   *

This new policy is good in that it is an attempt to foster mature thinking in student organizations. The University, of course, cannot grant autonomy to student groups because the average student is too immature to be able to successfully guard against overt acts which may be damaging to the University. Therefore, some inter-relationship is necessary between the University and the student groups. However, the University should not guard against possible damaging overt behavior by *suppressing* the activities of student organizations, although their method is admittedly the most expedient. The University *should* extend its program to foster mature thinking in student organizations so that they may then have *some* sort of *functional* autonomy. This is possible if leadership in student organizations is strong and mature enough so that, in their functioning, the organization will never want to damage their own, or the university's, reputation.

In summary, the student organization should not be told just what they may or may not do, but should instead be shown how to come to the proper conclusions themselves, so that the University will be protected but at the same time the students will be learning to think for themselves. This can only be done by creating a constant awareness of the damage which can be done to the University, and so to the students, by unthinking overt behavior. Basically, the students must first consider themselves a *part* of the University.

In Opposition to the Proposed Policy

We decided that the statement is very vague about just what is to be done and what is not to be done by various organizations. We feel that in its present form this statement has little application to our organization.

*   *   *

The general consensus questions the motive for the changes in the light of recent administrative trends.

We feel the basic policy and change of procedural method is commendable both as a time saver and because it is generally against sin. A consultation with the SAB, rather than waiting for action by the SCSA, could eliminate a long waiting period—and this, we recognize, is in accord with practices in industry.

However, many students sincerely feel that the University has overemphasized the importance of student actions on public opinion—for this reason, and others, we lack confidence in the administrative personnel, particularly the SAB.

It must be recognized that the proposed policy is not materially different from the 1946 policy as far as the administration of the policy is concerned. Pinpointing responsibility is recognized whenever authority to do or not to do a thing is given. Thus, we question the motive of proposing this change in policy.

We question the advisability of expressly giving the SAB punitive powers (Point 5, "or its agents") when it must be clear that there will be a considerable time lag between punitive action by the SAB and review by the SCSA.

We would appreciate hearing more about this matter.

*   *   *

I believe this draft, if accepted, would only give the University in general, and the SAB in particular, more control over student organizations as well as individuals. If organizations were held responsible, one student's action may cause "punishment" to be inflicted on the entire organization. Most organizations do not plan things which might affect their reputation or the University's. I feel that students at the University are old enough to discipline themselves.

It is impossible for an organization to dictate to its members what to do and what not to do. Nearly all students are aware of the rules, and the student who would knowingly break these rules would probably not respect the organization either.

*   *   *

We are unanimously opposed to the amendment for the following reason:

1. The proposed amendment is unacceptable because of the restraints it places on the organizations and individuals. It is our belief that there is a need for *less control* of our actions—not more.

2. It is ridiculous to assume that a group can be held responsible for one individual's action. Certainly it is one of our purposes to guide our members' behavior, but to bind ourselves in an agreement to any eventuality of behavior is not legally sound. Although any constructive suggestions are appreciated, we consider ourselves capable of maintaining the proper decorum in our school life without forming a contract with the SAB on set rules of conduct.

＊　＊　＊

With very little discussion—none in favor of the proposed policy—we voted that the policy was against the policies of our organization, and it was generally felt that such a policy would make it more possible for more impingement of a student's liberties by the SAB.

Why graduate high school kids from college?—Let's let the students have a few responsibilities of their own. Let them worry about their mistakes and not you—I think that's part of an education.

＊　＊　＊

Requests for Clarification, and Suggestions for Change

Precisely what the policy was or is, I must confess that I am not well aware. It has been the policy of Phi Chi in my recollection to act, in group manner at least, with the interest of the University in mind. Liaison with the Student Activities Bureau may well not have been as great as you would desire, but we have tried to cooperate and will continue to do so. The officers have been aware of the implication of any organization's activities on the university, and are willing to take responsibility for Phi Chi's group action. It thus would appear that we are in complete agreement with the proposed policy, and feel that if the inherent responsibility of any organization needs to be clarified, the proposed policy does so.

＊　＊　＊

Regarding the tentative draft of the responsibilities of student organizations, we comment on:

1. We reserve the right to engage speakers for our group meetings on topics of comparative religion. We do not feel that this will "adversely affect the good name and reputation of any other student organization."

2. The interest of the University shall always be *a* major consideration, never *the* major consideration in planning the activities of our group. For us, the major consideration is God.

We hope that these comments will receive consideration and will aid in drawing up the final Policy.

o   o   o

. . . is in agreement with the proposed clarifying statement of the SCSA Policy on Student Organizations with the exception of Number 5, "Failure to comply with the above Policy will call for action *by* this committee or its agents."

We would like to see a more definite explanation of extent of control by SCSA over activities and members of such organizations, and a more complete description of what types of misdemeanors would require the action of SCSA.[31]

These comments proved to be helpful in the revision of the circulated draft.

THE REVISION PROCESS

At its meeting on May 11, the committee tentatively approved the revised draft of the new policy and set the date of May 21 for final action, following a final consultation with student organizations about the wording of the proposed final draft. The *Minnesota Daily* reported in these words:[32]

SCSA CLARIFIES POLICY ON GROUP RESPONSIBILITY

University student organizations will be directly responsible for conduct of their members under a clarified policy tentatively approved last week by the Senate Committee on Student Affairs (SCSA).

Final approval will be made May 21 after student organizations have time to respond to a consultative letter to be mailed by the Student Activities Bureau (SAB).

The policy clarification calls for elected officers to exercise responsibility for the "individual and collective conduct of its members" in all group-sponsored activities and functions.

Each group will be responsible for implementing a code of ethics for its activities. SAB officials will ask what measures have been taken to cope with any misconduct on the part of persons attending a group-sponsored function when the function is registered.

---

[31] *Memorandum*, attached to *Minutes of the Senate Committee on Student Affairs*, Apr. 22, 1954.

[32] The *Minnesota Daily*, May 11, 1954.

But SCSA stressed the idea that every organization does not have to draft a code of ethics immediately. All disagreements between the organization's officers and the SAB could be taken to the Senate Committee or even to the Board of Regents.

Dean of Students E. G. Williamson said his office has been holding groups responsible for the conduct of members in past cases, and the procedure will continue unless the Senate Committee desire to change the policy.

Dean Williamson and James Borreson, SAB director, said the initiation of codes would be up to the group in view of its peculiar problems. Each group will be asked if it has the proper "machinery" to carry its responsibilities.

The committee said the present draft is not a basic policy change— just a clarification of the 1946 Senate-approved policy for student organizations.

The present policy clarification proposal was sent to 350 student organizations during winter quarter. Seventy-five of the groups responded with varied criticisms.

Twenty-one groups made no comment, 39 favored the proposal, nine favored it with reservation and six groups said it was unfavorable.

General criticisms of the policy statement were:

1. It contains ambiguous statements and does not clarify the 1946 policy.

2. The new policy can be interpreted to mean greater policing power for the University.

3. The portion that calls for self-regulation, and still requires reports to the SAB, is contradictory.

Some groups questioned the extent to which a group should bind itself to answer for an individual's action.

SCSA members felt that rules laying down specific codes of conduct would be impossible because each group has its own problems and has to judge its members on that basis.

And the minutes of the committee contain this account of the action of May 11:[33]

Final report and discussion on consultation with student organizations on the Policy Clarifying and Extending the Responsibility of Student Organizations for the Conduct of Members in Group Sponsored Activities and Functions.

Professor Clark reported that the responses received from student

[33] *Minutes of the Senate Committee on Student Affairs,* May 7, 1954, pp. 1–5.

organizations on the first draft of the policy seemed to fall generally into two categories: (1) Those that felt the policy failed in its stated purposes of *Clarifying* the responsibilities and (2) Those that interpreted the policy to be an extension of administrative control rather than a placing of more responsibility in the hands of the organizations. The latter group misunderstood the intent of the policy to the extent of suggesting that the University move to a position of complete anarchy with regard to student organizations. Since the Committee cannot relinquish the responsibility placed upon it by the Senate, the only thing it can do is to clarify the proposal. In view of the many justifiable complaints, he and Mr. Borreson drafted a proposed revision.

"Acting in the belief that the governing of student affairs should at all times be as close to the governed as possible, each student organization shall be responsible for the individual and collective conduct of its members in all of its group-sponsored activities and functions.

"This responsibility shall be exercised on behalf of the organization by the appropriate elected officers of each group under the following conditions:

1. "In all group sponsored activities and functions the best interests of the University as well as the interests of the organization shall be a basic consideration in planning and conducting programs.

2. "Each student organization shall be responsible for securing and maintaining compliance of its members with the aims and purposes of this policy. An organization will not be held responsible for the conduct of individual members outside of its group sponsored activities.

3. "Each organization or the appropriate governing council shall initiate the establishment of policies governing conduct. Such policies shall be developed and carried out by joint consultation between officers and the Student Activities Bureau with appeal rights to the SCSA. Such policies are subject to the review and approval of the SCSA."

✿   ✿   ✿

Mr. Borreson suggested that the covering letter invite interested groups to air their opinions at an open meeting of representatives of the Committee, held specifically for this purpose, prior to the meeting of May 21, when final action would be taken.

MOTION 66

It was moved and seconded that the Committee give preliminary approval to the tentative draft of the policy as revised:

"Acting in the belief that the governing of student affairs should at all times be as close to the governed as possible, each student organization shall be responsible for the individual and collective conduct of its members in all of its group sponsored activities and functions.

"This responsibility shall be exercised on behalf of the organization by the appropriate elected officers of each group under the following conditions:

1. "In all group sponsored activities and functions, the best interests of the University as well as the interests of the organization shall be a basic consideration in planning and conducting programs.

2. "Each student organization, or the appropriate governing council, shall have the right and responsibility for initiating policies governing conduct. Such policies shall be developed and reviewed through joint consultation between the officers of the organization and the Student Activities Bureau with the usual right of appeal to the Senate Committee on Student Affairs in instances of disagreement.

3. "Each student organization shall be responsible for securing and maintaining compliance of its members with the aims and purposes of this policy and with the rules established by the group for the governing of conduct, except that an organization will not be held responsible for the conduct of individual members at other than group sponsored activities."

The policy is to be sent to student organizations whose reactions shall be invited; and it shall be voted on by this committee for final approval on May 21.

Motion 66 was passed.

John French asked what would happen if the policy formulated by the student organization did not meet with the approval of the Student Activities Bureau.

Mr. Borreson indicated that there would be two recourses for arbitration: the Dean of Students and the Senate Committee on Student Affairs.

John French stated that Congress was particularly concerned about items 4 and 5 in the first draft of the policy. He said disagreement between the SAB and the organizations might occur in the working out of an agreeable program. In this event, Congress suggested a subjudiciary composed of three members of the ODS staff and three from the student organization be set up with the chairman of the Senate Committee voting in case of a tie. This would prevent a case of disagreement going to the Senate Committee on Student Affairs unless absolutely necessary.

*   *   *

Gordy Smith said several of the letters gave him the impression that what some of the groups wanted was for "the University to tend to its affairs and the organizations to theirs." He feels a basic issue is the lack of awareness by some groups that they depend upon the University for their very existence. These groups don't subscribe to the basic theory that they are part of the University.

Carl Zietlow feels it is unnecessary to try to have every organization set up a control system ahead of time; rather, it should be set up for the particular occasion as it arises.

Mr. Borreson indicated there will be groups who won't ever make use of a code but they will have a plan in case something does happen.

On May 19, 1954, the *Minnesota Daily* carried the following news story:

SCSA GROUP TO EXPLAIN NEW CONDUCT POLICY

A "skeleton crew" of Senate Committee on Student Affairs (SCSA) members will answer questions on the revised edition of the committee's student group responsibility at 3:30 p.m. today in 109 Nicholson Hall.

The committee has invited all student organizations to ask questions or make suggestions about the policy which makes each organization responsible for the conduct of its members at all group-sponsored activities.

The new proposal was approved tentatively last week. It is scheduled for final approval when the committee meets again at 3:30 p.m. Friday.

And on the following day this story appeared in the *Minnesota Daily*:[34]

ALL-U CONGRESS APPROVES GROUP DISCIPLINE POLICY

A tentative draft policy on the responsibilities of student organizations for the conduct of members was approved by All-University Congress last night.

The policy, drafted last week by the Senate Committee on Student Affairs (SCSA), will be acted on by that body tomorrow.

Discussion of the policy took on aspects of a debate throughout a good part of the abbreviated meeting. Bancroft Henderson, graduate school representative, attacked the policy as clarifying nothing, while John French, Congress secretary and an SCSA member, defended it.

The other 27 members of Congress present, although silent, seemed to agree with French. Only one member voted against recommending the policy; Henderson abstained from voting.

French said the policy is an invitation to organizations to govern themselves. He said it gives groups more disciplinary power over

[34] The *Minnesota Daily*, May 20, 1954.

their members by asking them to set up their own rules of conduct.
This, he added, side-steps the SCSA and the Student Activities Bureau
in all but the most flagrant disciplinary cases.

Henderson said the policy does not give organizations more power to
govern themselves, only responsibilities and no rights or tools to enforce
them.

Henderson called the policy "more restrictive than alleviating," but he
added he didn't think there was anything harmful in it.

A NEW POLICY IS ADOPTED

After five months of active discussion, consideration, and consultation, the new policy was almost ready for committee action.
But at the last moment the dynamic student life added a fortuitous
accent which illuminated the principles and concepts underlying
the policy. The *Daily* reported in these words:[35]

GROUP RESPONSIBILITY POLICY EFFECTED BEFORE APPROVED

The new group responsibility policy of the Senate Committee on
Student Affairs was put into effect before the policy actually was
adopted, James Borreson, Student Activities Bureau Director, revealed
last week.

SCSA Friday approved the 1946 policy clarification which makes
organizations responsible for the conduct of members at all group
functions. The action was taken after Borreson related the details of
Engineer's Day festivities.

Borreson told of oil paint, rumored use of rotten eggs, flour bags
and damaged hedges in an informational report on the results of E-Day
festivities. Two persons were admitted to the health service after the
parade and fight in front of the law school, according to Borreson.

The groups responsible for E-Day festivities immediately took steps to
combat such action next year, Borreson said. Representatives from the
E-Day committee, Tech commission, foresters, and law school met
May 17 to adopt a set of stronger rules for the carrying on of E-Day
activities next year. Final action was delayed until next fall, however,
because of law school exams.

The new policy clarification did not get approval without opposition,
however.

Jack Estes, committee member, said action taken by student groups
should be taken with the idea of educating and rehabilitating. "When

[35] The *Minnesota Daily*, May 25, 1954.

a student tries to punish another student, punishment is usually more punitive," Estes said.

It is dangerous and unwise for organizations to set up their own judicial boards in cases of major crimes, Estes said.

Do students have the capacity to educate and rehabilitate? Estes asked the committee.

Dean of Students E. G. Williamson said the University has to operate on the basis that "students have the capacity to learn." A compulsive desire to punish is bad, Williamson said, but students have in the past responded when rehabilitation is brought to their attention.

The new policy does not delegate "exclusive" control over punishment to the student group, Williamson said.

Estes asked what would happen if the University felt the group was too lenient in punishing a member who stepped out of line at a group-sponsored function.

Williamson replied that consistent refusal also would be a basis for SCSA action.

The committee's minutes contain the following account:[36]

POLICY ON RESPONSIBILITY OF STUDENT ORGANIZATIONS FOR THE
CONDUCT OF THEIR MEMBERS

Mr. Borreson reported that Congress has endorsed the policy without modification. Letters inviting those who had suggestions on the revised policy to attend a meeting with Committee members on May 19 were sent to all recognized student organizations, and about five groups sent representatives to the consultative session.

Larry Smith asked if this would mean that each organization ought to revise its constitution to provide for the exercise of responsibility.

Dean Williamson stated when a group comes in to register a program they will be asked what they plan to do *as a group* if anyone gets out of hand. If they show evidence of not having considered this problem, the Student Activities Bureau will insist that they do so before a program is approved.

*   *   *

MOTION 71

It was moved and seconded that the Committee give its approval to the Policy Extending the Responsibility of Student Organizations for the Conduct of Members in Group Sponsored Activities and Functions.

[36] *Minutes of the Senate Committee on Student Affairs*, May 21, 1954, pp 5–6.

The new policy as adopted by the committee on May 21, 1954, reads as follows:

POLICY ON THE RESPONSIBILITY OF STUDENT ORGANIZATIONS FOR THE CONDUCT OF MEMBERS

Acting in the belief that the governing of student affairs should at all times be as close to the governed as possible, each student organization shall be responsible for the individual and collective conduct of its members in all of its group sponsored activities and functions.

This responsibility shall be exercised on behalf of the organization by the appropriate elected officers of each group under the following conditions:

1. In all group sponsored activities and functions the best interests of the University as well as the interests of the organization shall be a basic consideration in planning and conducting programs.

2. Each student organization, or the appropriate governing council, shall have the right and responsibility for initiating policies governing conduct. Such policies shall be developed and reviewed through joint consultation between the officers of the organization and the Student Activities Bureau with the usual right of appeal to the Senate Committee on Student Affairs in instances of disagreement.

3. Each student organization shall be responsible for securing and maintaining compliance of its members with the aims and purposes of this policy and with the rules established by the group for the governing of conduct, except that an organization will not be held responsible for the conduct of individual members at other than group sponsored activities.

THE POLICY IS APPLIED TO STUDENT AFFAIRS

Judging from the controversy and consultation of the preceding five months, it was apparent to the staff of the Student Activities Bureau that it faced a tremendous task of further stimulation of thinking about the basic problem of relationships implicit within the judiciary policy. And by September, 1954, a systematic plan for the introduction of the judiciary program was drawn up by the staff indicating as the goal for the academic year 1954–1955 which organizations would be approached and in what order. Specific plans included staff responsibilities for leading discussions and stimulating thinking. Plans were also formulated for further clarification of the implications of the program. In addition, sample statements, bylaws which could be copied by student organizations, sample instances of misconduct in which group jurisdiction is either clearly established or questionable were drawn up.

Staff work continued with satisfactory results. On October 21, 1955, the director of the bureau sent a letter to each organization outlining more specifically how it could comply with the policy as adopted by the Senate Committee on Student Affairs in compliance with the committee's adopted plan as of May, 1954.[37]

Your organization may fulfill its obligations as set forth in the "Conduct Control Policy," by writing me a letter including the following steps:

1. The provisions of the Conduct Control Policy have been read, discussed, understood, and accepted by your organization.

2. A committee has been designated by the organization to prevent misconduct by members while participating in group activities and to take proper judicial action when it does occur.

3. Provision has been made for communicating with the Student Activities Bureau about cases of misconduct and judicial actions taken on them.

4. Provision has been made to review the policy annually for the information of all members of the group.

The staff worked diligently with different student organizations at full meetings or at meetings with the executive officers and by May 25, 1956, Paul Bloland, then directior of the Student Activities Bureau, reported to the Senate Committee on Student Affairs as follows:[38]

Out of a total of 347 recognized student organizations, 110 had complied with the requirements of the plan; 26 groups were in process; 107 groups had made no response; 28 were inactive; 79 were residential groups in some stage of compliance.

On January 8, 1957, the director of the bureau made a final report concerning each organization which had not so far signified its acceptance of the responsibilities as indicated in the policy adopted in 1954. For the most part, these were organizations that were

[37] Letter from Student Activities Adviser to each Organization, Oct. 21, 1955.
[38] Minutes of the Senate Committee on Student Affairs, May 25, 1956.

inactive, carrying on little programing of any kind, especially little programing of a social nature. As will be recognized by experienced personnel workers, many student organizations are run in such a haphazard, ineffective, and inefficient manner that sometimes replies are not written, actions are not presented to the group, or taken by them. The attitude of members of such groups may very well be friendly, and the group may desire to comply with requirements, but it simply does not answer communications—often not even after the officers are reached by telephone or in person. The problem of communication with such groups is a puzzling one, but we feel that it is worthwhile to maintain some personal relationship with them in order to assure the continuance of some kind of program.

SUMMARY

As a result of our efforts to develop shared judiciary functions, we anticipate that the Conduct Control Policy, which originated as a judiciary plan, will continue to be a major responsibility of the staff of the Student Activities Bureau. To date, we have found it to be effective as a means of involving all student organizations in the formulation of a policy, in its adoption, and in securing compliance with its requirements. We believe that students and staff of the university have undergone a worthwhile educational experience in rethinking the nature of the relationships between an organized group of students and the university. What began as a sharing of judiciary responsibilities has proved to be a worthwhile educational experience. We now have in the *Rule Book* an explicit policy which may be useful in clarifying each year for new organization officers their group's responsibilities and privileges concerning group-sponsored events and affairs. And we believe that a new and major concept has been structured in student government—shared responsibility for securing compliance with policies and regulations adopted after joint review and consultation of all interested parties, including students, faculty, and administration.

CHAPTER 12

Students and Their Relations with the Administration

Since establishment of universities eleven centuries ago in Italy, students and the college administration have experimented informally, and usually chaotically, with various forms of organizational relationships. Strict supervision within the classroom and riotous living outside the classroom and hospices characterized much of student life in the early centuries.[1] The extracurricular life of most students seems to have been one happy and continuous round of revelry, and the goliardic verses reflected that carefree gaiety of the "perennial student."[2] No doubt there were many serious students of the day but, as Rashdall says, "The life of the virtuous student has no annals. . . ."[3] The virtuous student practiced writing precepts, attended lectures, and practiced his disputations vigorously.[4]

In colonial colleges of America, established on a strict foundation of piety, the regimentation of students was equally intense.[5]

[1] Haskins, Charles H.: *The Rise of Universities.* New York: Peter Smith, 1940. (Copyright 1923 by Brown University.)
Rait, R. S.: *Life in the Medieval University.* London: Cambridge University Press, 1912.
Rashdall, Hastings: *The Universities of Europe in the Middle Ages.* London: Oxford University Press, vol. 3, 1895, rev. ed., 1936.
[2] John Addington Symonds, *Wine, Women and Song.* London: Chatto & Windus, 1925.
[3] Rashdall, *op. cit.*, p. 441.
[4] Haskins, *op. cit.*, pp. 120–121.
[5] Henry D. Sheldon, *Student Life and Customs.* New York: D. Appleton & Company, Inc., 1901, chap. 2, "Student Life in Colonial Colleges."

Following the medieval model of repression and regimentation, faculty authorities established detailed lists of prohibitions concerning behavior, dress, amusements, out-of-class activities, and language patterns, especially concerning vulgarity and profanity. Students were thought to be morally depraved [6] and, therefore, their behavior was severely curtailed and regimented. In part, these repressions were no doubt a reaction against the riotous frontier life of the day. As a defense against corrupting influences, serious attempts were made to enclose students within a life of Calvinistic piety and morality. In fact, the schools and colleges of the colonial period were specifically charged by the frontier citizenry with the dominant responsibility of moral training.[7] Thus colonial colleges, to a large extent, took the form of Puritan morality schools. And the relationships between students and administration was that of regimented learner with strict and often repressive teacher. Indeed, it was not until the latter part of the nineteenth century that the influence of state universities and the accompanying secular revolution in higher education substituted new relationships for the regimentation and repression that produced riotous outbursts. Riots were the students' technique for compelling some lessening of strict regimentation. This type of conflict established the faculty as the natural enemy of the students. Writing of the period of 1828 at Harvard, Peabody described the relationships between faculty and students as "mutually hostile." "If a student went unsummoned to a teacher's room, it was always by night." [8]

A fellow dean stated the same point in these plaintive words: "The dean is often puzzled by the sternness with which the ad-

[6] Richard Hofstadter and Walter P. Metzger, *The Development of Academic Freedom in the United States.* New York: Columbia University Press, 1955, pp. 282–283.

[7] Eugenie A. Leonard, *Origins of Student Personnel Services in American Higher Education.* Minneapolis: University of Minnesota Press, 1956.

[8] Andrew P. Peabody, *Harvard Reminiscences.* Boston: Technor and Company, 1888, p. 200.

Writing of grading and examinations in use today, Smith used the same word, "enemy," to describe students' attitude toward teachers. How depressing it is, many decades later, to discover this contemporary observation: "I suspect that largely as a result of the grading system a majority of the students regard the professor as, in a sense, the enemy. . . ." See C. Page Smith, "Human Time and the College Student," *Journal of Higher Education,* vol. 28, no. 2, p. 72, February, 1957.

ministration and faculty are viewed as natural foes, and by the contrasting sympathy, understanding, and loving kindness which the students show for each other." [9]

With the expanded mission of state universities in 1862, students from lower-economic-level homes enrolled in larger numbers. These students were vocationally oriented and motivated, and appeared to be more serious, as a whole, in their roles as students and learners.[10] During this same period of change in higher education, efforts were initiated to modify and humanize the relationships of students and administration. One of the early attempts to find a substitute for the guerrilla warfare of earlier periods was made by Jefferson in writing the charter of the University of Virginia. This attempt took the form of delegating to students some measure of control over misbehavior. Six students served as a court of inquiry concerning offenses and misbehavior. After one year's trial, the scheme was abandoned because students avoided the acceptance of responsibility for other students' behavior.[11] But some form of student management of behavior continued in the institution. Many other institutions followed this new model of relationships during the middle and later part of the nineteenth century. Most forms of the newly structured participation in university government centered on problems of discipline and control of student behavior. Sheldon referred to the most comprehensive scheme of student government, which was inaugurated in the University of Illinois in 1868.[12] This experiment was another effort to establish more orderly and constructive relationships between faculty and students through student control of behavior. But that system proved unwieldy, and students were loath to accept responsibility for disciplining each other. A second attempt was reported in 1873, at the University of Maine.[13] From that day on, serious attempts were made to involve students in the control of behavior. This centering of relationships upon discipline has given coloring to the form of student

[9] Everett Hunt, "The Dean and the Psychiatrist," *Bulletin of the American Association of University Professors*, vol. 39, no. 1, p. 28, 1953.
[10] Edward Danforth Eddy, Jr., *Colleges for Our Land and Time*. New York: Harper & Brothers, 1957, pp. 79–80, 89.
[11] Sheldon, *op. cit.*, p. 148.
[12] *Ibid.*, pp. 256–257.
[13] *Ibid.*, p. 259.

government; we shall reemphasize this conditioning at several points.

But progress has not been rapid nor extensive, as is shown by Friedson's recent investigation.[14] Lunn's informal survey of recent patterns of student participation in college policy making indicates that much remains to be accomplished, and that on many campuses students still deal with trivial extracurricular matters rather than with the basic and important policies confronting the institution.[15]

TWO PERCEIVED UNIVERSITIES

As one reads and rereads successive redefinitions of the role of students in universities and colleges, in this country and elsewhere, one searches for explanations of the persistently hostile, aggressive relationships which, even today, are the basis of the prevailing climate of opinion on many campuses. In effect, one may distinguish two separate universities;[16] the division[17] in large part defines the need for search of more satisfactory forms of relationships. Two universities seem to exist side by side, often in an unintegrated fashion, and they are frequently perceived by students as being in conflict with each other. Such a perception of conflict and competition may seem to justify maintenance of a disruptive form of relationship between students and administration.

Clearly, these two universities actually do exist to some extent on many, if not most, campuses. On the one hand, one soon identifies the often overpowering legal and fiscal administrative hierarchy in which trustees are the topmost authority, supposedly possessing the final veto vote and, therefore, the final power. Subordinate only to the trustees is the central administration. Under the administration in certain respects, one identifies the faculty—but a

[14] Eliot Friedson, *Student Government, Student Leaders, and the American College.* Philadelphia: U.S. National Student Association, 1955.

[15] Harry H. Lunn, Jr., *The Student's Role in College Policy-making.* Washington: American Council on Education, 1957.

[16] E. G. Williamson, "The Dean of Students as Educator," *The Educational Record,* July, 1957, pp. 230–240.

[17] Another type of divided campus, the curriculum classroom versus the extracurriculum, is described. See Burgess Johnson, *Campus versus Classroom.* New York: Ives Washburn, Inc., 1946.

faculty with a growing urge to attain equality and thus share some power with the administration. Then come the lowly students, at the bottom of this legal and fiscal administrative hierarchy. The clear perception of the student's status in this hierarchy undoubtedly gives rise many times to the student's apprehension that, upon becoming a student, he has lost any civil liberties he may have possessed as a citizen in his home community.

A second university competes effectively for the student's acceptance. From his perspective, reinforced by orientation programs and by a variety of services offered and, indeed, thrust upon him to improve his lowly life, the student is the center, the central authority of his own university. And this personal university center is surrounded by a number of subservient services to be used or exploited by him for his own enhancement and development. If one were to read freshman handbooks, one would see evidence of this perspective—the freshman is informed that he will be given, 'even persuaded to use, every conceivable kind of service to help him achieve optimal adjustment in the college. It would be natural for him to conclude, after reading these bulletins and conferring with counselors, that he is the Ptolemaic center of the university, the object of concern of everyone who stands ready to serve him. His welfare is held to be first in importance, and, in fact, he is inferentially encouraged to view himself as the real reason for the university in its every function.

This schema of two radically differently perceived universities, sometimes in conflict with each other and always needing careful appraisal and integration, may well be the central problem in the relationships between students and administration. Moreover, if this formulation has validity, then we may have readily available an approach to substituting new relationships for riot, conflict, demonstration, antagonism, and resentment. We believe that the history of the past half century, particularly since the First World War, will someday be rewritten in terms of students' and administrators' often fumbling search for new relationships which would preserve the two universities functioning harmoniously in a new form of integration.

NEW FORMS OF RELATIONSHIPS

Over the past few decades, many, many new forms of relationships have evolved, some of great promise for positive contributions to the achieving of the educational objectives of an institution. Lunn's and Friedson's surveys described many such new forms. Falvey's study also adds to our understanding of the variety of such experiments during the recent past.[18] One of these forms seems to be well established. For almost a century, students have gained for themselves increasing responsibility for management of their own extracurricular, social, and other activities. To be sure, most universities and colleges appoint a faculty-student committee with general supervision over policies governing such affairs; yet the students themselves are granted wide latitude in the day-to-day management of these affairs. It is true that, in most institutions, finances of such activities are supervised. And students' conduct is subject to administrative and faculty review; but the content of the activities, for the most part, is left to the ingenuity of students.

But the major conflicts over relationships usually do not arise from problems of the extracurricular activities. Rather does controversy stem from students' insistence that they participate in policy making and in actual governing of university affairs—as opposed to students' extracurricular affairs—both academic and nonacademic. That is, students are increasingly requesting, and are sometimes being granted, some opportunity to participate in deliberation concerning university policies. Sometimes these deliberations concern financial matters. They certainly involve public relations, and students are even interested in discussions concerning academic matters.

One may identify five types of structured relationships in varied states of development on different campuses. The first and perhaps most prevalent type is characterized as *advisory* to student organizations; staff members are perceived as available for advice upon the option of student leaders of affairs and activities. That is, they

[18] Frances E. Falvey, *Student Participation in College Administration*. New York: Bureau of Publications, Teachers College, Columbia University, 1952

may or may not be consulted, and their advice may or may not be accepted as the basis of actions and plans.

The second is the *formal demarcation of areas of autonomy.* Concerning certain specified problems and policy questions, students officially are declared to have the right to settle for themselves what they wish to establish in the way of ground rules. With respect to other defined problems and aspects of college life, the faculty is declared to possess demarked areas of autonomy.

A third type is reserved for the administration. This third type of structure is involved in the practice of *appointing students to university and college committees* with full powers of discussing issues and voting on proposed actions. In some institutions, full membership is granted only with respect to certain types of committees; in other institutions, students have representation on most committees, including committees in control of disciplinary and scholastic matters.

A fourth type of structure is being perfected. In this structure, *full partnership* between students, administration, and faculty is established through joint boards with wide powers over projects. In such partnerships, students sometimes have a majority membership. These joint boards are widely established for student publications, student unions, student judiciaries, and for those committees which govern or supervise all organized student affairs and activities. Usually, these joint boards are established in the charters of student organizations and enterprises. Joint partnerships differ from the second type in the manner of establishment and in the integration of the several separate jurisdictions—administration, faculty, and students.

Still a fifth type of structure involves the practice of *consultation.* This form of relationship is organized around issues and problems arising from policies or actions established administratively or by faculty action and which are determining with respect to student affairs and behavior. Decision making in this type of relationship often remains a prerogative of the administration or the faculty, but by practice, agreement, and consent, students are consulted prior to the making of a decision. In many such cases, students, who are without legal power, actually help to formulate and certainly influence the content of a particular decision.

THE LEGALITY OF SUPERVISION OF STUDENTS
AND THEIR ACTIVITIES

Students and some faculty seem to be uninformed of the legal foundation underlying all relationships between students and an educational institution. Thus they continually refer to students' rights to this or that status when the record clearly reveals that the so-called "rights" are in reality *privileges* granted by the institution. And when they often assert that an educational administrator has "no right" to take a certain action, they clearly are innocent of understanding of the legal authority of institutional officials. Bakken has compiled, from statutes and court decisions, some of the legal rights and responsibilities of educational institutions.[19]

It is clear that the legality of student-institutional relationships in no way weakens the paternal character of the relationship so long described as *in loco parentis*. Indeed, the parental relationship is intimately related to the legal responsibility the institution bears for the instruction, development, and welfare of its students. While experience over the centuries clearly indicates that this paternalism frequently has rigidified into Orwellian "Big Brotherism," [20] the record is by no means a dismal chronicle of parental oppression. In earlier sections of this chapter, and in several other chapters, we have traced some of the evolution from fatherly repression to benevolent and humane parenthood parallel with and, no doubt, influenced by the revolutionary changes in Western familial relationships.

But we return to the current point that the parental tradition has been reinforced by legal decisions and legal reasoning. In other

[19] Clarence John Bakken, *An Analysis of the Legal Basis for Operating Selected Student Personnel Services in State Tax-supported Four-year Colleges and Universities in the United States*, Ph.D. Thesis, University of Colorado, Denver, March, 1959. (Dean D. D. Feder, major adviser.) Bakken studied the legality (statutes and court decisions) of admissions, housing and food services, scholarships, loans, tuition and fees, health and counseling services, discipline, and student activities.

There is parallel study of the legal responsibilities of secondary school teachers, with limited attention to counselors. See Warren E. Ganerke, *Legal and Ethical Responsibilities of School Personnel*. Englewood Cliffs, N.J.: Prentice-Hall, Inc., 1959.

[20] George Orwell, *1984*. New York: Harcourt, Brace and Company, Inc., 1949; Signet Books, The New American Library of World Literature, 1950.

chapters we analyzed and appraised the application of the concept, tradition, and policy of civil liberties and academic freedom to the relationship of students in the institution and their status as students; this was contrasted with their separate status as citizens in the community. We hope that further exploration will clarify the many ways in which the legal responsibility of an institution modifies the student's political and civil liberties. This issue seems to us to be one of the most confused, as well as controversial, sources of conflict and acrimony in American student life today. The recent bulletin of the American Civil Liberties Union is a significant exploration of the complex set of relationships. Similar explorations of the topic would add significantly to orderly clarification of the issue. Hopefully, they would provide a substitute for dogmatic demands and assertions by those favoring parental control and claims fcr licentious freedom by those opposed to it.

FIDUCIARY RELATIONSHIPS AND RESPONSIBILITIES

While awaiting definitive clarification, we add two authorities to be reviewed: the fiduciary capacity of the institution and the long history of precedents. Seavey used the concept of fiduciary capacity to describe the responsibility of an educational institution over students:[21]

. . . to act for the benefit of another as to matters relevant to the relationships between them. Since schools exist primarily for the education of their students, it is obvious that professors and administrators act in a fiduciary capacity with reference to the students.

Elliott and Chambers quoted a court opinion concerning the force of institutional regulations upon students:[22]

Every student, upon his admission into an institution of learning, impliedly promises to submit to, and be governed by, all the necessary and proper rules and regulations which have been, or may thereafter be, adopted for the government of the institution.

[21] Warren A. Seavey, "Dismissal of Students: Due Process," *Harvard Law Review*, vol. 70, p. 1407, 1957.
[22] Edward C. Elliott and M. M. Chambers, *The Colleges and the Courts.* New York: The Carnegie Foundation for the Advancement of Teaching, 1936, p. 14. Quoted from *Court Opinion, State ex rel. Stallard v. White.* 82 Indiana 278, 42. *Am. Rep.* 496 (1882).

In further support of the assertion of the responsibility of an educational institution to establish and enforce regulations governing students in respect to academic matters as well as behavior, we cite the long history of actual regulation and supervision itself. To be sure, as we have indicated repeatedly, the historical record is replete with unwise, unjust, and unreasonable actions controlling students' behavior. Some of these efforts should not, we contend, have been made by faculty or administrators. And Seavey's plea and argument for reasonable due-process procedures is not only pertinent; it is long overdue as a governing principle and guide line. One must readily agree to the obvious need—indeed, the moral and fair-play requirement—for *judicious, reasonable,* and *reviewable* governing of students by regulations established through proper administrative, legislative, and consultative procedures which involve, in some substantial manner, the students who are to be governed.

Having made these pertinent and significant points, we then can point to the substantial precedents of the past three centuries of American higher education and also those of eight centuries of European universities. From the founding of universities, faculties, administrators, and students themselves have exercised authority over students. They have acted as though they had a right to do so. And it is likely that such historical precedents have some relevancy when the issue of institutional rights is debated today. Rashdall, for one, told the story for ancient European universities; Hofstadter and Metzger related the account for the colonial colleges.[23] The legal right of the institution to govern students would seem to be well established. But, to repeat, the manner of exercising that right is constantly in need of more delineation. The point made years ago by Elliott and Chambers is pertinent today:[24]

There are divisions of judicial opinion on such questions as what administrative procedure is necessary to safeguard the student's rights in expulsion cases, and whether the institution may reserve the right to expel a student without stated cause.

[23] Rashdall, *op. cit.*
Hofstadter, Richard, and Metzger: *op. cit.*
[24] Elliot and Chambers, *op. cit.*, p. 25.

Thus it is clear that the institution's rights in governing relationships with students need to be modified in terms of other factors, including the rights of students. These have not yet been definitively formulated and established in many instances and in some institutions.

We now turn from the issue of legality to explore the ways through which a variety of forms of relationships of students and institutions are established. We contend that both the manner of establishment and the substance of these relationships are as urgently in need of exploration and formulation—in consultation with students— as are the unresolved conflicts over rights of both institution and students.

THE CONCEPT OF ACCOUNTABILITY

The relationships of students to a college or university is usually defined in terms of legalities or rights, civil or academic. Some additional illumination of the relationship is afforded by exploring the implications of *privilege* of attendance and the inherent *accountability* of a student to the institution for his behavior. Perhaps the nature of the relationship will be even more meaningful educationally if we appraise the obligations assumed by the student upon admission.

Clearly, it is assumed by the institution that enrolled students will seek to profit from the college's instructional program. It is no breach of logic to deduce that the student is expected, reasonably, to make an effort to learn from classroom exercises and to discharge the attendant responsibilities—attend classes, take examinations, maintain standards of learning, and fulfill other inherent obligations of a student.

It would seem to be consistent with the institution's societal mission that certain other obligations are inherent in student membership. Among these other responsibilities one can identify propriety of behavior; the image represented to the public by decorum and behavior; the manner in which he speaks for and represents the institution and its students; and similar appropriate behavior. Presumably the definition of these areas of accountability is an established right and responsibility of the institution.

But unilateral definitions of accountability will produce resistance and resentment similar to reactions following institutional rule making. It is evident that important and mature learning is possible concerning this concept of student accountability to the institution. Learning is most likely to take place in periodic joint explorations with responsible student leaders and in open consensus-taking meetings. The exploration could well center on the following topics:

"In order to achieve both institutional and students' goals, what are reasonable standards of accountability concerning the many aspects of student life?"

"What behavior, if any, in off-campus situations is of concern to the institution?"

"What political behavior, on or off campus, is of concern?"

"What opinions held and expressed are matters of legitimate interest to the college?"

"What forms of behavior are of concern only to the student in his citizenship status?"

Such an approach may well clarify and define community policies and expectancies in a way that achieves approximate self-enforcement among students. Moreover, and this is of major importance, such a consensus-taking approach to definition of relationships will serve to identify forms that are sensitive and conflicting, and vague or complex in nature. The latter issues are in need of careful study before formulation of policies is attempted. But when consensus on such issues is achieved, it will win support; the relationship will then be removed from some of the associated controversy.

SAFEGUARDING STUDENTS FROM
UNREASONABLE REGULATION

One may well inquire, as students persistently and periodically do, what reasonable and fair safeguards are available for students if administrators and faculty committees possess, and exercise, legal rights to supervise and regulate the activities and affairs of students, individually as well as collectively? Such a valid question should be asked repeatedly about all types of relationships of students with the university—discipline, political behavior, expression of opinions and beliefs, protest and mass demonstrations, demands for redress of grievances, student government activities, and many others. In fact, we could discuss this topic relevantly in several other chapters—Chapters 5, 6, 7, 8, 9, 10, 11, and 13. Indeed, our discussion of this vital issue should be generalized to the topics discussed in these other chapters.

Since freedom is not self-maintaining, we turn to the pivotal query: What upholds freedom of all types for students? In discussing the freedom of student government, Johnson gives expression to a cynical point of view: "Complete student self-government does not and cannot exist in any American undergraduate college. So-called self-government by a student body is actually no more than a limited movement away from stubborn administrative autocracy." [25]

Johnson did mention the immaturity of most students and the centering of faculty and student efforts upon things intellectual as additional reasons why students' self-government is not possible. But no doubt "stubborn administrative autocracy" is, on most campuses, the most entrenched source of opposition to students' exercise of freedom, initiative, self-management, and other strivings for maturity. We do not hold that this is the only, or the most serious, obstacle to the free play of student initiative (see Chapter 11). Neither do we hold to the doctrine of freedom as autonomy for students. However, autocracy is indeed well established in the legal-fiscal-administrative hierarchy of authority which is spelled out in the charters of universities, and implicit in the day-to-day functioning of administrators in their relationships with students.

And, to return to our topic, students may well query: What is the shield of defense of students from autocratic and dictatorial intrusion and infringement on reasonable, fair, and just freedom of individuality? In reply to the query, and generalizing from the broad sweep of development of student life in American colleges over the centuries, one can identify at least four major institutional practices, traditions, and emerging mores which serve to uphold and safeguard students' freedom. Since we have referred to these four in many of our discussions in these chapters, we shall mention them briefly at this point.

[25] Burgess Johnson, *Campus versus Classroom.* New York: Ives Washburn, Inc., 1946, p. 71–72.

The first, but not necessarily and universally the most important and prevalent, safeguard may be captioned by the hackneyed phrase "freedom of the student press." Usually discussion of this safeguard is confused by analogous identification of the student press or newspaper with the commercially managed, subscription-supported daily newspaper. The professional tradition of the community press serves as a relevant model in many ways, but the captured audience of fee-paying students scarcely is analogous to the subscription readers of the daily newspaper. Nevertheless, a student newspaper that operates as a public commentator on everything taking place on a campus can be a most effective, oftentimes irritating and immaturely irresponsible instrument in identifying and criticizing things gone wrong in the relationship of students and the institution. By avoiding the cheap and irresponsible smears of yellow journalism, mature student editors serve an important cause in commenting on and criticizing the day-to-day operations of a university. Such a mature free press can serve the cause of higher education, and does not represent unaccountable and irresponsible license, but rather the kind of responsible freedom we have discussed throughout this book.

A second and most basic safeguard of freedom grows out of the practice of widespread *consultation* by institutional officers and students in identifying problems and difficulties before they become inflamed causes dominated by charismatic[26] leaders. Since this

[26] The term "charism" (adjective charismatic) was used by the German social scientist Max Weber "to characterize self-appointed leaders who are followed by those who are in distress and who need to follow the leader because they believe him to be extraordinarily qualified. The founders of world religions and the prophets as well as military and political heroes are the archetypes of the charismatic leaders. Miracles and revelations, heroic feats of valor and baffling success are characteristic marks of their stature." See H. H. Gerth and C. Wright Mills (trans. and eds.), *From Max Weber: Essays in Sociology*. New York: Oxford University Press, 1946, p. 52. See also Max Weber, *The Theory of Social and Economic Organization*. London: William Hodge and Company, Ltd., 1947, pp. 329, 332, 337, 340.

The reader will enjoy the use of this concept of charism in the Gullahorns' interpretation of the difficulties experienced by foreign students, coming from underdeveloped countries in which political causes are prevalent invitations to the emergence of charismatic leaders, in understanding the political apathy of American students. See John T. Gullahorn and Jeanne E. Gullahorn, *Foreign Student Leaders on American Campuses*. Philadelphia: U.S. National Student Association, March, 1958.

safeguard is discussed elsewhere at length, elaboration at this point is unnecessary, except to assert that continuous and widespread consultation yields many advantages. Not only are issues resolved before they become inflamed, but the morale of students is enhanced through the feeling of self-respect and dignity that consultation fosters.[27]

A third safeguard of freedom is related to the second. Periodic and systematically organized *reviewing* of regulations and policies serve also to reduce the need for explosive and disruptive revolutions, demonstrations, and sit-down strikes to redress real or imagined grievances. To wait until grievances are exaggerated is to provide "true believers" with a ready-made cause. While their needs for causes are real, psychologically the cause of education need not be sacrificed in meeting these psychological needs. And serious students are again encouraged in their efforts at leadership by administrator-initiated reviews of regulations.

A fourth safeguard takes the form of documented and established channels and procedures of *appeal and review* of decisions made by administrators and committees, student and faculty, in the application of established regulations to specific situations and incidents. The American tradition of fair play involves the right to appeal a decision—to the highest legal or administrative authority of the institution, if need be. While such appeal procedures are seldom used, their availability quiets the uneasy apprehension of students that higher authority of administrators and committees, of faculty or students, will be exercised in arbitrary and unilateral manner. One can understand that, without available appeal channels, students may succumb to apathetic despair and submission or to the method of violent revolt.

We believe that variations of these four safeguards not only will

[27] We refer again (see chap. 3) to the intriguing practice used in Benedictine monasteries: the abbot is required to consult everyone on matters of vital importance. Such consultation does not erode lines of administrative authority and decision making. While such requirements for consultation are sometimes restrictive and irksome to an harassed administrator faced with demands for prompt action, in a community of scholars, more frequent observance of such a practice might be salutory. See James D. Mooney and Alan C. Reiley, *The Principles of Organization.* New York: Harper & Brothers, 1939, p. 120.

provide for adequate protection of legitimate freedoms, but that heightened morale and orderly, constructive citizenship will improve the quality of higher education.

ADMINISTRATIVE PROCEDURES INVOLVED
IN CHANGING RELATIONSHIPS

In this present chapter we are not so much concerned with describing the variety—the encouraging variety—of experiments and attempts to perfect new and desirable types of relationships which will substitute for the old relationships of conflict, repression, and rioting. We are rather concerned with analyzing and describing the administrative processes by means of which these new forms of relationships are initiated and established. That is, we are interested in the administrative processes of change, search, and experiment, rather than in the results of such search. Our interest stems from the fact that restless search for improved structures and relationships seems to be the order of the day. In fact, it seems evident that it is permanent in this area of student life. Each student generation—in fact, the leaders of each academic year— demands a reexamination of the inherited structures for relationships. Thus it is that the administrators of a student personnel program are constantly faced with a necessity, the forced continuance of a fruitful search for new and improved forms of relationships.

This is indeed a curriculum of teaching and learning that is repeated year after year. Clearly the university, in its legal capacity, can adopt any structure it pleases, defining areas of competence and areas of jurisdiction. Nevertheless, as far as each new student body is concerned, nothing can be taken for granted and everything must be examined again each year. It is for this reason that administrators need to become expert in the processes of change and in the annual reexamination of relationships between students and the administration. Since this is the number-one item on each year's agenda, we should consciously help students organize and plan their critical evaluation rather than to wait until an explosion announces to us, rudely, that students demand that the sacred structure of the past be reexamined with respect to its alleged current inadequacies.

As we have indicated elsewhere in this book, we hold to the point of view that the dynamic of an American university inevitably requires periodically *organized* opportunities to reexamine those policies and rules and procedures established in preceding years. Sometimes we may wish that some perennial problems could be firmly established, at least for a few years. We steal some fleeting comfort while the prevalent interests of students are directed elsewhere than toward the traditional perennial issues. But usually the role of the student in his relationship to the university is a perennial problem which appears on every dean's agenda for the new year.

We shall turn now to an analysis and description of some processes by means of which one institution undertook—initially with considerable reluctance—to reexamine and to reformulate its relationships with students. And we repeat, we are not concerned, as were Friedson and Lund, with an inventory of the various forms of relationships; we are concerned with the processes by means of which some of these forms were originated and appraised as to effectiveness.

A CASE OF PROGRESSIVE REFORMULATION
OF RELATIONSHIPS

Under date of May 11, 1951, the Board of Regents defined a new relationship with students concerning the establishment of policies defining students affairs.[28] This policy later became the *Consultation Policy*. The establishing of the policy itself was the culmination of a movement which erupted in 1944, at the time of an administrative decision refusing permission to a student political organization, officially recognized, to use the then available student post-office boxes for the distribution of political campaign literature. The eruption of the peaceful campus scene took the following form of 'barking in" on the fight. To describe the stage setting and the dramatis personae of this exciting event, we quote extensively from the record:[29]

[28] *Policy Manual for Student Organizations.* Minneapolis: University of Minnesota, 1956, pp. 13–14.
[29] The *Minnesota Daily,* Oct. 12, 1944.

STUDENT PROTESTS POST OFFICE BAN

To the Editor:

I would like to add my protest, as a revolutionary socialist (Trot-skyist), to the chorus of protests already voiced against the arbitrary and undemocratic action last week—in banning the meeting announcements of the Campus Committee for Roosevelt from the Union Post Office system. . . . University students are old enough to be conscripted to fight; they are old enough to make their own decisions between different groups of ideas.

It is not my purpose to suggest for one instant that a "Democratic" state administration would act any more democratically. There are the major parties of capitalism, and capitalism in its economic decline turns ever more against democratic principles and the workers rights. I cannot forget that it was the "Democratic" Roosevelt administration which dictatorially imprisoned 18 socialist (Trotskyist) and trade union members for nothing more than the expression of their socialistic ideas. Nor can I forget that, as a preliminary to this frame-up, under fire from the Republican state legislature of 1941, the University administration refused Grace Carlson, one of the imprisoned 18, the right to speak on our campus.

While I cannot take seriously the imaginary political differences between the capitalistic in and out parties, I am seriously concerned with the struggle for genuine democracy. Therefore, I protest this undemocratic action by the University administration and warn the student body against this dangerous precedent. For freedom of speech and press on the campus! For freedom of the University mail from censorship!

Phillip Theo. Clark
Arts Junior

Following the decision to disallow the use of the post office for general distribution of political campaign literature to students, there was a wave of protest. We quote extensively from stories and editorials appearing in the student newspaper, the *Minnesota Daily*, to indicate both the temper of the student body at this particular time and what the student body defined and perceived as the essential issue at stake. It is apparent that our "guests from the left," as usual, took full advantage of the issue to add condemnation of the national scene and thus distorted the controversy. Nevertheless, there was a very real issue at stake as to the manner in which restrictions should be placed upon students' political activity. As we shall see in the following pages, from this beginning there evolved a new frame of reference, a new perspective, and, finally, a new policy which defined more liberal limitations upon students and also provided for systematic, and frequent, review of these limitations. Indeed, a basic written charter defining the privileges and responsibilities of student organizations ultimately evolved from this explosive incident.

DISCUSSION ON BAN WILL BE CONTINUED BY POLITICUS

The recent ban on use of the University Post Office boxes for circulation of meeting notices will be discussed as part of a Spotlight meeting of the Campus Committee for Roosevelt at 3:30 P.M. today in 343 Union.

Approximately 700 people have signed a petition protesting the ban. One hundred fifty copies of the petition are in circulation.[30]

* * *

COUNCIL URGES IMMEDIATE ACTION ON POST OFFICE BAN

A recommendation that immediate action be taken to open University Post Office boxes to general circularization by campus organizations will be made to the Senate Committee on Student Affairs at its meeting today by Jean Danaher, president of the All-University Council.

The recommendation will be stated in the form of a general motion as follows: That all policies governing student activities on the campus within the bounds of authority of the Senate Committee on Student Affairs be evaluated by the senate or by a committee designated by the senate from the point of view of the post-war campus.

The All-University Council will also recommend specifically that the following resolution be passed by the Senate committee: That until such time as the evaluation of policies relative to student activities on campus can be studied by the University senate, the senate committee move to reinstate the former broad interpretation of policy governing the use of University Post Office boxes; that all organizations again be permitted to generally circulate notices; that there be no discrimination against any organization through a strict interpretation of the ruling.[31]

* * *

[30] The *Minnesota Daily,* Oct. 13, 1944.
[31] The *Minnesota Daily,* Oct. 31, 1944.

SENATE TO STUDY EFFECT OF BAN

The Senate Committee on Student Affairs yesterday unanimously carried the All-University Council proposed motion that the University Senate study the effect of the recently imposed ban on general circularization of University Post Office boxes.

The Senate Committee also unanimously adopted the resolution which proposed that the present Post Office box ruling be interpreted leniently until the University Senate study can be completed. The Senate will meet next quarter.[32]

Following months of study of the issue, the Senate Committee on Student Affairs Minutes of December 13, 1944, contained the following information:[33]

At the last meeting of the Senate Committee on November 28, 1944, a set of operating principles regarding the uses of the Post Office boxes was adopted and forwarded to President Coffey. Under date of December 6, Dean Williamson received a letter of reply from President Coffey which was read. The letter gave approval to all the principles adopted; however, President Coffey suggested a change in principle number four: "Recognized student organizations, on special occasions, may circularize the student body or any segment of the student body members, for disseminating information of interest to students and for announcing such meetings as are deemed of all-University interest." The committee discussed at length the advisability of changing the wording of this principle: it was of the opinion that no substantial change should be made. Two groups would be restricted by a change in the principle—religious groups and political parties. President Coffey's suggestion was that the definition be more explicit, limiting Post Office use to programs that were sponsored by all-University organizations or by groups of organizations promoting an all-University event.

MOTION 23

Dean Henry Schmitz moved that the chairman be permitted to make editorial suggestions in the phraseology of Item 4 and be instructed to write the President a letter in the defense of the slightly modified statement in light of discussion. Motion seconded and passed unanimously.

[32] The *Minnesota Daily*, Nov. 1, 1944.
[33] *Minutes of the Meeting of the Senate Committee on Student Affairs,* Dec. 13, 1944.

Under date of December 14, the *Minnesota Daily* contained the following story:[34]

SENATE SETTLES ISSUE OF U POST OFFICE REGULATIONS

The Post Office circularization issue was settled yesterday. Principles adopted and established by the Senate Committee on Student Affairs will allow the Student Activity Bureau to determine what can be circulated in the Union Post Office boxes by using the same principles used before the issue arose.

In addition it was decided that all uses of the Post Office by students and student organizations shall be reviewed and approved by the Office of the Dean of Students. Appeals from the ruling of this office will be made to the Senate Committee on Student Affairs.

In situations not covered by the operating principles, the Dean of Students Office may formulate a ruling, that ruling to be subject to the approval of the Senate Committee on Student Affairs.

There are operating principles which have been reviewed by the All-University Council, approved by the President's Office and by the Senate Committee on Student Affairs:

1. Commercial or personal advertising by non-University organizations or individuals, and by students, shall be prohibited.

2. Off-campus institutions . . . either public or private, shall not be permitted the use of the Post Office boxes to publicize programs.

3. Non-commercial publicity materials . . . furnished by non-University organizations established for charitable or social service purposes may be used by recognized student organizations for circularizing the student body as part of an acceptable student project, i.e., Red Cross Drive, Christmas Seal Sales.

4. Recognized student organizations, on special occasions, may circularize the student body or any segment of the student body beyond its constitutional membership for the purpose of soliciting members, for disseminating information of interest to students and for announcing such meetings as are deemed of all-University interest.

5. Recognized student organizations may circularize their memberships as defined by their constitutions.

6. Recognized student organizations may circularize the student body publicizing an all-University event, program, or project, i.e., Homecoming, Gopher sales, Spring Festival, non-partisan political rallies.

[34] The *Minnesota Daily*, Dec. 14, 1944.

A NEW EXPLORATION OF RIGHTS AND PRIVILEGES

Following the settlement of the issue by the adoption of the new senate committee rules for that use, the All-University Congress petitioned the president of the university, requesting that the proper committee of the senate review all policies concerned with student activities in the light of problems of the postwar campus. This task was assigned to the senate committee on education. Before this committee had completed its mission, a new incident erupted which indicated the desirability of adopting a formal statement of privileges and responsibilities of organized and recognized student groups.

Under the leadership of mature veteran students, an organized protest was undertaken by students concerning the impending action of the state House of Representatives for the erection of a memorial to war veterans in the form of a monument and landscape approach to the state Capitol. In view of the great difficulties currently experienced by veterans in finding adequate rooming houses for themselves and their families, such an impersonal memorial was sufficient to trigger explosive reactions. The *Minnesota Daily* had this to say:[35]

Democracy went into action yesterday afternoon.

Two hundred and fifty students met in a rainstorm on the steps of Northrop auditorium and then proceeded as a group to the state legislature in order to register their opposition to the proposed Veterans' Memorial Bill which was scheduled to come up in the House.

Aroused at the proposal to erect an office building and to beautify the approach to the state capitol in the name of returning veterans, many students had spent Tuesday evening organizing, circulating petitions and informing the students of the special order placed on the bill which would move it up on the House calendar.

These students took their objections to the capitol, filling the House gallery. In small groups, they waited outside the door of the House, talking to representatives wherever they found them, asking opinions and comments. During the noon recess period, students joined with members of the campus Veterans' club and selected representatives with whom to talk.

[35] The *Minnesota Daily*, Apr. 12, 1945.

But democracy was having a hard time. Students found it difficult to exercise their rights as citizens of the state (and many of them were voting citizens).

One representative told students that he had been in the legislature 40 years and didn't think that he should have to discuss his convictions on the Veterans' office building. Others brushed students aside, in a hurry to answer "important telephone calls" and then failed to appear again. Some representatives simply excused themselves and disappeared within the impenetrable house chamber.

A few representatives, though, welcomed the students, inviting them to attend legislative sessions more often. They praised the demonstration as exemplifying an honest desire to present one side of a question and to listen to the other. They were pleased that students were interested enough in legislative action to spend long hours sitting in the gallery or talking to the House members who would listen.

Then up rose John Kinzer, representative from Stearns county; addressed the House in the afternoon, angrily spoke against the students. He was indignant about their presence and declared that he would not be told what and how to legislate by "high schoolish students."

Considering their arguments of worth, and believing that having members of their families serving in the armed forces gave them the right to speak, the students remained in the gallery during the presentation of the bill. There was no unnecessary noise, other than that unavoidable in a packed gallery. If they briefly applauded a few speeches, it was because there was no other way for them to show their approval.

Not until late in the afternoon did they leave the session—not until the final vote was taken at 6 P.M. . . .

As is biennially true in this state university, the effects of students' actions upon appropriations are seriously appraised. To state this fact is not to argue that students should be repressed during legislative periods, or that freedoms and liberties should be curbed. On some basic issues, both university and student spokesmen must speak out in spite of the risk of retaliations from any source. Nevertheless, unthoughtful representations to the Legislature, as well as to other responsible groups in the state, need to be thoughtfully appraised in anticipation of their effectiveness in achieving desired, as well as undesired, results. After all, there are ways and ways of achieving objectives. And surely one may argue— at least, a dean of students *does* argue—that one of the learnings desired in mature students is skill, as well as forcefulness and vigor, in presentation of convictions, with due consideration to the rights and privileges of others, from whom demands are made and on whom sometimes unforeseen effects are projected.

It was from such a perspective that the Dean of Students wrote a long letter to the editor to describe his efforts to dissuade non-veteran students from pressuring for veterans' legislation and his attempt to dissuade veterans from using high-pressure methods of persuasion.[36]

To the Editor of the *Daily:*

You state that I have been "strongly against students expressing their sentiments on the bill at this time." This is not my position. I believe that students should express their opinions, beliefs and attitudes at any time on any and all issues. I have expressed myself on numerous occasions to numerous groups with respect to the concern of my staff that students do not discuss, debate and argue the fundamental issues facing citizens. Unless students do learn to discuss issues, especially those which are characterized as "controversial," then there is not the slightest possibility that students will ever become enlightened and effective citizens and, as far as citizenship is concerned, it will have made no difference that these students have graduated from college.

What I believe with respect to the controversial "War Memorial Bill" and what I stated to every student I was able to contact is that students should exercise judgment, care, caution, restraint and other desirable marks of an educated man in the way they discuss such controversial issues and the place in which they discuss them. In my judgment, the proper place was on the campus and not in the State Capitol, and I so stated as definitely as I could to all that I could reach. Unless the Dean of Students is not entitled to have any personal opinion about such matters, I will continue to state such a point of view. I believe that it was proper for the students who are war veterans to petition the legislature as they did on two occasions, since they had a personal stake in the matter, and Mr. Johnson[37] and I explicitly approved their proposal to so petition the legislature. I do not think that it was timely, appropriate, wise or otherwise desirable for non-veterans to "cut" their classes, go to the State Capitol and run the risk of creating the impression among the harassed members of the legislature that they were out for a lark.

[36] Letter from E. G. Williamson to the editor of the *Minnesota Daily*, Apr. 13, 1945.

[37] Theron Johnson, Director of the Student Activities Bureau, University of Minnesota.

As I explained to the editorial writer and to the student leaders, the University appropriations were at stake, that the situation was delicate, as it always is at this period in the legislature's session, and that I felt that it was unwise to run the risk of jeopardizing the University's appropriations in this manner for this particular issue on the part of non-veteran students. . . .

The march on the Capitol appeared to have had little effect as reported by the *Minnesota Daily* under date of April 12, 1945:[38]

The house of representatives approved the St. Paul Veterans Service Building and Capitol Approach Bill, 69–59, yesterday after a long and heated debate.

The house earlier approved a motion changing the bill's title from "War Memorial" to the present one. The motion was made by Representatives Hans Pedersen, Pipestone county, and Wilhelm Holm, Lincoln county, immediately after the bill was put up for debate.

Mr. Holm, in presenting the amendment, stated, "The intention of this amendment is merely to call a spade a spade. The present bill is drawn too much to play on sympathy rather than to present facts. I think we need a new office building—and let's call it that."

Claude Allen, representative from Ramsey county, one of the authors of the bill, led the fight for it and gave a long, dramatic speech saying, "We have known for years that in the State of Minnesota there was a necessity for this building. It is sufficient to take care of any further needs that may arise. Let's give them (the veterans) this one building so when they come to Minnesota to get information, they need not go from city to city or from building to building but will have it all at one door."

At one point in the debate, the gallery, in which several hundred University students were packed, applauded a speech against the passage of the memorial and Speaker Lawrence M. Hall, St. Cloud, rapped the gavel, demanding quiet. He got it, for the students were afraid of being ejected from the house.

CAPITALIZING UPON THE INCIDENT—A NEW "BILL OF RIGHTS"

The march on the Capitol concerning the War Memorial bill proved to be an excellent, but unplanned, trigger to initiate consideration of a basic policy concerning student organizations, their

[38] The *Minnesota Daily*, Apr. 12, 1945.

privileges and responsibilities. Such a new formulation had been under consideration for the past several months. But the *Minnesota Daily*, and many students, expressed their point of view in anticipation of the presentation of what was called by the *Daily* a "Bill of Rights."

In the uproar following the student lobbying trip to the state legislature recently, the *Daily* commented on the sad condition of rules governing the activities of student organizations and individual students.

But the importance of this confusion regarding when to act and how cannot be overestimated.

There have been times when certain student organizations have been allowed to go "off campus" on some project; but there have been times, too, when other student organizations were denied this right.

In addition, it's common knowledge in most student groups that if the Dean of Students Office refuses permission to go "off campus" for the organization as such, then the members can "act as individuals" and achieve the same results.

As far as the activities of individual students are concerned, the only usable rule to be found, comes under the heading of "Discipline" and says that students are liable to expulsion or suspension by the University Senate when they are guilty of "misconduct of any kind which is unbecoming a student of the University and detrimental to the welfare of the student body." [39]

The *Daily* has indicated the need for a Student Bill of Rights which will serve as a guide for student organizations—and, perhaps, for individual student action. Particularly in the case of the latter, however, the *Daily* would be flatly against any rule which prevented the development of citizenship responsibility.

As more and more students return to the University and as situations in which students act as individuals or otherwise multiply in number, the confusion regarding activities will grow in accordance.

Here is a problem which such student organizations, as the All-University Council, the Liberal Society, the Forum (and any other interested student group) would do well to consider.

It must be stated here, however, that if students do get a Bill of Rights—and one which allows them great freedom, the University's public relations policy must be altered considerably.

An informed, active public relations policy could go a long way

[39] This was indeed a bit of overexercise of editorial license since such an item (Senate Minutes, Dec. 20, 1917) was embedded in a definition of gross misbehavior of theft, misdemeanor, and other actionable misbehavior.

in convincing the public (and the legislature, too!) that every time student properly called attention to certain contradictions and not for the University.[40]

At this juncture in the community consensus taking, a graduate student properly called attention to certain contradictions and unresolved conflicts in the position taken by the Dean of Students. By calling attention publicly to these weaknesses, both the *Daily* and the students brought to the attention of the entire university community the danger involved in using anticipated public relations risks as the principal, if not the sole, yardstick by means of which to appraise students' both activities and enterprises, both individual and organized.

To the Editor:

There are many who feel that Dean Williamson's letter to the *Daily* leaves certain basic questions unanswered. Dean Williamson admits that unless students participate in the fundamental issues of the day they will never become "enlightened and effective citizens." Yet in the very next paragraph he states that it was "unwise" for the students to run the risk of jeopardizing "the University's appropriation in this manner for this particular issue."

What the students would like to know is whether there will ever be a time that is "wise and appropriate." The legislature meets every two years. Every two years University appropriations are considered—too often near the end of the legislative session. To say that students must refrain from protesting against legislation at a time when University appropriations are being discussed is to say that students must almost never participate in the issues of the day. There is, therefore, seldom a "wise and appropriate" time.

The next unanswered question involves the relation of a student to the University. Dean Williamson states that the student as a member of the University has certain obligations, among which are accuracy, self restraint, respect for the opinion of others, and an obligation to make it clear that he—the student—is not an "institutional spokesman." No one would disagree with this statement but it is hard to see how the students who actively opposed the War Memorial Bill in any way failed to fulfill these obligations.

The fact that certain members of the legislature did not realize that the students were speaking as individuals is not the fault of the students. The answer lies, as the *Daily* has suggested, in a better public

[40] The *Minnesota Daily,* Apr. 18, 1945.

relations policy that will make it clear to the legislators that the University is in no way responsible for its members when those members speak as individuals. It is difficult to see how the students in opposing the War Memorial Bill violated any obligation implicit in their status as students of the University of Minnesota.

Esther Seeman
Graduate Student [41]

The stage was now set for serious consideration of a formulated policy which would define, more or less specifically and as best could be understood at that time, the privileges and responsibilities of organized student groups. The document, prepared by a committee in consultation with faculty, staff, and students, was sent to the president of the All-University Congress, with the request that the congress give very careful and critical scrutiny to this document. The document was also mailed to the *Minnesota Daily*, with the request that it be published in full for the purpose of stimulating widespread discussion leading to desired revision.

Under the date of April 26, 1945, the *Minnesota Daily* ran the following story: [42]

A statement of principles defining the place of student activities at at the University was presented to the All-University Council last night by the University Senate's sub-committee of the Committee on Education.

The attitude of the council was generally receptive although several points were questioned and discussed. The question of a policy to govern student activities originally was asked for by the council when the Post Office controversy rose last winter.

At that time the All-University Council petitioned the President of the University to have all policies governing student activities reviewed in light of the problems of the post-war campus.

Earlier in the day, the statement presented to the council was reviewed by the Senate Committee on Student Affairs.

Edmund G. Williamson, Dean of Students, pointed out that the statement presented was only the first draft and would be subject to changes before it is finally approved by the University Senate.

"The committee has released and published the statement in order that students may discuss it, criticize it and make suggestions to the committee for improvement," Mr. Williamson said. . . .

[41] The *Minnesota Daily*, Apr. 18, 1945.
[42] The *Minnesota Daily*, Apr. 26, 1945.

Most discussed and questioned by the council was the problem of the right of the student as a citizen in the community and as a member of the University.

Jean Danaher, president of the council, stated she believed the statement did not clearly delineate the rights of the student as an individual and as a member of a group.

Mr. Johnson said that by the original request of the council the work of the group clearly was delineated to a policy on student organizations. A similar charter for individuals might be necessary, he added. Maynard Pirsig, professor of law, and another member of the sub-committee, said that the policy statement might well be renamed for clarification: "The place of organized student activity."

And the *Minnesota Daily* commented editorially as follows:

From the point of view of student organizations, the drawing up of a statement of principles defining the place of activities at the University is a step in the right direction.

The presentation of this policy to student organizations is only the ground work for a student bill of rights and it has the virtue of being written. But it still leaves room for interpretation where interpretation is not particularly desirable.[43]

This policy was not drawn up by students. The subcommittee responsible for the statement was composed of faculty members and administrative personnel. Consequently, the students will have to study this statement, talk it over, and express their views.

Suggestions may be sent directly to the sub-committee, to the All-University Council or expressed in letters to the *Daily*.[44]

[43] This comment revealed a troublesome area of the relationships of students with universities. At times it seems that students desire regulations and policies which are so specific and clear that no interpretation is necessary or possible in their applications to incidents and situations. No doubt such a never-never land would be perceived by students as protecting them from the vagaries of a feared administration. Seldom do students perceive that the administration might well wish also for such automatic reaction in the punishment by rule, with no judgment making required. But, alas, neither wish is possible in this empirical world of testimony conflicting as to fact and confusing interpretation of rules and regulations. Each freshman law student learns that out of these realities, courts, attorneys, and judicial rules and procedures have evolved because of confusion and conflict in interpretation and application.

See Edward H. Levi, *An Introduction to Legal Reasoning*. Chicago: University of Chicago, series 9, 1948. (Reprint and pamphlet.)

[44] The *Minnesota Daily*, Apr. 26, 1945.

One student would have none of it, and commented as follows:[45]

To the Editor:

Your support of the principle of a policy statement by the administration regarding student organizations is not only surprising, but alarming. Yesterday's editorial pointed out that changes in the published policy would undoubtedly be demanded by students, but you seem to have overlooked the possibility that such a statement of policy might be undesirable on principle and completely contrary to the interests of student organizations.

In the first place, if students trust the administration, there is no point in such a statement. The acclamation of one, as a Bill of Rights, implies a deep mistrust—which would not be healed by such a feeble measure.

Second, the policy of the administration toward students is essentially an equilibrium, based on variations of power and opinion and influence, which is sensitive to all the yearly variations in these factors. It is fantastic to think that such an equilibrium could be summarized in a statement and alarming to think what would be the effect of such a written statement, if conditions arose which might allow a shift of this equilibrium "to the left."

Third, the existence of such a document would lead to endless legalistic quibbling and to arguments and hesitations which would be more likely to benefit the forces of reaction than of progress.

No, a written statement could become a noose around the collective necks of student organizations.

There is, in the Student Activities Bureau, a pile of rules and "guides" and whatnot, which is the administration's policy toward student organizations. Some of these rules, however, are redundant, some contradictory, and some of questionable legal power.

What should be done is quite clear:

1. There should be a clear statement of the channels wherein legal power is delegated by the Board of Regents.

2. All rules and regulations made in exercise of such legal power should be published and readily available to all student organizations.

In this way, the policy would become clear beyond question, and the principles underlying the policy would rest on their own merits, rather than being based on the dictatorship of a piece of paper.

John McFie
Medical Senior

[45] The *Minnesota Daily*, Apr. 27, 1945.

And another student commented, properly, on the serious mistake in judgment which did not assign full membership[46] to any students on the committee that formulated the policy.[47]

To the Editor:
The recent presentation of the "Text of Student Activities Policy" by a Senate committee involves a principle more basic than the merits or demerits of the provisions which the text contains. Although the statement dealt with the activities of campus organizations, no student or representative of these organizations was included in the committee which formulated these highly important principles.

It is difficult to understand how the very Senate which objected to the fact that it was not allowed an adequate voice in the choice of the University President, could a few months later take exactly the same stand toward a matter of student policy.

Democratic postulates, if they are to have any value, must be applied at all levels of activity regardless of the questions or persons concerned. A truly democratic philosophy must mean that any comprehensive formulation of student policy should be a cooperative venture of students and faculty.

Esther Seeman
Graduate Student

The discussion continued in somewhat of a desultory fashion through the spring and into the Fall quarter. And on October 26, the *Minnesota Daily* commented in these words:[48]

Texts of the student activities policy drafted last spring by a subcommittee of the Senate are being circulated by the All-University Council for amendments and endorsement by campus groups.

This statement defines all aspects of University policy towards student activities. The *Daily* feels that the last four sections of the text—student privileges, responsibilities, definition of types of activities and relation of students to the University family—should be eliminated.

It is impossible to define these parts, even with the best of intentions in mind, without leaving clauses open which can be misconstrued willfully if sudden curtailment were deemed necessary.

Students may exercise "rights *similar* to those enjoyed by responsible

[46] The committee did meet frequently in consultation with student leaders from a number of organizations.
[47] The *Minnesota Daily*, May 23, 1945.
[48] The *Minnesota Daily*. Oct. 26, 1945.

citizens in every community . . . through *recognized and established media of expression."* The deck has jokers, and the administration could decide easily what cards are wild.

Why not strengthen the first section, Purpose, and use it in the future as a yardstick by which to judge specific University action on specific occasions involving organizations? Also, a well-worded addition to the *Purpose platform is needed to strengthen the position of the Dean of Students Office. No trespassing, please.*

A formal statement by the Senate recognizing the important place of activities in education, combined with a re-checking and revamping of existing University rules, would be sufficient. Also, if new regulations are added, after the old are retreaded, the judgment would be on worth, not protective coloring.

The policy was revised in the light of some comments, oral and written, from students and faculty, and was presented to the university senate for action on October 31, 1946, at which time it was approved. The final approved draft of the basic policy concerning student organizations and their activities is included in the *University Policy Manual for Student Organizations,* published by the Student Activities Bureau in the office of the Dean of Students, 1956, pp. 14–17. For better or for worse, and for the first time in almost one hundred years of functioning, student organizations at the University of Minnesota began operating under an explicitly formulated policy stating their privileges and responsibilities, and, what is perhaps more important, spelling out the proper channels of appeal for review of administrative decisions concerning organized student affairs.

A CHANGE IN PUBLIC RELATIONS POLICY

Tension among students was further eased by means of a newly formulated policy encouraging students' efforts to express their individual and common opinions and desires about public and national affairs. The steps involved in this significant change of policy and practice are summarized here.

Under date of May 23, 1946, the Senate Committee on Student Affairs passed a resolution which established a reformulation of the university's traditional attitude toward public relations as a criterion for appraising student events and affairs. The *Minnesota Daily* carried the following story about this resolution:[49]

The resolution, passed by the Senate Committee last Friday, was handed to the President for review and final approval following that meeting.

Student organizations are given permission by the resolution, "to publicize their own actions, views and decisions, taken by vote of the members, through the usual media of publicity such as newspapers, petitions, letters, telegrams, and the radio."

The resolution also cautions student groups to avoid giving the impression that such actions carry the endorsement of the University or the general student body. Each group must make it clear, the resolution states, that it is responsible for its actions and statements.

All publicity concerning such actions, views and decisions, the resolution provides, must be referred to the student activities bureau, for clearance before it is released.

"This resolution was passed," said Barbara Clark, assistant director of the Student Activities Bureau, "after considerable study by the Senate Committee on Student Affairs.

"It represents a concrete step forward in establishing a procedure allowing students to publicize their actions, views and decisions in a manner which is consistent with the purpose of a university."

The resolution itself read as follows:[50]

A motion was made by Dean Schmitz that the resolution be put into effect concerning publicity of decisions, views, and actions of student groups, amended to read as follows:

Be it therefore resolved:

That student groups and organizations may publicize their own actions, views, and decisions, taken by vote of the members, through the usual media of publicity such as newspapers, petitions, letters, telegrams and the radio.

That the publicity employed should avoid giving the impression that such actions, views, and decisions carry the endorsement of the University or the general student body and should be in such form as to indicate clearly the organization's responsibility for its actions, views, decisions, and statements and that the University bears no such responsibility.

[49] The *Minnesota Daily,* May 24, 1946.
[50] *Minutes of the Senate Committee on Student Affairs,* May 23, 1946.

That before publicity concerning such actions, views, and decisions is released it shall be referred to the Student Activities Bureau, Office of the Dean of Students, for clearance as to form consistent with the above paragraph.

AN ORGANIZED COMPLAINT SESSION

Following the post office incident and prior to the march on the Capitol and the subsequent adoption of a bill of rights for student organizations, still another movement began. This was another effort to organize a new form of relationship between students and the central administration. This form proved to be highly effective in many respects.

At its meeting on February 21, 1946, the Senate Committee on Student Affairs, composed of faculty and students, aired at length and with great seriousness the general problem of student morale as evidenced by continuing comments and criticisms published in the *Minnesota Daily* and by critical remarks reportedly heard among student groups. Frequent references were made in the discussion to the stresses and strains caused by the postwar period, and the general restlessness of students concerning restrictions on social behavior carried over from prewar days. The contributions of mature veterans to students' unrest and the reactions of student veterans to prewar restrictions on students and student affairs were very important in the discussion. Repeated reference was made to resentment and impatience as a reaction of postwar students to regulations, restrictions, administrative decision, and the general state of affairs among students. No doubt, unrest was experienced on many, many campuses, and it was indeed a tense and most difficult readjustment period not only for students, but for the university staff as well. Repeatedly, references were made in this particular session to the resentment of students prevented from playing a more serious role in the formulation of rules and regulations governing their own enterprises. Of course, reference was naturally made to the huge size of the student enrollment and to the impersonality of the university as perceived and reported by many students. The frequent expressions of hostility and aggression were said to be but symptoms of the underlying unrest which needed to be alleviated in some way. This particular committee discussion was summarized in ten typewritten pages filed with the committee minutes of that date. As a result of this open and uninhibited discussion, the following motion was passed by the committee:[51]

Moved by Raeder Larson that the chairman of the Senate Committee on Student Affairs be directed to arrange a dinner meeting with President J. L. Morrill, Vice Presidents Malcolm Willey and W. T. Middlebrook, this committee and such other responsible student leaders and faculty members as should be invited. The agenda shall include discussion of general student problems, to point up the problems and dissatisfaction involved, and to suggest procedures whereby remedies may be eventually provided. Said meeting is to be called at such time within the next few weeks as may be determined by the Chairman and President Morrill. The Chairman shall be responsible for such preparation as is necessary by himself and the committee to have all available information ready for this meeting. The motion was carried unanimously.

The first historic meeting was held on April 1, 1946; subsequent meetings are now commonly called the "joint meeting." The meeting consisted of the Senate Committee on Student Affairs, the All-University Congress, selected staff members of the Office of the Dean of Students, and selected student leaders. Almost continuously since that date, similar meetings have been held with great profit, both to the administration and to the students. A summary of the somewhat tense meeting of April 1 contained the following points:[52]

1. Student help with Legislature re appropriations.
2. Need for more communications between administration and students, e.g., re budgets and appropriations and other problems.
3. Student political actions particularly off-campus because of fear of bad public relations.
4. Why don't we get more money for faculty salary increases?
5. Faculty repression re expression and teaching of personal beliefs —which may not be approved by the administration.
6. Confusion in student government, e.g., All-University Council has no powers or no real powers.

[51] *Minutes of the Senate Committee on Student Affairs,* Feb. 21, 1946.
[52] *Summary Notes of Discussion of Joint Meeting of Senate Committee on Student Affairs,* Apr. 2, 1946, by E. G. Williamson.

7. Need for program of public relations to change attitudes of legislature and rural public.

8. Use of students from particular communities in developing better understanding and favorable attitudes toward the University.

9. Need for more frequent face-to-face contacts and communications to overcome such obstacles as size to face-to-face relationships.

10. Need for more "common causes" or projects on which students, faculty and administration can join in discussion and action.

11. Need for some organization constantly available to the administration for consultation on problems and policies.

ORGANIZED STUDENT PARTICIPATION IN UNIVERSITY AFFAIRS

For a number of years after adoption of the new basic policy, new procedures used by the Senate Committee on Student Affairs concerning student enterprises, together with the periodic joint meetings, improved morale and resolved many conflicts before they became open ruptures. In the meantime, a student-faculty committee of the senate was studying the general character of participation by students in the making of plans and policies of the university.[53] Over a period of two years, the committee explored participation by students in college as well as in university affairs. It reviewed the responsibilities of college councils, the representativeness of students' reactions, the relationships of student councils

[53] This development of a program of systematic rather than episodic consultation between students and the central administration parallels the more elaborate practice of consultation in many, if not most, industrial corporations. It is a sad commentary that institutions of higher learning followed rather than led in developing consultation as a new form of relationship with clientele. If the colonial tradition held sway of judging students too young and immature to deal with as junior partners in the educational enterprise (a likely hypothesis), then probably the return to campuses of mature veterans as students accelerated the reform. Perhaps in time it would have been widely accepted; indeed its advent preceded the Second World War on some campuses, notably Antioch College.

There is a somewhat parallel industrial practice. See Robert Tannenbaum and F. Massirk, "Participation by Subordinates in the Managerial Decision-making Process," *Canadian Journal of Economic and Political Science,* vol. 16, pp. 408–418, 1950.

This article was also issued in 1950 as Reprint no. 14 by the Institute of Industrial Relations, University of California.

See also Chris Argyris, "Organizational Leadership and Participative Management," *Journal of Business,* vol. 28, pp. 1–7, 1955.

with students at large, the membership of students on committees and the educationally desirable avenues of communications with students. In its final report of February 15, 1951, to the senate, the committee made the following general recommendations:[54]

1. That the Senate endorse the principle of student participation in the making of educational policies and plans within the separate colleges and with respect to University-wide matters.

2. That the President explore with each of the standing committees of the Senate the desirability of adding student members or increasing the number of student members on each committee and in other ways establishing a greater degree of communication with student organizations.

3. That departments and divisions not directly concerned with educational matters but which provide services to students endeavor to develop effective relationships with student organizations, including the All-University Congress.

4. That instructional divisions and colleges continue and extend their programs of consultation with student organizations.

5. That the college student councils and intermediary boards explore the possibility of increasing effective communication with their student constituents.

Through regular administrative and committee channels, the search continued for means of improving communications and of increasing the effectiveness of student participation. As a result of these further explorations, the president of the university wrote to the then president of the All-University Congress, under date of April 23, 1951, as follows:[55]

Mr. Allen A. Kaufmann
President, All-University Congress
Coffman Memorial Union 228

Dear Mr. Kaufmann:
I am certain you will understand my unavoidable delay in acting upon the suggestions outlined in your helpful letter of March 9. Apart from our time-consuming obligations at the State House, which only

[54] *Minutes of the University of Minnesota Senate*, Feb. 15, 1951, p. 63. Approved.
[55] Quoted in *Policy Manual for Student Organizations*. Minneapolis: Student Activities Bureau, Office of the Dean of Students, University of Minnesota, 1956, pp. 11–13.

now have come to an end, I have needed time for reflection and consultation with my administrative associates. Now I am prepared to take action necessary to carry out in some measure our part of a program designed, as you suggest, to maintain University relationships with students at a high level of effectiveness.

In considering the proposals contained in your letter, I have also drawn upon the four points contained in Mr. Marvin's letter of March 13. I assume that you are working out the internal organizational matters within the All-University Congress as referred to in both letters, and I shall not concern myself with these matters except to say that such an extension of your program to include interpretation of the University and its problems to the "grass roots" of student life will, I believe, be helpful to all of us.

Let me first state my own conviction concerning the role that students play in University affairs. This University has long been committed to the use of its full resources for the development of leadership and responsible citizenship in its students. In the midst of an ever-broadening program of research and public service, this commitment to the instruction of youth remains our central objective.

Our experiences with the Congress have convincingly demonstrated that responsible student citizenship can be achieved. I am certain that consultation with students and sharing with them the backgrounds of University affairs and problems have developed a deeper loyalty to the University and have yielded continued high morale. But of equal importance, the Congress has shown that student ideas and perspective have vital significance in effective functioning of the University itself.

A university, like any other social institution, functions best when mutual understanding prevails among those who are its members. I have many times declared that the major administrative problem faced by a large and complex university such as ours involves the means and facilitation of more complete communications.

More than the negative avoidance of misunderstanding and friction is at stake. Especially in working co-operatively with students, the development of positive, responsible leadership and citizenship is a goal. That is what we want to achieve.

I have discussed this conviction of mine with the Administrative Committee and also with some of my advisers. Everyone agrees concerning the desirability of maintaining cordial, friendly, and co-operative consultative relationships with responsible student leaders. To underscore all of this, I am preparing a brief statement which later I shall present to the Regents, reaffirming our faith in the significance and the importance of common understanding with students, and bespeaking the continuous cooperating that insures it.

Furthermore, in order to give further substance to our wishes, I am designating Dean E. G. Williamson as the responsible intermediary in working directly with student leaders and University departments, especially those not engaged directly in instructional programs, in the search for effective relationships and for satisfactory solutions, if possible, of present and future matters of concern to students. Except for matters that the Congress may wish to take up with me directly, Dean Williamson will serve as the channel of communication between the organs of student government and the University's many departments to maintain a high level of co-operative and constructive relationships.

In moving forward in these ways, I am deeply grateful for the assistance you and your associates have contributed. I have high confidence, too, that these developments will make possible on a still firmer basis a continuation of the outstanding leadership the Congress has offered to student affairs and to the University at large.

Sincerely,
J. L. Morrill
President

And on May 11, 1951, the Board of Regents adopted the following resolution concerning relationships with students:[56]

The University of Minnesota has long been committed to the use of its full resources for the development of leadership and responsible citizenship in its students. In the midst of an ever broadening program of research and public service, this commitment to the instruction of youth remains a central objective.

Over the years the experiences of the administration and staff working with students have demonstrated that responsible leadership can be developed by students. Moreover, consulting and sharing with students the background of University affairs and problems have served to develop a deeper loyalty to the University and have yielded continued high morale. It is also apparent that the co-operation of student organizations, such as the All-University Congress, has contributed significantly in the effective functioning of many projects and activities sponsored by the University itself.

Such co-operative relationships are not easily attained for many reasons, among which faulty communication is of major significance. Experience indicates that a university functions best when mutual

[56] Ibid., pp. 13–14.

understanding and respect prevail among its many members, both staff and students. Indeed a major administrative need of any complex university involves the facilitation for more complete communication. In this undertaking more than negative avoidance of misunderstanding and friction is at stake. The development of positive and responsible leadership and citizenship is the goal to be attained.

It is therefore desirable that all members of the University endeavor to maintain cordial, friendly, and cooperative relationships between members of the staff on the one hand and responsible student leaders on the other.

Without implying that the ultimate authority for responsible decisions rests elsewhere than in the Board of Regents itself, by provisions of its basic charter, the Regents look with favor upon all efforts that are designed to improve the consultation, communications, and relationships between staff members and responsible student leaders. This statement is adopted to the end that encouragement may be given both to staff members and to student leaders in their joint efforts to further the welfare and services of the University as an agency of the state.

MUCH PROGRESS WAS ACHIEVED

There were many other encouraging indications that progress had been made over the years to develop better student morale, and to increase the effectiveness of student leaders in establishing and maintaining that morale. And the channels of communication apparently were increasingly effective between administration and students. The acting president of the All-University Congress wrote to President Morrill under date of March 9, 1951, as follows:[57]

I want to take this short opportunity to thank you and Mrs. Morrill for the most generous hospitality the other evening. The Congress was very pleased with the meeting and felt it has the possibility of a most fruitful session. . . .

The problems and examples presented Wednesday were not "fact problems" but they represented "feeling problems" of the students. We have extreme faith in the University and feel that the University is deserving of our full loyalty and support. Congress is partially to blame for not providing a link between the Congress and the student body at large. Perhaps Congress should sponsor a publication containing interpretations of the whys behind certain actions. Students are

[57] Letter of Allen A. Kaufmann, President of the All-University Congress to President J. L. Morrill, Mar. 9, 1951.

sincerely interested in the problems and decisions of the administration. They may, at times, not agree with the reasoning, but we feel understanding can only come through knowledge.

The solution is deep rooted. The solution does not lie entirely with you and your office. We should be able to achieve better relationships and resolutions of difficulties on the secondary level without channeling through your office. We definitely realize the many burdens you have each day and hope we will not increase the burden. . . .

I have merely vocalized my inward thoughts and hope the Congress may be able to help you arrive at a solution. I feel these problems can be solved through the continued good relationships between your office and the Congress. I am looking forward to discussing the problems involved with you in the near future.

Congress is behind you 100%. The sole purpose in raising these questions with you is in the hope that we might be of some help and assistance to you in maintaining the best possible internal public relations.

The *Minnesota Daily* commented editorially concerning the president's letter in these words:[58]

The two important words in Pres. Morrill's letter—which appears on this page today—are "mutual understanding."

As the President so correctly points out, nothing can be achieved without the students, faculty and administrative staff understanding each other's problems.

There must be a will to find the ways to work out individual problems as they arise. Often this is even more important than understanding.

Pres. Morrill has led the way in showing his willingness. Now it remains for the rest of the members of this community to follow his lead.

From the students must come the realization that the overwhelming majority of the University staff is trying to run this University for the benefit of the student. Those students who feel that the faculty considers them "just students" must put such an attitude aside. . . .

Pres. Morrill has taken two positive concrete steps toward achieving the goal: "the development of positive, responsible leadership and citizenship."

So in terms of solving actual problems, what does this statement mean?

[58] The *Minnesota Daily*, May 3, 1951. Editorial. Based on a letter to Allen A. Kaufmann from President Morrill. See *Policy Manual for Student Organizations*, 1956, pp. 11–13.

It means that when problems—like the changing of convocation programs—arise, people representing the three areas involved will know they can sit down and reach a solution.

It means that in the near future more information should be made available on a variety of topics which have student interest—parking lots for instance.

It means that a broad base has been established for achieving a more workable and responsible student government on this campus.

The goal once again has been pointed out. There are obstacles ahead. But if the students provide responsible leadership; if they are willing to understand and to work for the goal, there should be no obstacle which can't be overcome.

And the new president of the All-University Congress wrote to the president on June 13, 1951, expressing the prevailing sentiments of the student body and staff concerning the great progress made in the preceding seven years:[59]

On behalf of myself, the All-University Congress, and the student body, I would like to extend our heartfelt thanks to you and your advisors for the large advances which have been made this year in the student participation and representation areas.

Your fine letter to the Congress on April 23, 1951, stating your conception of the problem was widely circulated and the subject of very favorable comment. Secondly, the "Basic Policy Regarding Student Participation," approved by the Board of Regents on May 11, was a landmark in this area and the occasioned sacrifices of time and energy are sincerely appreciated. This issue, coming at the same crucial moment as the Legislative review of the budget, called for considerable diversification of interests.

The approval by the University Senate, of the Education Committee's Report "Student Participation in Educational Planning and Policy-making," opens myriad avenues of possibilities for responsible students. These possibilities are limited only by the student's interest, the faculty's willingness and the desire to cooperate on the part of all three groups—student, faculty, and administration.

This step, taken by the Senate, indicates that the present trend of student-faculty-administrative relationships meets with the approval of the majority of the faculty.

I believe that the University of Minnesota has shown that it not only has one of the most advanced student relationship and participation

[59] Letter of James R. Riley, Jr., President of the All-University Congress, to President J. L. Morrill, June 13, 1951.

programs in the Big Ten, but also in the Nation. Only the future will tell how successful this new policy will be, but it opens the door for more efficient and effective working relationships between the students, faculty, and the administration.

Our sincere thanks and best hopes for the future.

Sincerely,

James R. Riley, Jr., President
All-University Congress

A NEW STUDENT JUDICIARY

One more forward step can be reported to complete this illustration of administrative processes involved in progressing from a state of continuous unrest to a state of more orderly resolution of conflicts of interests and points of view. In the first place, the senate, acting on a recommendation of the Senate Committee on Student Affairs, adopted appeal procedures based upon the substance or application of established policy or based upon actions of administrators in connection with the application of policies to programs or incidents.[60] These new procedures spelled out in detail the protections available to organized student groups with respect to their rights and privileges in case action has been taken against them as a result of violation of university policies and regulations governing student groups. These appeal procedures round out the regularization of this type of relationship between the university and organized student groups.

An action having still greater implications completes this review of some processes involved in redefining students' relationships with the administration. In May, 1955, the Senate Committee on Student Affairs established an all-university judiciary with two principal functions. The first was to handle judiciously cases referred by the Senate Committee on Student Affairs concerning alleged violation of rules and regulations by organized student groups. The thought behind this form of judiciary was that a specialized group, having student majority but full faculty representation, should be removed from administrative decision and policy making to act in a detached manner about alleged violations of regulations. Such an orderly handling of alleged violations would,

[60] *Senate Minutes,* June 4, 1956.

it was assumed, again protect the basic rights of student groups as well as the interests of the university.

The second function of the new judiciary may prove, in the long run, to be equally important, if not more so. The judiciary was given authority to act, upon request, in an advisory manner concerning the alleged violations of administrative rulings and policies established by agencies of the university, other than the Senate Committee on Student Affairs.[61] Either party involved in such an alleged violation or nonconformity may ask the all-university judiciary to review the situation and present an advisory opinion. While this would not be binding upon the parties involved, it would nevertheless serve as the voice of a disinterested body with respect to a conflict situation. Since its organization, the judiciary has to date (1960) handled only two cases. The first case was the alleged violation of a senate committee's policy concerning discriminatory clauses on the part of a sorority. A second case was described by the *Minnesota Daily* in the following words:

It looks as though University students who once used the underground tunnels to go from one class to another will have to fasten the top button on their overcoats and brave the winter winds.

Andrew R. Vernes, Assistant Director of Protection and Safety (P and S), said yesterday he doubts there will be any change in the strict enforcement of the "patrons only" policy in the tunnels.

Some tunnel doors were locked and new signs forbidding pedestrian traffic—except by University garage patrons—have been erected.

Why the strict enforcement? Vernes cited two reasons.

"For one thing," he said, "we've had quite a few complaints from patrons of the garages. Pedestrians have been blocking traffic. And some car owners complain their radio aerials have been bent.

"And another thing. We're afraid somebody will be run over down there. We've had some very close calls, although we haven't had any accidents yet."

A Northrop garage parking attendant said he noticed some garage patrons were irritated because after all the maneuvering required to get in and out of the tight parking spaces in the garage, they still had

---

[61] *Constitution of the All-University Judiciary Council,* art. 2, sec. 1, adopted Apr. 1, 1955. See *Policy Manual for Student Organizations, op. cit.* pp. 10, 40. Procedures for appeal from decisions affecting student organizations were adopted Apr. 1, 1955. See *Policy Manual for Student Organizations, op. cit.*

the blocs of pedestrian students to contend with before getting out of the garage.

Oscar Peterson, University parking facilities supervisor, said yesterday that the "patrons only" signs had always been on the doors, but they have never been strictly enforced.

"It seems that the pedestrian traffic has finally gotten out of hand," he added.[62]

HANSCOM DEFENDS TUNNEL CLOSING

Spring may be on its way, but the underground transportation issue is still being debated at the University.

C. B. Hanscom, director of University Protection and Safety (P and S) yesterday defended the closing of two doors leading to Northrop garage "as a necessary safety factor. . . ."

Hanscom said that the doors locked were those connecting Northrop Auditorium and the garage (not those leading to tunnels). He added that all the tunnels could still be used—at the expense of a "small inconvenience."

Congress had requested the hearing because it believes, according to Gary Filerman, SLA Junior and Congress vice president, that there was a lack of evidence that the doors should be closed and because students were not consulted, as required by University policy. . . .

Hanscom apologized for not consulting Congress, and said: "We knew nothing about the policy. Although we don't anticipate closing any more doors, we shall consult with Congress before doing so."

Hanscom said the garage problem—involving the safety of student pedestrians—had become more acute in the past six months because more students than ever before were using the tunnels and the garage to walk between class.

He claimed that "Students just laughed at garage attendants and told them to go to the dickens when the attendants requested their cooperation in staying clear of a motorist's path. . . .

"Students also left doors open and turned off light switches which left some areas in complete darkness—another safety hazard. In fact, we had to put a lock on one light switch."

L. L. Wood, assistant supervising engineer for the physical plant, said that an industrial commission ruling forbids pedestrian traffic in the garage.

"But the ruling is difficult to enforce," he added, "and, after all, we have to live with the students too."

"We didn't make this move arbitrarily," said Hanscom, "but only

[62] The *Minnesota Daily*, Feb. 11, 1958.

after a meeting of P and S with the University safety engineer and the physical plant representative."

A recommendation—on the basis of the hearing—will be given by the Council in the near future.[63]

Upon petitioning the All-University Student Congress and after properly hearing interested parties, the judiciary brought in an advisory opinion which requestaed that further consultation be held between interested parties and that the president remind all university departments of the desirability of cooperating with student groups, in line with the basic policy of consultation as adopted by the Regents.

The President issued such a request under date of May 21, 1958.[64]

A NEW STAGE IN REDEFINING RELATIONSHIPS

An incidental part of the judiciary's report may prove, in the long run, to be a significant contribution to the defining of more productive relationships between organized student groups and the university administration. In this connection, we recall Thwing's summary of student-college relationships during the nineteenth century and we project a summary into our future: "The history of the government of students in American colleges is a history of increasing liberality and orderliness." [65]

The student chairman of the judiciary wrote an opinion which we believe points cogently and clearly to the fundamental strategy of the practice of consultation. In fact, we believe this to be the most mature and noteworthy formulation of the importance of continually redefining the relationship between students and the administration that we have seen anywhere. This concurring opinion was advanced:[66]

The general disposition of the recent tunnel controversy by the All-University judicial council is, in my judgment, a fair and balanced

[63] The *Minnesota Daily,* Mar. 11, 1958.

[64] Published in the *Minnesota Daily,* May 21, 1958.

[65] Charles Franklin Thwing, *College Administration.* New York: D. Appleton & Company, Inc., 1900, p. 113.

[66] Bruce Smith, Chairman, All-University Judiciary Council, *A Concurring Opinion.* (Mimeographed.)

decision. However, I am obliged to elucidate some of the points not fully explained in the formal report. This is done because of the grave implications with which this case is fraught, not only for the future of the body of which I am presently chairman, but for the whole development of student-administration relationships on this campus as well.

There is apt to be a tendency on the part of responsible persons, student, faculty and administrators alike, to regard this case with an air of amused complacency, and hence to ignore the far-reaching ramifications involved therein. After all, the snow is gone, no one is using the tunnels any more, and few students seem to evince any interest anyway. One need only recall that some of the most important constitutional issues in our country's history have been decided in ostensibly trivial cases. Indeed, the whole doctrine of judicial review as established in the well-known landmark case, *Marbury* v. *Madison,* was largely an accident. . . . Similarly, the tunnel controversy touches the very heart of a portentous issue for the University in the coming years, namely, the cooperative status of student groups and administrative personnel. Are we to have a peaceful and harmonious relationship, or a bitter and incessant feud? As the number of students grows, and the University of necessity becomes larger and more impersonal, this problem will take on increasingly alarming proportions.

With the statement of facts appearing in the first two sections of the majority report I have no quarrel. My first query concerns the painful contortions through which the majority of the Council felt obliged to go in order to establish "non-compliance" by a student organization with a University administrative decision. The majority decision relied upon Article II, Section 1, of the Judiciary Council's constitution, which permits review by the Council of cases involving "non-compliance of a student organization . . . with decisions by University officers based on other than Senate Committee on Student Affairs' regulations or policies." In such a case the Judiciary Council is empowered to "make recommendations to either or both parties for resolutions of the problem." (Article II, Section 2.)

Clearly, any sensible interpretation of "non-compliance" should embrace "non-acceptance." Otherwise one would assume that there would have to be a well-publicized scandal, or an outburst of violence and destructive defiance of a regulation, before the Council would ever have jurisdiction to hear a case. It would be a curious and dangerous legal doctrine indeed that would require a student organization to flaunt a University regulation and thereby put itself in jeopardy and endanger the peace and good order of the University community, in order to test whether that regulation were in accord with University policy or enacted according to proper procedures. But aside from this obvious point, it seems clear to me that it is not even necessary to rely exclusively upon Article II, Section 1 to establish basis for jurisdiction. The creator of the Judiciary Council, the Senate Committee on Student Affairs, has declared that the "Basic Policy Concerning Student Organizations and Activities," approved by the Senate, grants to student organizations the right of appeal from decisions and actions affecting their operations. "Appeals may also be made on the substance of a policy." This unequivocal assertion is followed by equally forthright statements which make it abundantly clear that the Senate Committee on Student Affairs intended student organizations to have unobstructed channels to secure redress of their grievances, concerning administrative decisions affecting the operation of their organizations, in a peaceable and orderly manner. In fact, an elaborate classification of appeals procedures was laid down which was surely intended to apply to the jurisdiction of the All-University Judiciary Council. It cannot be seriously maintained that the jurisdiction of a judicial body which is the creature of a University legislative committee cannot be expanded or contracted by subsequent pronouncement, irrespective of the original provisions found in the judicial body's constitution. The governing provision then would seem to be Article II, Section C, Paragraph 3 of the Senate Committee Minutes for April 1, 1955.

"Appeals from decisions made by administrative officers, but not based on a Senate or Senate Committee on Student Affairs policy shall be referred only to the All-University Judicial Council and not to lower bodies."

And the criterion would then simply be whether the rule or regulation "affected the operations" of a student group, rather than involved a case of "non-compliance" with the rule or regulation. The Senate Committee minutes can be construed as a type of amendment to the actual constitution of the Judiciary Council. Whether or not the minutes were formally incorporated into the written constitution as amendments is largely irrelevant, since they were so obviously intended to clarify the duties and procedures of the Judiciary Council. In interpreting the written provisions of a judiciary body, it should always be remembered that rules of procedures are designed to promote, and not to obstruct, justice.

Clarification of this jurisdictional point may help to clear the atmosphere for future cases.

Secondly, the question arises as to the fancied prospects that a recommendation from the Judiciary Council in cases of this nature would seriously interfere with administrators' freedom to do their jobs. It is erroneously supposed that, if a student organization is permitted to petition this Judiciary Council for a recommendation by way of redress of grievances, every administrative decision will fall under the scrutiny of a clamoring horde of disgruntled students. The fact is that there are certain rigid conditions which must be met before the Judiciary may hear any case and issue any recommendation. These conditions include:

1. A student organization must be involved. No individual student may decide to challenge any administrative decision because he was not consulted. And where large numbers of students are involved, who have no recourse through group action, they may seek to convince the All-University Congress that it is being affected as an effective representative of the student body. The Congress then carefully considers any such request, and acts as a rigorous screening device to weed out the empty protestations of cranks and crackpots.

2. A student organization must be directly and adversely affected, in such a palpable manner as to imperil the very existence of the organization as a viable entity. The impact of the administrative decision must be immediate and forceful, and it must be clearly apparent that the student organization has, or will, suffer significantly from the decision.

3. No administrative decision or rule may be appealed on an ex post facto basis. If an appeal is not submitted within ten days, as provided by Senate Committee minutes, it is presumed to be in accordance with University policy and procedures. Thus no long-standing policy ruling can be challenged through appeal to the Judiciary Council.

4. Strictly academic matters do not fall within the jurisdiction of the Judiciary Council. If a student group dislikes new course requirements in a certain college, for example, it must seek different channels in which to air its grievances.

5. There must be unmistakable abuse of the consultation policy.

Once these five criteria have been satisfied, the Judiciary Council may hear a case and issue appropriate recommendations to either, or both, parties by which the dispute may be amicably resolved. Rather than being hampered, administrators may find their jobs considerably easier and more pleasant as a harmonious and cooperative working relationship with student groups develops. There is clearly no basis for assuming that the Judiciary Council's exercise of the recommending authority rightfully given it would disrupt the administrative arm of the University community.

As one of its recommendations in the present case, the Judiciary Council urged the Senate Committee to suggest to the office of the President that the "consultation policy" be circulated to department heads. The fact that he was unaware of the existence of such a policy would appear to support the wisdom of such a recommendation. Never-theless, the recommendation would prove less than useful if there were not basic agreement on the meaning of the term "consultation." Through-out the years it has been a most abused term, administrators and students alike glibly tossing it about with little or no understanding of its true significance. Consultation is not a mere shibboleth, a phrase to be dragged forth as a substitute for thought. It does not mean that an administrator informs a student group of what he is about to do be-fore he in fact does it. It does not mean that students passively defer to what they are told is best for them. Nor does it mean that the tra-ditional prerogatives of administrative responsibility become captive to the passing inclinations of succeeding generations of students. Neither does it infer that administrative competence be thrust aside for student experimentation in the arts of management. Consultation implies mutual concession and cooperation, a common struggling with a common burden, a joint effort toward a joint end. It implies a status of dignity and vitality for men who must in future years show dignity and vitality if self-government is to survive across a troubled earth. It suggests patience and understanding, without complacency and smugness. It demands statesmanship and dedication by all, according to recognized norms of orderliness.

If student groups are denied peaceful recourse to settle grievances, their likely reaction will be organized displays or violence, designed to achieve by coercion what was denied them by law. An important prece-dent will be established here by the present tunnel dispute.

SUMMARY

We have reviewed a case relevant to basic principles in the continuous search for effective forms and structures of relationships within a university community. This search and research operates *within* the legal authority of the institution's charter. The adminis-trative officers continue to act as the agents of the trustees, who possess ultimate authority. The faculty continues to exercise its hard-won delegated authority over educational policies and regula-tions. And students continue to enjoy their rights and privileges as citizens of the wider community. But within the community of scholars, orderly consultation, review, and joint planning of changes in regulations, freedoms, rights, activities, and enterprises are slowly evolving to substitute for rioting, revolt, invective, and disruptive conflict. And the search will no doubt continue in future years, thus defining a continuing service and function of the student personnel staff, especially those members who work with student leaders of activities and organizations.

CHAPTER 13

The Extracurriculum as Higher Education

Shoben has formulated a comprehensive rationale of student personnel work, essentially a philosophic orientation of our program of services. Though we have sometimes been charged with anti-intellectualism, he argued that we do have a philosophy of education which embraces the objective of *full development of students.* He reasoned that, therefore, there is "no contradiction between the objectives of personnel officers and their instructional colleagues." [1] In describing the objectives, as well as the content, of our program of services, perceived as higher education, Shoben referred to such educational objectives as—[2]

. . . helping students to gain greater personal maturity through reflected-upon experience, increasing their interpersonal effectiveness, deepening their sensitivity to human needs including their own, clarifying their long-range objectives in both vocational and more personal terms, and assisting in their interpretation of education both in their active student careers and their lives after graduation.

Shoben continued his statement with reference to the campus as—[3]

. . . a kind of social microcosm in which students acquire the knowledge, skills, motivations, values, and personal attributes useful for productive participation in American life.

[1] Edward Joseph Shoben, Jr., "A Rationale for Modern Student Personnel Work," *Personnel-o-gram,* vol. 12, no. 3, p. 10, American College Personnel Association, March, 1958.
[2] *Ibid.*
[3] *Ibid*

Now we subscribe heartily to Shoben's philosophy of higher education which embraces the development of knowledge *and* interpersonal relationships, sensitivity to human needs and to the rich development of humane lives. But we believe Shoben agrees that we do not make a good case for the relevancy of personnel work to higher education when we give indication that our philosophy is thus so radically opposed to that of our faculty colleagues. They, too, recognize that human needs and problems must be dealt with in organized society, but not within the university. Indeed, they assert vigorously that to equate interpersonal skills with intellectual development is to miss the point of *higher* education. They point to the record indicating that Western education has long centered upon intellectual development. And we personnel workers *seem* to some critics—humanists especially—to have broken with that tradition of intellectual emphasis by substituting personality for intellectual development and by treating personal adjustment as the core of higher education.[4]

We might not be so critically chastised if we had *added* personality development to intellectual emphasis. But we appear, perhaps incorrectly, to have *substituted* one for the other. This supposed offense brings forth the charge of soft education and many other scathing characterizations. We personnel workers are thus identified with that philosophy of education which elevates *interpersonal skills* and *affect adjustment* above intellectual and rational development as the important objectives sought in the community of scholars.

To be sure, the telling argument is not quite so one-sided nor is the division of opinion quite so sharply opposed in all cases. Some intellectuals have paid sober tribute to at least one segment of the personnel worker's domain—the extracurriculum. For example, Charles Seymour, former president of Yale University, characterized the extracurriculum as relevant to our distinctly American pattern of higher education. While recognizing that extracurricular activities tended to become divorced from the scholastic or intellectual, nevertheless he contended that ". . . the college has provided

⁴ Howard Mumford Jones, *The Pursuit of Happiness*. Cambridge, Mass.: Harvard University Press, 1953, chap. V, "The Technique of Happiness." See also Jones's "Campus: Echo or Criticism," *Harvard Alumni Bulletin*, vol. 63, no. 4, p. 161–164, Nov. 5, 1955.

the free opportunity whereby in their associations of living, in their activities and competitions, the young can discover themselves in relation to their fellows, can learn to adjust in all liberty their individual interests to those of the community." [5]

Another intellectual, former President Lowell of Harvard University, made a similar pronouncement in the following words: ". . . the object of the undergraduate department is not to produce hermits, each imprisoned in the cell of his own intellectual pursuits, but men fitted to take their places in the community and live in contact with their fellow men." [6]

While taking comfort and even courage from these educators, yet we must note several limitations in generalizing from their statements to the entire range of personnel services. Both were paraphrasing the Oxford-Cambridge goal of educating gentlemen and scholars. We may conjecture, therefore, that neither held to a concept or program of social adjustment such as that seemingly implicit in Shoben's philosophy of education. The very restricted social class and the economic and cultural origins of the students then enrolled in their institutions would seem to influence their special meaning of learning "to adjust" to others and to "live in contact with their fellow men." Both presidents were referring to undergraduate student life within residential colleges and they probably had in mind what Woodrow Wilson referred to as "pupil to pupil in a comradeship of studies." [7] Like Wilson, Lowell sought to increase intellectual emphasis in the collegiate way of living, the theme of our chapter.

To return to our analysis of the resistance and opposition to personnel services within higher education, it is clear that those services are indeed infused with their own philosophy of education. It is equally true that we are a type of educator. But, to repeat, there are wide, perceived differences between our philosophy of education and that held by some members of the faculty with respect to the emphasis, importance, and status given to intellectual

[5] Charles Seymour, "The Tradition of the Liberal Arts College," *Association of American Colleges Bulletin*, vol. 36, no. 4, pp. 471–472, December, 1950.

[6] A. Lawrence Lowell, *At War with Academic Traditions in America*. Cambridge, Mass.: Harvard University Press, 1934, p. 32.

[7] John A. Garraty, *Woodrow Wilson*. New York: Alfred A. Knopf, Inc., 1956, p. 30.

development. As perceived through the medium of our written and spoken statements, we personnel workers seem to be principally concerned with the *well-rounded development* of the student *as an individual student*.[8]

Our faculty colleagues usually speak and write as though they concentrate their efforts on developing rational powers as their central emphasis. And Shoben's formulation seems to contrast sharply with Boyd's scholarly history of classical learning from the Hebrew, Greek, and Roman schools to the European schools of this century.[9] Lowell carved the basic charter in these words: "Universities stand for the eternal worth of thought. . . ." [10]

While we do not concur with those who currently advocate a return to the classical curriculum, yet today *we do hold to an educational point of view that enthrones reason as the center of education—but reason fully integrated with a social ethic and a healthy personality*, in the mode of ancient Greek thought. We hold to the

---

[8] In an earlier statement on the extracurriculum, we wrote only of nonintellectual content, emphases, and objectives. Difficult as it is to recapture an earlier mental framework, we did not intend to exclude intellectual content but rather to highlight those parts of student life which had been long neglected or relegated to the periphery of campus life, largely as a direct result of the German experiences of some American educators. For our earlier statement, see "The Extracurriculum and General Education," *General Education*, Fifty-first Yearbook of the National Society for the Study of Education, Chicago, 1952, part I, pp. 230–249.

[9] William Boyd, *The History of Western Education*, London: A. & C. Black, Ltd., 1954.

The reader who is interested in contrasting American higher education with that of other cultures will find these two older books will serve as a simple introduction:

Bradby, Edward (ed.): *The University outside Europe*. New York: Oxford University Press, 1939.

Kotsching, Walter M., et al.: *The University in a Changing World*. New York: Oxford University Press, 1932.

A simple characterization of contemporary student life in a number of countries is contained in "The Student in Society," *News Bulletin*, vol. 34, no. 5, Institute of International Education, New York, January, 1959.

American education was influenced by several European prototypes, and in this sense it is an extension and projection of the European modification of classical education of Rome and Athens. Yet, as Cowley established so clearly in his analysis of origins, "the University in the United States is *sui generis*." See W. H. Cowley, "The University of the United States of America," in Edward Bradby (ed.), *The University outside Europe*. New York: Oxford University Press, 1939.

[10] Lowell, *op. cit.*, p. 64.

social ethic stated by Gabriel in his provocative study of the philosophy of American democracy with these relevant words: ". . . to be effective, reason must be disciplined by an ethical code, the code of freedom, honor, mutual aid, and the complete subordination of the individual will to the cause of truth." [11]

We do not even suggest that Shoben's formulation of the core of higher education is wrong or even less desirable than the formulations of others. In fact, as stated above, we subscribe heartily to it. Our point may be made clearer by reference to this quotation from Boyd in reference to the utility and content of education in a political democracy in which individuality is held to be precious: "After all that can be said as to the virtue of classical learning has been admitted, it still remains true that the central principle of the old tradition is that literature in any form and in any language is the means of intellectual salvation." [12] This formulation of the strategy of the humanities centers major emphasis upon intellectual development as the basic purpose of education.

If we were to search for points of similarity and continuity between such a statement of objectives and those found in the literature of personnel work, we might discover much of substance. Perhaps then we would no longer rest the whole case for the relevancy of our work to higher education upon the utility of vocational guidance, or student loans, or crisis-centered and problem-oriented services for students. Moreover, we might then come to perceive that our own case for relevancy need not rest so solidly upon Thorndike's doubt of the generalized transferability of mental discipline and the consequent assumed uselessness of classical languages and studies. Indeed, we might even come to hypothesize that

[11] Ralph Henry Gabriel, *The Course of American Democratic Thought.* New York: The Ronald Press Company, 1940, p. 465.

The reader is urged to review John Dewey's educational philosophy. The therapist and progressive educators have distorted his philosophy by substituting "togetherness" and "affect" for his concept of "rational inquiry" as the goal to be achieved through education. Many of his concepts are freshly relevant as foundations for our program of services—if we abandon that form of anti-intellectualism which enthrones feeling as the foundation of the happy and adjusted way of living. See John L. Child, *American Pragmatism and Education.* New York: Henry Holt and Company, Inc., 1956. See also "John Dewey Centennial: A Special Section," *The Saturday Review,* Nov. 21, 1959.

[12] Boyd, *op. cit.,* p. 381.

the empty shell of formalism[13] in teaching classical languages, "gerund grinding," [14] was the real target of an earlier and too severe revolt against intellectualism. Indeed this empty formalism in teaching was also the source of our search for a new philosophical outlook which focused upon the dynamic and humanely developing students. In turn, we might relax our rejection of the content of past higher education and review our efforts to educate the whole student, *intellect and all*. This would be a welcome reform that might win some degree of support from our academic colleagues.

To continue this polemic against the narrowness of our own educational perspective, we believe that periodic reading of *The College Charts Its Course* by R. Freeman Butts[15] will sharpen perspective as well as refresh identification of our work with the changing direction, coverage, and emphases of education in America. This book documents the dynamic interplay of the classical tradition, liberal arts, the elective system, mental discipline, Prussian *Wissenshaftlehre,* the land grant college revolution, progressive and essential dogmatism, intellectualism, Rousseau-Dewey pupil centeredness, vocationalism, and the bursting expansion of enrollment of new types of students differing from earlier students in ability, interests, and objectives. We need recall that student personnel work arose during the recent dynamic half century of violent debate and disruptive change in higher education. Our work cannot be clearly understood or evaluated except

[13] Boyd, *op. cit.,* pp. 195–197. John Sturm (1507–1589) of Strasburg is credited with creating the long-continued rigid pattern of instruction in the classical languages for the chief purpose of learning oratorical style and verbal forms of the Ciceronian pattern. Such preoccupation with verbal forms was said to drain life out of the humanistic studies and made them formalities, empty of humanistic teachings.

Alfred Whitney Griswold said of formalism in teaching: "Form without substance, polish without purpose, have always been a 'distemper of learning' to the liberal arts." See Alfred Whitney Griswold, *In the University Tradition.* New Haven, Conn.: Yale University Press, 1957, p. 21.

[14] Charles W. Eliot, "Educational Reform," in David Andrew Weaver (ed.), *Builders of American Universities.* Alton, Ill.: Shurtleff College Press, vol. I, p. 18. An inaugural address delivered on Oct. 19, 1869. See also the inaugural address by Andrew Dickson White, Oct. 7, 1868, which is also contained in vol. I, p. 267.

[15] Published by McGraw-Hill Book Company, Inc., New York, 1939.

See also R. Freeman Butts and Lawrence A. Cremin, *A History of Education in American Culture.* New York: Henry Holt and Company, Inc., 1953. Note especially chaps. 1, 15, and 16.

with the background and interplay of these competing concepts which contend even today for partisan advocacy. Unfortunately, most of us have narrowed our historical and societal perspective to a few stages of development derived from restricted courses in psychology and education. But a new widening of understanding of our own program development within the changing educational enterprise will serve to clarify much of our professional confusion and will also aid in the perception by our academic colleagues of our relevancy to higher education.

To return to our central point of argument, it is clearly evident that we who operate services do indeed have a philosophic point of view concerning the relevancy of our work to higher education. But this point of view is usually stated in such different wording from that of the faculty that we are often perceived as working at cross-purposes with instructional programs. For this reason, student personnel work has been characterized, sometimes accurately, as *marginal* to the main educational relationship of teacher and student involved in mastery of the formal classroom curriculum.[16]

A CRITICAL SELF-EXAMINATION

It would seem desirable that we critically examine our relationships with the educational enterprise, not only as they are defined by student personnel workers, but even more as they are perceived by the faculty. And this query would soon lead us to a critical examination of the basic question: Do we make essential contributions to the intellectual development of students? Or are we indeed peripheral to that one objective of education and thus unknowingly, perhaps, committed to nonintellectual aspects of students' development? In the latter case, if this were true, it would not necessarily follow that our services were irrelevant or unnecessary, since some nonintellectual dimensions of students' development are indeed essential, both in their relevancy to American democracy and as supportive and preparatory steps in intellectual development.

Indeed, the purpose of this present chapter is to examine one part of the student personnel program—the extracurriculum—not

[16] *The Edward W. Hazen Foundation: 1925–1950.* New Haven, Conn.: Report of the Foundation, p. 34.

merely to delineate and justify its worthwhile nonintellectual outcomes, such as learning to live and work in a teamwork situation
with other individual students. We have no question but that such
an objective is a worthwhile outcome of the extracurriculum. But
we need also to appraise our program to see whether it does, in
effect and in fact, contribute significantly to the strictly intellectual
accomplishments of the institution. We will also, at the same time,
need to appraise our efforts in the extracurriculum to determine
whether we perchance do contribute to anti-intellectual emphasis
and to other student-established mores. If we were contributing
to anti-intellectual results, or if we are perceived, even erroneously,
as being anti-intellectual, then we would need either to change our
content and emphasis or attempt to restructure the way in which we
are perceived by our faculty colleagues and by students.

The disturbing likelihood that our program of services is incorrectly perceived by faculty in terms of value systems other than
our own is suggested by an analogous study of the differences in
perceptions of educational values held by faculty and students in
one university.[17] The study found that the faculty was markedly
concerned with intellectual and related activities, while students
ranked intellectual growth as fourth in importance. That is, students
ranked vocational preparation, self-fulfillment, and self-understand-
ing higher than intellectual values and activities. Moreover, rank-
ings of seniors did not reveal any marked movement toward the
academic value orientation of the faculty. One may hazard a guess
that personnel workers would tend markedly to agree with these
students rather than with the faculty members involved in this
study. The point is clear that studies of the perceptions of students
and faculty—and of workers themselves—toward personnel services and workers are needed as a basis of organized efforts to change
perceptions and program content in regard to the intellectual emphases in the university community of scholars. In the absence of
such studies, we proceed in our present discussion on the assumption that our program content is understandably, but often erroneously and unnecessarily, perceived as nonintellectual, if not anti-
intellectual, in orientation and consequences.

[17] Frederick M. Jervis and Robert G. Congdon, "Student and Faculty Perceptions of Educational Values," *The American Psychologist,* vol. 13, no. 8,
pp. 464–466, August, 1958

OUR REACTION AGAINST FORMALIZED INTELLECTUALISM

Perhaps most personnel workers have habitually defined their function in the university largely in terms of a protest against the pattern of impersonalism which seemed to characterize higher education during the past half of the nineteenth century. Ours was but a small part of the organized movement to re-establish the *live* child and his optimum and healthy development as the center of the educational enterprise. In this sense, redevelopment of modern student personnel work paralleled certain aspects of progressive education, but our efforts involved more than a philosophic point of view geared to new classroom techniques. We sought to apply to the extraclass problems of adolescents and to the learning of classroom materials the knowledge that the psychologists, psychiatrists, and others had gained about human development—beyond mastery of the formal curriculum.

One signal point in this return to the "whole" student was the actions of reform against the Germanic pattern of higher education. Much has been written about the efforts of President Tappan at the University of Michigan to remodel that university after the German pattern. Dormitories were turned into classrooms, students lived with townspeople, and the university concerned itself with things intellectual.[18] This American transformation of the German concept of a university as a place for research and advanced learning with reoriented concern for students as individuals, was just that—an American interpretation. Many neglected facts tell the full story of the transformation of American undergraduate colleges into research stations. If one reads the personal accounts of American students in German universities, one discovers that there were indeed highly personal relationships between professors and students at the advanced-seminar level.[19] In the seminar, a friendly

[18] Charles M. Perry, *Henry Philip Tappan, Philosopher and University President.* Ann Arbor, Mich.: University of Michigan Press, part III, 1933.

[19] The reader may be richly rewarded with glimpses of these personal relationships. See Lincoln Steffens, *The Autobiography of Lincoln Steffens.* New York: Harcourt, Brace and Company, Inc., 1931, chap. 19, "Heidelberg: There Is No Ethics."

Many other instances of the humanness of teacher-student relationships in our own and other national universities are related in a delightful compilation. See A. C. Spectorsky (ed.), *The College Years.* New York: Hawthorn Books, Inc., 1958.

comradeship was enjoyed—in large part because the German universities had early freed the faculty from the disruptive and hateful disciplinary control of students' behavior, a burden which earlier plagued our American colonial colleges and almost ruined them as effective instructional institutions.[20] Having thus freed themselves from the petty, irritating, and antagonizing responsibilities for behavior and decorum, the German professors could develop a comradeship with their students in terms of things intellectual. And there was no universal, impersonal concern for the individual advanced student. Rather was he dealt with as an intellectual apprentice, and given every conceivable intellectual challenge and encouragement. It is true that the professors did not concern themselves about the student's personal and social life, but there was a highly personalized concern for the intellectual life of the student.[21]

We personnel workers have too long misinterpreted this narrowing of the professor's concern to things intellectual as a cold indifference to the student as an individual. And the American educators, such as Tappan, who transmuted the German formulation of higher education, undoubtedly contributed to the subsequent American pattern of impersonalism. Granted that it was a great gain to free the college faculty, in the German pattern, of responsibility for immature misbehavior, yet the preoccupation with scholarly efforts and with classroom instruction turned into the American pattern of impersonal concern for other facets of the American student's life. The American pattern of reduced concern for students' out-of-class life was later to produce a reaction that led to the development of the variety of personnel services for students as extra-instructional responsibilities of the institution.

And as a part of that general movement which rejected impersonalism in American institutions and sought to recapture the earlier colonial concern with the whole individual student, personnel workers seem to have unknowingly rejected intellectualism. This blind spot in the complex crosscurrents sometimes produced

[20] Richard Hofstadter and Walter P. Metzger, *The Development of Academic Freedom in the United States.* New York: Columbia University Press, 1955, pp. 306–309.
[21] Charles Franklin Thwing, *The American and the German University: One Hundred Years of History.* New York: The Macmillan Company, 1928.

a faddish concern with a narrowly redefined function, oblivious to important but neglected areas of concern in education. And as a result, the literature of personnel work does seem to be limited to nonintellectual aspects of development. In part, this limitation may be a reflection of the progressive education movement which sought to recapture concern for the child's emotional and social development. In part, it may also be a reflection of the fact that personnel work originated on the edge of the educational enterprise, the campus. By its very nature, it operated away from the classroom and was concerned in part with matters not immediately and intimately related to instruction—housing, finances, and activities.

Whatever the factors involved in this complex movement, today we do find ourselves largely concerned with nonintellectual aspects of the student's development. We contend that it is not that we are actually indifferent to the fact that the student is attending classes and developing intellectually: we do help him to select his course of study, his vocational objective; we help him learn to read, to study for examinations, and we perform a host of related functions, many directly and intimately related to the academic responsibility. Since we do not organize our services in the classroom form, we are usually thought of as nonacademic, and therefore probably nonintellectual in our interest and effort.

But the present state of separated affairs need not continue. Indeed, we contend that a case can be made for our relevancy to higher education and for our significant contributions to the achievement of academic objectives. Shoben cogently argued that ". . . student personnel workers are the collaborators of instructors and research workers." [22]

In the present chapter we will examine one part of the student personnel program, the extracurriculum, in an appraisal of its present state of concentration on nonacademic and sometimes anti-intellectual objectives. We shall also examine its possibilities for contributing immediately and directly to the intellectual life of the student body. Unfortunately, there is no extensive literature available describing efforts to achieve these objectives through the extracurriculum. But there are sufficient testimonies and a few

[22] Shoben, *op. cit.*, p. 11.

accounts of experience which will serve to highlight the problem and perhaps to stimulate a more intensive exploration of new program developments. Such deficiencies can be readily corrected, as is illustrated by the fact that in the past quarter of a century we have made tremendous improvements in vocational guidance as a result of intensive program and research efforts, A quarter of a century hence, one would hope that the extracurriculum will have been subjected to a similar effective reconstruction.

UNIVERSITIES AND THINGS INTELLECTUAL

At this point we need to define our use of the term "intellectual," both as it concerns program content and students as intellectual beings. Taylor provided the simplest and most precise concept, having first expressed the hope that no separate intellectual class would arise in America: "An intellectual . . . is a person who is interested in ideas and carries on a serious intellectual life of his own. If he has no private world of ideas, he is merely a practitioner or a technician in the field of ideas. . . . The ideal for American society is one in which the intellectual and aesthetic interests of the citizens are an element in the daily life of the country."[23]

The point needs little elaboration. A university is a special type of public institution dedicated to learning the old and discovering the new in the world of concepts and ideas. This is an intellectual pursuit, and it is a professor's hope that most students will come, in time, to enjoy the excitement of pursuing truth. Sir James Jeans concluded that ". . . to many it is not knowledge but the quest for knowledge that gives the greater interest to thought. . . ."[24]

Ortega y Gasset has delineated the function of a university as "the teaching of culture, the system of vital ideas."[25] In further discussing the intellectual task of the Western university, he described the use of the metaphor of ideas as paths or roads in these words:[26]

[23] Harold Taylor, "The Intellectual in Action," *Bulletin of the Atomic Scientists*, vol. 14, no. 9, pp. 368–373, November, 1958.

[24] Sir James Jeans, *Physics and Philosophy*. London: Cambridge University Press; New York: The Macmillan Company, 1943, p. 217.

[25] José Ortega y Gasset, *Mission of the University*. Princeton, N.J.: Princeton University Press, 1944, p. 59. Translated, with an introduction by Howard Lee Norstrand.

[26] *Ibid.*, p. 85.

When we find ourselves in a perplexing, confused situation, it is as though we stood before a dense forest, through whose tangles we cannot advance without being lost. Someone explains the situation, with a happy idea, and we experience a sudden illumination—the 'light' of understanding. The thicket immediately appears ordered, and the lines of its structure seem like paths opening through it. Hence the term *method* is regularly associated with that of enlightenment, illumination, *Aufklärung*. What we call today a "cultured man" was called more than a century ago an "enlightened man," i.e., a man who sees the paths of life in a clear light.

The metaphor is itself illuminating of the function of education as a whole and of universities in particular. And the function of instruction, in fact the function of the entire institution's program, is geared to the objective of assisting students in illuminating what was foggy, distorted, and unclear in the world of ideas and concepts. In contrast with the use of *satori* by the Zen Buddhist to accomplish illumination and enlightenment of the universe, in Western culture higher education uses the method of the classroom, the library, and the laboratory to secure intellectual illumination.

But illumination and enlightenment are not, we hope, place-bound to the extent that they do occur and can occur only in certain behavior postures or in certain places, such as laboratory and library and classroom. President Lowell's incisive words expressed his hope for the radiation and generalization of things learned in the university classroom: "It is the ambition of every earnest teacher so to stimulate his pupils that they will discuss outside the class-room the problems he has presented them." [27]

Harold Taylor has repeatedly emphasized that "the involvement of the student in the entire life of the college is the key to improvement in the quality of individual education." [28] Taylor is readily identified with the *immersion* concept of that education in which the student utilizes his enlightenment experiences, not only in the classroom, laboratory, and library, but literally everywhere. This is a twenty-four-hour-a-day concept of learning, in which

[27] Lowell, *op. cit.*, p. 39.
[28] Harold Taylor, "The Individual Student," *Essays in Teaching*. New York: Harper & Brothers, 1950, p. 226.

there is no sharp division between the curriculum and the extra-curriculum, as far as learning is concerned. This is the community of scholars in which learning is the thing to do—learning that is casual, informal, and highly personal. Taylor said that ". . . education is not something administered in lumps but something which grows in the warmth of a friendly community." [29] He continued: "We must make the life of the college student an immersion in a total environment of learning where the companionship of the scholar, the athlete, the wit, and the artist are sought naturally and eagerly at various times and according to various needs." [30]

President Lowell sought to establish throughout university halls a climate of opinion and an intellectual atmosphere which would raise the level of enlightenment and also cultivate enjoyment of the pursuit of learning among students.[31] In support of his reform of students' attitudes toward scholarship, Lowell employed one of the early statistical studies of this problem, the high degree of persistence of high scholarship among students. In his famous essay "Examinations and Respect for Rank," he established statistically that the honor students in the undergraduate college persisted in high scholarship when they entered law and medical schools. He was engaged in combating the established mores at Harvard that the "Gentleman's C" grade was sufficient for an undergraduate and, in fact, would be followed by an improvement in scholarship once one really turned earnestly to studies in the professional school.[32] What Lowell accomplished in Harvard College should serve as a continuing model for the efforts of all student personnel workers. This is one of the measures of our potential relevancy in higher education.

[29] Harold Taylor, *On Education and Freedom.* New York: Abelard-Schuman, Inc., Publishers, 1954, pp. 65–66.
[30] Harold Taylor, "The Future of American Education," *The American Scholar,* vol. 18, no. 1, pp. 38–39, January, 1949.
See also Ordway Tead, *The Climate of Learning.* New York: Harper & Brothers, 1959.
[31] Lowell, *op. cit.,* pp. 39 and 279.
[32] A. Lawrence Lowell, *What a University President Has Learned.* New York: The Macmillan Company, 1938, chap. IV, "Examinations and Respect for Rank."

OBJECTIVES—CONTENT OF THE EXTRACURRICULUM

Let us turn now to a program review of the extracurriculum with respect to its emphasis and content. Since no definitive research analyses are presently available, we are limited to individual judgments and characterizations. For our initial examination, these sources are sufficient to indicate a general evaluation of and point to pioneering efforts to redress the present imbalance of the extracurriculum. A number of fruitful research projects will be uncovered and indicated.

First, let us make a simple identification of some of the presently observed emphases and objectives of the extracurriculum. The history of higher education in Western culture is, of course, replete with accounts of the proliferation of student activities and enterprises. Most histories of education and perhaps all autobiographic accounts of collegiate experiences contain at least one chapter on student life.[33] In these chapters, we are given some description of students' extraclassroom activities and interests, informal and casual, as well as organized. Keppel characterized students' activities in these words: "College life is likely to be an elective rather than a prescribed course." [34] That is, student life was thought of in such terms as "off duty," "informal," "voluntary," and "casual." At various periods in the history of American institutions, these activities have been viewed with concern and aided; at other times they have been suppressed. Such activities over the centuries have been both constructive and destructive at different periods, and sometimes on the same campus at the same period of time. We have indicated elsewhere that, in the early American colonial college, rioting and riotous living seemed to be the principal major activities outside of the classroom, centered in dormitories. But one reads of rich experiences in debating and literary society ac-

[33] Canby, Henry Seidel: *Alma Mater: The Gothic Age of the American College.* New York: Rinehart & Company, Inc., 1936, chap. II, "College Life."

Keppel, Frederick Paul: *Columbia.* New York: Oxford University Press, 1914, chap. VI, "Students and Student Life."

Sellers, James B.: *History of the University of Alabama,* vol. I, *1818–1902.* University: University of Alabama Press, 1953, chap. VI, "The Students"; chap. VIII, "Student Organizations"; chap. XXII, "Extracurricular Activities."

[34] Keppel, *op. cit.,* p. 173.

tivities in the same colonial colleges. Repeatedly we have noted references to the American campus as a reflection of general societal conditions prevailing in the outside world. It may well be that a rigorous study would identify and analyze contemporary reflection in American colleges of the general anti-intellectualism of the American culture at large.[35]

If one generalizes from the many published descriptions of student life and activities, one can identify the following objectives of the extracurriculum—not in equal proportions, and certainly in varying intensities on different campuses and at different periods in history. Nevertheless, we may well conclude that some parts of the extracurriculum have been organized around efforts to achieve the following objectives:

Recreation, or the contemporary pursuit of happiness through relaxed off-duty and non-credit fun activities, is one of the most dominant of observed emphases.[36] The college adolescent has, throughout the centuries, placed *the pursuit of happiness*—with appropriate aggressiveness —as a legitimate and accepted objective of higher education outside of the classroom. And one may observe an orderly change from the riotous pursuit of happiness of the early periods, with an occasional current outburst, to increased commercialized and University-sponsored recreational facilities and organized programs. In fact, the development of the institution-sponsored and -organized recreational programs is currently accepted as a positive and desirable substitute for traditional riots, feuds, and other disorganizing outbursts.

Personal development, especially respecting interpersonal relationships through group memberships and team work operations has also been a dominant characteristic of the extracurriculum.[37]

[35] As we have repeatedly stated, such a hypothesis undergirds Coulter's graphic description of some aspects of student life in the early years of the University of Georgia. See E. Merton Coulter, *College Life in the Old South*. New York: The Macmillan Company, 1928.

[36] Ruhlman, Jessie, and Jean Swensen: "Leisure Activities of a University Sophomore Class," *Educational and Psychological Measurement*, vol. 12, no. 3, pp. 452–466, Autumn, 1952.

Williamson, E. G., et al.: *A Study of Participation in College Activities*, University of Minnesota, Studies in Student Personnel Work, no. 5, Minneapolis, 1954.

[37] Coyle, Grace Longwell: *Group Experiences and Democratic Values*. New York: Women's Press, 1948.

Mayo, Elton: *The Social Problems of an Industrial Civilization*. Boston: Harvard University Bureau of Business Research, 1945.

*   *   *

We Americans apparently prize highly learning involved in becoming an effective member of a group and, in fact, we are sometimes said to overstress conformity through group membership. Regardless of whether we overstress it, this objective is stressed repeatedly in descriptions of the extracurriculum.

The extracurriculum is also full of cultural and aesthetic programs with content paralleling some of that of the classroom. The *Belle Lettres* are readily identified in the extracurriculum, but surveys show that this type of activity is less well patronized than are others, such as recreation.[38]

*   *   *

There is also much academic content in the extracurriculum as represented in the programs of technical speakers sponsored by professional clubs. The content is of a technical sort, and sometimes constitutes advances over the formal curriculum of an informal seminar type. This type of program is organized around professional curricula.

We have referred in previous chapters to learning another type of content, learning fundamental principles of democratic consensus in times of institutional crisis in the extracurriculum. In the present chapter we propose to examine other aspects of the program which could be organized and administered more explicitly, and perhaps more effectively, to achieve intellectual objectives.

STUDENT LIFE THROUGH THE CENTURIES

Many accounts of student life in medieval universities have created the impression that it was one continuous bibulous and violent carousal, interrupted infrequently by organized disputations and formal dictations by teachers of books by the ancient authorities.[39] Inferring the character of student behavior from the overwhelming multiplicity of rules and regulations governing behavior,

[38] Williamson et al., *op. cit.*, pp. 80, 84.
[39] Haskins, Charles H.: *The Rise of Universities.* New York: Peter Smith, 1940, chap. III, "The Medieval Student."
Kibre, Pearl: *The Nations in the Medieval Universities.* Cambridge: Medieval Academy of America, 1948. The nations were *collegia* or associations of students (particularly foreign students) and masters banded together

dress, and decorum, one would judge that such a generalization was justified. And the annals of student life in the early colonial college are similarly dotted with rebellions, riots, destruction of property, and other evidences of violent reaction against regimentation.[40] Riots caused by bad food and discipline brought forth by riotous drinking did much to set the general pattern of the extracurriculum well into the latter part of the nineteenth century.

But a more careful examination of the record reveals that the extracurriculum was not always or in all ways riotous and distracting, even though "student rebellions peppered the annals of every college in America."[41] A hundred years ago or more during the period of repeated rioting there were other types of extracurricular activities. Every campus had its devout and phrenetic religious conversions reflecting the *zeitgeist* of the frontier society at large. About one hundred years ago the student YMCA movement was organized as an outgrowth of the missionary spirit and the impulse to take Christianity to heathen countries.[42] Frequent religious revivals paralleled those of the frontier community.

The historians also record cultural aspects of student life— literary societies, disputations, and oratorical displays. Rivalries between literary societies became the center of student life and gave considerable intellectual depth to out-of-class affairs.[43] Clubs, secret societies, and fraternities provided some cultural experiences and atmosphere within the separate dormitories and houses.[44] Coulter described the elaborate oratorical contests held in connec-

for mutual help with problems of housing, studies, health, and other conditions of student life.

Rashdall, *op. cit.*, vol. 3, chap. 14, "Student Life in the Middle Ages."

Schachner, Nathan: *The Medieval Universities.* London: George Allen & Unwin, Ltd., 1938, chap. XXXII, "Student Life and Customs."

Sheldon, Henry D.: *Student Life and Customs.* New York: D. Appleton & Company, Inc., 1901, pp. 81–82, 88–89.

[40] John S. Brubacher and Willis Rudy, *Higher Education in Transition.* New York: Harper & Brothers, 1958, pp. 50–56.

[41] *Ibid.*, p. 39.

[42] Shedd, Clarence P.: *Two Centuries of Student Christian Movements.* New York: Association Press, 1934, chaps. VI and VII.

————: *A Century of Christian Student Initiative.* New York: Association Press, 1945.

[43] Brubacher and Rudy, *op. cit.*, pp. 47–48.

Sheldon, *op. cit.*, sec. 2, chap. 3, "The Debating Society."

[44] Brubacher and Rudy, *op. cit.*, pp. 122–126.

Sheldon, *op. cit.*, chaps. 4 and 5.

tion with commencements at the University of Georgia.[45] Commencement time was truly an intellectual feast, with its day-long oratorical contests. Amateur dramatics flourished, even in the crude frontier communities, and student orchestras and singing clubs were active in programs of enlightenment and entertainment. Organized gymnastic exercises and intramural sports became an important forerunner of modern athletics.[46] Every college had its own literary magazine and sometimes a student newspaper. These intellectual activities and programs expanded greatly in the late nineteenth century along with expansion of athletics and sports and many other types of activities. To many educators, things seemed to be in a state of imbalance, and strenuous efforts were made to strengthen the one and deemphasize the other. This became the pattern prior to the First World War, but many obstacles to such a correction were encountered.

OBSTACLES TO INTELLECTUALISM

If one approaches the task of cultivating the pursuit of learning as a continuing dominant emphasis in the extracurriculum, one usually faces certain serious obstacles to be appraised and overcome in the development of an effective program. A study of these obstacles will also serve to highlight many possibilities of developing new forms of extracurricular activities of a new character.[47]

Possibly the most dominant obstacle, and the one most difficult to modify or circumvent, is the general tradition of students—perhaps influenced by society at large—to organize their activities *with a minimum of intellectual content*. One must recognize that to be intellectual is not a popular posture in many American circles. Yet one would conclude from reading evaluations of the literature and movements of this period that considerable progress has been made

[45] E. Merton Coulter, *College Life in the Old South*. New York: The Macmillan Company, 1928, pp. 63–64.

[46] Brubacher and Rudy, *op. cit.*, pp. 126–131.

[47] David Reisman has appraised a number of obstacles operating within the academic program. See David Reisman, "The Intellectual Veto Groups," *Constraint and Variety in American Education*. Lincoln, Neb.: The University of Nebraska Press, 1956, pp. 53–106.

during the past centuries.[48] H. L. Mencken may have been partly justified in coining the phrase "homo boobiens" [49] to characterize the low level of intellectual thought in some circles. Krutch later referred to "The Age of the Common Denominator." [50] Yet one must balance Mencken against Mead, Gabriel, and other commentators to arrive at a reasonable and fair estimate of the American scene. Cowley's brilliant account of the growing intellectual content and emphasis in higher education during the past century is most heartening to those who seek to reconstruct the university's curricula.[50a]

In searching for parallel increases in intellectual content within the extracurriculum, one must guard against the temptation of caustic characterization of the level of intellectual content.[51] While the intellectual depth, or level, of conversation in fraternities and

[48] Beard, Charles A., and Mary R. Beard: The Rise of American Civilization, rev. ed. New York: The Macmillan Company, 1933, chap. XXV, "The Gilded Age."

Brogan, D. W.: The American Character. New York: Alfred A. Knopf, Inc., 1944.

Butts, R. Freeman: A Cultural History of Education. New York: McGraw-Hill Book Company, Inc., 1947. See especially chaps. XVI–XXII, the cultural development of America in the nineteenth and twentieth centuries related to developments in education.

Commager, Henry Steele: The American Mind. New Haven, Conn.: Yale University Press, 1950.

Gabriel, op. cit.

Lerner, Max: America as a Civilization. New York: Simon and Schuster, Inc., 1947, chap. X, "Belief and Opinion."

Mead, George H.: Movements of Thought in the 19th Century, Merritt H. Moore, ed., Chicago: University of Chicago Press, 1936.

Parrington, Vernon Louis: The Beginnings of Critical Realism in America. New York: Harcourt, Brace and Company, Inc., 1930.

[49] See H. L. Mencken, The American Language. New York: Alfred A. Knopf, Inc., 1949, p. 560. Mencken here related the circumstances of his coining of this phrase, first as "booboisie," and referred to by others as "Boobus Americanus." See also Harvey Wish, Contemporary America. New York: Harper & Brothers, 1955, p. 331. Wish appraised Mencken's anti-egalitarian role in the postwar 1920–1930 era in these biting words: "Confident that he and his fellow intellectuals were among the elect chosen to create all art and civilization, Mencken popularized the aristocratic game of ridiculing the mob with 'Boobus Americanus,' and the 'Bible-belt Fundamentalists.' Absolute truth and progress were illusions; hence there remained only the superior man's privilege of laughing at the antics of the herd."

[50] Joseph Wood Krutch (ed.), Is The Common Man Too Common? Norman, Okla.: University of Oklahoma Press, 1954.

[50a] W. H. Cowley, "College and University Teaching, 1858–1958," The Educational Record, October, 1958, pp. 311–326.

[51] Jones, "Campus: Echo or Criticism?" op. cit.

dormitories is by no means equivalent to that of the classroom, yet here and there on most campuses one would discover some acceptance of the intellectual life as a normal part of student mores. And each personnel worker must maintain an optimistic approach if he is to make progress in adding to that intellectual depth through his relationships within the extracurriculum.[52] We can always keep before us the successful effort of President Lowell to change the student mores at Harvard concerning the "Gentleman's C" grade. Other reforms of this type surely are possible elsewhere if we but accept the challenge to make such reforms a dominant part of our personnel services to students. We can take encouragement from Griswold's dictum found in his delightful essay "On Conversation Chiefly Academic": ". . . though it may begin anywhere, even in the realm of trivia, it should try to get somewhere and carry everyone with it as it goes." [53]

Left to themselves, many students pursue happiness through organized recreation, and those who have intellectual interests frequently retreat to the library. Now the pursuit of happiness as organized or unorganized recreation is an established and justified part of the mores of our Western culture, and we should not decry and undervalue its importance in the maintenance of morale. This pursuit also serves as a positive and constructive substitute for traditional riots and feuds, and it effectively obviates repression and regimentation of students. We need to remind ourselves that the mental hygiene movement of the past half century has demonstrated clearly the necessity of emotional maturity, part of which is attained through balancing recreation and off-duty activities.

But the adolescent's need for recreation does not in any way justify our neglect of things intellectual and cultural. The development of human normalcy can issue as much from intellectual activity and cultural and aesthetic experiences as from social contact and hobbies. Possibly we may have needlessly and superficially interpreted the psychology of mental health as requiring nonintellectual activity of a play character. But such partial interpretation of the needs of adolescents does not follow from the facts. It is true that one's recreational activities, or off-duty activities, proceed from

[52] E. G. Williamson, "Students' Residences: Shelter or Education?" *The Personnel and Guidance Journal*, vol. 36, no. 6, pp. 392–401, February, 1958.
[53] Griswold, *op. cit.*, p. 42.

active to passive forms at progressive stages of maturity. Yet we are not justified in concluding that a student who works at intellectual activities under compulsion in the classroom necessarily must move to the opposite universe and be unintellectual in his off-duty recreation and relaxation. Such a concept of an *alternation psychology* is unnecessary. One can relax, recreate, and maintain morale by shifting from reading one book to reading another. And there is seldom danger of mental overwork and breakdown if a student reads the same textbook for pleasure and also in preparation for examinations.

But the prevailing mores which dictate the necessity of *alternation* in maintenance of normal morale and mental health seems to be usually lurking behind justification of an extracurriculum which is overloaded with nonintellectual content. Indeed, it is the dominant folkway on some campuses, and in some dormitories and fraternities, to deride intellectual conversation as an evidence of snobbery and an imitation of a professor. All such trappings of "boobism" are unnecessary and, when they do occur, they indicate that the personnel workers, and other workers who operate in the extracurriculum, have failed to exercise effective leadership concerning academic and cultural matters. In fact, some of these workers may not even have thought that this function was within their range of responsibility. Perhaps in self-defense, they may assert that things intellectual are reserved to those who are licensed to teach, the professors.

A second obstacle facing the initiation of intellectual and cultural exercises in the extracurriculum arises out of the *concept of segregation of learning*. Human beings seem to overlearn *place-time-situation linkages*. It is as though the student early in his school life learned that in the classroom one studies books; everywhere else, except in the library and the laboratory, one avoids books, or bookish postures and behavior. Some students seem to give evidence of such a concept. In fact, some derisive remarks by students would seem to indicate that one violates the acceptable mores if one makes an intellectual remark or shows a cultural interest in the absence of a professor. Such a linkage would be tragic in higher education, as it is anywhere. The traditional community of scholars should be a way of life in which learning takes place casually, everywhere, and at all times. The intellectual life and, indeed, the cultural life is not linked to time or place. It is rather a universal posture, possible and desirable not only for the student of high intellect but at all ages and all levels of competence. Intellectual and cultural activity should be as casual and informal as are the expressions of interest in athletics, human relationships, and other natural topics of conversation.[54]

A third obstacle to the development of effective services concerning academic and intellectual matters is to be found in the prevailing *concept of on- and off-duty life*. This view stresses the point that students work hard at their studies and, therefore, they want to refresh themselves through activity which places less mental strain upon them. This concept is understandable because every kind of activity, including intellectual, does produce fatigue requiring some relaxing intermittent behavior. But sometimes this concept of on and off duty masks a feeling that it is much more natural to be nonintellectual and relaxed than it is to be tense in an intellectual experience. It is as though the so-called "natural

[54] This concept of education is borrowed from the insightful writings of Harold Taylor. References to his many essays appear throughout this book. The author has been thankfully moved by Taylor's seminal and humane concepts. His own bias will be revealed by the admonition to the reader to contrast such a concept of the role of education in human development with that described, satirically, by Nietzsche as characteristic of some European university professors:

> Now that I have once more seen the teeming brood of philologists of our day at close quarters, now that I have observed daily the whole of the mole-hill activity, and the animals with their cheek-pouches full, their eyes blinded, rejoicing over the captured worm and showing absolute indifference to the true and the pressing problems of life; now that I have seen these things not only in the young brood but in their elders as well, I become ever more clearly convinced that we two, if we wish to remain true to our genius, will not be able to pursue our life task without many a conflict and many an obstacle. [See Elizabeth Foerster-Nietzsche, *The Life of Nietzsche*. New York: Sturgis and Walton Company, 1912, vol. 1, pp. 183–184. (Trans. by Anthony M. Ludovici.)]

Elsewhere the author has quoted the phrase "gerund grind" to recall to the reader the nineteenth-century American caricaturing of the "greasy grind" type of college student. To further clarify his bias, he holds that while every scholarly effort is commendable, the subject of education is not inert knowledge but that rather, as Whitehead asserted, learning is the result of complex interactions of student, teacher, and subject matter within a warm, human relationship. Such a concept can embrace the relationships of personnel workers with students, and the author believes firmly that we must remodel our services in accordance with such a concept of education.

posture" of students were to be characterized as nonintellectual, if not anti-intellectual. In extreme form, this viewpoint might justify the conclusion that, after fifty minutes of forced intellectual effort in a classroom, a student is justified in regressing to his natural posture of unintellectual vacuity. It is regrettable that such a point of view seems to motivate some individuals, because it may have been caused by some unfortunate experience in which intellectual and cultural exercises were not enjoyed and, thereafter, were to be avoided, except for necessary swallowing of bitter medicine in the formally required classroom exercise.

More mature testimony indicates that intellectual activity, as well as recreation, can be fun, even though we seem to have associated learning with disagreeable effort rather than with enjoyable consequences. It is clear that, if we are to make any unique contribution in the extracurriculum, we must strive to help students experience enjoyable off-duty intellectual activities rather than a continuation of the painful experiences some of them seem to associate with classroom exercises.

A fourth obstacle of a more serious character stems from the fact that so many students are understandably, but still undesirably, *practical-minded*. They want to learn only the minimum of things which they can immediately use, and their concept of use is very, very limited. They want practical knowledge which will help them increase their standard of living through salary increases, and they have been unduly influenced by aspects of our American culture with its anti-intellectual attitude toward the impractical egghead, ill-equipped to compete in the market place with the practical businessman. We Americans are pragmatists, and we want to know what use knowledge has. We thus tend to oppose theorists as impractical, even though our American democracy is squarely built on a unique theory of government. This latter fact is a measure of how theoretical we really are in our practicality! It is also a measure of the practicality of a good, sound theory, but this lesson seems to have escaped most of our anti-intellectual critics.

The *limited expectation* of some students concerning what they will experience in a university is, of course, an additional obstacle in the extracurriculum. But it is not one incapable of solution. Such a limited expectation of a university education fades away if and when students are intellectually stimulated and thus become excited about ideas. Then the pursuit of learning becomes integrated with the pursuit of enjoyment, and a student is well on the way to generating his own momentum in educating himself. The solution for this obstacle is to make education exciting. Now this is a difficult task, because some learning is difficult, dull, and uninteresting, although necessary. But there are many other kinds of learning that can be exciting, and such excitement is just as possible in the extracurriculum as it is in the lecture hall, in which a scintillating dialectic is carried on by a brilliant professor. Great ideas and theories can be tested, examined, manipulated, and analyzed in the extracurriculum as in the classroom, *but different methods are required in the two situations.* A university, as a *summa dialecticum*[55] in which big problems are analyzed, is possible anywhere in a community where scholars and students are capable of learning an integrated approach to learning the soundness of ideas. It is as possible to generate "the winnowing breeze of freedom"[56] which separates the kernels of truth from the chaff of untruth in a fraternity as it is in a classroom. But we have seldom tried the winnowing technique in the first-mentioned place, perhaps having concluded that it was a function restricted to the other locus.

A fifth obstacle to the introduction of intellectual and cultural emphases in the extracurriculum is to be found in the prevailing concept that "I am too busy learning my classroom assignments to waste time thinking about great questions that have no answers, or that are unrelated to my required curriculum." Some students do bog down with their required learning, and thus fail to attain a method of learning beyond the classroom assignments. These "greasy grinds,"[57] these "Philistines"[58] make a difficult and tiring full-time occupation out of what should be the pursuit of learning for enjoyment, as well as erudition. Concerning such unfortunate collegiate ways of living, the extracurriculum has a decided tactical advantage over the classroom. In the extracurriculum one experi-

---

[55] Griswold, *op. cit.*, p. 35. The author quoted Whitehead in support of academic conversations: "Outside of the book-knowledge which is necessary to our professional training, I think I have gotten most of my development from the good conversation to which I have always had the luck to have access."

[56] Eliot in Weaver (ed.), *op. cit.*, p. 36.

[57] Canby, *op. cit.*, p. 125.

[58] White in Weaver (ed.), *op. cit.*

ences a generally relaxed air. In such social context, it should be much easier to approach learning in a relaxed mood of enjoyment. We have now appraised five serious obstacles to the integration of learning in students' lives. We turn to another important aspect of our reform of the extracurriculum and pose the question: What forces have caused the division of the campus and the collegiate way of living into curriculum and extracurriculum? [59]

WHAT DIVIDED THE CAMPUS?

Throughout the centuries one finds many diagnoses of the difficulties encountered by teachers in arousing and maintaining students' efforts in the pursuit of learning. Howard Mumford Jones diagnosed the situation as caused by too many personnel workers who specialize in adjustment. He said: "Today we do not cut the leading strings, we merely lengthen them. It is not true that an American lad cannot make a significant mistake as a young collegian, but it is true to say that an entire battery of adjusters is happily at work to see that his mistakes shall never, never harm him." [60]

[59] The term "divided campus" was used in describing that phenomenon. See Burgess Johnson, *Campus versus Classroom*. New York: Ives Washburn, Inc., 1946.

[60] Howard Mumford Jones, "Undergraduates on Apron Strings," *The Atlantic Monthly*, vol. 196, no. 4, p. 47, October, 1955.

See also Jones, *The Pursuit of Happiness*, chap. V, "The Technique of Happiness." Here, in a more stimulating work, Jones gives some indication of disdainful misinterpretation, or limited understanding, of modern psychology as applied in counseling therapy and the mental hygiene movement to adjust inner emotions and impulses with external societal forces and circumstances. One seems to experience an impression that our contemporary pursuit of happiness as the freeing of individuals from anxiety and misery is, perhaps, for Jones a debasing of the Greco-Roman search for contentment, which became the English colonial philosophy of finding *and accepting* one's station in life. If this impression is accurate, then such an antiegalitarian point of view would find much ground for criticism in the current American scene. If, however, we are in America experimenting with a spreading of culture from the monopoly of the patrician class of colonial days to today's new masses, then one may, with some confidence, anticipate that desirable upgrading of standards of taste will follow—if planned and executed—the thinness of the initial spreading. Mencken clearly thought otherwise but Ortega y Gasset and Parrington seem not to have been pessimistic about the long-range results, but rather about the danger of arrested standards at the low level of the masses. If one reads Karl R. Popper's *The Open Society and Its Enemies* along with *The Pursuit of Happiness*, one can find justifica-

Elsewhere Jones asserted, correctly, that the campus is a minia-
ture of life outside the campus. "Traditionally, the American campus
is an echo, not a criticism, of American society." [61] Since the community is divided into the practical and the intellectual, the campus
reflects that same division. Burgess Johnson made a candid appraisal
of the American college, and traced the development of the divided
campus.[62] The colonial college was a residential college, and with
considerable effort partly succeeded in immersing students in an
intellectual atmosphere. Unfortunately, there was often more concern for piety and righteousness than for intellectual development. Moreover, behavior was regimented and misbehavior severely
punished. And students continuously revolted, with the result that
maintenance of decorum diverted emphasis away from things intellectual. So the campus became a unified campus around a religious
theme, rather than around an intellectual pursuit. But the rowdyism
and violence of students' behavior almost wrecked the college, even
as an institution of confinement.

At a later period, Woodrow Wilson characterized the divided
campus in the following words:[63]

---

tion of hopeful results of the long struggle to find and forge *new* standards of
taste and conduct rather than a futile effort to return to some earlier Golden
Age or to freeze society, at any age, in its current mold.

By and large, student personnel workers, as educators, find congenial the
open society with its restless search for improvements for all individual members. They do not serve as society's agents in assigning (through classification testing and counseling) students to their proper station in life. To us
adjustment means evolving and developing one's potentiality within the
necessary societal limitations imposed by the requirements of other evolving
individualities. This adjustment is *not* the mechanistic mass conformity to
imposed stations in life and contentment with one's lot found in Plato's
Republic. Our philosophy is an extension of the Renaissance emphasis on
individualism, but with this essential difference—we consider *every* citizen
to be eligible by right to develop his full potentiality, not merely the educated
or the free citizen or some other chosen people. And modern psychology,
as it finds expression and utility in counseling therapy, especially within
institutions of education, is a new theoretical and technological underpinning
of such an egalitarian open society.

[61] Jones, "Campus: Echo or Criticism?" *op. cit.,* p. 163.
[62] Johnson, *op. cit.*
[63] Woodrow Wilson, "The Spirit of Learning," *Selected Literary and
Political Papers and Addresses of Woodrow Wilson,* vol. 1. New York:
Grosset & Dunlap, Inc., 1926, p. 260. Oration delivered before Phi Beta Kappa
chapter at Cambridge, July 1, 1909.

Life, at college, is one thing, the work of the college another, entirely separate and distinct. The life is a field that is left free for athletics not only, but also for every other amusement and diversion. Studies are no part of that life, and there is no competition. Study is the work which interrupts the life, introducing an embarrassing and inconsistent element into it. The faculty has no part in the life; it organizes the interruption, the interference.

A. Lawrence Lowell referred to Woodrow Wilson's point of view in these terms, and added a relevant quip to the original remarks:[64]

Woodrow Wilson, when President of Princeton, remarked that the side shows had overshadowed the main tent; whereas an alumnus is said to have complained that the President had turned that dear old college into a damned educational institution.

Earlier, Eliot of Harvard had declared it necessary to build colleges with "common rooms and dining halls" so that "students of all sorts" could mix freely. The social life of the residence hall had become "unrelated to the intellectual life of the classroom and laboratory." [65] The divided campus was characterized as one in which "two philosophies of life saluted in passing, and sometimes even stopped for a chat." [66] Santayana described an earlier educational system in these words, which indicate one important source of the divided campus:[67]

The young had their ways, which on principle were to be fostered and respected; and one of their instincts was to associate only with those of their own age and caliber. The young were simply young and the old simply old, as among peasants. Teachers and pupils seemed animals of different species, useful and well disposed toward each other, like a cow and a milkmaid; periodic contributions could pass between them, but not conversation.

With varying degrees of relevancy these diagnoses of the divided campus, the curriculum and the extracurriculum, all have their validity. Overeager personnel workers no doubt do sometimes interfere with and interrupt intellectual activity, even if there is some

[64] Lowell, *At War with Academic Traditions in America*, op. cit., p. 186.
[65] Charles W. Eliot, *University Administration*. Boston: Houghton Mifflin Company, 1908, pp. 216–220.
[66] Brubacher and Rudy, *op. cit.*, p. 135.
[67] George Santayana, *Character and Opinion in the United States*. New York: W. W. Norton & Company, Inc., 1921, pp. 52–53.

justification in terms of the related problem situations confronting a student at a particular time. And personnel workers must accept some responsibility for failing to find effective ways of diverting students from the pursuit of happiness at the expense of the pursuit of learning. Jones scored pertinent points in his stimulating analysis and historical account of man's restless search for happiness through a variety of activities, only a few of which were intellectual in content or emphasis.[68] Perhaps the responsibility for the divided campus is no more one for the personnel worker than it is for that teacher who has failed to make his teaching so exciting as to divert students from the pursuit of pleasure.

And it may very well be that larger forces are at work outside the campus, some of them identified by Jones, which encourage students to focus upon their personal adjustments and their happiness and to forego intellectual pursuits. Indeed, many critics have referred to the debasing of culture and civilization by the masses, and the pursuit of happiness which produces anti-intellectualism is a case in point. In discussing the role of religious pluralism in America, Niebuhr relevantly characterized some phases of our culture in these words: "The final vulgarity is to equate the ultimate ends of life with the dubious goal of 'happiness' and to equate happiness with creature comforts." [69]

While it is true that the colleges were long ago established as specialized institutions for intellectual activity, nevertheless the influences of the surrounding culture frequently seep into the campus and corrode students' motivations. Moreover, students bring to the campus their earlier learned motivations and interests, and when they come from nonintellectual homes, or homes of limited intellectual and cultural interests and tastes, then the college faces a tremendous, *but not impossible,* task in awakening the individual to the meaning of the pursuit of learning and higher standards of taste and culture.[70]

[68] Jones, *The Pursuit of Happiness, op. cit.*
See also Duncan Aikman, "What We Pursue," *The Turning Stream.* New York: Doubleday & Company, Inc., 1948, pp. 421–432.
[69] John Cogley (ed.), *Religion in America.* New York: Meridian Books, Inc., 1958, p. 45.
[70] Krutch, Joseph Wood (ed.): *Is The Common Man Too Common?* Norman, Okla.: University of Oklahoma Press, 1954, pp. 3–19.
Ortega y Gasset, José: *The Revolt of the Masses.* New York: W. W. Norton & Company, Inc., 1932; Mentor Books, The New American Library of World Literature, 1950.

All these, and many other forces, operate to make the task of the university a most difficult one, and it is most urgent that the personnel worker should assess his obligation, and opportunity, to aid in the pursuit of excellence as the basic task of the university. Frequent reading of the Rockefeller report on education will stimulate him to the task of encouraging students to pursue excellence in their personal and intellectual lives rather than comfortable but dangerous mediocrity in their studies.[71]

STUDENTS AS THE MEASURE OF EDUCATION

The point of view implied in the literature of student personnel work centers attention upon the individual and his development as the subject of education. Such a narrowing of focus sharpens our attention upon the individual in isolation from other individuals. While it is not implied that the individual is independently and socially isolated, nevertheless, in our work we do isolate the individual, operationally, to concentrate on his own individual, peculiar problems as distinct from those of other individuals. It is true that there is a so-called "group movement" in student personnel work, and many programs are organized for groups of individuals. But when we wax philosophical in describing the point of view, purpose, and objective of our programs, we define them almost exclusively in terms of the unique growth of each individual student in all his unique potentiality. He may exhibit commonality in problems and potentiality with other individuals, but the particular individual we are serving is our chief concern at any one moment. And in some instances we have gone so far as to imply, if not to state explicitly, that all the potentialities of the individual for his optimum development lie within him alone. This is to say, so it seems, that society is not crucially necessary to the individual, except when he encounters difficulties in unfolding his own potentiality.

It is high time that we examine critically such an implied point of view, because of some evident insufficiency in the potential of the individual for his own bootstrap development.

Many students do not, in fact, contain within themselves suffi-

[71] *The Pursuit of Excellence: Education and the Future of America.* New York: Doubleday News Books, Rockefeller Brothers Fund, Special Studies Project Report V, 1918.

cient potential for full growth. The individual is indeed dependent upon the culture for the realization and unfolding of his potential and for the acquisition of new potentials that he may not possess in isolation. Education, as an organized societal function, would be unnecessary if the individual could, alone, unfold his own potentials, or if he had all the required potentials within himself. We have argued this point elsewhere, but it needs emphasis again. Herberg phrased the point: "The human self emerges only in community and has no real existence apart from it." [72]

This point of view, congenial to an anthropological approach to the education of an individual, is by no means unmentioned in the literature of student personnel work. But neither is it a dominant emphasis. Rather is the dominant emphasis placed upon autonomy and self-sufficiency of the individual. We need to modify such a doctrine of extreme individualism with frank recognition of the interdependency of the individual and the groups in which he holds membership and from which he derives so much of his own individuality. Our argument proceeds in the following manner. To be effective, and because of his habitual narrowing of attention upon individual students, a personnel worker needs to review frequently the historical account of the development of human freedoms and liberties. This glorious story embraces the thinking of Jeremy Bentham, through John Stuart Mill, to the Oxford idealists T. H. Greene and F. H. Bradley. Such a broad review is presented in Irwin Edman's *Fountainheads of Freedom*.[73] Edman summarized this, the sweep of man's development, in these words: "Even individuality it turns out, is determined by social relations, even private good is really social in essence; the good life is for all and with all. However abstract the formulations of the Oxford idealists, they were reminding liberal minds everywhere, in the language of St. Paul, that we are all members one of another." [74]

A periodic rereading of Gabriel's story of the development of intellectualism and the American concept of freedom will serve as an effective backdrop for the worker who must deal with indi-

[72] Herberg, Will: "Freud, Religion, and Social Reality," *Commentary*, vol. 23, no. 3, March, 1957.
Mead, *op. cit.*, chap. XVIII, "Individuality in the Nineteenth Century."
[73] Published by Reynal & Hitchcock, Inc., New York, 1941, "The Growth of the Democratic Idea."
[74] *Ibid.*, p. 131.

vidual students in the matrix of the educational scene. It would seem desirable, and even necessary, to maintain a balanced perspective in dealing with individual students, to lift up one's eyes frequently to the broader and more remote scene of which the college community of scholars is only a small, but vital, part. Otherwise one becomes so preoccupied with the problems of the individual that he fails to see the societal matrix that plays such a vitally liberalizing and humanizing force in the very life of each individual.

There are still further important reasons why we should not focus narrowly on the immediate desires—and their gratification—of the individual or on his immediate problems and their solution as the sole, or even as the most important, determinant in the direction and configuration of his full development, including things intellectual.[75]

Reisman resurrected the old German university "Philistine norm" which was earlier used to describe "greasy grinds" who took no interest in taste or other measures of gentlemanly cultivation.[76] Let us examine another line of argument. It may come as a shock to some personnel workers to admit frankly the unpleasant fact that some human beings do not contain within themselves, at any given point in their development, some of the virtues and attributes of which man in general is capable. Personnel workers are basically optimistic in their view of the potentiality for development of the humanity of all students. Nevertheless, the hard realities of the day-to-day program indicate that not all students have perceptibly progressed in the direction of humane stature. In an address delivered at Melbourne University in Australia, Dr. I. L. Kandel, of Teachers College, Columbia University, had this to say on this very point:[77]

As the bonds of authority and tradition were loosened, as faith declined, as ideals and standards of conduct and taste became confused even in the minds of leaders, the common man in turn had nothing to fortify him against the bombardment of new sensations and *without a sense of any categorical imperative the individual became the measure*

[75] Lotus Delta Coffman, *Freedom through Education.* Minneapolis: University of Minnesota Press, 1939, p. 15.
[76] David Reisman, *The Lonely Crowd.* New York: Anchor Books, Doubleday & Company, Inc., 1953. (Abridged.)
[77] Coffman, *op. cit.,* p. 12.

of all things. The growing contempt for intellectualism and the constant jibes at culture or the Genteel Tradition as the marks of bourgeois liberalism compelled the intellectual to seek the approval of the masses on their own terms. . . . In the end it almost looks as though the desire to disseminate culture has resulted in spreading only a thin veneer. . . . Hence an illusion of knowledge and an illusion of power without any penetrating influence upon character or enlightenment, and *on those illusions each man claims the right to philosophize.* Rationalization has taken the place of reason and emotions have usurped the place of intelligence, and as a result of both, the emphasis has been placed upon the satisfaction of rights rather than upon the assumption of obligations.

Coffman continued Kandel's dictum in similar vein—that the debasing of culture [occurred] when "some" individual standards and tastes were adopted as the "measure"of that culture.[78] Similar dicta have been reasserted, pertinently, throughout the ages.

We will make the point less painfully if we turn to the broader scene for elaboration. Ortega y Gasset referred to the capacity of the mob to debase culture and to lower standards of taste and behavior to the level of the common man.[79] To quote him is not to agree that the common man is necessarily debased; it is rather to acknowledge that frequently some external educative leadership is necessary to assist some individuals to achieve the full stature of humanity. Joseph Wood Krutch sounded the same note in his question: "Is our common man too common?" [80]

If one takes the point of view that the inner resources of an individual are fully adequate for his own full development, without external assistance, then education becomes a mockery and an unnecessary one, as Ortega y Gasset argues clearly. Standards of culture and civilization put demands on individuals in their growth, both with respect to the pattern of that growth and the degrees or complexity of it. To be sure, we readily agree that inner-directed growth provides a highly desirable and necessary, though not a sufficient, source of motivation and pattern of development. This is clearly discernible in dealing with individual students in an educational setting when one sees the crippling effect of growth-destroying influences which bear upon the individual. Concerning

[78] Taylor, *On Education and Freedom, op. cit.,* p. 21.
[79] José Ortega y Gasset, *The Revolt of the Masses.* New York: Mentor Books, The New American Library of World Literature, 1950, chap. 8, "Why the Masses Intervene."
[80] Krutch, *op. cit..* p. 26.

the necessary contribution of the societal context for the full development of the individual, Taylor had this to say:[81]

There are many things learned which are not taught, and some which cannot be unlearned. Children catch their values through the atmosphere, and are infected by courage and cynicism, love and hate, generosity and meanness, snobbery and kindness, selfishness and unselfishness. The formal part of most college programs has very little to do with such values, the life on the campus very much. Students are on the whole tolerant and liberal, and wish to do what the college expects of them in the matter of their attitudes. They will fit themselves to the social situation which the college arranges for them. Since liberal education is intentionally designed to liberalize and humanize each generation of the young, it is essential that the social situation be one congenial to liberal and democratic attitudes.

If education is to be more than endless circularity of individualism feeding upon itself, and if it is to influence the individual's development to *full humanity*, then it must be value oriented and value saturated. We do not deny to the individual his moral right to self-determinism and to the final choice of commitment as to what values he wishes to live by. Nevertheless, an educational institution must be value saturated, and personnel workers in education must exercise their value influences explicitly and overtly, much as the faculty maintains a posture of academic integrity and professes overtly and persuasively the basic conviction that the search for learning is the basic value of the educational experience. We have argued elsewhere that it is high time for all personnel workers to turn some attention to the largely unexplored or naïve formulations of the function of value orientation in their educational efforts.[82]

The crucial test of validity of our point is to be found in the stature which some students achieve in things intellectual. Education is achieved by the student's own efforts, or not at all. But such a conclusion does not remove from teachers their responsibility for serious efforts to stimulate the desire for learning and to aid students in achieving it. The teacher's stimulus and example serve to expand and deepen the student's concept of, and aspiration to,

[81] Taylor, *On Education and Freedom, op. cit.*, p. 21.
[82] E. G. Williamson, "Value Orientation in Counseling," *The Personnel and Guidance Journal*, vol. 36, no. 8, pp. 520–528, April, 1958.

fuller education to a great degree—greater than the student might have acquired if left to his own resources and efforts. Williams's scathing indictment of college teachers for failure to inculcate the feeling that "learning is a delight," documented, perhaps too fully, "one of the saddest weaknesses of the entire system of higher education." [83] Ortega y Gasset's admonition about the danger of debasement of culture is pertinent for education and for student personnel work as well. We must not serve merely as technical aids in helping students to achieve only those experiences which they presently perceive as their own chosen goals of personal development. To be sure, students, at their closest approximation to maximum potentiality, do serve as the measure of both education and personnel work. But some students do need to be challenged to restructure their perspectives, their value commitments, and their aspirations *beyond* those they initially identified within their self-concepts. And these concepts are most pertinent with regard to the need for increasing emphasis and content in students' intellectual life.

THE ROLE OF THE PERSONNEL WORKER

The initiation of any reform or any reorganization of a program must follow upon the crystallization of a firm conviction and a plan for that reform. For example, we may operate on the assumption that personnel workers can exercise leadership for things intellectual in their advisory and other relationships with student leaders of organizations. The reform movement may be as simple as that. That is, when the president of a student organization comes to a dean of students or to any staff worker to ask for suggestions—as frequently happens—for program events, it can be suggested that the organization consider inviting a professor or a competent advanced student to discuss informally a particularly exciting topic. It does not make any difference what topic is chosen from the many currently of interest to students. Or it may be suggested that a professor of philosophy be invited to discuss religion and theology —one of the perennial items on the agenda of every bull session. The list of things to be explored is endless, and the talent to raise

[83] George Williams, *Some of My Best Friends Are Professors.* New York: Abelard-Schuman, Inc., Publishers, 1958, p. 74.

the intellectual content of the discussion is readily available among the faculty and graduate students who specialize in higher-level thinking about the human problems frequently discussed at a much lower level in student residences.

This is not to say that only the professor can carry on an intellectual discussion in a student residence, for example. If this were the case, then we would have another form of place-agent linkage which would teach the student that only when a professor is visible should one attempt to be intellectual. We want to avoid such linkages with time, place, and agents. To be sure, we may need to begin our program with the professor and a formal monthly intellectual evening, systematically organized for the school program each year. But we hope that students will generalize from experience and themselves assume the posture of a professor at the breakfast table on Sunday morning, for example, when no professor is around. Parenthetically, we note that the degree and the speed with which generalizations are made, of course, is a well-known measure of the maturing process in students. That is, no professor expects everyone in his class to receive an A. In similar manner, no personnel worker should expect that every member of a group, or that all groups, will eagerly progress toward the intellectual Utopia, where only learned conversations take place. But a simple beginning must be made by someone and, strange as it may seem, probably the response of students will be much more enthusiastic than was even anticipated.

All this means that personnel workers themselves must become at least somewhat competent in suggesting and initiating intellectual activity, although not so fully competent as the professor. Perhaps this will dislocate temporarily some workers, since they had not anticipated, or even imagined, that they had such a role to play. They, too, may have been subject to linkage, in that they thought only the professor could be academic, or was exclusively licensed to be intellectual. Without implying any criticism, we note that some workers may have been so technically trained, and so preoccupied with technical and administrative matters of program development, that they have forgotten how to carry on an intellectual conversation on any topic other than a technical problem. If this be the state of affairs, then the personnel workers may have to return to the classroom to recapture some of their own earlier academic experiences, or they may need to take adult off-the-job retooling training. Some such needed changes would occur more readily if intellectual and cultural topics were placed on the agenda of all staff meetings. This would leave the topics discussed and remind us continually that we operate in an academic institution in which intellectualism, it is contended, is the dominant characteristic.

SOME ILLUSTRATIONS OF ACTIVITIES

The following illustrations will serve as simple examples of transposing from the classroom to the extracurriculum some intellectual content and emphases:

At an annual "retreat," one of the topics for discussion was "learning versus fun on the campus." [84] The selected student leaders listened to a lecture on the topic, presented with some historical materials, as a psychological and educational analysis of the obstacles to the integration of learning. The program event was organized to stimulate students to explore the problem with the expectation that they might generalize and initiate their own organization programs of a similar character. At the same retreat, another program event consisted of an organized debate by the dean of students and a professor of political theory on the troublesome problem of reconciling authority and control in a democratic form of government, and in particular in a university. In both instances the discussion was lively, and there was some indication that the students reacted pleasurably and favorably to the introduction of such intellectual topics into the weekend camp retreat.

Annually freshmen of superior achievement and capacity are invited to a weekend retreat. These retreats are organized as intellectual fun-weekends. In the relaxed, casual camp environment, with no telephonic or other distractions, selected professors carry on intellectual conversations with freshmen at a "high" level of thought.[85]

In the first such retreat, the textbook and the topic was Whitehead's *Theories of Education*. At another retreat, the topic of "conformity" was discussed by a professor of sociology and by a professor of anthropology. At another retreat, a professor of the humanities discussed the general topic of "language and thought."

[84] E. G. Williamson, "Learning versus Fun in College," *Journal of Higher Education*, vol. 28, no. 8, pp. 425–433, November, 1957.

[85] George Charles Mohlke, Jr., "Stimulating Intellectual Interests," *School and Society*, vol. 85, no. 2114, pp. 226–227, June 22, 1957.

As part of the organized orientation for new students, a series of classroom previews were conducted by selected professors. On a rotational basis on the first day, a sample lecture is given from one of the natural sciences or from mathematics. On the second day, a sample lecture, or organized discussion, using sophomores, from one of the social sciences is conducted. On the third day, a sample lecture or discussion is conducted by one of the humanities professors, or language professors. These were actual, shortened lectures, or discussions, designed to demonstrate clearly both the general procedures in the classroom and also to establish a high expectation on the part of the freshmen that in the University *it is the thing to do* to be "academic" and "intellectual" in interest and behavior. Thus, the motif or theme was transposed to the extracurriculum and served to make the transition from high school to college an initiation into the Western tradition of intellectualism.

Within college residences, dormitories, fraternities, and sororities, selected counselors were trained in helping student organizations to conduct discussions, inviting professors and sometimes others from the community competent to lead a discussion on a particular topic of foreign policy, religion and theology, human relatons, racial integration, and similar current topics of interest. Systematically, these programs were introduced as a normal part of the schedule of activities, integrated with recreation.

Under a liberal policy governing inviting to the campus of non-university speakers, personnel workers both encouraged students and assisted them in selecting speakers from the community and at large who might have something to contribute to the students' understanding of a current topic, such as academic freedom, tariff problems, international tensions, and similar current topics. "Hot" issues and conflicts served thus as seminars for learning how to identify basic issues, to appraise alternative solutions, and sometimes to achieve community consensus on emotionally charged issues that divided the campus. Disputes and conflicts within the institution were dealt with in these seminars, thereby illustrating to the student the virtues of the intellectual approach as opposed to the "feuding" way of dealing with conflict situations. This was a difficult type of instructional program to conduct, especially in a tense, angry division of campus opinion. Nevertheless, the opportunity was available for those who had sufficient ingenuity to exploit it for educational, as opposed to disruptive, objectives.[86]

[86] Williamson, E. G.: "The Dean of Students As Educator," *The Educational Record*, vol. 38, no. 3, pp. 230–240, July, 1957.
———— and B. J. Borreson: "Learning to Resolve Social Conflicts," *The Educational Record*, vol. 31, no. 1, pp. 26–38, January, 1950.

SUMMARY

Thus we experiment in creating and maintaining a community of scholars, a community in which students are totally immersed in the cordial, warm, casual learning relationships of scholar with scholar within the extracurriculum. And, to some extent at least, learning as personal development of students becomes an *integrated experience of living* as contrasted with the segregation of intellectual activity in the classroom, laboratory, and library. This is, one hopes, the wave of the future in student personnel work—not a program of technical and necessary services to student clientele, but rather a furthering of integrated learning with strong intellectual components, as well as affect maturity.

We have presented the case for reconstruction and reorganization of the extracurriculum by personnel workers in cooperation with students. We did not propose that the extracurriculum be reconstituted with academic content alone and no recreational emphasis. Rather did we argue for the transposition to activities of some of the content and atmosphere of the curriculum without destroying its casual and informal character. Such informality, we contended, makes possible the integration of learning with pleasure, and facilitates the mature development of wide generalizations of learning habits and aspirations. This reform, we contend, offers new and significant opportunities for personnel workers to add to their present service new functions which are clearly educative in their effects upon the totality of learning.

Index

BT
ASHC

Williamson, Edmund Griffith, 1900–
    Student personnel services in colleges and universities;
some foundations, techniques, and processes of program administration. New York, McGraw-Hill, 1961.

    474 p. illus. 22 cm.

1. Personnel service in higher education.   I. Title.

LB2343.W53   371.422   60–11967 ‡

Library of Congress   [30]